Presidents
under fire

PRESIDENTS UNDER FIRE

COMMANDERS IN CHIEF

IN

VICTORY

AND DEFEAT

BY JAMES R. ARNOLD

ORION BOOKS
NEW YORK

"Cedant arma togae (Let arms yield to the law)."
—Cicero (executed by soldiers in 43 B.C. for his adherence to
republican principles during the civil wars that destroyed the
Roman republic)

E
181
A77
1994

Copyright © 1994 by James R. Arnold

Published by Orion Books, a division of Crown Publishers, Inc., 201 East 50th
Street, New York, New York 10022. Member of the Crown Publishing Group.

Random House, Inc. New York, Toronto, London, Sydney, Auckland

ORION and colophon are trademarks of Crown Publishers, Inc.

Manufactured in the United States of America

Design by Lauren Dong

Library of Congress Cataloging-in-Publication Data
Arnold, James R.
    Presidents under fire : commanders-in-chief in victory and defeat
/ by James R. Arnold.—1st ed.
        p. cm.
    Includes bibliographical references and index.
    1. United States—History, Military—Case studies. 2. Civil
-military relations—United States—History—Case studies.
3. Presidents—United States—History—Case studies. 4. Executive
power—United States—History—Case studies. I. Title.
E181.A77   1994
353.03'22—dc20   93-38182
                                                            CIP

ISBN 0-517-58863-3

10 9 8 7 6 5 4 3 2 1

First Edition

CONTENTS

ACKNOWLEDGMENTS

I am profoundly appreciative of the contributions made by friends, family, and associates. Thank you all.

Joyce B. Arnold once again provided emergency assistance. John Carland offered references for the Ia Drang campaign. At a time when book editing skills are on the decline, along comes a gifted editor to restore one's faith: Peter Ginna combined conscientious editing with insightful critiques and friendly comment. Robert Gottlieb, my agent, combines a keen interest in history with business acumen. Christina Houston and the staff of the Lyndon Baines Johnson Library, Austin, Texas, guided me with great professionalism through the collection and, like the archivists with whom I've worked in the past, helped make the research exciting and rewarding. General Hal Moore took time from his own book tour to answer some queries. Ralph Reinertsen shared information from his Revolutionary War archives. John Slonaker helped launch me in the right direction at the fabulous library of the U.S. Army Military History Institute. Carl Teger employed his photographic skills to provide illustrations. Jim Wade had the confidence to support this project. Bernard Wiener suggested the title during a thought-provoking conversation.

I continue to marvel at the public library system. My old friends—the reference librarians at the Handley Library, Winchester, Virginia—and new ones at the Parachute Branch of the Garfield County, Colorado, Library system—courteously processed my interlibrary loan requests.

The publication of this book coincides, more or less, with the beginning of the second half of my life. As I prepare to set sail, I want again to acknowledge my fellow explorer, soul mate, and wife, Roberta, who labored hard on this journey while helping make the trip such a joy.

INTRODUCTION

"Despite all the new and terrible techniques of killing that our generation has devised, the foot soldier is still the ultimate weapon. Wars are still fought for little bits of bloody earth."
—GENERAL MATTHEW B. RIDGWAY, 1956[1]

Every four years one American citizen's public pledge to defend the nation places him in the position of "President and Commander in Chief." The rousing processional "Hail to the Chief" gives symbolic voice to a change in stature that is immediate and immense. Henceforth, every member of the armed forces from rawest recruit to successful, heroic, four-star general must defer to this man's orders. The commander in chief is exactly that, the individual at the apex of the military chain of command, and he occupies this position regardless of his prior knowledge or ignorance of military matters. The president can now lead the country into mankind's darkest undertaking, war.

The Founding Fathers recognized the tremendous power invested in the commander in chief. They devised a system of government intended to limit reasonably his ability to plunge the nation into conflict. It has not worked as planned. American historical experience is replete with instances of American soldiers and sailors engaging in armed conflict by direction of the president without prior approval of Congress, let alone the public. Quite simply, historical precedent yields to the modern president a nearly unlimited power to begin war.

The agonizing decision-making characteristic of modern presidents when they confront the realization that their decisions kill fellow citizens seems to be a twentieth-century phenomenon. Certainly leaders such as President James Polk, about whose conduct of the war against Mexico we will read, expressed little remorse about the deaths that would result from his actions. Similarly, President George Washington—who had no illusions about the nature of combat but was neither a cruel nor an unfeeling man—reported to Congress the news of an unprecedented massacre with the pragmatic observation that "although the national loss is considerable . . . it may be repaired without great difficulty, excepting as to the brave men who have fallen on the occasion."[2] In contrast, President Lyndon Johnson did agonize about the consequences of his decisions. Shortly after committing U.S. ground forces to Vietnam, he visited a ward of wounded Marines. Full of emotion, he told them that he felt "pretty blue at night" after having issued the orders sending American fighting men into battle.[3] Perhaps the ability of earlier commanders in chief to accept the human costs of war indicates they were made of sterner stuff than more recent presidents, or perhaps they simply lived in a more callous era. But they, like their successors, entered war only after deep reflection and only when, by their lights, the situation demanded the "last full measure" of their citizens' devotion to country.

When a president chooses war as an instrument of policy, he fully assumes his constitutional role as commander in chief. Then he must address what the great Prussian strategist Karl von Clausewitz called the "first of all strategic questions," by establishing the kind of war upon which he is embarking.[4] Having crossed the threshold to war, his duties are the same whether the year is 1792, 1846, 1861, or 1965. The presidents considered in this book—George Washington, James Polk, Jefferson Davis, and Lyndon Johnson—confronted two surpassing tasks: to formulate a war-winning strategy; and to find men to implement it. Devising a strategy necessitates selecting national objectives and determining means and methods of obtaining them. In turn, the relationship the president forges with his top officers was and remains the link between high strategy and the bloody business of carrying it out. The successful conversion of intention into action is what being a commander in chief is all about. Throughout it all, the president must consider how to maintain public support.

Does the way a president assumes this role influence a war's outcome? Is there a presidential style that contributes to victory?

What follows examines the performance of four presidents under fire, four men who led their country during war. In addition, it shows the human consequences of presidential decision making by examining battles where young Americans fought and died to implement their president's strategy. As has been true throughout American military history: "At the end of the most grandiose plans and strategies is a soldier walking point."[5] Here we see whether the commander in chief's strategic vision can still be recognized at the sharp end: on the banks of the Wabash, in the Mexican arroyos, along the slopes of Gaines's Mill, and in the Ia Drang jungle.

The nation's first commander in chief acquired great knowledge about Indian warfare during his service on the Virginia frontier. When he took office, George Washington enjoyed an unmatched military reputation gained during the Revolutionary War. Nonetheless, as president his initial campaigns against the Indians living in the Northwest Territories failed totally. The first campaign conducted under his stewardship ended in stumbling, ignoble retreat; the second resulted in massacre. We will see how Washington responded to these setbacks and how he organized ultimate victory.

Unlike Washington, James Polk, a political creature born of Jacksonian party machinery, seemingly possessed exceptionally few qualities relevant to service as commander in chief. He was the first civilian to serve as president during a war and the first to direct a war fought on foreign soil. When hostilities with Mexico commenced, his intense animosity toward the nation's ranking general colored all he did. Yet, by justifying his actions in the name of national interest, which it was for him as president to define, Polk showed what an industrious, if unscrupulous, war leader could accomplish. Almost alone he determined the size and disposition of the army and navy, directed wartime finances, and most important, crafted the winning grand strategy. By so doing he proved that a civilian could effectively direct a major war effort.

In contrast, Jefferson Davis seemed a model choice to lead a nation at war. West Point educated, he had been a successful combat leader. Thereafter he served as Secretary of War to near-universal approbation. To the extent Davis's qualities as a commander in chief have been examined, historians have made wildly divergent assessments, generally according to regional bias. The consensus seems to be that Davis was unequal to the demands of being commander in chief and squandered the South's morale and manpower resources. Yet, at one critical juncture, he implemented the nation's first draft and with the resultant manpower devised the South's only multiarmy offensive of the war, an operation that gave the South its best chance for victory and independence. Thereafter, amid a revolution based on states' rights, he centralized power in the interest of efficiency, and thus became vilified by many southern politicians as a tyrant equal to Lincoln. Using words that might have been spoken by Lyndon Johnson, Davis complained that malcontents, including prominent politicians and newspaper editors, capitalized upon military difficulties by magnifying every reverse and prophesying ruin. Their words discouraged the public and made the successful prosecution of the war problematical. Despite his resultant loss of personal popularity, and in the face of terrible battlefield losses, Davis kept his nation fighting until the enemy occupied his ruined capital and his principal armies surrendered.

Some one hundred years later, this Lyndon Johnson could not do, even while his soldiers gained their greatest battlefield successes. Within two months of the Tet Offensive, he announced he would not run for reelection and thus became the first commander in chief driven from office by war. Afterward, critics blamed his "micromanagement" of the war effort for the first clear-cut defeat endured by the United States. Yet, several earlier presidents had acted much like Johnson and enjoyed victory. Moreover, at every key decision point of the war, he availed himself of a massive government bureaucracy built to provide expert advice to the commander in chief. What went wrong?

Johnson's Vietnam legacy had a large bearing on how President George Bush conducted the war against Iraq. Bush drew certain strategic lessons from the Vietnam War regarding the perceived wisdom of leaving military matters in the hands of the generals; the importance of fighting with great force, unfettered by political constraints; the desirability of applying unrelenting force without pauses for discussion and negotiation; and the importance of managing the press to try to control public response to the war. He established the broad strategic outline and apparently made several crucial decisions—when to start the war, when to end it—on his own. Postwar revelations hint that there was much more strain in the relationship between Bush and his generals than was apparent during the course of the war. If so, this is very typical, and indeed may be inherent in the way the role of the commander in chief has evolved. The Gulf War is merely the most recent example of the dynamic tension between civilian leadership and the military when war comes.

Sadly, although we consider ourselves a peaceful people, during the two-hundred-year-old American experiment, no nation has sent its young men to battle more frequently. Since the end of the Civil War, American commanders in chief have sent forces to fight on foreign soils more often than any other nation. It is a pattern that does not appear likely to change any time soon.

Of the four war leaders examined in this book, two achieved their objectives and two failed. They all contributed to the historical experience that has molded the modern role of the president as commander in chief. A nation should ponder this experience when electing a president because, whether by historical accident or presidential intent, conflict can occur during any term of office. Whether to engage the nation in this conflict, and whether and how to send America's children to contest "little bits of bloody earth," is a presidential decision of unsurpassed importance.

PART ONE

GEORGE WASHINGTON

AND HIS REVOLUTIONARY

TIMES

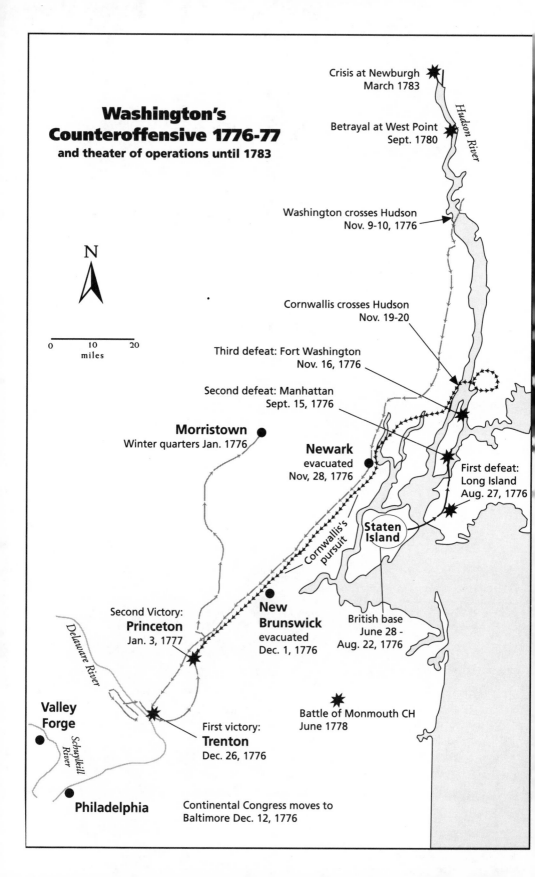

Washington's Counteroffensive 1776-77
and theater of operations until 1783

Crisis at Newburgh
March 1783

Betrayal at West Point
Sept. 1780

Hudson River

Washington crosses Hudson
Nov. 9-10, 1776

Cornwallis crosses Hudson
Nov. 19-20

Third defeat: Fort Washington
Nov. 16, 1776

Second defeat: Manhattan
Sept. 15, 1776

Morristown
Winter quarters Jan. 1776

Newark
evacuated
Nov, 28, 1776

First defeat:
Long Island
Aug. 27, 1776

**Staten
Island**

Cornwallis's pursuit

N

0   10   20
miles

Second Victory:
Princeton
Jan. 3, 1777

**New
Brunswick**
evacuated
Dec. 1, 1776

British base
June 28 -
Aug. 22, 1776

Delaware River

**Valley
Forge**

Schuylkill River

First victory:
Trenton
Dec. 26, 1776

Battle of Monmouth CH
June 1778

Philadelphia

Continental Congress moves to
Baltimore Dec. 12, 1776

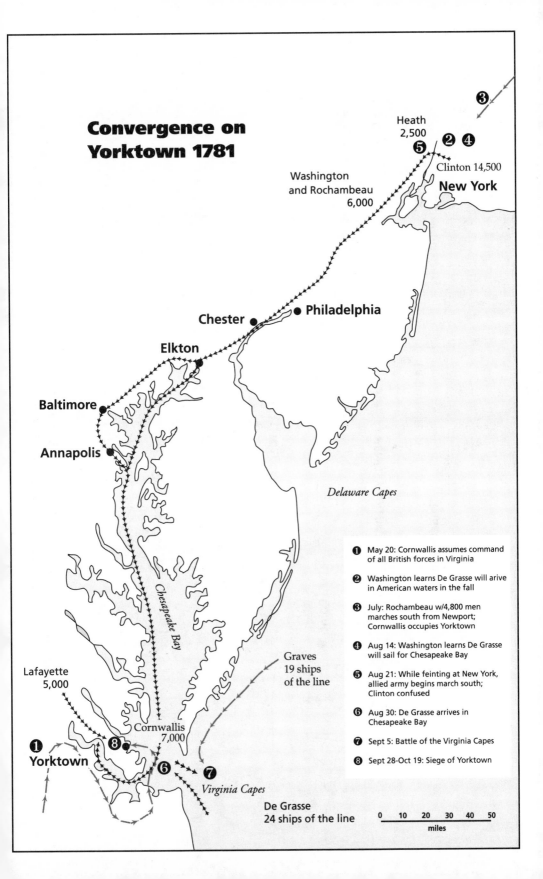

Convergence on Yorktown 1781

Heath
2,500

❸

❷ ❹

❺

Clinton 14,500

New York

Washington
and Rochambeau
6,000

Chester ● ● **Philadelphia**

Elkton

Baltimore ●

Annapolis ●

Delaware Capes

Chesapeake Bay

Lafayette
5,000

Graves
19 ships
of the line

Cornwallis
7,000

❶
Yorktown

❽

❻

❼

Virginia Capes

De Grasse
24 ships of the line

0   10   20   30   40   50
miles

❶ May 20: Cornwallis assumes command
of all British forces in Virginia

❷ Washington learns De Grasse will arive
in American waters in the fall

❸ July: Rochambeau w/4,800 men
marches south from Newport;
Cornwallis occupies Yorktown

❹ Aug 14: Washington learns De Grasse
will sail for Chesapeake Bay

❺ Aug 21: While feinting at New York,
allied army begins march south;
Clinton confused

❻ Aug 30: De Grasse arrives in
Chesapeake Bay

❼ Sept 5: Battle of the Virginia Capes

❽ Sept 28-Oct 19: Siege of Yorktown

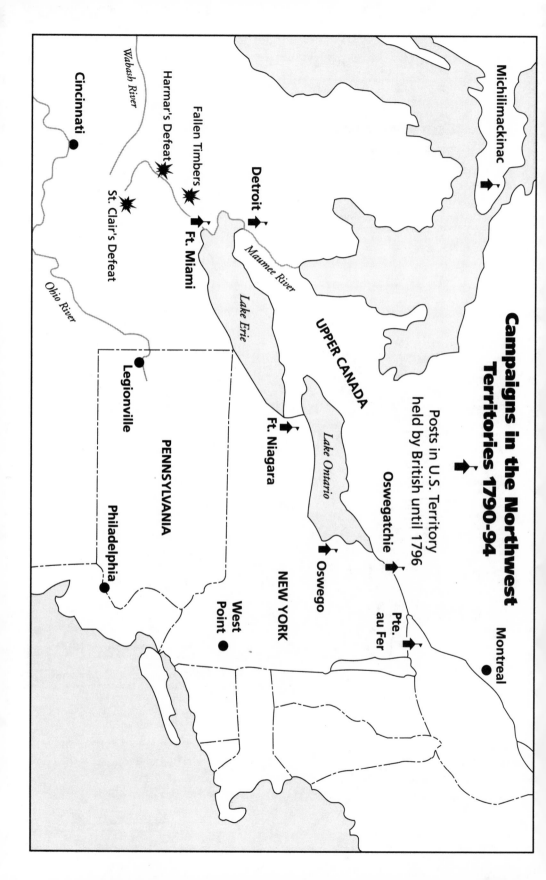

Campaigns in the Northwest
Territories 1790-94

Michilimackinac

Montreal

Posts in U.S. Territory
held by British until 1796

Oswegatchie

Pte.
au Fer

Oswego

Lake Ontario

NEW YORK

West
Point

Ft. Niagara

UPPER CANADA

Lake Erie

PENNSYLVANIA

Philadelphia

Detroit

Maumee River

Legionville

Ft. Miami

Fallen Timbers

Harmar's Defeat

St. Clair's Defeat

Wabash River

Cincinnati

Ohio River

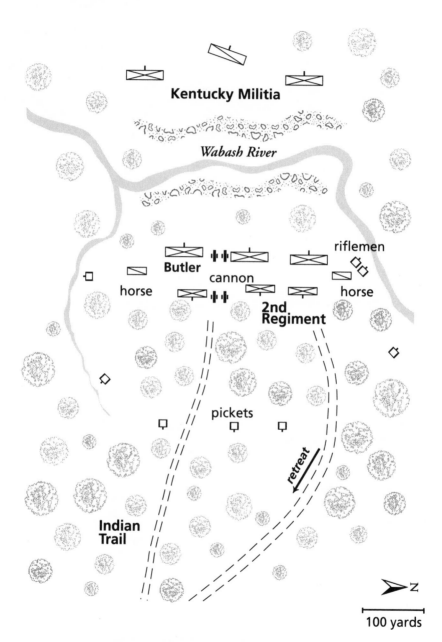

Kentucky Militia

Wabash River

riflemen

Butler

cannon

horse

2nd
Regiment

horse

pickets

retreat

Indian
Trail

N

100 yards

St. Clair's Camp
Dawn, November 4, 1791

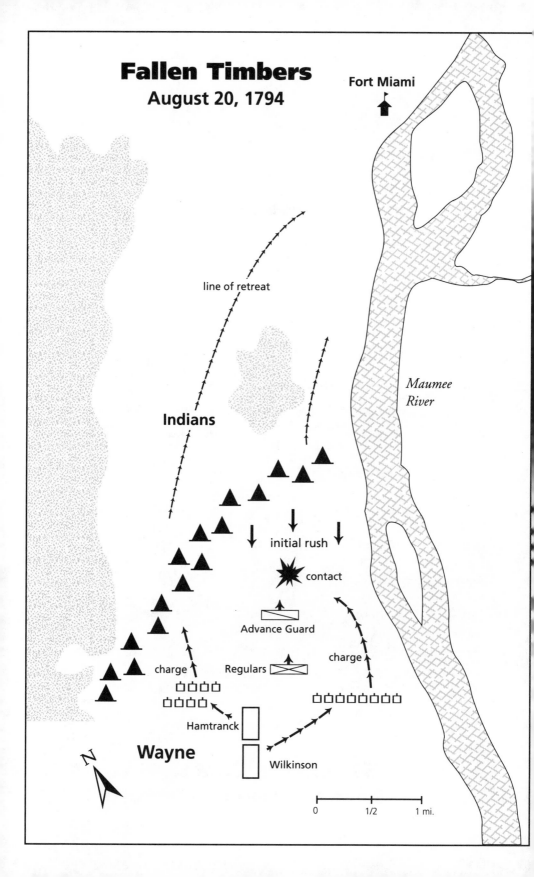

Fallen Timbers
August 20, 1794

Fort Miami

Maumee River

line of retreat

Indians

initial rush

contact

Advance Guard

charge

Regulars

charge

Hamtranck

Wayne

Wilkinson

N

0   1/2   1 mi.

1

DATELINE TO
INDEPENDENCE

THE DELEGATES OF THE UNITED COLONIES IN CONGRESS UNANIMOUSLY resolve to appoint Colonel George Washington "to be General and Commander in chief, of the army of the United Colonies . . . for the Defence of American liberty."[1] The Virginian comes before them to give his response: "Tho' I am truly sensible of the high Honour done me in this Appointment, yet I feel great distress from a consciousness that my abilities and Military experience may not be equal to the extensive and important Trust."[2]

Washington's modesty is not feigned; quite simply, the appointment overwhelms him. It has been sixteen years since he last served in a military capacity. Heretofore, his military experience has been confined to woodland fighting versus Indians and the French. He has never seen short-range volley fire between rival lines of close order troops, the hallmark of eighteenth-century warfare, a style exemplified by the matchless discipline of the British regular. Most important, he possesses neither training nor experience in devising and executing strategic operations.

3

PHILADELPHIA, JUNE 18, 1775

Two days after his appointment Washington writes to a friend: "I am now Imbarked on a tempestuous Ocean, from whence perhaps, no friendly harbour is to be found . . . I can answer for but three things, a firm belief of the justice of our Cause, close attention to the prosecution of it, and the strictest Integrity."[3]

NEW YORK, JUNE 25, 1775

Washington appreciates that there are important political duties associated with his position. He recognizes that the colonies have entered uncharted waters and, absent landmarks, his personal conduct sets precedent. Henceforth, for as long as he serves, he carefully considers every order and every action in this light. Of paramount importance is the colonies' deep suspicion of a standing army, permanent government forces supplied by the public treasury in peace as well as war. The ancestors of most colonists had left England at the time authorities used the standing army to take away their civil and religious liberties.

A spokesman for the New York Provincial Congress underscores American sensitivities about the threat of militarism. In his welcoming remarks he wishes Washington a glorious success and urges that when the contest ends, "you will cheerfully resign" and return to civilian life.[4] He has not yet taken command of his army and already many worry that a tyrant is in the making.

ARMY HEADQUARTERS, CAMBRIDGE, JULY 10, 1775

Inside Boston are elements of the British army. Outside, investing the city, is a ragtag rebel force of militia and volunteers. Although he has been with his field command a mere eight days, Washington detects a major flaw in the newly forged chain of command. The twin mandates of a commander in chief are to devise a war-winning strategy and to select officers to execute this strategy. Toward this end Congress vests him "with full power and authority to act as you shall think for the good and welfare of the service."[5] It then proceeds to promulgate orders that sharply limit his real power. Equally bad, Congressmen who fancy themselves strategic thinkers begin hatching plans and issuing orders—a handful practical, most naive—without regard to the nominal commander in chief.

ST. JAMES PALACE, AUGUST 23, 1775

The thirty-seven-year-old English monarch received his most important inheritance from his father via a set of "Instructions for my son George." These urge him to control his ambitions and avoid war while preserving his honor and that of the nation. King George III interprets this to mean he must prevent the dissolution of the empire. Observing "I wish nothing but good," he concludes "therefore everyone who does not agree with me is a traitor and a scoundrel."

His reply to the events at Lexington, Concord, and Bunker Hill is published. Entitled "A Proclamation for Suppressing Rebellion and Sedition," it calls upon the king's North American subjects to remember the allegiance owed to him and to ignore those "dangerous and ill-designing men" who challenge lawful royal authority. He reminds his subjects that they are required by law to assist in the suppression of rebellion and to inform royal authority of "all treasons and traitorous conspiracies" so the perpetrators can be punished.[6] He rejects the colonists' last effort at compromise. There can be no gradations in sovereignty. In effect, the proclamation is a declaration of war and a message to rebel leaders about the consequences of failure. They fight with a noose around their necks.

ARMY HEADQUARTERS, CAMBRIDGE, SEPTEMBER 21, 1775

The commander in chief's urgent appeals to Congress concerning the onset of winter have met silence. He writes Congress again:

> *My Situation is inexpressibly distressing to see the Winter fast approaching upon a naked Army, The time of their Service within a few Weeks of expiring, and no Provision yet made for such important Events. Added to this the Military Chest is totally ex-*

> *hausted. The Paymaster has not a single Dollar in Hand . . . and*
> *the greater part of the Army in a State not far from mutiny.*[7]

Unflinching deference to civil authority characterizes Washington's command style during the crucial formative days outside Boston. Yet it angers him to sit helplessly while his army melts away. Privately he rails against the lack of patriotism and predicts disaster. Publicly, instead of adopting coercive measures to force his citizen soldiers, the militia, to stay, Washington perceives that a precedent of vast importance is at stake. Heavy-handed British militarism had brought on the Revolution. To act in a similar fashion, no matter how grave the crisis, would cause civilians to equate the rebel army with the British oppressors. So Washington tries persuasion and embarks upon a voluminous letter-writing campaign to local officials asking for new militia levies. In this way he keeps faith with the revolution's basic tenets.

ARMY HEADQUARTERS, CAMBRIDGE, WINTER 1775

Examining returns that document the army's declining strength, Washington sees that the winnowing process has begun. Poorly clad, poorly fed, the first wave of enthusiastic volunteers sickens and many die. It is a breakdown in the chain of command, with authority ill defined among Congress, its commander in chief, and the individual colonies. The confusion accurately mirrors debate in Congress over issues substantive and trivial, but regardless, it is the soldiers who suffer.

ARMY HEADQUARTERS, CAMBRIDGE, MARCH 17, 1776

By the narrowest margin, Washington holds enough of a force together to continue the blockade of Boston. His stewardship over its investment is crowned with final success when the British fleet evacuates the port. It is a stupendous achievement for the former provincial colonel. Untutored in the higher aspects of war, Washington has maintained a rebel army composed mostly of civilians against the professional military might of the world's strongest nation.

The rebel occupation of Boston changes the nature of the contest: the campaign to deny the British a base in New England is over; the competition for control of the Hudson River, whereby the British hope to isolate New England from the colonies to the south, begins.

PHILADELPHIA, JUNE 18, 1776

Although their ranks include no outstanding military genius and no delegate has more experience than that acquired from supporting a few hundred militia or constructing a frontier fort, Congress continues to provide strategic direction of a continental war effort through its Board of War. The board hampers its generals by spasmodically interjecting detailed directives about small issues that prove disruptive and out-of-date. It ignores larger issues, disregarding Washington's warning that the next British blow is likely to strike New York. John Adams, whose back room plotting led to Washington's appointment, explains to one of Washington's subordinates, "We don't choose to trust you Generals, with too much Power, for too long Time."[8] Yet, when a huge British fleet appears in New York Harbor, laden with incomparable red-coated infantry and stout German mercenaries, the commander in chief is informed "that Congress have such an entire confidence in his judgment, that they will give him no particular directions about the disposition of the troops."[9] Washington stands alone at the top.

ARMY HEADQUARTERS, NEW YORK, SEPTEMBER 8, 1776

To confront a British army numbering over 30,000 trained and well-equipped soldiers backed by 10,000 sailors and a battle fleet, Washington commands some 19,000 men, 9,000 of whom are regulars of the Continental Line. The balance are untested militia. Inexperienced in field command, Washington fragments his forces and sends his main body to Long Island. In the subsequent debacle, he is badly outgenerated and barely escapes back to Manhattan with an intact army after losing some 1,407 men while managing to inflict only 367 casualties.

His subsequent resolution to avoid battle clashes with his sensitivity to critics who complain about his leadership. This sensitivity, coupled with fears that another retreat will demoralize his men, induces him to defend Manhattan. Given British control of the adjacent waters, it is a foolish choice that puts everything to risk. One week later the British land on Manhattan, rout the defending militia, and capture the rebels' heavy cannon, and a considerable part of the army's baggage, tents, and stores, for a loss of about twenty men. It is a second humiliating defeat.

HARLEM HEIGHTS, SEPTEMBER 24, 1776

Following another discouraging day during which he witnesses the continued poor discipline of his troops, particularly the militia, Washington pours out his feelings in a late-night letter to the president of Congress. He describes his embarrassment at repeated defeats and says he will not be surprised if Congress should censure him. But he tries to explain that the existing Rules and Regulations of War are inadequate to discipline the army and that continued failure to recruit soldiers for long-term service forces him to rely upon the militia, which is "assuredly, resting upon a broken staff." He continues: "The Jealousies of a standing Army, and the Evils to be apprehended from one, are remote . . . but the consequences of wanting one . . . is . . . inevitable Ruin." In the strongest language possible he says there must be "a thorough change in our Military Systems."[10]

PHILADELPHIA, OCTOBER 8, 1776

After much deliberation, Congress has finally responded to Washington's queries regarding the raising of the new army. When Washington learns of Congress's plan, he immediately appreciates that it is a great mistake. Not only will the process take overly long—committees will appoint committees who will make recommendations that will be studied by committees—but local politics rather than military merit will intrude upon the selection of officers. Experienced and proven officers will be passed over because they lack political clout.

As he explains to Congress, "the Season is late, and there is a material difference between voting of Battalions and raising of Men."[11]

AMBOY, NEW JERSEY, OCTOBER 14, 1776

Like many officers, the man whom Washington considers the army's most able, experienced officer, Major General Charles Lee, blames Congress for the army's troubles.[12] Lee confides that "Congress seem to stumble every step—I do not mean one or two of the Cattle, but the whole Stable." He adds that Washington "is much to blame in not menacing 'em with resignation unless they refrain from unhinging the army by their absurd interference."[13]

A month later Lee writes a friend in Congress that "had I the powers I could do you much good—might I but dictate one week—but I am sure you will never give any man the necessary power." Referring to the Roman practice of appointing a dictator in times of crisis, Lee concludes, "did none of the Congress ever read Roman History?"[14]

NEWARK, NOVEMBER 24, 1776

The commander in chief is very tired and it shows. An aide describes how he hesitates "more than I ever knew him on any other occasion, and more than I thought the public service admitted."[15] Consequently, the British capture Fort Washington and its 2,818-man garrison along with vast amounts of supplies and artillery. It is the third American defeat in a row. Washington's army is now so scattered that it cannot resist a mere enemy advance guard let alone the main British army.

PHILADELPHIA, DECEMBER 1, 1776

The British pursuit of Washington's flying army gains momentum. In spite of the gravity of the situation, Congress, through its myriad committees, continues to try to manage the war effort at a level of near-bewildering detail. Thus: the Committee of Treasury studies a doctor's bill for medicines to sick Virginia soldiers of "67 37/90 dollars"; the Secret Committee appoints "trusty persons" to travel to the eastern states to oversee the collection of clothing, this in response to Washington's repeated pleas that his naked men need protection against the coming winter; and the Board of War orders an infantry battalion to march immediately to join Washington and then alerts Pennsylvania's council of safety to guard the public stores against the battalion's anticipated looting.

PHILADELPHIA, DECEMBER 12, 1776

The British advance through New Jersey draws nearer to Philadelphia. Congress resolves—"Whereas the movements of the enemy have now rendered the neighbourhood of this city the seat of war, which will prevent that quiet and uninterrupted attention to the public business"—to adjourn to Baltimore. Before taking flight, the delegates give Washington "full power to order and direct all things relative to the department, and to the operations of war."[16] Washington employs his power to concentrate his army, informing a subordinate, "If we can draw our forces together . . . we may yet effect an important stroke."[17]

ARMY HEADQUARTERS ON THE
DELAWARE, DECEMBER 18, 1776

The commander in chief has often confided feelings to his brother that he will not share with others. Pursued by British forces he estimates to number 10,000 men, reduced to less than 3,000 fit men in his own army; he doubts his ability to save the capital. He tells his brother: "If every nerve is not strain'd to recruit the New Army . . . I think the game is pretty near up."[18]

PHILADELPHIA, DECEMBER 19, 1776

The recent immigrant from England has accompanied the army on the long retreat across New Jersey. He has shared their suffering and been inspired by the soldiers' exhibition of fortitude. Reflecting upon what he has seen during cold nights around the camp fires, he writes a manuscript that is printed this day in the *Pennsylvania Journal.* Titled "The American Crisis—Number One," Tom Paine's message begins: "These are the times that try men's souls."

ARMY HEADQUARTERS ON THE DELAWARE, DECEMBER 20, 1776

Washington's urgent appeals made in October have received no response from Congress. He reminds the president of Congress that the army will essentially dissolve by year's end. He must have immediate authority to recruit. Moreover, if all decisions have to pass through Congress, so much time will elapse as to "defeat the end in view."

He understands congressional sensitivity over an expansion of his powers and assures Congress "that I have no lust after power but wish with as much fervency as any Man . . . for an opportunity of turning the Sword into a plow share." But the terrible problems caused by short-term enlistments and dependence upon militia "have been the Origin of all our Misfortunes." He elaborates that the militia arrive for a six-week period, "consume your Provisions, exhaust your Stores, and leave you at last in a critical moment. These Sir are the Men I am to depend upon Ten days hence."[19]

Revolutionary rhetoric describes the militia as "the only security of a free government." In the breach, Washington concludes that the patriot cause necessitates a large standing army.

THE MERRICK HOUSE, DECEMBER 24, 1776

The commander in chief arrives for supper and a conference. Heretofore, he has followed congressional advice and used councils of war to plan his maneuvers. This time it is different. The plan is his alone. He has concentrated all available forces after a harrowing month-long retreat. These 2,400 men are the Continental Army, men who hail from Virginia to New Hampshire, and unless there is a dramatic change, the majority will depart when their term of enlistment runs out at month's end. So Washington resolves to try to cross the Delaware River and attack the Hessian garrison occupying Trenton tomorrow. Washington hopes that the Christmas festival—with its traditional feasting, drinking, and revelry—will allow his men to surprise an unwary opponent.

He makes careful preparations, but the venture is fraught with risk. His maneuver columns, comprised of poorly trained and largely inexperienced soldiers led by officers who were civilians themselves not long ago, must exhibit great discipline so as to arrive at Trenton nearly simultaneously following a night march. Then, there is the weather. After a heavy snowstorm there have been two days of intense cold. If the river's ice is too thick the boats on which the army will cross will be useless. As he makes his final plans, clouds thicken and the wind shifts to the northeast, promising another storm.

TRENTON, DECEMBER 26, 1776

The two supporting militia columns are thwarted by ice from crossing the river. Ferried across the Delaware by skilled fishermen serving in a Massachusetts regiment, the Continentals advance alone. After a nine-mile march through wind and sleet, two columns converge on Trenton, overrun the surprised outposts, and continue toward the town center. Washington's artillery, ably commanded by Henry Knox, a self-taught former New England bookseller, dominates the action.

The firing stops. An officer spurs up to the commander in chief to announce that the last German unit in the town has surrendered. Washington extends his hand, saying, "Major Wilkinson, this is a most glorious day for our country."[20]

TRENTON, JANUARY 1, 1777

After the victory at Trenton the army retreats over the Delaware to escape British retribution. Two days later Washington leads them into Trenton again. This time their numbers are reduced by half because many have left camp in anticipation of the year-end expiration of their term of enlistment. Many more plan to leave the army tomorrow. George Washington reins in his horse before the center of a New England regiment. He is no orator, and the occasion demands eloquence. Briefly, he describes the meaning of the recent victory and why it is important that they, the army's veterans, remain in service. If they will stay for another six weeks they will render the country an inestimable service. He offers a ten-dollar bounty to encourage them to stay. The regimental officers ask them to stride forward at the sound of the drum and re-enlist. The drum rolls and not a man moves.

This cannot be! Washington renews his appeal, imploring the men to stay, reminding them of their country's need and their opportunity. The drum rolls. A few men step forward, followed by more and more. The crisis is met. Enough veterans remain with the minuscule army to provide a solid nucleus around which new recruits can rally. Relieved that he retains an army, if only for another six weeks, Washington begins planning a new offensive.

PRINCETON, JANUARY 3, 1777

Nearly trapped at Trenton by an overwhelming British force led by Lord Cornwallis, Washington eludes the enemy host and marches against Cornwallis's rear to attack a British detachment at Princeton. As the battle begins, some of his troops break in panic:

> *At this moment Washington appeared in front of the American Army, riding towards those of us who were retreating and exclaimed, "Parade with us, my brave fellows! There is but a handful of the enemy and we will have them directly."*[21]

The commander in chief rides between the rival firing lines, placing himself a mere thirty yards from enemy musket fire. One of his staff watches with awful anxiety: "So recklessly did he expose himself that I was sure the General would fall and I raised my cloak over my face to shut out the dreadful sight."[22]

A crash of musketry, the smoke clears, and Washington is untouched. He leads the Americans to a second victory, captures a large quantity of badly needed military stores, and nimbly marches out of danger when the fuming Cornwallis storms back to Princeton.

Thereafter, Washington occupies a flanking position threatening the British line of communication. In response the British evacuate all their garrisons in central and western New Jersey. In ten days

Washington has entirely reversed the strategic situation in a bold display of generalship of the highest order. Frederick the Great will characterize this campaign as one of the most brilliant in military history. The commander of the British army in North America, Lord Howe, acknowledges the setback: "I do not now see a prospect of terminating the war, but by general action, and I am aware of the difficulties in our way to obtain it."[23]

The campaign along the icy Delaware demonstrates something that many in London, Paris, and the thirteen colonies, had doubted: if the rebels persist they have a fighting chance to win what they set out to achieve. The French court greets news of Trenton and Princeton with unconcealed glee. Washington's victories also have an immense effect upon public morale in America. A traveler observes: "The minds of the people are much altered. Their late successes have turned the scale and now they are all liberty mad again."[24] The success changes the American commander in chief as well. Henceforth, he can remember two solid victories earned by his determination and leadership. They will help fuel future resolve when all seems bleak.

2 ⟡⟶

AN INDISPENSABLE MAN

*"Few people know the predicament we are in ... I have
often thought how much happier I should have been,
if, instead of accepting of a command under such circumstances, I had taken my musket on my shoulder and
entered the ranks, or, if I could have justified the measure
to posterity and my own conscience, had retired to the
back country, and lived in a wigwam."*

GEORGE WASHINGTON, 1776[1]

THE TEMPESTUOUS OCEAN

IN 1775 THE YEAR OF REVOLUTION, THE CONSTITUTION'S CLEAR DELIN-
EATion of military authority was still twelve years away. To fight the
Revolution, the fledgling nation relied upon its Continental Congress,
an untried political body that combined what would later be defined as executive and legislative authority. Having renounced British rule, it had to fill the resultant administrative vacuum simply
so the American people could continue their daily business. Simultaneously, the Continental Congress had to invent a system of government while conducting a war against the world's foremost
military power. Of the myriad challenges, the military effort had
to stand foremost. If the war was lost, all else became moot, since
those who stepped forward to lead the Revolution, the congressmen themselves, would be hung as traitors. So daunting was the
task, the remarkable thing is that they began a Revolution at all.

They lived at a time when a recognizable body of knowledge
constituted an education. The revolutionary leaders' study and
contemplation taught a profound fear of a standing army, a permanent establishment maintained by government and supplied by
public treasury in peace as well as war. They well knew that 122

15

years earlier, two years after the end of the English Civil War, a triumphant army led by Oliver Cromwell had grown ever more dissatisfied with Parliament. That army believed Parliament corrupt, and although Cromwell tried to mediate, his sympathies were with his soldiers. Finally, convinced that this "Long Parliament" had to be dissolved, Cromwell ordered his musketeers to expel members from the House. The story of a victorious general using his soldiers to evict the government made an indelible impression upon American politicians in the next century.

Then there was the struggle against the Stuart kings that climaxed when Parliament declared a Bill of Rights in 1689. This document charged the late King James II with subverting the kingdom's laws and liberties by several actions, including "raising and keeping a standing army within this kingdom in time of peace without consent of Parliament."[2] This history solidified the notion in the minds of America's revolutionary leaders that standing armies lead to the despotism of military dictatorship. Most concluded that a democratic nation should instead depend upon its militia, armed and trained yeomen and landholders who had a large stake in society. They would never seize power or overturn legitimate rule unless that rule was tyrannical. According to this view, a militia could perform necessary military tasks while simultaneously acting as a democratic force against tyranny. In theory, reliance upon the militia ensured military subordination to civilian authority. The effort to fight a war commanded by politicians using citizen soldiers proved to be the salient struggle of the American Revolution.

When delegates gathered at the Second Continental Congress in the spring of 1775, events forced them to make hard decisions. Not yet recovered from the shock of learning that American militia had fought against British regulars at Lexington and Concord, they received dramatic news from Joseph Warren, acting president of the newly named "Provincial Congress" of Massachusetts. Warren informed delegates that the establishment of an army was indispensable to protect against British depredation.[3] Consequently, Massachusetts had unilaterally raised nearly 14,000 militia, a colossal amount of manpower. Warren acknowledged that Massachusetts unaided could not stand up to England and so requested help from the other colonies. His request created a profound dilemma for many delegates. They believed that a fair chance for reconciliation with Mother England remained. However, the bloodshed outside of Boston changed attitudes and hardened enough delegates' resolve so that a predominant viewpoint emerged: the colonies must not yield to British military coercion. Resistance to coercion required military planning. At this point a heretofore overlooked delegate from Virginia emerged as an important figure.

George Washington had sat through the entire first Congress and the opening days of the second without formally speaking or being called to committee. Although silent, he was an unmistakable military presence simply because he alone of all delegates wore a military uniform. It was his long-unused service uniform from the French and Indian Wars. Among many, Washington impressed John Adams, who observed that "Colonel Washington . . . by his great experience and abilities in military matters, is of much service to us."[4] There was less to Washington's experience than met Adams's eye.

Encouraged by his older brother to participate in Virginia's military life, George Washington had entered military service in 1754 when rising tensions with the French over control of the Ohio River Valley caused the colony to ready for war. Sent with a militia detachment to build a fort at the junction of the Allegheny and Monongahela, the young officer found the French already in possession of this key point. Showing commendable initiative, Washington built a fort in western Pennsylvania to counter the French presence. Aptly named Fort Necessity, it fell to an overwhelming French attack after a vigorous resistance.

The next year, the arrival of General Edward Braddock, the new British commander in chief in America, inspired Washington to volunteer as a special aide in Braddock's military family. During Braddock's ensuing disaster along the banks of the Monongahela—a battle featuring concealed French soldiers and Indians shooting apart a rigid British line and mortally wounding Braddock himself—Washington exhibited great personal courage. Enemy bullets pierced his clothes and killed two horses beneath him. Having volunteered in anticipation of learning formal war at the hands of a master, instead Washington saw the ineffectiveness of European infantry tactics in the wilds of North America. Moreover, as Benjamin Franklin wrote: "This whole Transaction gave us Americans the first Suspicion that our exalted ideas of the Prowess of British Regulars had not been well founded."[5]

Following Braddock's debacle, British troops withdrew from the colonial frontier, leaving Virginia exposed to the ravages of Indian raiding parties. In this emergency, Virginia's House of Burgesses voted money to raise a regiment for frontier defense and commissioned Washington "Commander in Chief" of all forces raised. He was twenty-three years old. He served on the frontier for three more years but never saw action again beyond a minor skirmish. Thus the sum total of his military service, during which he never commanded more than one thousand men, amounted to a few skirmishes, a short siege culminating in his honorable surrender, surviving a catastrophic Indian ambush, and supervision of a chain of frontier forts. Limited as it was, his experience surpassed that of virtually every other southerner of his era.

Thereafter he managed his Mount Vernon plantation, and it was there in 1774 that he heard the electrifying news that Parliament intended to punish Boston for its unlawful destruction of tea by closing its port. After conferring with the members of Virginia's General Assembly, Washington concluded that Americans would not tolerate taxation without their own consent and would adopt Boston's cause as their own.[6] He became convinced that efforts to reconcile American differences with the king would fail. "I shall not undertake to say where the line between Great Britain and the colonies should be drawn," he wrote, "but I am clearly of opinion, that one ought to be drawn, and our rights clearly ascertained. I could wish, I own, that the dispute had been left to posterity to determine, but the crisis is arrived when we must assert our rights."[7]

He attended the First Continental Congress and endured its seven long weeks of debate. Cognizant of his awkward writing style, aware that he was no great orator, Washington remained in the background. However, the proceedings changed him. He echoed the Congress's rhetoric when he described events to his friends, and, for the first time, entertained the notion of American independence. His active social life outside of the Congress broadened his views. Like many southerners, Washington was mistrustful of New England. His private visits introduced him to men such as John and Samuel Adams and John Hancock. Although their accents and background were different, their patriotic zeal impressed the Virginian. Equally important, many delegates, who only knew Washington by reputation as someone who had fought the French and Indians and had served with Braddock, had a chance to measure the man himself.

A half year later, when the Second Continental Congress began to confront military issues, it appointed Washington to head a committee for the defense of New York City. Next he chaired a committee to consider ways and means of obtaining ammunition and military stores. Then, at the beginning of June 1775, events in distant Massachusetts again forced this Congress to make difficult choices. The Provincial Congress of Massachusetts had pondered the implications of its decision to raise an army and concluded that, "as the sword should in all free states be subservient to the civil powers . . . we tremble at having an army (although consisting of our countrymen) established here without a civil power to provide for and control them."[8] Asserting that the army being collected was for the general defense of America, Massachusetts asked that the Continental Congress assume its "regulation and general direction." If Congress accepted this responsibility, then it had to appoint a military leader.

For the next two weeks, every post brought letters explaining the impossibility of maintaining the rebel army outside of Boston without the assistance of the Continental Congress. But moderates in Congress were embroiled in fashioning a petition to the king seeking reconciliation, and this made it hard for them to focus on active military preparations. More radical members were riven by sectional disputes with southern delegates holding "a jealousy against a New England army under the command of a New England General." Massachusetts delegate John Adams appreciated that the south could be rallied behind one of their own but that southerners could not agree whom it should be. Adams also knew that the New England–bred president of the Congress, John Hancock, harbored a concealed desire to be named commander in chief and that his ambition divided New England delegates.

Consequently, Adams secretly conferred with "our staunchest men" to assess the situation. Cutting through anxieties and confusion, he concluded that George Washington was the best choice even though Hancock's patriotic services had been "incomparably greater." Adams conducted a private canvass of key delegates to determine their attitudes toward Washington and found them divided and irresolute. Undaunted, and "determined to keep a step which would compel them and all the other members of Congress to declare themselves for or against something," Adams addressed fellow delegates to urge them to adopt the army outside of Boston and to appoint a general.

After enumerating reasons this should be done, Adams stated that he had "but one gentleman in my mind for that important command." At these words John Hancock brightened visibly, certain that his fellow Massachusetts delegate was about to call his name. Instead, Adams continued: "A gentleman from Virginia." A striking change came over Hancock, "mortification and resentment" as strong as his face could exhibit. Simultaneously, from the back of the chamber, Washington, overcome by embarrassment, darted from the room. Plunging ahead, Adams completed his speech: "A gentleman whose skill and experience as an officer, whose independent fortune, great talents, and excellent universal character, would command the approbation of all America, and unite the cordial exertions of all the Colonies better than any other person in the Union."[9]

Cousin Samuel Adams seconded the motion and Adams's coup de main was complete, a decisive first step toward providing the colonies with a unifying commander. Although there was mild dissent, John Adams's behind-the-scenes negotiations held up. That night a Virginia delegate wrote: "Colonel Washington has been pressed to take the supreme command of the American Troops encamped at Roxbury, and I believe will accept the appointment, though with much reluctance, he being deeply impressed with the importance of that honourable trust, and diffident of his own ... abilities."[10]

The prospects of high command frightened Washington. Always sensitive to his reputation, he predicted to fellow Virginian Patrick Henry: "Remember, Mr. Henry, what I now tell you: From the day I enter upon the command of the American armies, I date my fall, and the ruin of my reputation."[11]

For the next several days delegates pondered the man who would lead their army. Silas Deane spoke for many when he noted that the more he saw of Washington, the better he thought of him.[12] Eliphalet Dyer weighed Washington's merits and decided that although he lacked military accomplishment, his appointment cemented the south to the north and relieved southern fears that a victorious army led by a New Englander would dominate the colonies and "give law to the Southern or Western Gentry." Moreover, Washington did not fit Dyer's New England stereotype of a southern cavalier. Washington was "no harum Starum ranting swearing fellow but Sober, steady, and Calm."[13]

When General Washington departed Philadelphia to join the army he took with him limited military experience. However, his life at Mount Vernon had required him to keep business records, to allocate scarce financial resources, and to plan for both the short run—the next harvest season—and the long term. These were skills directly relevant to the task ahead. In addition, his background included lengthy membership in the Virginia House of Burgesses. This taught him the workings of the legislative mind. It provided to be vital knowledge as he embarked upon what he foresaw would be a "tempestuous Ocean."[14]

TO COMMAND A WAR

During the American Revolution many factors conspired to make Washington's leadership of the rebel army almost impossibly difficult. Whereas future leaders enjoyed established precedent, Washington and the Continental Congress had to grope toward some workable system while trying to outlast the world's mightiest military machine. For the war's eight long years, conflict between Congress and its general revolved around two great, interlocked issues: command authority, the power to issue orders and have them carried out; and army formation, creating and maintaining an effective military force.

When Washington took command outside of Boston, he soon realized that his position lacked essential authority. Congress insisted that no troops could be disbanded without its approval. Yet Washington found that many regiments were hollow, having a full complement of officers filled by political patronage, and insufficient men. Future commanders in chief—Abraham Lincoln, for one—would face the same problem, but they possessed vastly greater resources to support such profligacy. Such units cost almost as much as combat-worthy formations—already Washington's military chest was running out of money—yet contributed little to the army's battle strength. Military and financial logic dictated that they be consolidated and surplus officers sent home. Instead, Washington had to argue endlessly with a distant Congress.

Consumed by a first major firestorm between emerging political factions, Congress failed to address its general's concerns. The tinder was the related question of who could appoint the field officers in the new Continental Army, Congress or the colonies? Congressmen recognized that they, too, were setting a precedent by laying the foundation for an American army and defining that army's relationship to civil rule. Backers of a strong central government argued that since Congress had responsibility for the army, then it was entitled to appoint officers. By such appointments they wanted to cement the army's dependence upon Congress. John Jay explained: "The Union depends much upon breaking down provincial conventions." Opponents described this suggestion as "extraordinary and big with mischief." They wanted to preserve the colonies' autonomy, believing that the union existed to protect individual colonies. In the ensuing days, the debate expanded to the question of who should control the militia. Samuel Adams, fearing the ultimate character of a central government, urged "that the militia of each colony should remain under the sole direction of its own [legislature] . . . history affords abundant instances of established armies making themselves the masters of those countries, which they were designed to protect."[15] In the end Congress reached a compromise regarding the appointment of field grade officers, and required General Washington to obtain permissions from the executive authority of each colony before calling up its militia. The long-term implications of the congressional debate lay in the revelation of a schism of opinion regarding the role of central government. It would widen to form contending political factions and give birth to political parties. It was the issue that dominated American politics for the next forty years. In 1775 it was an issue whose debate did nothing to advance Washington's struggle against the British.

*   *   *

At the close of 1776, Congress was safely ensconced in a provisional capital in Baltimore. Although not yet informed about Washington's strike across the Delaware, it vested the commander in chief with complete powers to raise another sixteen battalions of infantry, three thousand light horse, three regiments of artillery, a corps of engineers, and to appoint their officers under the rank of brigadier general. Henceforth he could call upon any state militia he desired. The former was an enormous step toward placing the regular, or Continental, army on a sound basis. The latter helped Washington to respond to enemy maneuvers without the time-consuming need to go through civil channels. The authority to call out the militia became one of the key powers of all subsequent presidents and commanders in chief.

There was more. Congress authorized Washington "to take . . .

whatever he may want" from private sources for the army if the inhabitants would not sell, and to arrest anyone who refused to accept the debased continental currency or was "otherwise disaffected to the American cause."[16] Congressmen recognized that these were surpassing powers. To some it was a straightforward matter: "We have given Genl. Washington large and ample powers . . . Thus the Business of War will for six months to come move in the proper channels and the Congress be no longer exercised about matters of which it is supremely ignorant."17 To others it was an act of desperation: "Congress have given up most of their Power to the Generals . . . if this don't save your City [Philadelphia] nothing we can do will."[18] On the other hand, Washington's inner circle believed the general's accretion of power overdue. Had he possessed such powers months ago, affairs would not have reached such desperate straits.[19]

No one took this step lightly. When the commander in chief used his emergency powers to require suspect civilians to take an oath of allegiance to the United States, it alarmed some thoughtful patriots. The oath represented the general's effort to deal with the difficult problem of distinguishing loyalists from rebels, for in truth there were as many of the one as the other. In response, one of the original signers of the Declaration of Independence observed that the rebellion set out "to oppose tyranny in all its strides." He perceived fatal consequences flowing from the fact that the commander in chief "hath assumed the Legislative and Executive powers of Government in all the states."[20] In the end, enough congressmen believed they knew the measure of the man and could entrust him with great power without endangering the nation's liberty.[21]

While specifying that the commander in chief was to have emergency powers for six months, it repeatedly reauthorized them for the remainder of the war. Even so, congressmen continued to observe closely the ebb and flow of civil-military power. After Trenton and Princeton, patriotic publications praised Washington. Typical was the *Pennsylvania Journal*:

> *Washington retreats like a General and acts like a hero. If there are spots in his character, they are like the spots in the sun, only discernible by the magnifying powers of a telescope. Had he lived in the days of idolatry, he would have been worshipped as a god.*[22]

Such popular praise upset many delegates. John Adams, for one, explained why he lacked an "exalted Opinion of our Generals."

He cited Dr. Jonathan Swift's assertion that history had witnessed only six military geniuses. Thus, Adams noted, it was unlikely that one should arise at the present time. He concluded: "When such shall appear I shall certainly have an exalted opinion. Until then I believe my Opinion of our Generals will continue not very exalted."[23]

The core military force striving to terminate America's bid for independence was composed of red-coated British regular infantry and German mercenaries. They drilled for years to achieve the necessary discipline to fight on the eighteenth-century battlefield. The era's inaccurate muskets and their slow rate of fire dictated that soldiers stand shoulder to shoulder in order to generate sufficient firepower. Firefights typically occurred at a range of less than fifty yards. Victory demanded that a soldier be able mechanically to load, fire, close ranks when the adjacent soldier fell, and advance with lowered bayonet into a wall of opposing fire for a decisive charge. In sum, the tactics of the day required an individual to become a "walking musket," capable of performing these tasks regardless of the noise, smoke, and slaughter that surrounded him. To ask this of the militia, civilians summoned from their farms and shops during an emergency, was to ask too much. In spite of repeated defeats and disasters, often caused by militia failure, numerous congressmen failed to comprehend this battlefield reality. Consequently, Washington and his generals had to find ways to meld the militia into a military machine, a task requiring considerable trial and frequent error.

They much preferred relying upon the regular soldiers of the Continental Line. However, simply designating a soldier a "regular" does not make him so. It was something that necessitated relentless, often brutal, training—and it took time. Here American antimilitarism affected matters as well. Congress, reluctantly, granted the need for regular soldiers but then limited the term of enlistment to prevent the creation of a threatening standing army. As early as the winter of 1776, during the investment of Boston, Washington recognized the evils thereof. It took two to three months to acquaint a recruit with his duty, longer to instill in him the habit of discipline. Before this training was complete, the recruit's time for dismissal approached and it was necessary to relax discipline in hopes of encouraging the recruit to re-enlist.

This relaxation undid what was first accomplished.[24] Washington concluded that there was only one solution: enlistment for the war's duration.

Congress debated whether to accept this proposal by using offers of money and the promise of land in the western territories to attract long-term enlistments. Although John Adams personally favored this approach, he, too, was ambivalent: "Although it may cost us more, and we may put now and then a battle to hazard by the method we are in, yet we shall be less in danger of corruption and violence from a standing army, and our militia will acquire courage, experience, discipline, and hardiness in actual service."[25] In the spring of 1777, the consequences of erratic congressional policy toward long-term recruitment put much more than merely a battle "to hazard."

Washington's winter victories at Trenton and Princeton had preserved the rebel cause, but they were mere pinpricks relative to the formidable enemy host preparing for a new campaign. From Canada came an invading army led by "Gentleman Johnny" Burgoyne, an aggressive, confident general who made book in a fashionable London betting parlor that he would bring the war to a successful conclusion in short order. From New York came an even larger British army commanded by Lord Howe. Its objective was the rebel capital in Philadelphia. To oppose it, Washington had a small force whose ranks had yet to be filled by new recruits. Although Congress had authorized the raising of new regiments, the states found myriad reasons to fail to comply. Yet Congress believed that the army was stronger than ever and held high expectations for the coming campaign.

As the British juggernaut ground forward, congressional anxiety increased. Unwilling or unable to see that their own actions had limited the effectiveness of Washington's army and thereby precluded offensive possibilities, many congressmen grew restive over Washington's defensive strategy. It reminded Samuel Adams of the Roman Fabius, who preferred to retreat before an enemy in order to overextend the enemy's resources rather than standing and fighting. Sam Adams was not "pleased with what is called the Fabian War in America." For the moment, however, he acknowledged "I have no Judgment in military Affairs, and therefore will leave the Subject to be discussed . . . by those who are Masters of it."[26] That "master," George Washington, in turn assessed the situation bluntly: "The campaign is opening, and we have no men for the field."[27] It almost turned out that he had too few qualified subordinates to officer the men that he did have.

In July of 1777, letters from Washington's three top lieutenants—Generals Sullivan, Knox, and Greene—stirred an enormous controversy over the relationship between civil and military rule. The three generals threatened to resign if a recently arrived foreign general—one of a host of such officers, some qualified, others charlatans attracted by the prospect of quick and undeserved rank—received promotion over them. Congress, seeing in this threat a deadly challenge to its authority, sniffed that it was not "accustomed" to being "controlled" by its officers.[28] It debated whether to dismiss all three or better yet to arrest and try them. Cooler heads prevailed, and Congress merely demanded an apology from the offending officers.

On a personal level, John Adams and Nathanael Greene terminated their friendship over this issue. Adams tried to explain that had Greene considered "the Necessity of preserving the Authority of the Civil Powers above the military," he would never have threatened to resign. If Congress backed down, Adams continued, it would establish a precedent and "one Breach of the Privileges of Congress after another will be made, and one Contempt of its Authority after another will be offered until the Officers of the Army will do as most others have done, wrest all Authority out of civil Hands and set up a Tyrant of their own."[29] As principled a patriot as any American, Greene still did not agree. More generally, the controversy demonstrated that although Washington had few competent subordinates, Congress was willing to sacrifice three of them in order to establish a precedent even at a time when an enormous enemy offensive threatened to snuff out the rebel cause.

As had occurred the previous year, when the threat was distant Congress limited its commander in chief's power, when the menace loomed large it relinquished authority to him. So, in August of 1777, with the British army again drawing near, Congress provided the clearest definition to date of Washington's mandate. It ingenuously explained that all of the impediments it had erected to limit Washington were "never intended . . . to supersede or circumscribe the power of General Washington as the commander in chief of all the continental land forces within the United States."[30]

It is the business of an army to fight. Knowing that Congress and the army itself expected it, sensitive to criticism of his Fabian strategy, for the first time since his ill-fated decision to offer battle in Manhattan, Washington violated his own strategy. Instead of avoiding major battles, he occupied a defensive position behind Brandywine Creek from where he hoped to block Howe's entry into Philadelphia. However, he failed to assess correctly battlefield intelligence, allowed his flank to be turned, and in spite of stout fighting by his Continentals, suffered defeat.

Grumbles about his leadership, even among his heretofore most devoted subordinates, mounted. Many political leaders wondered if Washington was equal to the military challenge at hand. John Adams poured his own anxieties out in his dairy:

> *Oh, Heaven! grant Us one great Soul! One leading Mind would extricate the best Cause, from the Ruin which seems to await it . . .*
>   *We have as good a Cause, as ever was fought for. We have great Resources. The People are well tempered. One active masterly Capacity would bring order out of this Confusion and save this Country.*[31]

For the second time, Congress decided to evacuate the capital. Five days later, against no opposition, the British marched into Philadelphia.

A wholesale turnover in the membership of Congress occurred before delegates reconvened in safety in York, Pennsylvania, in the autumn of 1777. Of the twenty-plus members who had elected Washington to highest command, only six remained. Some had died, others terminated their service, and still others took leave with or without their colleagues' consent. Few members of the new Congress were personally acquainted with Washington and fewer still had useful experience to apply to the support of the army.

They could not help but compare General Horatio Gates's performance with that of Washington. Gates had won a stunning triumph at Saratoga, where he forced the surrender of Burgoyne's army. A Washington critic wrote John Adams to praise Gates and note that Washington, in contrast, had been "outgeneraled and twice beaten" and forced to give up the nation's capital. The critic concluded: "If our Congress can witness these things with composure and suffer them to pass without an inquiry, I shall think we have not shook off monarchical prejudices."[32] John Adams himself welcomed Gates's success with particular pleasure since it was due neither to the commander in chief nor to southern troops. By Adams's lights, Gates's success moderated excessive public adulation. Referring to Washington, Adams concluded: "Now, we can allow a certain citizen to be wise, virtuous and good without thinking him a deity or a savior."[33]

The new Congress did not possess Adams's mature perspective. The cause had suffered unexpected setbacks and shocking defeats, and delegates intended to do something about it. They resolved that henceforth when any land or sea expedition failed or an important post or fort was lost, it would "be an established rule in Congress to institute an enquiry into the causes of the failure . . . or loss . . . and into the conduct of the principal officer or officers conducting the expedition so failing."[34] Their resolution marked the origin of the congressional inquiry.

Highly focused on the contrast between Gates's success and Washington's failure, congressmen failed to appreciate that the war's strategic calculus had altered. When news of Burgoyne's surrender at Saratoga reached Paris, it gave great pleasure to the court at Versailles. It was the decisive event that triggered overt French intervention on behalf of the American rebels. An American diplomatic team led by Benjamin Franklin negotiated a treaty by which France pledged to support American sovereignty. A French naval squadron began preparation for a voyage across the Atlantic, where it would seek to coordinate its operations with the Americans. When London learned of the Franco-American alliance, King George III's advisers considered it an act of war. Thereafter, the rebellion in America shrank in importance, with British strategists viewing it as one theater subsumed within a larger world war.

Strategic planning in faraway Europe took time to have an impact on operations in North America. In the meantime, there was a real possibility that the rebel cause would collapse, for the winter of 1777–1778, the first encampment at Valley Forge, was the worst yet endured by Washington's army.

*   *   *

The soldiers' somber cries echoed off the bleak, windswept ridge: "No meat, no meat!" Indeed, it was only the truth. With the British comfortably housed in winter quarters in Philadelphia, Washington established his own winter quarters at Valley Forge. It soon became clear that it would be a time of immense hardship.

When Washington prepared marching orders, he received a chilling reply. The soldiers could not stir from camp. They lacked the basic apparel, shoes, and warm clothing for a winter march. Even if they could march, there was not enough food to sustain field operations. The camp's only Commissary officer reported that he had no animals for slaughter and could count only twenty-five barrels of flour to feed the entire army. Nearly three thousand men were unfit for duty. Although Congress had authorized the delivery of essentials such as blankets, soap, and vinegar, they did not arrive.

A soldier wrote:

> *I am sick—discontented—and out of humour. Poor food—hard lodging—cold weather—fatigue—nasty cloaths—nasty cookery— vomit half my time . . . why are we sent here to starve and Freeze.*[35]

Many officers complained of low pay, salaries in arrears, inadequate living allowances, and lack of a plan for postwar compensation. They saw a home front growing rich as civilians concentrated on profiteering, hoarding, and avoiding conscription. They discussed seizing supplies from the civilian population and forcibly drafting men to fill depleted ranks.

Meanwhile, congressional critics blamed Washington for the army's suffering, and his influence fell to a nadir. One commented privately that the commander in chief had been guilty of "such blunders as might have disgraced a soldier of three months' standing."[36] Others sneeringly styled him a "Demi God" while treating his request for a reform of the Quartermaster's Department with jokes and sarcasm. Some delegates predicted his imminent resignation and suggested that Gates should succeed him.

They greeted with great skepticism Washington's letter stating that unless there was an immediate change "this Army must inevitably be reduced to one or other of these three things. Starve, dissolve, or disperse."[37]

In contrast, a Virginia delegate who visited Valley Forge saw the army's paralyzing distress. He heard the commander in chief enumerate his problems and responded, "My dear General, if you had given some explanation, all these rumors would have been silenced a long time ago."[38] Two years earlier Washington had faced a similar situation when his ill-supplied army outside of Boston dissolved. Then, as now, to describe his situation candidly and in public would give the enemy too much valuable information.[39] At Valley Forge he confronted the British by bluff alone. Accordingly, he replied to the sympathetic fellow Virginian, "How can I exculpate myself without doing harm to the public cause?"[40]

By the narrowest the army endured. Finally allowed to reform the Quartermaster's and Commissary departments, Washington partially corrected the administrative chaos that had caused the winter shortages. Simultaneously, his congressional opponents lost influence, and his rival generals lost stature. In large measure all of this was because Washington's devotion to the cause and basic integrity could not be gainsaid. The army that prepared for a new campaign season was very much Washington's army. A gifted martinet, Baron Friedrich Wilhelm von Steuben, had drilled the Continental Line to nearly the same state of efficiency as that of crack British regiments. Trusted subordinates now led Washington's fighting formations. His own appointees headed the all-important administrative posts. Thus were the soldiers' sacrifices at Valley Forge partially redeemed.

CAMPAIGN FOR A CONTINENT

In July of 1778 the British evacuated Philadelphia. Occupation of the rebel capital had proved a strategic dead end. The soul of the rebellion did not lie in any one geographical place. Rather it resided with the army, and because of Washington's leadership it had proved an elusive target. The American general's pursuit of the British led to a major battle at Monmouth Courthouse in New Jersey. Monmouth was an inconclusive encounter. As at Princeton one year earlier, Washington rode along the lines where "his fine appearance" and "calm courage" rallied the American army, thereby permitting the Continentals to do something they had never done before: fight the British to a standstill in a field action.[41] Monmouth was the war's last battle between the American and British main forces. In three years of war Washington had failed to defeat the British in a set piece battle. This failure obscured his more important triumph: he had baffled the efforts of a much stronger British army to reconquer America and forced that army to return to its base in New York City, the city from which the campaign of 1776 had begun.

During the Monmouth campaign came the welcome news that

a French fleet had appeared off the Delaware capes. Congress instructed Washington to cooperate with the French in offensive operations as he saw fit.[42] This broad mandate reflected the trust Congress now invested in its commander in chief. Henceforth, Washington's major strategic challenge was to coordinate the Franco-American war machine toward some productive end. It was not easy, for most Americans possessed an antipathy toward the hereditary enemy. Indeed, since the time of Washington's first exposure to the French, when they had been his sworn enemy on the Virginia frontier, until now, when he had to cope with prideful French volunteer officers swarming his headquarters in pursuit of a high rank they could not obtain in Europe, Washington's experience with the French had been unhappy. Language, religion, and habits all conspired to impede the forging of a successful relationship with the new ally.

Furthermore, supply, as always, was difficult, and communication with a sail-driven fleet subject to the vagaries of weather, tenuous. Lack of money forced a defensive strategy, for without money the army could neither accumulate supplies nor recruit. Congressional indolence, coupled with its choke of administrative detail, caused most important measures to be deferred. In sum, it was to be a fateful experiment in cooperation fraught with real military obstacles, diplomatic difficulties, and stupefying bureaucratic impediments.

In spite of Washington's efforts to hold diverse factions steady toward the main goal, another campaign season ended in frustration with little accomplished. Summoned to Congress, the commander in chief confirmed his suspicions that Congress was grossly mismanaging the country's affairs. Congress's most gifted leaders had returned to their states to engage in local concerns. In their wake they left a body populated, not with great statesmen like those of 1775, but with mediocre men. The result, in Washington's view, was "that our Affairs are in a more distressed, ruinous, and deplorable condition" than at any time. It was particularly galling because Washington believed that French intervention promised ultimate victory if the country could persevere. His solution was to suggest to state authorities that they send their "ablest and best Men to Congress," where they could correct public abuses and work a thorough reformation.[43]

*　　*　　*

While a war remained to be won, old fears lingered. In March of 1779, on the ninth anniversary of the Boston Massacre, Massachusetts's former judge advocate general addressed a patriotic crowd. He looked to the future and warned that "at the close of a struggle for liberty, a triumphant army, elated with victory, and headed by a popular General may become more formidable than the tyrant that has been expelled."[44] The judge's anxieties seemed well-founded when the ensuing summer witnessed a controversy involving accusations that Washington's aide, Alexander Hamilton, had said that the people should rise, join the commander in chief, and oust Congress.

The army's recurring distress triggered Hamilton's latent authoritarian instinct. The army relied upon requisitions to the states for food and supplies, requisitions the states were slow to fulfill. Even when they did comply, there was no money to hire wagon teams to haul supplies from distant regions to army camps. Consequently, after eating up local supplies, the soldiers were again without forage and food. Under such circumstances, history, as patriot leaders well knew, was replete with instances of military revolt. A congressional committee reported that such were the army's accumulated distresses, "the effects of a repetition of want . . . Their starving condition, Their want of pay, and the variety of hardships" that mutiny was possible.[45] So another campaign season wound down with little evidence that the patriot forces were approaching victory.

Through it all Washington tried to retain a balanced perspective. In answer to his brother's question how he could endure, the Virginian replied, "There is one reward that nothing can deprive me of, and that is, the consciousness of having done my duty."[46]

He pondered the political obstacles impeding victory. Even when cooperating harmoniously with Congress, he remained stymied to his efforts to create a military capable of winning the war. By 1780 it was the states who obstructed the war effort. Washington believed that Congress lacked the power to prosecute the war. He saw each state acting independently of the others; some fulfilling congressional requisitions and some neglecting them, "one head gradually changing into thirteen."[47] Congress had been surrendering powers to the states until it reached the point where it was little more than the medium through which the wants of the army were conveyed to the states.[48] Expectations of French intervention had caused most states to reduce their contributions to the common cause. The states competed not to see "which shall do most for the common cause, but which shall do least."[49] Lacking forceful leaders who could overcome provincial interests for the benefit of the whole, Congress slipped into impotence.

By midsummer 1780, the army was at a near-fatal low ebb: unfed, poorly supplied, unable to maneuver against the British army around New York while a new British strategic offensive overran the southern states. Writing to his brother, Washington explained why so little had been accomplished since the welcome news of French intervention two years ago:

> *We are, during the winter, dreaming of Independence and Peace, without using the means to become so. In the Spring, when our Recruits should be with the Army and in training, we have just discovered the necessity of calling for them. and by the Fall, after a distressed, and inglorious campaign for want of them, we begin to get a few men, which come in just time enough to eat our Provisions, and consume our Stores without rendering any service; thus it is, one year Rolls over another, and with out some change, we are hastening to our Ruin.*[50]

The winter of 1780–1781 marked the nadir of patriotic American spirit. A soaring inflation, the loss of Charleston, the British rout of the southern field army, Benedict Arnold's shocking treason, and mutiny in the ranks of the Pennsylvania and New Jersey Continentals combined to discourage the nation that victory was ever obtainable. Undaunted, Washington fixated on the main chance, cooperation with the French. Such cooperation, in turn, hinged upon a decisive naval superiority.[51] Absent a significant American naval force, this superiority could only be won by the French.

*   *   *

Since his arrival in America, Lieutenant-General Comte de Rochambeau had obeyed his king's instructions to cooperate loyally with the American commander in chief. But, by the spring of 1781, Rochambeau sensed that time was running out on the rebel cause. He believed that British operations in Virginia posed a mortal peril and was unpersuaded by Washington's logic that the best way to relieve Virginia was by attacking New York City. In May, a frigate arrived in Boston carrying dispatches from France. Written at Versailles in early March, they included two pieces of information too secret to share with Washington. First, a second French fleet was bound for the West Indies and then for the American coast sometime in July or August. Second, if the American cause collapsed, Rochambeau was to cease accepting orders from the Americans and to abandon them to their fate. Rochambeau wrote Washington that it was "indispensable" that they confer.[52]

In the subsequent meeting, Rochambeau shared with Washington the exciting news that a large French fleet commanded by Comte de Grasse had left France to sail to the West Indies. More than this he did not say. He asked Washington where the French should take the field. The commander in chief replied that experience had shown that the long march from New York to Virginia involved a heavy attrition and therefore the campaign should focus on New York City. Rochambeau then inquired, if French naval reinforcements appeared on the coast, how did Washington think they should be employed? Washington answered that plans depended on the size of the reinforcement, but that it could either assist against New York or perhaps be used for operations in the south. The allies agreed that in any event Rochambeau's army should march from New England to join Washington along the Hudson.

Rochambeau had played a deep game. Required to keep secret the fact that the French fleet under de Grasse would certainly come to the American coast, he tried to advance campaign planning by posing hypotheticals. It was clear that Washington strongly preferred a campaign against New York City, but Rochambeau remained skeptical about its feasibility. Five days later he made a momentous decision. He wrote de Grasse about "the very grave crisis" affecting America "and especially the southern states." Without help from de Grasse nothing could save the situation. "There are two points to take the offensive against the enemy: Chesapeake and New York. The south-west winds and the condition of distress in Virginia will make you probably prefer the Chesapeake Bay, and it will be there where we think you can render the greatest service."[53]

Henceforth, everything hinged on the circumstances of de Grasse's arrival. Washington's patience had been often tried during the war, teaching him how to wait. In spite of uncertainty, the commander in chief was confident. He wrote a despondent member of Congress:

> *But we must not despair; the game is yet in our own hands . . . A cloud may yet pass over us, individuals may be ruined; and the Country at large, or particular States, undergo temporary distress; but certain I am, that it is in our power to bring the War to a happy Conclusion.*[54]

*   *   *

New York or Virginia? As the summer progressed Washington pondered the options knowing that the only hope for an offensive campaign in 1781 rested on the arrival of significant French reinforcements.[55] He carefully monitored the naval balance, its fundamental equation a matter of numbers of rival ships of the line, the battleships of the age of sail. When a sudden storm struck the British anchorage, damaging some ships of the line, Washington asked, Does this give the French a sufficient superiority to strike? When his spies reported the departure of a British ship of the line from New York Harbor, he considered, Is it now time? He could only answer no, not yet, not until de Grasse appeared with reinforcements.

Again he met with Rochambeau at a formal conference of war. Rochambeau was certain that the campaign should be directed against Virginia. He guided Washington toward his own point of view by posing a series of questions regarding future actions. Having listed all the reasons against an attack on New York, he inquired if instead the two leaders could "turn our ideas to Virginia, direct de Grasse to the Chesapeake Bay, and march there" with both the French and American infantry. In this manner, would not the allies be able "to intervene with success against Lord Cornwallis and force his evacuation?"[56] Washington acknowledged the plausibility of this plan, but still preferred to attack New York if possible. However, given the uncertainties, he ordered his heavy artillery—weapons crucial to any attack against an entrenched position, and currently located in Philadelphia—to suspend its movement north in case he should require it for operations in the south.[57]

Finally, on August 14, 1781, Washington received the most welcome news since he first had learned of a French alliance back in

1778. Admiral de Grasse was coming, not to New York, but to the Chesapeake, with twenty-nine ships of the line and three thousand infantry! This, by the narrowest, could give the French naval supremacy. It was glorious news, but—and Washington had learned to expect always a "but"—de Grasse intended to remain on the American coast only until October 15. Furthermore, one of his detached subordinates planned to take his squadron off to Newfoundland instead of joining the main fleet.

With "matters having now come to a crisis," the commander in chief set to work; first to dissuade one French admiral from the Newfoundland diversion, second to describe a plan of operations to de Grasse.[58] Washington abandoned the effort against New York, canceled the departure of forces from Virginia, and concentrated everything, including his siege cannon at Philadelphia, against Cornwallis, who was reported entrenching near the small port of Yorktown on the Chesapeake Bay. Then he rode south to join the movement against his old foe.

En route, the eagerly awaited news reached him: de Grasse had arrived and had landed his men on the Virginia coast. A Frenchman described Washington's reaction, his

> *natural coldness and . . . serious and noble approach . . . his features, his physiognomy, his deportment—all were changed in an instant. He put aside his character as arbiter of North America and contented himself for the moment with that of a citizen, happy at the good fortune of his country. A child, whose every wish had been gratified, would not have experienced a sensation more lively.*[59]

On September 5, 1781, the decisive conflict of the war occurred. No American serviceman participated in the naval battle off the Capes of Virginia, yet the fact that it took place was due to the persistence of George Washington. Admiral de Grasse engaged the British fleet and thwarted the British effort to relieve Cornwallis.

No sailor is comfortable on a lee shore, particularly when the world's most powerful fleet could appear over the horizon at any time and attack. Even as the allied vise embracing Yorktown began to tighten, de Grasse proposed taking his main fleet to open water to find maneuvering room. Washington well knew that an adverse wind could scatter the French fleet and thus save Cornwallis. He implored de Grasse to stay put, explaining that if the admiral held his position, victory was certain. A British defeat "must necessarily go a great way towards terminating the war."[60] Washington's argument prevailed. On October 18, 1781, the general sent Congress the happy news that Cornwallis had surrendered.

By the following spring most active campaigning had ended, but peace proved elusive. A formidable British host remained in New York, checked only by the presence of Washington's depleted army, and that army again stirred toward mutiny. This time it was the officers who led the discord. A veteran Continental colonel, who explained he represented many other officers, described to Washington the army's plight and attributed it to congressional inefficiency: "This war must have shewn to all, but to military men in particular the weakness of republicks." The colonel continued by observing that the same abilities that had triumphed over apparently insurmountable odds at Yorktown and elsewhere would be most appropriate to guide the nation at peace. He added that some people failed to comprehend this and thus mistakenly associated tyranny and monarchy. He concluded by suggesting that Washington should become king.[61] It was exactly the nightmare feared by the first delegates to Congress.

Washington issued a stern response: "Be assured Sir, no occurrence in the course of the War, has given me more painful sensations than your information of there being such ideas existing in the Army ... I must view with abhorrence, and reprehend with severity ... if you have any regard for your Country, concern for yourself or posterity, or respect for me ... banish these thoughts."[62]

While diplomats squabbled over vital issues of territory and influence, Washington tried to hold the remnants of the army together. The soldiers endured a Valley Forge–like winter of hunger and deprivation. Then, in mid-March 1783, two anonymous papers, the Newburgh Addresses, circulated through the Continental Army's camp. They asked soldiers whether, after seven years of trial, the country was "willing to redress your wrongs, cherish your worth and reward your services," or was it "a country that tramples upon your rights, disdains your cries and insults your distresses." After reminding the soldiers that Congress had repeatedly ignored its sufferings, the addresses challenged them "to oppose tyranny under whatever garb it may assume" and resist disbandment until justice was delivered.[63] A manifesto invited officers to attend a meeting to ponder the proposition that the army disband if war should resume or, if peace came, retain its arms and retire to the frontier.

Here was the crisis that many had feared when authorizing a standing army. Some recalled that in similar fashion Roman legions had marched against their government to demand back pay. The commander in chief recognized the merit of the complaints articulated in the Newburgh Addresses. He also recognized mutiny. He preempted the meeting of officers by summoning them to a meeting of his own.

Standing before them, he drew his written address from his coat pocket and, with his other hand, reached for his spectacles. "Gentlemen, you will permit me to put on my spectacles, for I have not only grown gray, but almost blind, in the service of my country." At these words many fought to keep their composure, a few unabashedly cried.

The commander in chief described the manifesto as shocking, unmilitary, subversive, an insidious attempt to sow "the seeds of discord and separation between the Civil and Military powers." He stated his confidence that Congress would deliver full justice to the army because that body was aware of the army's merits and its sufferings. He explained that like all deliberative bodies having a variety of different interests to reconcile, Congress had to proceed slowly. He pledged himself to justice and asked his officers not to sully the army's glory by overturning civil rule. He requested that they

> give one more distinguished proof of unexampled patriotism and patient virtue, rising superior to the pressure of the most complicated sufferings; And you will, by the dignity of your Conduct, afford occasion for Posterity to say, when speaking of the glorious example you have exhibited to Mankind, had this day been wanting, the World had never seen the last stage of perfection to which human nature is capable of attaining.[64]

Shamed and silenced, the insurrection died stillborn.

Finally, by the end of 1783, Washington saw the last British forces evacuate New York. With that, he had accomplished all of his duties except one. The nation born by revolution and war would experience no Roman emperor, no Cromwell. Instead, as the triumphant commander in chief informed a friend, he would journey to Annapolis, where he expected to "get translated into a private Citizen."[65]

On Friday December 20, the day after his arrival in Annapolis, five days before Christmas 1783, Congress received his letter asking whether he should resign his commission by private letter or public audience. Recognizing the transcendent symbolism of the occasion, Congress choose the latter.[66] A team of three writers, led by Thomas Jefferson, prepared Congress's formal response for the coming Tuesday, while at nearby Mann's Tavern, a worthy tavern-keeper frantically arranged a sumptuous feast to be held the day before.

Mr. Mann proved equal to the occasion, serving close to three hundred gentlemen in "elegant and profuse style." Good cheer flowed amid the burble of contented voices and the clang of silverware. Guests drank the customary thirteen toasts, yet so important was the occasion that not a soul exhibited drunkenness. To climax the dinner, the general proposed a fourteenth toast, a salute to Congress that urged qualified, dedicated men to join that body to lead the young nation into the future.[67]

Monday evening, gentlemen and ladies alike rode to the State House to attend a ball in the general's honor. A brilliant illumination shone from the mullioned windows, reflecting the guests' excitement and hopes. During the ball, the general proved tireless, dancing every set so the ladies might have the pleasure of getting "a touch of him."

On Tuesday, Congress convened, its members wearing their most formal clothes. At precisely noon the great man was announced. It took time to silence the expectant throng—men packed in every nook and cranny behind the seated congressmen, women overflowing the gallery—but once silence befitting the solemn occasion reigned the general rose and bowed to Congress. The congressmen, in turn, doffed their hats in salute, but did not return the bow. This symbolic subordination of military to civilian rule was unmistakable.

The general began his address. Normally, he spoke in a deep, penetrating voice, but his audience realized that this would be different. His hand holding the paper shook as he began: "The great events on which my resignation depended having at length taken place; I have now the honor of offering my sincere Congratulations to Congress and of presenting myself before them to surrender into their hands the trust committed to me." When he spoke of those devoted officers who had served in his military family from Valley Forge to Yorktown, he choked with emotion and grasped his paper with both hands. Many in the audience stifled sobs, and not a few, overcome by emotion, shed tears. In faltering voice he continued until, commending the interests of his country, and those who superintend them, to God, "his voice faultered and sunk, and the whole house felt his agitations." He regained his composure and in strong voice concluded: "Having now finished the work assigned me I retire from the great theatre of action, and bidding an affectionate farewell to this august body under whose orders I have so long acted I here offer my commission and take my leave of all the employments of public life."[68] He reached into his breast pocket, drew out his commission, and delivered it to the president of Congress.

A revolution completed, a new nation begun. The commander of a victorious army, a man of near-unchallenged popularity at the apex of his career, through word and action underscored a newborn American tradition of civil supremacy over the military. It was this historic theme that Jefferson emphasized in the short speech the president of Congress now delivered: "You have conducted the great military contest with wisdom and fortitude invariably regarding the rights of the civil power through all disasters and changes."[69]

Thanked, dismissed, having conducted himself for eight weary years in such a way that he won independence and then left it to civilians to consolidate the gains of the Revolution, George Washington hurriedly departed for home to spend Christmas dinner at his beloved Mount Vernon.

3 ☞

TO LEAD A NATION

> *". . . while there are knaves and fools in the world, there will be wars in it; and that nations should make war against nations is less surprising than their living in uninterrupted peace and harmony."*
>
> JOHN JAY TO GOUVERNEUR MORRIS, SEPTEMBER 24, 1783[1]

LESSONS FROM A REVOLUTION

WHEN, IN 1783, THE SAILS OF THE LAST BRITISH TRANSPORTS DISAPpeared over the horizon east of New York City, the Continental Army and its commander in chief had finished their job. Like the vanquished, the victors then returned to their homes. This was a remarkable event, unlike previous historical experience. History taught that once a revolution triumphed, the rebels employed armed force to consolidate victory. Instead, the American army dissolved back into the populace. Thus, the military, as a force unto itself, did not shape the new nation's post-Revolutionary domestic and foreign policy.

During the war, the Continental Congress had been a combustible political group united in only one belief: the war must be won. There had been little agreement as to how this should be done, which was why Congress gave General Washington increasing latitude to conduct military operations. However, Congress always retained ultimate control by defining the war's objectives, specifying the number of troops and the extent of their supplies, and financing the whole effort. Back in 1776, John Adams had acknowledged that the ways of Congress were costly in both treasure and blood, but they were necessary to avoid the "corruption and violence from a standing army."[2] Indeed, it was a triumph of congressional planning that the military establishment was no threat to the young republic. What is remarkable is that a Congress representing diverse and parochial interests, populated by many who were more afraid of national government than of the British, should have succeeded as well as it did. What is unremarkable is that at the war's conclusion, different politicians drew very different lessons from their recent history.

When the Revolutionary War began, patriot leaders recognized the efficiencies flowing from a concentration of power. However, Congress could not operate in a style exhibiting any taint of tyranny, so it chose a system featuring a remarkable number of committees formed to address the myriad needs of a nation at war. To name only a few is to underscore the fragmentation of power: committees on saltpeter; spies; musket manufacture; hospitals; the health and discipline of the army; clothing; beef; salt; a committee to draft instructions for recruiting officers and another responsible for putting the militia on a war footing. Furthermore, Congress did not delegate authority to the committees. Rather, the committees examined the issues, devised solutions, and then reported to the whole Congress.

A year of this was enough to prove it unworkable. Congressmen simply did not have enough time no matter how hard they worked. John Adams recalled working every morning and evening for a solid four months on committees, with afternoons spent attending to legislative matters. By the fall of 1777 a new arrangement formally began: a Board of War comprising noncongressional members who would handle the war's executive business. Congress retained ultimate authority over the new board, but the reform represented an important change in how Congress utilized its executive powers.

The new Board of War turned out to be a hotbed of anti-Washington sentiment, featuring such unsavory characters as Thomas Conway, of Cabal fame, and the ambitious Horatio Gates, who believed himself better suited for the role of commander in chief than Washington. Even after Congress purged the anti-Washington conspirators, the board still failed to function in a satisfactory manner. Essentially a clerical agency, it easily became engrossed in military minutiae to the detriment of more important issues.

While Congress never developed a satisfactory mechanism for administering land forces—the Continental soldiers' suffering at

Valley Forge is only the best-known example of congressional ineptitude; it was an experience American soldiers shared time and again during campaigns from Georgia to Canada—it had a different experience with the fledgling American navy. This was because the challenges associated with turning citizen soldiers into regular infantry were novel problems whereas converting a fast-sailing merchantman into an armed privateer was not.

In happy contrast to the tedium and intractable problems faced by committees dealing with army affairs, the Naval Committee's sessions began at six in the evening and continued until midnight amid "diversions marked by a rich flow of soul, history, poetry, wine, and Jamaica rum."[3] Such conviviality did not prevent the hard-eyed New England Yankees, and in particular Governor Hopkins of Rhode Island, from keeping a weather eye on the main chance. Their attention ensured that the governor's relatives and friends led the new fleet, with Hopkins's son becoming "Commander in Chief of the Fleet of the United Colonies" while his grandson received command of one of the fleet's vessels. Reorganized as a Marine Committee, it enjoyed considerably more authority than its army counterparts. It issued specific instructions to naval officers that defined their cruising stations. Much like the German U-boat admiral Karl Doenitz, who, during World War II positioned his wolf packs along vulnerable British convoy routes, the Marine Committee sent its ships to intercept England's West Indian sugar ships, Newfoundland fishing vessels, the Hudson Bay fur fleet, and Guineamen laden with ivory, gold, and slaves.

In spite of such relative efficiencies, even in naval affairs the committee system ultimately failed. By the spring of 1779, a leading opponent of the committee system, John Jay, wrote Washington that the Marine Committee had exposed "all the Consequences of Want of System, Attention and Knowledge."[4] As part of the subsequent reform, in the winter of 1781 Congress resolved that there should be a Secretary at War.[5] It equated the position with that of a high-level clerk whose department would serve as a clearinghouse for administrative matters. In a similar manner the Marine Committees's successor, the Board of Admiralty, administered naval and marine affairs. Neither board planned grand strategy.

General Benjamin Lincoln, a revolutionary veteran of modest abilities, served as the first Secretary of War. Lincoln was responsible for record keeping and transmitting congressional resolves to the field. A different man might have made much more of the position, but as a contemporary congressman later said, it "was fortunate for the United States, that the Secretary of War, was a true Republican, & totally oppos'd to Intrigue & aristocratical Measures."[6] When dealing with the commander in chief, Lincoln sought Washington's "approbation" before establishing a policy. Washington, out of respect for congressional authority, reciprocated the secretary's deferential style. The relationship worked so well that the next year Congress expanded the Secretary of War's powers: he was to give his opinions on subjects referred to him. In this way a semblance of military professionalism entered the counsels of Congress.

*   *   *

The war had been the formative experience for the men who were to lead the new nation for the next quarter century. George Washington had seen the racking consequences of shortage in his army. However, his legislative experience had taught him that deliberative bodies required time above all else to reach a decision. Lawmakers' belief in the need to distance the army from civil authority, to prevent the former from exercising undue influence, exacerbated the problem. So, too, the reluctance of many states to meet congressional requisitions for men and supplies, a reluctance based on ideological grounds connected with the emerging schism between state and federal authority as well as on purely selfish reasons, had posed an enormous impediment to Washington's operations. In spite of the fact that Congress and the states frequently ignored the army's just concerns, Washington had held the army together while displaying subordination to civil rule. Because he could do this, he was truly the indispensable man of the Revolution. Because he knew how close he had come to failure, he wanted to make changes so that future commanders in chief would not have to confront the same problems. This desire put Washington at odds with the antimilitary attitudes shared by most Americans.

By and large the public believed that the militia, motivated by a sense of public virtue, had won the war. Adherents of this view coalesced into the Anti-Federalists, a faction that evolved into the Democratic-Republicans, or Jeffersonians. It is a testament to their persuasive efforts that the myth of the patriotic militia—sharpshooters all (in fact, they were anything but) possessing native field craft (a talent most, excepting the southern frontiersmen, had long lost)—persisted into modern times. In the war's immediate aftermath, their combination of revisionist military history and revival of the Whig fear of standing armies, the Anti-Federalists helped gut the American military by arguing that the future security of American independence should rest on public virtue, not on a military establishment.

These, then, were the military issues—the standing army and regulation of the militia—that became part of the larger political battle for control of the Revolution's legacy between the Federalists and Anti-Federalists.[7] Politicians extracted the lessons they preferred from the historical record and argued their cases with great fervor.

As he left the army, Washington wrote to fellow patriots about the future. He said that now was the time to establish national character and create an effective Federal government. In addition to believing that the militia should be placed upon a regular establishment, which he understood to mean that each state's militia should receive the same training, discipline, arms, and equipment, Washington believed that lack of adequate congressional authority had frustrated too many campaigns and thus lengthened the war and made it much more expensive. In these conclusions he was joined by many of the nation's most penetrating thinkers.

They included ex–Continental Army officers, men who had served at the highest levels of command or who had assisted Washington as personal aides and secretaries. Most of them had been young men in 1775 and so the wartime experience made a tremendous impression. Typical among them was Henry Knox, who had been a twenty-five-year-old Boston bookseller when war began. Throughout the war Knox struggled to make the most scientific of the three branches of the army, the artillery, an effective military force. Congress and state governments seemed to undermine constantly his efforts by pursuing policies that fostered supply shortages, civilian profiteering and apathy, and raging inflation. On the eve of the climactic Yorktown campaign, Knox wrote his brother: "The vile water-gruel governments ... are totally disproportioned to the exigencies of the war."[8]

Then there was Alexander Hamilton. Aged twenty years at war's outset, he displayed brilliant talents that made him one of Washington's indispensable aides. Aware of the army's true posture during the war, Hamilton intimately understood how close it had come to perishing, and with it America's chances for liberty. He too concluded, as he wrote in 1780, that the "fundamental defect is a want of power in Congress."[9] Like Knox, he would become a Secretary of War in the postwar government.

For these ardent Federalists there was no ignoring that what had happened during the war did not accord with Whig theory. It had not been the citizen soldier, the militia, who had carried the bulk of the burden of defending the nation. After the first bloom of patriotism, it had not been the nation's best—its freedom-loving farmers and artisans—who filled the ranks of the Continental Army. Rather, the army comprised those on the bottom who had joined because of the inducement of bounty and reward. Sharing this clear-sighted understanding of what had taken place, Knox, Pickering, McHenry, and Hamilton, along with their beloved commander in chief, became the driving force urging the nation to create a national military establishment. They received an opportunity in 1783.

In the spring of that year, Congress appointed a five-man committee to ponder future military requirements. Guided by Hamilton, the chairman, the committee solicited Washington's thoughts. His response, "Sentiments on a Peace Establishment," articulated four needs: a regular army; a militia trained and equipped to the same standard; arsenals; and military academies.

Washington understood the nation's continuing fears of a large army in times of peace, but maintained that a few troops—his recommended number was 2,631—were "indispensably necessary," primarily to garrison certain key posts and awe the Indians. A larger force was neither needed—the wide Atlantic buffered against major surprise attacks and gave enough time to mobilize the militia—nor affordable. Washington recommended that once the national debt had been paid off, extra funds should be used to build and equip a navy. With peace at hand, he thought it proper to introduce some "new and beneficial regulations." First and foremost, he advised abolishing promotion by seniority. That system destroyed "the incentives to Military Pride and Heroic Actions. On the one hand, the sluggard, who keeps within the verge of duty, has nothing to fear. On the other hand, the enterprising Spirit has nothing to expect. Whereas, if promotion was the sure reward of Merit, all would contend for Rank and the service would be benefited by their Struggles for Promotion." He believed an examining board of superior officers who made recommendations to Congress would be a great stride toward a meritocracy.[10]

Washington observed that the United States was unique in being equally prejudiced against the military regardless of whether the nation was at peace or at war. Indeed, for many delegates to the postwar Continental Congress the question of civilian control of the army had been subsumed by a larger question of whether to have an army at all. The submission of "Sentiments" began a decade-long struggle pitting Hamilton and his fellow Federalists against the Anti-Federalists over the issue of how to implement the nationalist program in face of public and congressional fears of a standing army. The debate featured the familiar arguments, frequently mounted by the same politicians who had participated in the earlier wartime debates.

However mightily the antimilitarists labored to prevent the formation of an army, events kept demonstrating the irreducible need for some kind of military. By 1784 it was clear to all that the flood of settlers to the lands west of the Allegheny Mountains could not be dammed. The settlers flowed into a strategic no-man's-land, an ill-defined area lying west of the mountains and east of a chain of British forts. It was an area of tension and potential conflict between America and Britain. It was also an area populated by some of the most warlike Indian tribes on the North American continent. Soldiers were needed to protect the settlers, to impress the hostile Indians with the might of the new nation, and to occupy the forts that Britain was supposed to cede as part of the peace terms ending the Revolution.

And then, as would recur time and again, military security fell second to budgetary considerations. Although negotiations with the Indians of the Northwest were at a critical juncture, and no less a figure than George Washington in his "Sentiments" had recommended retaining a sizable force to influence favorably these negotiations, congressmen focused on the issue of which states should pay how much to maintain existing forces. The nation was poor, soldiers were expensive, and so by the summer of 1784 Congress reached a compromise whereby it discharged all its soldiers except an eighty-man guard for military stores and authorized the recruitment of a new seven-hundred-man regiment for frontier defense.

The leader of the newly raised 1st Regiment, Lieutenant-Colonel Commandant Josiah Harmar, reported both to Congress and to Pennsylvania's chief executive, because Pennsylvanian troops made up the majority of his command. Indeed, the command had been reserved for him both because of talent displayed during the Revolution and his good connections with prominent state politicians. Congress exercised only limited authority over this 1st Regiment. The states controlled officer appointments, recruiting, and promotions. Although in time this regiment would become the nucleus of a new regular army, in its birth year it hardly sufficed as a border constabulary. Seriously limited by external political competition, internally flawed by inappropriate regulations and poor junior leadership, the 1st Regiment's manifest failures contributed to a sense that the Articles of Confederation were flawed themselves.

AN "ASSEMBLY OF DEMIGODS"

From 1777 until 1787, the nation operated under the Articles of Confederation. The Articles were the country's first constitution. The principle of state sovereignty formed their basis, but precisely what this principle implied was open to debate. What it meant in practice became ever more clear as time passed: states disregarded inconvenient congressional legislation with impunity. During the war states had blithely ignored requisitions for men and supplies until the conflict approached their own borders. Once peace came, no state wanted to incur the costs associated with military defense.

Under the articles there was no executive and thus no commander in chief. Instead, Congress performed the dual legislative and executive functions. Only when nine states agreed could Congress appoint a commander in chief, and even then Congress would still direct military operations. The Articles gave Congress "the sole and exclusive right and power of determining on peace and war."[11] The Articles foresaw war as a defensive response to foreign attack.

With its emphasis on the sovereignty of the states, one thing the Articles of Confederation explicitly did not do was give Congress the power to enforce its requests on the states. By 1786, army veterans joined many veterans of Congress—notably John Jay, the Morrises, John Adams, and James Madison—in the conclusion that this one thing was everything. To them it was plain that the nation's core political structure required change, change on a scale as revolutionary as that which had initiated the break from

England in 1775. Most Americans opposed such sweeping change. Typical white American males, at this time of limited enfranchisement the only group that had political power, were self-sufficient individualists who cherished their freedom and possessed a strong suspicion of all authority. The violence of 1786 did much to persuade everyone that sweeping change was indeed essential.

It began in the south. There, the national border was the Georgia frontier. Georgia's southern boundaries abutted Spanish Florida. West lay thinly populated land claimed by Georgia but occupied by the Creek Indian Nation. From Florida, Spanish officials cheerfully supplied the Creeks with arms, ammunition, and sanctuary. Similarly, the British, who had never abandoned their border forts as called for in the war-ending treaty with the United States, retained great influence among Indians all along the U.S. border. So arose a gifted, twenty-four-year-old Creek leader, Alexander McGillivray, the issue of a Tory father and a Creek mother, to lurk with his warriors along Georgia's border. When it seemed that McGillivray intended to send his war parties raiding against Georgia, Congress declared Georgia "in danger of invasion." With some satisfaction, that strong Federalist Secretary of War Henry Knox reminded congressmen that the threatened district happened to be land claimed by Georgia but not within the central government's actual jurisdiction, and consequently Congress lacked the authority to do anything. In the event, the Creeks refrained from attack, but the scare underscored the central government's helplessness.

It was a situation made plainer when Daniel Shays, a Bunker Hill veteran and ex-Continental captain, took up arms against the state of Massachusetts. Throughout the nation a recession had followed the postwar economic boom. Hard coinage was scarce and becoming scarcer, prompting seven states to begin to print paper to pay debts and taxes. This was a controversial activity from a variety of vantage points, but one immediate impact was to widen the distance between debtor and creditor. Britain still provided most essential manufactured goods to the United States. Alarmed at the spread of loosely secured paper, British manufacturers demanded hard currency payment from American importers, who, in turn, leaned on local storekeepers. Heretofore, merchants had operated on a barter economy with their clients. Now they required money from farmers who had none, and so sent sheriffs out to enforce their demands. In rural farming areas of western

Massachusetts ugly scenes of debtors' jails and eviction, entire families cast out into the winter's snows, became common.

Debtors and their sympathizers resisted, blocked country courts from conducting business, and as a last resort took up arms. Soon rebels printed manifestos reminding one and all that on similar terrain during the war they had beat Burgoyne and the British and by God they could "Burgoyne Lincoln [the former Secretary at War, now a Massachusetts militia commander] and his army" as well.[12] With over two thousand rebels in arms, this did not seem an idle boast.

Shays's tax revolt would have remained a local matter except for the existence of a national arsenal in Springfield that housed powder, muskets, shot, and shell in abundance. With their own revolutionary experience fresh in mind, it did not require great perception for congressmen to see that the arsenal offered Shays a very inviting target indeed. The Articles of Confederation did not give Congress authority to intervene in internal state disorders unless Congress declared that a state of insurrection existed. Unwilling to take this first step, Congress could not raise, support, and direct a military force to squash the rebels. However, the protection of national stores like the Springfield arsenal was something that probably provided grounds for sending the army. Except, and here was the rub, there was no available army to send.

Secretary Knox, who would have rather enjoyed performing as de facto commander in chief, relentlessly laid out the situation to Congress: "Were there a respectable body of troops in the United States . . . Or were the finances of the United States in such order, as to enable Congress to raise an additional body of four or five hundred men," the arsenal would be secure and anxieties about a rebellion springing up from nearly the same soil that had produced the first one could be laid to rest.[13]

Lacking help from United States regulars, Massachusetts confronted Shays with its own volunteers and militia. Foreshadowing the divided loyalties of the regular army on the eve of the Civil War, their ranks included many Continental Army veterans and at last one who had served under Shays at Bunker Hill. Following a series of skirmishes, including a successful defense of the Springfield arsenal by Massachusetts militia—a defense that left three rebels dead in the snow and thereby answered in no uncertain terms the question whether civilian militia would obey orders and fire on their neighbors—Shays's rebels dispersed, the flare of rebellion extinguished before it reached critical dimensions. Congress had finally managed to authorize the raising of a 1,340-man force to meet the threat, the first Federal augmentation of the army since the Revolution, but before any of them reached Massachusetts the rebellion ended. Retaining two companies to guard West Point and Springfield, Congress happily dismissed the balance.

McGillivray's Creek warriors, rising tensions with the British in the territories west of the Allegheny Mountains, and, most important, Shays's rebels highlighted the central government's military impotence under the Articles of Confederation. Before these events, only six states had sent delegates to the Constitutional Convention at Annapolis. Catalyzed by Shays's Rebellion, all except maverick Rhode Island sent delegates to Philadelphia for the session of 1787.

At least one delegate embarked on the journey to Philadelphia with considerable reluctance. He did not doubt the need for substantial reform—and, indeed, had written often on the subject. Content at age fifty-seven to remain on his plantation, he resisted until he could resist no longer. At the end of 1778, a year of extraordinary congressional bungling and inattention, George Washington had urged the states to send their "ablest and best Men to Congress."[14] Nine years later, when Knox, Madison, and others told him that news of his own attendance would stimulate the states to dispatch their most distinguished men, he bowed to persuasion. So the former commander in chief crossed the Potomac again and rode north to perform his duty. When news of Washington's attendance spread, it had the desired effect. A New York paper asserted: "A Washington surely will never stoop to tarnish the luster of his former actions, by having an agency in anything capable of reflecting dishonor on himself or his countrymen."[15]

*   *   *

No nation had ever been formed through a social compact, or contract. Instead, nations issued from the haphazard workings of history. James Madison believed that America offered a unique place to test the theory of the social contract. Its basic tenet held that the people possessed power by natural right. They freely could use this power to contract among themselves a union. Then, they could make a second contract delegating specified powers to their rulers while reserving all other power unto themselves. Madison went to Philadelphia with very specific ideas how this contract should be written.

He believed that the major impediment was the human tendency to form factions, by which he understood interest groups. Although an individual's conscience acted as a check against wrongdoing, a group who all desired the same thing, a faction, reinforced each other's self-righteousness. Having thereby lost restraint, a faction acted unfairly and tried to acquire ever more power:

> *If men were angels, no government would be necessary . . . In framing a government which is to be administered by men over men, the great difficulty lies in this: You must first enable the government to control the governed; and in the next place, oblige it to control itself.*[16]

In the final analysis, it was the control of power that dominated Madison's thoughts. At the pinnacle of power was whoever controlled the military.

Thirty of Madison's fifty-five fellow delegates to the Constitutional Convention had served in either the Continental Army or in the militia during the Revolution. Forty-four had been or still were members of the Continental Congress. As a group they were conversant with the military aspects of the late war. They were not representative of American opinion in general. Madison would have denied it, but they were a faction united in the belief that the nation required a stronger central government. The most articulate opponents of this Federalist view—the Anti-Federalist leaders Patrick Henry, Richard Henry Lee, George Clinton, and Sam Adams—stayed away from the convention and thereby committed a colossal tactical error. At several times the convention nearly collapsed. Had the Anti-Federalists been present they could have ensured this result. In their absence a new system of government was born.

The convention that begat a democrat government began in secrecy. Although it was summer, delegates insisted on closing the windows before discussion began so no one could overhear. Whether this contributed to the candid discussion is uncertain. It certainly made meetings uncomfortable, and eventually delegates had the good sense to move the proceedings upstairs where the windows could be thrown open and they could escape the stifling air of a humid Philadelphia summer.

Having successfully cast over British monarchical rule only to see the frightening possibilities of disunion as exemplified by Shays's Rebellion, those who attended the Constitutional Convention were eager to explore the consequences of building a national executive. While the framers disagreed about much, they generally agreed that if the American democratic experiment was to endure, the central government needed coercive powers. Many of them had studied the law and so understood Madison's clear distillation of the Confederation's defects: "a sanction is essential to the idea of law, as coercion is to that of Government." Intertwined with the question of who would control the powers of coercion were several related and profound issues.

Delegates grappled with whether the new Congress should be based on proportional representation or on the principle employed under the Articles of Confederation—namely, one state, one vote. They also debated how the very different economic needs of the various states—exemplified by the emergent fault line between the north and the slave-holding south—could be cared for by one central government. And finally, they addressed the largest question: how could a government be made effective without infringing upon the peoples' liberty?

Through it all, many at the Constitutional Convention believed that they walked a perilous path alongside the chasm of despotic rule. Accordingly, they examined the merits of a plural executive and the value of having the states retain most military power. Virginian George Mason, an ardent states' righter, spoke for many when he asked, "What, would you use military force to compel the observance of a social compact?"[17] Alexander Hamilton gazed into the same chasm but was untroubled. He challenged the critics of a strong executive, damned states rights, and demanded action.[18]

Arguments about the wielding of coercive power centered on control of the militia, who were supposed to be the foundation for the nation's defense. Gouverneur Morris, who chaired the committee examining military powers, recalled: "Those, who, during the Revolutionary storm, had confidential acquaintance with the conduct of affairs, knew well that to rely on militia was to lean on a broken reed."[19] To improve them, Washington, and others, wanted the militia placed under national control. This badly frightened states' righters, who believed that the militia represented a despot's most likely path to domination. The ensuing colossal debate reduced to the essential issue: delegates could grant the government paper powers; it was something else again to give it the armed might with which it could enslave the people. Delegates addressed this great question with passion and with a remarkable absence of bias. Sectional and economic interests had little bearing on this question of control of the militia. Delegates made principled judgments, each according to his own lights, and all with awareness that history would judge their work. In the end, they gave the president only one power over the militia: he would be in its commander in chief but only after Congress called the militia into national service. This seemed a satisfactory check against an executive's potential monarchical tendencies.

The Constitution defined specific war-making powers granted to the new national government. As a group, the framers believe that wars stemmed from the inherent excesses of monarchical rule. A republic's popular rule would contribute to a pacific future. To institutionalize this belief, they placed war and peace powers in the hands of the people's representatives, Congress. When a delegate proposed a clause stating that "the military should always be subordinate to Civil power," the majority rejected it on the grounds that it merely stated the obvious. While empowering Congress "to subdue a rebellion in any state, on the application of the legislature; to make war; to raise armies; to build and equip fleets; to call forth the aid of the militia," the draft Constitution did not squarely address the question of a standing army. Some delegates, such as George Mason, argued against a standing army in times of peace. Elbridge Gerry moved that the army be limited to two or three thousand men, to which, tradition has it, George Washington replied in a stage whisper that the Constitution should then also limited invading forces to the same size.[20] Delegates eventually agreed that the check on an overly powerful standing army would be the same as practiced in England: military appropriations for land forces, but not for the navy, would be limited to a two-year term so Congress could cut them off if necessary. This careful separation of the sword and the purse was a safeguard designed to prevent any chance of the army's growing because of bureaucratic momentum or parliamentary maneuvering. While this constraint would

seem insufficient to ardent Anti-Federalists during the ensuing ratification struggle, it seemed adequate to the majority of the delegates in Philadelphia. So the nationalists had achieved their most
important goal: empowering the government to create a standing army.

After deciding there would be a standing army and that state
militia would be subject to national government control, the framers turned to the remaining outstanding military questions: who
would command the army; who would have the right to send it to
battle? The context of the debate was much different than it is in
modern times. The delegates never foresaw an American army
invading a neighbor in order to conquer, as occurred in the
Mexican War. Nor did they envision overseas military operations.
The command and control system they established stemmed from
a belief that the American army would be a purely defensive force.
So, with little debate, because everyone agreed, they wrote into
the Constitution that Congress could "declare" war and the
executive would command the military through his position as
commander in chief. Originally, delegates considered granting
Congress authority to "make" war. But in recognition of the possibility of a surprise enemy attack, they changed the wording to
"declare." As Madison explained, this provided "the executive the
power to repel sudden attacks."[21] On August 27, 1787, the convention agreed that the president should be "Commander in Chief
of the Army and Navy of the United States."

*   *   *

The drafting of the Constitution was merely a first step. The convention delegates had represented a distinctly minority viewpoint.
They returned to their homes to persuade their fellow citizens that
ratification of their work was in everyone's best interest. Having
just codified what they hoped would be the nation's new national
charter of government, they proceeded to ignore the existing character. Article XIII of the Articles of Confederation clearly specified how alterations could be made. Inconveniently, it required
all thirteen state legislatures to confirm change. The Anti-Federalists had stayed away from Philadelphia. They would not repeat
this error at the state level where their opposition might prove
insurmountable. So the farmers hit upon a clever parliamentary

ploy to outflank the state legislatures. They established special conventions to ratify the Constitution, with ratification approved when only nine states assented.

Nonetheless, regardless of the forum, a wild controversy ensued. George Washington observed: "A few short weeks will determine the political fate of America for the present generation and probably produce no small influence on the happiness of society through a long succession of ages to come."[22] Those weeks saw Americans displaying their unsurpassed zeal for pamphleteering. As sign posters put up the Constitution for public scrutiny and papers and gazettes disseminated it to a keen readership, protest swelled. Many argued that standing armies were "Engines of despotism," the "bane of freedom," and would "subvert the forms of the government under whose authority they [were] raised."[23] Noting that a chief executive would have control of the army, Patrick Henry asked: "If your American chief be a man of ambition and abilities, how easy is it for him to render himself absolute!"[24] Anonymous citizens hotly debated the Constitution under noms de plume like Brutus, Cato, Caesar, Constant Reader, and Publius, the name jointly chosen by Alexander Hamilton, John Jay, and James Madison when they authored *The Federalist*.[25]

The searching analysis of the Constitution's military sections continued into the coming decade as newborn political parties used the issue to define themselves. But during the constitutional ratification process, a majority decided that in the end, the military could be safely restrained as long as the people retained popular control over the government through elections. Although a few people expressed a generalized fear of the concentration of power within the executive, there was no specific anxiety over the commander in chief clause.

The framers had deliberately avoided "fettering the government with restrictions that cannot be observed" because, as Hamilton explained, when necessary the nation would do what was required for survival regardless of legal constraints. If such actions breached fundamental laws, the reverence for the Constitution and the rule of law itself would be weakened. Moreover, such a breach "forms a precedent for other breaches where the same plea of necessity does not exist at all, or is less urgent and palpable."[26] Hamilton well anticipated the future competition for power and the future temptation for abuse once the Constitution was breached.

Yet future conflict between Congress and the executive sprang from the framers' design. The separation of power could only lead to competition for power. In that competition, each branch would cite the Constitution and take a broad view of its own powers and a corresponding narrow view of the powers of the other branch.[27] As mandated by the Constitution, only Congress could declare war. All measures short of war, including "protecting" various interests, rested with the discretion of the executive. The future would reveal that the president's war powers exceeded those conferred on Congress.[28]

The delegates at the convention in Philadelphia comprised those who were to make the new Constitution work or fail. Their ranks included future presidents, vice presidents, congressmen, ministers, Supreme Court justices, and Secretaries of State and Treasury. They and their fellow delegates understood that they were grappling with profound issues. The compromise they issued from Philadelphia gave the country a military system capable of meeting the needs of defense without loss of civil control. It also left much unsettled, for the framers had deliberately avoided defining all possible contingencies. Regarding the authority essential to the common defense, Hamilton explained that powers to raise armies and fleets and to direct their operations "ought to exist without limitations, because it is impossible to foresee or define the extent and variety of national exigencies."[29] This meant that the actions of the nation's first president and commander in chief would set all-important precedents.

4

DISASTER AND REDEMPTION

"The first wish of the United States with respect to the Indians is to be at peace with them all, and to cultivate a good understanding to our mutual benefit. As we have not been able to obtain this without the effusion of blood, the next wish is, to pursue such measures as may terminate the hostilities in the speediest manner."

GEORGE WASHINGTON, 1792[1]

"The fortunes of this day have been as the cruelest tempest to the interests of the country and this army, and will blacken a full page in the future annals of America."

WINTHROP SARGENT, A PARTICIPANT IN
ST. CLAIR'S CAMPAIGN, 1791[2]

"OUR NATURAL ENEMIES"

THE ELECTORAL COLLEGE HAD VOTED BACK IN FEBRUARY. NOW, IN April 1789, Congress convened the joint session specified in the Constitution to open and count the ballots. To no one's surprise, the man who had previously been unanimously elected commander in chief of the Continental Army and unanimously elected as president of the Constitutional Convention won another unanimous election as the first President of the United States. Washington anticipated that he would receive great help from the Senate, which he believed would act as an English-style Privy Council.[3] The precedent-setting practical exploration of this vision revolved around Senate ratification of various Indian treaties.

The Creek, Cherokee, Chickasaw, and Choctaw Indians resided along Georgia's western and southern frontiers. Like the Indians in the Ohio Valley, they received material support and tacit encouragement from the British to act against the former colonies. With the

58

slender might of the regular army occupied in the Ohio Valley, Washington and Secretary of War Knox knew that this Indian threat would best be neutralized by diplomacy rather than by military means. Because the southern Indians presented such an important strategic threat, Washington carefully supervised Indian diplomacy.

All proceeded smoothly until a climactic late August day in 1789 when he decided to obtain the Senate's "advice and consent" on the proposed Indian treaties. He intended to present certain documents and then have the senators vote "aye or nay." After Vice President Adams and Secretary Knox presented the administration's position, a long silence ensued. Finally a senator said that the business was new and required further reflection. At this, Washington displayed "an aspect of stern displeasure" while Knox reread the relevant papers. This only produced more questions from the senators. After two failed attempts to carry the motion, the senators decided to postpone the matter. Exhibiting "a violent fret" Washington said such procrastination "defeats every purpose of my coming here" and withdrew in a huff.

Washington had violated his own sentiments regarding how to communicate with the Senate. He had recommended giving senators time to consider complicated matters such as treaties before consulting them in person. This he had failed to do. He returned once more and did indeed gain his objective, but only after a time-consuming and tedious debate. The entire experience forever changed his attitude. Henceforth the Senate's role as an executive council was undone. Instead it would be an independent legislative body.[4] So from the very beginning, a gulf between the executive and Congress emerged.

Denied a privy council, Washington turned to the heads of his administration's executive departments, his Cabinet, for advice, and by so doing established the precedent for all future commanders in chief. George Mason, a Virginian and leading Anti-Federalist, feared the worst. He observed that lacking a Constitutional Council, a president would be unsupported by proper information. Instead, he would receive advice from minions and favorites and thereby lead the nation to ruin. The Indian disasters of 1790–1791 put Mason's dire prediction to the test.

*   *   *

When George Washington became the nation's first president and commander in chief, he commanded very little military strength.

Henceforth, Americans would frame their own history using four-year presidential terms climaxing in reelection or change. But since the rest of the world does not so obligingly organize into tidy four-year cycles, presidents have often found that the decisions and actions of their predecessors severely circumscribe their choices. When an incoming president inherits an armed conflict, the need for action is even more urgent while his room to maneuver is more restricted. So it was for the nation's first president. In the land bordering the Ohio River that would become Kentucky, Ohio, and Indiana, George Washington found he had an ongoing war.

American ownership of the Northwest Territories, as they were then called, derived from the Treaty of Paris, which ended the Revolutionary War. The problem was that the original inhabitants of the land had had no say in the treaty provisions. During the Revolution, most tribes had cast their lot with the British. In turn, the British had stood loyally by the Indians. There had never been the slightest indication that King George, the Great White father across the ocean, would abandon his allies until news of the war-ending treaty spread along the riverine arteries of the Northwest Territories. The Treaty of Paris made peace between America and Britain. It left the Indians exposed and vulnerable.

One Indian understood the new strategic picture. Thayendanegea, a Mohawk chief, remembered in the histories of the victor as Joseph Brant, appreciated that, disunited, the Indians had no chance to resist successfully. Thayendanegea tried to form an Indian confederation, constituting the tribes of the upper Ohio and Great Lakes country, to defend native lands. British agents told the first great Indian council that met in Sandusky, in what would become Ohio, that the Ohio River marked the legitimate boundary between white man and Indian. Indian leaders did not realize that British advice was solely based on a desire to preserve the lucrative fur trade, and they did not understand that they were being used as pawns in a great contest between rival white nations. Meanwhile, the Americans had arrived at a quite different notion of where lay the boundary.

Back in 1783 Congress had announced that the Indians, because of their support for the British, had forfeited all rights to their lands under previous treaties. Then it forced upon the Indians a new treaty taking the Indian lands between the Ohio River and Lake Erie east of the Great Miami and Maumee rivers. Thus, while

Thayendanegea's Indians met in one part of Ohio, federal survey-
ors were actively laying off plats in another part of Ohio on lands
the United States alleged it now owned by virtue of the new treaty.
Supporting their efforts were federal troops who manned a series
of camps and border forts along the Ohio River. Simultaneously,
white settlers swarmed over the mountains and down the Ohio
River to settle in Kentucky and to raise new towns in such places
as Marietta and Cincinnati.

Kentuckians had greeted the newly adopted Constitution with a
special joy. Since the first white settlers had arrived, the land had
lived up to its Indian name, "dark and bloody ground." During
the years of the Confederation, in excess of fifteen hundred settlers had been killed or captured in Kentucky. A sporadic but
always savage battle of annihilation featuring raid and counterraid,
with terror tactics employed by Indian and settler alike, characterized the contest. It gave every indication of intensifying in 1789.
Thus, with considerable relief a Kentucky militia colonel predicted
that because of the Constitution the central government would
take up the struggle and "the next year will put an end to Indian
hostilities."[5] Instead, the next year brought more of the same.

This, then, was the situation George Washington confronted
when he became president. The combination of the British abandonment of the Indians, Thayendanegea's confederation, Congress's imperial resolve, and the influx of more white settlers
meant that conflict was unavoidable. Washington, whose outlook
had been shaped by the terrifying Indian raids along the Virginia
frontier when he was a young man, simply could not entertain the
idea that the settlers should relinquish disputed lands. In his heart
he also believed that all Indians preferred plundering the whites
to hunting, particularly when so encouraged by British traders.
They could continue this as long as they could war with impunity.
Washington did not consider the Kentuckians blameless for the
resurgence of Indian attacks, but overweighing this knowledge was
an awareness of Kentucky's strategic position. Unless the Federal
government succored beleaguered Kentucky, it was quite possible
that the settlers would turn elsewhere for relief, with Britain or
Spain—Spain because it controlled the Mississippi River outlet to
world markets, outlets that the settlers well knew they would someday need—being the most likely alternatives.

Late in 1789, Virginia's and Kentucky's leaders requested that
the Federal government assume the burden of sustaining frontier

scouts. The next spring Washington agreed. Having taken this first step, escalation of the Federal effort was all but inevitable. By April, the local commander of Federal troops cooperated with Kentucky militia in a filibustering expedition against the Indians. The Indians retaliated in May by attacking a Federal six-boat convoy on the Ohio River, killing six men and capturing eight. Exasperated, Congress authorized the president to call out the militia to protect the frontiers against the Indians. Thus empowered, Washington sent instructions to Arthur St. Clair, the governor of the Northwest Territory, to establish peace with the Indians if that could be done on "reasonable terms." However, if hostilities continued, Washington granted St. Clair the discretion to act in the president's name and call upon available forces for their offensive or defensive operations. Washington concluded his instructions to St. Clair by emphasizing that war should "be avoided by all means consistently with the security of the frontier inhabitants, the security of the troops, and the national dignity." Unless there was further Indian provocation, a war would be unjust on the part of the United States. However, if the Indians refused the United States's peaceful overtures: "The United States will be constrained to punish them with severity."[6]

St. Clair believed peace a hopeless quest. When the Indians rebuffed his emissary, the governor used the discretion granted by Washington to opt for war.[7] Washington approved of St. Clair's time-honored tactic of a vigorous, punitive campaign against the Indian home villages. The campaign would be led by the ranking federal officer, of whom Washington had no special knowledge, Brigadier General Josiah Harmar.

The thirty-seven-year-old Harmar was an unlikely candidate to lead the nation's first military campaign since the Constitution's ratification. Although brought up as a Quaker, Harmar had entered a Pennsylvania regiment at the outset of the Revolution. He served competently during the war, and Nathanael Greene thought so highly of him that he made Harmar adjutant general of the southern army by war's end. Unlike most officers at that time, Harmar expressed a desire to continue his military career. Impressed by this display of zeal, Congress selected him for the honor of carrying a ratified copy of the Treaty of Paris to Europe. Upon his return he received the appointment to the head of the only force of regular infantry retained in United States service and went to the Northwest frontier. He performed well enough to be promoted to brigadier general in 1789, making him the first commander of the first U.S. army under the Constitution.

Because he had only the roughest maps to consult, Washington merely offered the most general guidance for the coming campaign. He clearly defined Harmar's mission, to establish a fort at the Miami villages to dominate the area, but left it up to his field commander how to accomplish this. Instead, Secretary Knox relayed the commander in chief's sentiment that this expedition "is not only of great importance in itself but it may be attended with extensive and remote consequences," thus requiring "that it should be conducted in the most perfect manner."[8] Thenceforward, the campaign unfolded without close attention from the man at the top.

Washington spent August, the month before the campaign was to begin, on a visit to Rhode Island to congratulate that state for ratifying the Constitution, and then retired to Mount Vernon for September. During this time he handed over war business to Knox, who, with Washington's approval, also left his office for an extended absence. Careless as these measures seemed, the two combat veterans recognized that they could do little to affect affairs in the distant Ohio River Valley. It all depended upon the field commander.

Had George Washington visited the encampment of the forces assembled to "punish" the Indians, he would have viewed a scene all too reminiscent of his own experience during the difficult days of the Revolution. Harmar had a small nucleus of regular soldiers supported by Kentucky and Pennsylvania militia. The regulars were an indifferent lot; poorly paid, poorly supplied, and poorly motivated. Many had signed up in order to receive free Federal transportation to the frontier, where they had every intention of deserting at the first opportunity. The militia were even worse. They were not the Daniel Boone type of sharpshooting frontier scout but instead young boys, old men, drunkards, and petty criminals; society's restless castoffs no more able to succeed here on the frontier than in the East Coast society whence they came. At first glance Harmar said that "at least 200 are good for nothing."[9] Common sense dictated a pause to provide Harmar a chance to discipline this riffraff into an army. But the lateness of the season precluded delay, and so Harmar set out from his base at Fort Washington, the future site of Cincinnati, Ohio.

By October 3 he had a force of some 320 regulars and 1,133 militia assembled along a tributary of the Little Miami River. Harmar handled the advance toward his objective, the Miami Indian towns under the renowned Chief Little Turtle, well enough. Frontier scouts led the way, small bodies of mounted men protected the flanks, and at the end of the day's march, while it was still daylight, the army encamped in a defensive square with pickets alert for any surprise attack. The problem was that by necessity Harmar's column could not move very fast. The land north of the Ohio River was covered in heavy forest and completely devoid of means to sustain such a large force. Harmar had to bring all his provisions with him, which required 578 packhorses and 175 beef cattle. Moving them along narrow Indian paths, up and down hills, over streams, and through swamps was slow business and gave ample warning to the Indians.

By mid-October Harmar's men had toiled to within striking distance of Little Turtle's villages at the confluence of the St. Joseph and St. Marys rivers, the future site of Fort Wayne, Indiana. So far they had encountered few Indians. A detachment of Kentucky militia managed to burn out five deserted villages and destroy thousands of bushels of corn. On the morning of October 19, a party of 30 regulars and 180 militia set out to continue the job. The Indians had not yet shown any fight, and the officer in charge of this column proved overconfident and careless. Stumbling into an ambush, his militia broke in terror, with many casting their weapons aside without even firing. Only the 30 regulars and a few militia stood, but they were too few and were overrun. A surviving regular who managed to hide in neck-deep water in an adjacent swamp watched in horror as the victorious warriors scalped and tormented the wounded and prisoners.

Two days later Harmar sent out twice as many men to seek revenge. The intent was to surprise the Indians in their sleep but it did not work. Again the militia broke on contact, this time leaving some 50 regulars to be slaughtered in useless sacrifice. Deep in hostile territory, his army fully demoralized, Harmar resolved to retreat. It was difficult because the militia were in a state of near mutiny. Harmar resorted to the lash to try to restore discipline, but floggings merely turned the militia even more against him. Later militia leaders would spread the word that Harmar had been drunk throughout the campaign. Because the Indians did not pursue, the survivors managed to return to Fort Washington, where

Harmar lost no time in discharging the remaining militia. His ranks had been fearfully thinned. Of the 320 regulars, 75 had been killed and 3 wounded; 108 militia had been killed and 28 wounded. The ratio of killed to wounded underscored in terrifying arithmetic the consequences of receiving a disabling wound in Indian fighting. Downed and abandoned, a wounded soldier was certain to meet an ugly death. And so an expedition intended to teach the Indians to fear the military might of the United States ended in defeat and humiliation. Instead of suppressing the Indians, Harmar had managed first to infuriate them by his destruction of their villages and then to embolden them by his and his men's display of incapacity.

"BEWARE OF SURPRISE"

At the beginning of November 1790, lack of news from Harmar made the commander in chief anxious. Some three weeks later, as rumors of Harmar's failure reached Mount Vernon, Washington wrote to Knox that he feared the worst: "I expected little from the moment I heard he was a drunkard. I expected less as soon as I heard that on this account no confidence was reposed in him by the people of the Western Country. And I gave up all hope of Success, as soon as I heard that there were disputes with him about command." So far all he had heard was rumors, "but the report of bad news is rarely without foundation."[10]

Full knowledge of what had transpired confirmed Washington's fears. He greeted the news as a setback, frustrating and unnecessary, but hardly fatal. Harmar's campaign report came along with a request for a court of inquiry, which met the following year and fully exonerated his conduct. In fact, Harmar had committed numerous mistakes, the most important of which was to divide his army into detachments, thereby presenting his enemy with the opportunity to defeat him in detail. Knox attributed failure to a lack of good troops, insufficient discipline, and the lateness of the season.

Since the campaign began, Washington had kept Congress closely informed about what was being done and what was expected. In his second annual message Washington reiterated why Harmar's expedition had been undertaken. The Senate replied that they understood the president's motives and had confidence in "the wisdom of the dispositions" he had taken.[11] By the time Harmar's court of inquiry met, Harmar had passed into the shadows of history and the commander in chief and the nation at large had an even greater disaster to occupy their attention.

*   *   *

The nation's first commander in chief had ordered his first military campaign and now he had to cope with the first failure. In more modern times such a defeat would have yielded heavy criticism. Two factors helped prevent this: news of the debacle spread slowly, and this helped dull popular reaction; and the president was more concerned with preparing another effort than with explicating recent failure, and his resolve swayed many potential critics. As the president explained matters in a typical letter, Harmar's expedition had "not been productive of the consequences which were expected from it." Thus, further measures were need to convince the Indians of their folly and "that the enmity of the United States is as much to be dreaded as their friendship is to be desired."[12] Toward the end the president wanted Arthur St. Clair to lead the next expedition against the Indians.

Born in Scotland, St. Clair had come to America as a junior officer to fight in the French and Indian War. After seeing combat first at Louisbourg and then with Wolfe at Quebec, he had resigned his commission to settle in western Pennsylvania. In 1775 he sided with the rebellious colonists, rising to the rank of major general in 1777. He served as a loyal, if not always successful, subordinate under Washington all the way through to Yorktown. Peace came and St. Clair entered Congress, serving as its president in 1787. Then he accepted the office of governor of the Northwest Territory, a position he had filled since the summer of 1788. Washington selected St. Clair because he was an experienced, mature combat veteran with knowledge of the territory northwest of the Ohio, particularly of local resources that could support military movements.

St. Clair journeyed back east, met with the president, and lobbied for the expansion of the army. After much wrangling, Congress added a second regiment to the regular army and authorized recruiting to fill the depleted ranks of the 1st Regiment. The president and his Secretary of War expected that the new troops would be mustered at Fort Washington in time for St. Clair to launch an offensive by July of 1791. Before St. Clair returned west, Washington gave him some last advice: "Beware of surprise; trust not the Indian; leave not your arms for the moment; and when you halt for the night be sure to fortify your camp—again and again, General, beware of surprise!"[13]

By mid-May St.Clair arrived at Fort Washington. He found the country devoid of resources and incapable of supporting an assembly army. The only exception was a plentiful supply of whiskey, a commodity so valued that a hundred-gallon barrel still traded for two hundred acres of good land. He also found that the new levies were proving reluctant to join the army. In part this was because of national prosperity; an able-bodied man could easily find a job at better pay than the three dollars per month he might earn as a soldier. In larger part, most everyone now realized that the Indian foe was not to be taken lightly. The consequences of defeat, lifelong captivity at best, barbaric torture more likely, did not provide an inducement to join the army. So, once again, those recruits who found themselves assembling at Fort Washington were drifters and recent immigrants truly down on their luck.

Throughout history skilled leaders have been able to take similar men and turn them into crack soldiers. Here St. Clair proved lacking. He had grown large and slow, subject to crippling bouts of gout. But the Federal government proved lacking as well. Federal money for the military remained scarce. Indeed, efforts to subsidize frontier defense partially contributed to the tax on distilled spirits that triggered the so-called Whiskey Rebellion. Hamilton at the Treasury insisted on a level of economy that, if it prevented waste and abuse, also prevented the soldiers from receiving adequate rations. Knox failed to ensure that the army received the logistical support required. And the man at the top again failed to exercise appropriate oversight of his subordinates.

He confined his supervision to providing a clear definition of the objective, of what constituted victory. It was the same one that Harmar had failed to accomplish, establishing a strong post in the heart of the Indian territory for the purpose of "awing and curbing" the Northwest Confederation. Washington anticipated that the Indians would resist, but confidently told St. Clair that the "disciplined valor" of his force would triumph over the undisciplined Indians.[14] The president was woefully out of touch with reality. On the eve of departure, one of St. Clair's officers prayed that there would be no battle because he considered the army inadequately manned and composed of poorly disciplined troops, "the worst and most dissatisfied Troops I ever served with."[15] St. Clair would not have time to whip them into shape because his orders required him to march immediately.

On August 7, 1791, five weeks after the projected beginning of the campaign, St. Clair's army lurched forward. It moved very slowly, trying to build a passable supply road as it advanced. He encountered vexing delay caused by a lack of tools; those at hand were so poor that axes bent "like dumplings."[16] The army paused two weeks to build a fort the need for which a more energetic commander would have anticipated and had built before the campaign began. Militia continued to turn up to swell the army's ranks, including three hundred from Kentucky described as the "off scourings of large towns and cities, enervated by idleness, debaucheries and every species of vice ... badly clothed, badly paid, and badly fed."[17]

Provisions ran low as venal army contractors short-weighted wagon loads of flour. Desertion became common; even the hanging of three captured deserters failed to deter it. The militia grew unruly, their officers openly contemptuous of the regulars and St. Clair himself. As October came to an end, sickness, discharges, desertions, and detachments weakened the army even while ominous signs of Indian strength appeared. St. Clair had continually found himself having to detach ever-increasing numbers of troops to escort the supply convoys. Matters worsened when some sixty militia left camp swearing they would intercept the next convoy and take what they wanted. St. Clair sent a regiment of regulars, unwisely choosing his most experienced 1st Regiment to stop them and see the convoy to safety, and thereby depleting his field army of its best unit.

Finally the army advanced through a light snow to the banks of the Wabash River some ninety-seven miles from its base at Fort Washington. Here, on the evening of November 3, it made camp, chilled, tired, and hungry. The men established two parallel lines of tents some 350 yards long and 70 yards apart. Within this rectangle were the horses and supplies. The heavily timbered camp overlooked the Wabash, which was about 15 to 20 yards wide and covered in a skim of ice. In order to prevent desertions, the militia were sent across the river, where they camped amid an open wood. So poor was the army's reconnaissance that St. Clair did not know that less than three miles distant was a force of several hundred Indian braves.

In the bloody aftermath there was much talk about what might have and what should have taken place. An advance picket encountered numerous Indians massing in the forest during the night. Around midnight they reported this alarming information to three high ranking officers, including second in command Richard Butler. Butler, a militia officer who had little respect for St. Clair, dismissed the report. Two other officers, both regular army soldiers and Revolutionary War veterans, likewise failed to inform St. Clair of the danger lurking just outside the glow of the army's camp fires. Lastly, a regular army officer whom St. Clair ordered to send out a dawn patrol declined to obey, explaining that his men could not be trusted. In sum, so new and poorly forged was the chain of command linking the army's various components that routine security measures essential in guerrilla warfare were not performed.

The army slept uneasily with muskets within easy reach. Well before sunrise the long roll summoned them to arms. On prior mornings they had maintained defensive positions until daylight permitted them to distinguish objects three hundred yards distant. Inexplicably, on this morning their officers dismissed them early. Consequently, about a half hour before sunrise, they were huddling around their camp fires preparing breakfast when the Indian attack came. Heralded by war cries, which one survivor likened to the sound of an infinite number of horse bells ringing all at once, the Indians struck the militia camp west of the Wabash. A handful of militia fired their weapons; most fled in terror toward the main camp. They crashed through the main camp spreading panic and disorder only to recoil at the camp's eastern boundary when they saw Indians attacking from that direction as well.

Led by a chief in a British army jacket, the Indians pursued hot on the heels of the militia, tomahawking those who fell behind. In spite of all, Butler's battalion defending the main camp stood firm, allowing the militia to break through their line and then closing ranks and firing a controlled volley at the Indians. The adjacent American artillery began firing, covering the front with a ground-hugging pall of smoke. Typically, Indians showed no stomach for cannon fire, but these warriors were made of sterner stuff. "The Indians seemed to brave everything," wrote one American survivor.[18] They dispersed and took shelter behind trees and fallen logs and began to pick off the artillerymen. Many gunners were hit and not one artillery officer escaped unharmed. The firefight extended around the entire perimeter of the camp and the advantage was all with the Indians. Well led by Little Turtle, Simon Girty—the "Great Renegade" to frontier settlers, a hero to the Indians—and others, the Indians fought with great skill. Their fire and movement tactics made it "almost impossible to find them out, or to know whither to direct your fire."[19] Their tactics called for shooting down the officers first, and with relentless regularity St. Clair's leaders began to fall. As pressure built up against the defenders stationed on the camp's left, gout-ridden Arthur St. Clair tried to mount his horse. An Indian bullet killed it and another wounded an aide who was assisting the general. Whether it was the courage born of desperation or battle courage simple, St. Clair suddenly found he could move about unaided. To everyone's surprise the Scotsman overcame his gout long enough to lead a charge that temporarily restored the line. No fewer than eight bullets pierced his uniform and another brushed his hair.

The defenders had hit upon a tactic to gain relief from the deadly Indian sniping. Sharp, short bayonet charges would drive the Indians back. The newly raised 2nd Regiment made three such charges. But each time the defenders returned to their lines they found their ranks thinned. Slowly the perimeter shrank. Encircled, confused, and frightened, the defenders waited for the next onslaught. A survivor later wrote, "I wish I could describe that battle, but I have not the power.... It seems like a wild, horrid dream in which whites and savages ... were all mixed together in mad confusion ... melting away in smoke, fire, and blood amid groans, shouts, yells, shrieks—the flashing of steel and crackling of firearms—all blended into one loud, continuous roar."[20]

The Indians penetrated the lines, scalping the dead and wounded. Around the artillery lay more than thirty scalped defenders. A Captain Smith, "sitting on his backside, his head smoking like a chimney" as his freshly scalped head contacted the cold, moist air, dazedly asked if the battle was almost over. To another survivor the many freshly scalped heads "were reeking with smoke, and in the heavy morning frost looked like so many pumpkins [in] a cornfield."[21] Major General Butler fought like a man possessed, moving about his unit to encourage and direct, wounded first once and then again. His soldiers carried him to a tent for surgery. One of the surgeons fell mortally wounded while operating on Butler but still managed to shoot down an Indian who charged into the tent to scalp the stricken general.

The wounded and the camp followers, including numerous women, tried to find shelter in the middle of the fire-swept camp. But there was no safety here. A bullet killed Dr. Victor Grasson while he was attending the wounded, the first medical officer to die in action since the Revolution. An increasing number of dispirited soldiers milled about, ignoring their officers' orders. St. Clair drew his pistol and threatened to shoot those who refused to fight. Emboldened by his leadership, the camp women "Drove out the skulking militia and fugitives of other Corps from under wagons and hiding places by firebrands and the usual weapons of their sex."[22]

Believing it the only alternative to certain annihilation, around nine A.M. St. Clair resolved to lead a breakout. It was not well conducted, more the spontaneous rush of a desperate mass of men rather than any sort of ordered retreat. A survivor likened them to "a drove of bullocks."[23] Safety lay twenty-nine miles distant at a stockade fort. St. Clair tried to organize a rear guard but could not stem the rout. However, as had been the case with Harmar, the Indians chose not to pursue. Instead they fell to plundering the camp, tormenting the wounded, and preparing survivors for ritual torture. Even the women were not spared: some thirty were killed and only three escaped. To revenge themselves upon the white men who had taken so much land but wanted still more, the Indians stuffed dirt into the mouths of the slain Americans.

St. Clair did not try to halt the retreat at any of the forts built during the advance. He and his panic-stricken survivors covered nearly forty miles in the twenty-four hours following the battle. Reaching Fort Washington three days after the battle—the army proved considerably faster in flight than during the advance—the full dimensions of the disaster became apparent. Exclusive of the women and camp followers, at least 918 solders and civilian employees had been killed or wounded. Thirty-five commissioned officers died on the field; the 2nd Regiment, the only regular unit present, lost every officer killed or wounded. All the carefully stockpiled stores and equipment—wagons, tents, cannons, horses, tools, and medicines—were lost. St. Clair failed to provide the restorative leadership needed. Shocked and apathetic, he did nothing while his men wandered out of control around the fort, preying upon adjacent civilians. Drunkenness and disorder ruled.

A courier from the army reached Philadelphia on Friday, December 8, 1791. The news found the president at a dinner party. Washington excused himself, scanned the dispatches, and alighted upon one that began: "Yesterday afternoon, the remains of the army . . ."[24] His shock must have been considerable, for it was apparent that his chosen general had committed Braddock-like blunders in spite of Washington's cautionary words to beware surprise. Yet he returned to dinner revealing nothing to his fellow diners. Only after the guests departed did he explode, damning St. Clair for his conduct. Here was a second failure to explain to the nation.

The commander in chief had the weekend to determine what to say to Congress. He chose candor and simplicity combined with a forward-looking focus. He expressed "great concern" about the "misfortune which has befallen the troops," and went on to observe that "although the national loss is considerable according to the scale of the event, yet it may be repaired without great difficulty, excepting as to the brave men who have fallen on the occasion."[25] He appended copies of St. Clair's reports, although this he did only after wrestling with his conscience. St. Clair's dispatches included such ugly details as descriptions of soldiers throwing away their arms and fleeing in panic. Washington was unhappy that the public would learn about all of this and had he his druthers would have suppressed certain unflattering details. But he concluded that too much information had already leaked out and thus it was too late for even partial censorship.

Thereafter, Washington responded to St. Clair's disaster with composure. He had faced too many setbacks in the long war against the British to be overly troubled. Employing what modern political strategists would call "spin control," he wrote letters to friends and politicians that explained what it all meant. He told them that while the loss of life was regrettable, it was by no means a permanent setback. Then he applied his own energy and critical facilities to redressing the disaster.

In his own analysis, Washington chiefly attributed St. Clair's defeat to short enlistment terms. Short enlistments forced a general into action prematurely; long enlistments allowed a general to prepare and then choose an opportune time and place to strike. It was the history of the Revolution revisited. So, he set about using the defeat as a springboard for meaningful military reform.

First he had to contend with the nation's first constitutionally empowered congressional investigation of Federal military conduct. A House committee asked Secretary of War Knox for all federal papers relevant to the St. Clair disaster. Before obliging, Knox talked the issue over with Washington. Recognizing that he was setting a precedent, the president convened a meeting of his Cabinet. So, Knox, Alexander Hamilton, Thomas Jefferson, and William Randolph met to discuss just how open a government the Constitution intended. Fortunately for history, Jefferson described what took place in his diary. Washington gave no hint of his own belief. Instead, he listened to his Cabinet. The passage of time had seen those two brilliant adversaries, Hamilton and Jefferson, drift ever farther apart on most issues. The conflict between Hamilton's Federalism and Jefferson's vision of democracy would soon prompt Jefferson to depart the Cabinet. Yet on this crucial decision, there was agreement. As Jefferson wrote: ". . . we were of one mind . . . that the Executive ought to communicate such papers as the public good would permit, and ought to refuse those the disclosure of which would injure the public." Consequently, the president must "exercise a discretion."[26]

Here was the basis for what would come to be called executive privilege. It could be invoked to protect national military secrets and it could be used to cover up blunder and embarrassment. It depended upon the discretion of the president.

ENTER "MAD" ANTHONY WAYNE

During the congressional investigation of St. Clair's defeat, the issue of St. Clair's fitness for command became swallowed by partisan politics. The man himself died a pauper years later after being relieved from his post as governor of the Northwest Territory for political reasons by President Thomas Jefferson. Anti-Federalists focused the debate on the question, was this a just war? Indeed, many congressmen believed that whites had been the aggressors, an opinion partially shared by the president. The behavior of many frontiersmen irked the commander in chief. Even while the United States was trying to negotiate a new treaty, agents for the Tennessee Company were advertising for new settlers on Indian land. Washington believed that unless the executive possessed the means to penalize such land speculators, conflict with neighboring Indians was unavoidable. In addition, frontier attitudes would have to change. Washington observed that as long as settlers believed "that there is not the same crime (or indeed no crime at all) in killing an Indian as in killing a white man" peace was impossible.[27]

War supporters argued that simple justice demanded that this war be fought. Citing examples of Indian bad faith—during 1790, while a truce was in place and a treaty pending, Indians had still killed some 150 Kentuckians—these congressmen requested an expansion of the regular army. In the end the simple logic of several Federalist congressmen, who echoed Washington's opinion that regardless of the conflict's origins here was a war and it must be fought and won, held sway. In March 1792, Congress passed a law expanding the regular army to more than five thousand men. New recruits were to serve for a maximum of three years. To attract recruits a bonus would be given and the monthly pay raised from two to three dollars. No longer would operations in the Northwest depend upon ad hoc measures and short-term enlistments. Having made the necessary organizational changes, the issue turned to who would lead this new army.

The commander in chief plainly understood that the nation would not tolerate any more debacles. To retrieve national fortunes he had to find a new general. Washington considered proven "firmness" of character and a demonstrated history as an "oeconomist"—by which he understood the ability to manage the army's logistics without wasting federal funds—as two highly desirable traits. Together with his closest advisers, he examined the qualifications of all of the nation's living generals. He wrote short résumés of their characters, which provide fascinating thumbnail sketches of the top echelon of the American army and a retrospective glimpse of Washington's attitudes toward some of the military heroes of the Revolution.

The years had treated many aging Revolutionary veterans unkindly; physical decrepitude ruled them out. Addiction to drink eliminated several more. Then there was the troublesome problem of seniority. The complexities of rank—during the Revolution the Continental Congress had upon occasion handed out generals' commissions broadcast style and at other times shown extreme parsimony in promoting qualified men—meant that many preferred officer combinations would simply not work because one general would refuse to serve beneath another. This combination of prickly pride and sensitivity to rank ruled out the man Washington wanted, the governor of Virginia, Henry "Lighthorse Harry" Lee.

Washington wrote of the man he finally chose:

> *More active and enterprising than Judicious and cautious. No economist it is feared. Open to flattery; vain, easily imposed upon; and liable to be drawn into scrapes. Too indulgent . . . to his Officers and men. Whether sober, or a little addicted to the bottle, I know not.*[28]

Thomas Jefferson called him "Brave and nothing else." A leader who might "run his head against a wall where success was both impossible and useless."[29] This, then, was "Mad" Anthony Wayne.

A native Pennsylvanian, Wayne had exhibited great dash during the Revolution. However, many shared Comte Rochambeau's opinion that he was "very brave, but too aggressive," and thus well deserving the moniker "Mad" Anthony.[30] His great day occurred in 1779 when, acting under Washington's close scrutiny, he led the cream of the American army against a British fortified post on the Hudson River. In a well-planned surprise assault, Wayne's infantry carried the post at the bayonet. Leading from the front, Wayne received a near-fatal head wound. Subsequently, he took an independent command to Virginia, where, in the preliminaries to the Yorktown campaign, his rashness almost caused the destruction of his force. After the war he fell heavily into debt—thus Washington's fear that he was "no economist"—managed to recover through good fortune, and won a hugely disputed congressional seat as a transplanted Georgia representative. He served briefly and was helpful to the administration in promoting the expansion of the army. Then, in March 1792, the House of Representatives decided that he was not a duly elected member. With Wayne's reputation damaged, his career at a nadir, Washington's selection was a bold choice indeed. He knew his general would fight, but whether Wayne possessed the other attributes of command was uncertain.

Like the two failed generals before him, Wayne's mission was to defend the frontier in both directions, protecting settlers from Indian attack and, "in the name of the President," preventing whites from raiding Indian villages.[31] In addition, he had to restore confidence to the dispirited regulars garrisoning the frontier forts and train the newly raised units for Indian warfare. As was his custom, Washington left much up to his subordinate's discretion because of Wayne's "nearer view" of the prevailing situation.[32] However, departing from his practice during the previous two campaigns, the commander in chief carefully attended to the details surrounding Wayne's buildup. Washington did this because of his perception of national politics and the national interest, those two interwoven threads that have cloaked every commander in chief's decision making.

Wayne's preparation for a third campaign took place against a rising din of political criticism directed against the government. This annoyed Washington, who, like every subsequent commander in chief, believed that in matters of war, once embarked upon a certain policy, the commander in chief deserved unswerving support. He complained that internal dissension was "harrowing and tearing our vitals" and was a threat to the nation's very foundation:

> *I believe it will be difficult, if not impracticable, to manage the Reins of Government or to keep the parts of it together: for if, instead of laying our shoulders to the machine after measures are decided on, one pulls this way and another that, [the nation] must, inevitably, be torn asunder.*[33]

Washington understood that political differences were unavoidable and perhaps even necessary. But he could not understand why zealous patriots—a category he understood to include his critics—could not subordinate partisanship to the national interest. He predicted that unless those both inside and outside of government displayed "mutual forbearances and temporizing yieldings" the American experiment would fail because either the government could not carry out its mandate or the states would disunite.[34]

Frustrated with the nation's political timbre, Washington left Philadelphia to summer at Mount Vernon. There he received weekly reports from his Secretary of War regarding Wayne's activities and there he pondered upon the best route for advancing against the Indians once an offensive could be launched. Meanwhile, his chosen field general was busy vindicating the government's trust.

Wayne selected Pittsburgh as his first headquarters. Here he received the new recruits from the eastern seaboard. He also received advice from Mount Vernon regarding the importance of training his soldiers. The commander in chief placed high stock in the value of individual marksmanship. He understood that a soldier in the forest confronting a charging, tomahawk-wielding Indian brave had only one shot with his musket to defend himself and that he had best make that shot count. If soldiers lacked confidence in their marksmanship, they were likely to break and run, the fate of many of St. Clair's poorly trained regulars. Informed of Washington's opinion, Wayne set his men to target practice.[35]

Powder and shot were scarce, but still, each day, when a soldier finished standing guard he went to the shooting field, where he discharged his musket at a target. To encourage accuracy, Wayne rewarded the day's best shooter with a gill, a quarter-pint tot, of whiskey. In addition, he held regular shooting contests, instructing his men to aim and fire as individuals rather than to shoot in the European style of volley firing. The best shots received a whiskey bonus, the worst dug the lead from behind the targets so it could be reused. The general had the army's horses assembled nearby so they would become inured to the sounds of combat. He conducted mock engagements using his elite riflemen painted up like Indians to simulate the enemy while the balance of his force maneuvered in the face of repeated "Indian" charges.

Meanwhile, real Indian attacks continued. A raid into western Pennsylvania killed seven settlers; another north of Cincinnati picked off sixteen unwary soldiers gathering hay outside a fort. A third raid, near Pittsburgh itself in mid-August, underscored how unready were Wayne's men for real combat. Wayne reported that when the Indians approached, "such was the defect of the human heart, that from excess of Cowardice, One third part of the sentries deserted."[36] To prevent a recurrence, the general resorted to ferocious discipline, even contemplating branding the foreheads of deserters with the word *coward*. He authorized the execution of some deserters while others were "shaved, branded, & whipt" with up to one hundred lashes.[37] Later in the campaign, when a squad of dragoons ran from the enemy, Wayne arrested the lot and held a court-martial. While the court conveyed, he had a grave dug for the squad's leader in anticipation of the verdict. When the court duly condemned this officer to death, Wayne assembled the army around the grave, issued a pardon at the last minute, and used this shock theater to harangue the troops on the horrors of cowardice. Washington approved of most of this, only cautioning that branding as a punishment was of doubtful legality and should therefore be employed sparingly.

While Wayne grappled with the problems of turning civilians into soldiers, Washington concluded by late summer 1792 that slow recruiting meant an offensive campaign could not be mounted anytime soon. The nation's commander in chief had maintained only the loosest control over Harmar and St. Clair. Two shocking disasters had resulted. Now winter approached with the country's scant military resources committed to a third campaign. No living soldier possessed greater experience of the trials and tribulations of frontier winter encampment and the strategic direction of troops involved in an Indian campaign. Washington's wisdom shone as he sent instructions to Wayne.

The commander in chief had pondered what to do next and understood that ideally the army should be concentrated so as to perfect its training and discipline. But such concentration would leave too much of the frontier exposed to Indian raids. The conventional solution was to man a series of forts spread all along the frontier. Washington believed this a mistake. Forts were useful to protect supplies; otherwise, they drew soldiers into passive defense. Knowing they were safe behind the stockade, soldiers tended to avoid the dangers of patrolling. Indians, employing the tactics of lightly armed guerrillas, quickly assessed a fort's numbers and strength. They then had the option to avoid the fortified area or to isolate and attack it. Thus passive defense surrendered the initiative to the enemy.

Instead of a cordon defense along the frontier, Washington selected posts that could serve as springboards for next season's offensive while still protecting the frontier during the coming winter. By locating them on waterways, and having boats and supplies collected in advance, troops could quickly surge forward when the spring melt came. By locating many posts well to the rear, the supply line would be short and forces could be massed in secret. To help ensure a secret concentration, he recommended an active counterreconnaissance screen of far-ranging patrols to keep prying eyes distant from American camps. Such active patrolling would also deter Indian raids against civilian targets.

He well understood that previous failure stemmed, in part, from inadequate intelligence and took measures to obtain the best information possible about the strength of the Indian Confederation and the activity of the British. Since intelligence was difficult and dangerous to procure, and often proved unreliable, he urged the use of multiple sources so that reports could be compared in order to arrive at some approximation of the truth. Finally, Washington forwarded these plans not as orders, but as suggestions. He knew that the man in the field possessed more recent and better intelligence, and equally believed in the importance of granting subordinates command discretion.[38] Although the forces involved were tiny by European standards, Washington's clear exposition adhered to several of the great strategic principles that would be articulated by Europe's leading generals in the coming century.[39]

Accordingly, Wayne moved his main base camp twenty-two miles away from the fleshpots of Pittsburgh and established a Spartan camp he called "Legionville." The name reflected the army's new structure. It was to be a legion, a balanced force comprising the three arms; infantry, cavalry, and artillery. At Legionville, Wayne instilled martial pride among the new recruits by demanding that the officers themselves lead by example. Wayne did his part by attending to the myriad details—the siting of latrines, inspection of kitchens, organization of a laundry service—that made all the difference between a healthy camp of instruction and a pesthole. If the guard turned out in soiled uniform, he took away the soldier's daily whiskey ration, a loss keenly felt in the cold winter. If an entire company looked slovenly, Wayne ordered them to perform fatigue duty until they improved. Even the camp's civilian employees had to adhere to a set of standards or face a triplicate ducking in the icy Ohio River waters.

Washington questioned some of Wayne's decisions. But he masterfully tempered his criticisms with praise in a well-calculated mix designed to spur Wayne on to efficient performance. Although eager for decisive action, he understood the value of careful preparation. So he curbed his frustration and gave Wayne the time he needed to prepare his army for battle.

Simultaneously, Washington kept Congress well informed about events before they reached a critical impasse. His understanding of the Constitution led him to believe that no offensive operation could be undertaken without congressional assent.[40] As 1792 came to a close, he provided Congress with documents bearing upon Indian affairs. He asked Congress to consider whether the government should take any further measures, adding that his future conduct would "materially depend upon congressional advice."[41]

By reaching out to Congress he sought to ensure unity of purpose for the coming campaign.

In sum, since St. Clair's defeat, Washington had reflected upon past failure and changed his command style. His attention ranged form the detailed to the grand strategical and was thus much different than in the previous two failed campaigns. He clearly expressed himself to his Secretary of War. Knox, in turn, served as a good chief of staff, transmitting Washington's desires to Wayne. It was an ordered chain of command involving three veterans who understood the task at hand and, equally important, understood one another.

*   *   *

There would be a last attempt at peace. Although he thought the exercise futile, Washington carefully attended to the instructions given to his negotiators. In part he did this because he was an honest man, in part because he feared the political ramifications if the effort was not made. These ramifications were both domestic and foreign. Referring to domestic opinion, Secretary of War Knox explained to Wayne: "The public voice demands" a fair experiment to secure peace.[42] Regarding international opinion, Knox wrote that to continue a war with the Indians would likely lead to the destruction of many tribes. This was inconsistent with the country's honor and would attract foreign criticism because "The favorable opinion and pity of the world is easily excited in favor of the oppressed."[43] Accordingly, Washington distilled the essence of his Indian policy so that the U.S. negotiators clearly understood what "they are to insist upon . . . and what, for the sake of peace, they may yield."[44]

Here and henceforth, American commanders in chief believed that the public needed reassurance that the nation was embarking upon a moral, or just, war. Back in 1791 Washington had assured Congress that offensive operations were being conducted "as consistently as possible with the dictates of humanity."[45] The best tool to reassure the public was to at least seem to make good faith efforts at a peaceful solution. This cloaking of war inside of a moral justification was a peculiarly American aspect of war making, and it would baffle foreign observers. At the time of the 1793 peace initiative, a British military agent in Philadelphia cynically observed: "In a Government scarcely formed . . . [with] its origin built on opinion, it was found impossible to draw the strength of the country into action at once ... [therefore] the most artful measures have been pursued in order to ... lead the people into this business."[46]

In the late spring of 1793, Washington unburdened himself in a letter to Virginia's governor. The continuation of sporadic Indian raids along the western frontiers pained the president. But, he explained, for the moment his hands were tied by the ongoing negotiations with the Indians. Washington wrote that he had concluded that nothing would come of these talks, but felt compelled to wait their collapse before acting. It was necessary for the people to see "that the Executive has left nothing unessayed" to achieve a peace and "to remove those suspicions which have been unjustly entertained that Peace is not its object." Only after taking the long chance for peace would the people enable the sword of government "to strike home."[47] Secretary of State Jefferson heartily concurred that negotiations were for public consumption and that campaign preparations should proceed forthwith.[48]

Meanwhile, Anthony Wayne's legion had struck camp, sailed down the Ohio River, and arrived at Cincinnati on May 5, 1793. Wayne believed that it took a minimum of three years to make a reliable soldier. By the time his legion reached Cincinnati, he had had only one year. Yet he expressed satisfaction that they had become good marksmen and could rapidly perform the necessary battlefield maneuvers. What remained was "to make the riflemen believe in that arm, the Infantry in heavy buck shot & the bayonet, the Dragoons in the sword, & the Legion in their Un[i]ted prowess."[49] Aided greatly by the fact that his government had provided more support—better uniforms, more abundant supplies, and regular pay—than it had to Harmar's and St. Clair's troops, Wayne had taken the same raw material and turned them into a confident offensive weapon.

Wayne strengthened his outposts to the north in the direction of the Miami Indians, sent out scouts, and awaited the results of the government's peace initiatives. He wanted to do more, but Washington had specifically forbidden upsetting the pending negotiations through aggressive action. Wayne was in a position that would recur repeatedly in conflicts up to and including Vietnam and Iraq. It was the dilemma of limited war: the field general was responsible for military victory yet had to fight under diplomatic and political constraints. During this time, while his enemy suffered no such constraints, Wayne neither received large numbers of reinforcing militia—the militia simply would not turn out until peace initiatives had failed—nor was allowed to position his forces in advantageous advanced positions for fear of upsetting the peace talks. He wished "this business was decided" since he found the state of "Anxious suspence . . . almost intolerable."[50]

Finally, at the end of August 1793, Wayne received notice that efforts at a peaceful resolution had failed. He was free to begin the war. The president had impressed upon his Cabinet the fact that the prestige of the United States hung in the balance. Twice the Indians had humiliated the country, exposed in weakness, and thereby made every foreign negotiation difficult. Wayne's actions on the Ohio frontier would reverberate throughout Europe and most especially in London. A third failure must be avoided. Knox transmitted these sentiments to Wayne: "Let it therefore be again and for the last time impressed deeply on your mind that as little as possible is to be hazarded, that your forces be fully adequate to the objects you propose to effect, and that a defeat in the present time and under present circumstances would be pernicious in the highest degree to the interests of our Country."[51]

An autumn campaign was not one Wayne welcomed. A year ago, upon first assuming the command, he had told Knox that the Indian was a formidable enemy only when he could choose the time and place for battle. "In the fall of the year," he explained, "he's strong ferocious & full of spirits—corn is in plenty & Venison and other game every where." The time to strike was in the spring, when "he is half starved Weak and dispirited."[52] Wayne correctly understood that his opponent lived a subsistence life and that in the spring the Indians would lack food and supplies, the logistical sinews necessary for sustained campaigning. But politics had forced him to begin when enemy strength was at full flood. In the future some notable disasters would occur when presidents ordered premature military operations for political purposes. In 1793 this did not happen because the commander in chief understood and accepted the need for caution.

Wayne carefully managed his march north from Cincinnati so as to be secure from surprise attack. Each night he arrayed his legion behind rough breastworks and assigned each subunit a sector to defend. Unwittingly he emulated the tactics employed by the Roman legions when they fought in the German forests and foreshadowed the tactical method that would be used by American soldiers in the jungles of Vietnam. His ceaseless vigilance led the

Indians to say he never slept. In spite of these precautions, the legion covered the same ground over which St. Clair had marched in half the amount of time. However, the legion's first encounter was inauspicious. The Indians ambushed a wagon train escorted by regular riflemen, nominally the army's elite. The two officers in charge, a lieutenant and an ensign, and thirteen other ranks were felled by bullet, arrow, and tomahawk. The balance of the men, some ninety-odd, broke and ran.

Wayne reported to Knox that he had "experienced a little check" and predicted that it might be "exaggerated into something serious."[53] Indeed, when rumors of this encounter reached Philadelphia ahead of Wayne's report, they put Washington in a very anxious state. The first combat in any war always has a psychological impact disproportionate to its actual military impact. As far as the president could tell, here was another setback that might well presage something worse. Washington mastered his anxieties and waited Wayne's account of the action. Reading the report, he accepted that no more could be done this season and calmly contemplated plans for the upcoming winter.

In his fifth address to Congress, delivered soon after Wayne's "little check," the commander in chief did not dwell upon operations on the Ohio frontier. Instead, he spoke about the broader picture. Europe was again at war and it threatened to embroil the United States. American ships traded with those two great rivals, France and England, and individual Americans were actively taking sides. England continued to occupy forts on American territory. Against this background, Washington articulated what should be American policy:

> *There is a rank due to the United States among nations which will be withheld, if not absolutely lost, by the reputation of weakness. If we desire to avoid insult, we must be able to repel it; if we desire to secure peace . . . it must be known that we are at all times ready for war.*'[54]

Turning to Indian affairs, he explained that good faith efforts at a peaceful settlement had failed. However, the protracted talks had forced a late start to Wayne's campaign, and therefore little could be expected until the next season. The president's clear explanation of what was at stake, what had been done, and what could be expected impressed Congress. Just as Washington had been patient with Wayne, so Congress was patient with Washington.[55]

In Ohio, Wayne's legion was at the end of a precarious supply route. But the general judged that a retreat would be too demoralizing. Instead he established the aptly named Fort Recovery at the site of St. Clair's defeat and prepared for the long winter. Meanwhile, British agents stirred up the Indians. In February, the British governor general of Canada told Indian leaders that soon, no doubt, Britain would again be at war with the United States and this would allow them to regain their lands. The governor general intended his speech to remain a secret, but Quebec had as much difficulty holding a secret as Philadelphia, and word soon leaked to American ears. As if to put teeth in this pledge, the British restored a fort on the banks of the Maumee—nominally U.S. territory—and garrisoned it with three redcoat companies. In fact, this move was to protect the approaches to the great British base in the west, Detroit, a base that Wayne's buildup seemed to threaten. To the Indians it seemed a sure sign that the Great Father across the sea would support them in their war. To the Americans it seemed a most provocative challenge. So the frontier had all the ingredients for war: England and the United States, two prideful, edgy rivals who misinterpreted one another's defensive actions as offensive buildup for conquest.

The spring of 1794 came with bloody promise. As patient as Washington had been, he had to tell Wayne that this year must be decisive. Affairs in Europe had reached a critical stage. If Europe saw that the United States could not defeat some backwoods Indians, then American hopes to be treated as a diplomatic equal would disappear. Wayne had at his command over 80 percent of the entire U.S. regular army. The term of enlistment for many legonnaires would end during the coming year. There was little chance they could be replaced. After "the most mature" deliberation, the commander in chief had concluded that the time for action must be now.[56]

In the event, it was the Indians who struck the first blow. Led again by Little Turtle and Simon Girty, along with a rising, aggressive Shawnee chief named Blue Jacket, in excess of fifteen hundred Wyandots, Delawares, Shawnees, Miamis, and Weas attacked Fort Recovery. They caught a convoy of ninety riflemen and fifty dragoons outside the fort. Badly cut up, the survivors staggered back under the fort walls. Although the fort's perimeter had been cleared for several hundred yards, the tree stumps remained. The attackers crawled forward from stump to stump and began to shoot down the defenders. In spite of losses the Americans held firm. The Indians had expected to find and use the cannon abandoned by St. Clair to breach the fort's walls. Instead, the Americans had found them first and mounted them inside the fort. Lacking cannon, the Indians had to rely upon naked valor. That night they bravely pushed their assault up to the very loopholes of the fort. But they could not overcome the well-defended walls. Having suffered heavily, lacking the supplies to mount a siege, the situation Wayne had accurately anticipated back in 1792, they withdrew. The Northwest Indians' last, best chance of stopping the American invasion of their lands had failed.[57]

Some Indian leaders recognized this. After urging that peace terms be negotiated, the heretofore successful Miami warrior, Little Turtle, stepped down from command of the Indian Confederacy. Enough other Indians wanted revenge and their counsel prevailed. Accordingly, Blue Jacket took command and the war continued.

From Wayne's perspective the situation appeared dangerous. He had reports that the Indians were massing all their strength to resist his advance and that fifteen hundred British trappers and traders were gathering at Detroit to support the Indians. But rumors of near-overwhelming enemy strength confront most field commanders during times of war, and Wayne chose to ignore them. It was because he was aggressive that Washington had selected him, and with this decision to advance, Wayne vindicated the commander in chief's judgment. He gathered his legion and a large body of Kentucky Mounted Volunteers, some twenty-one hundred men in all, and drove deeper into Indian territory. His combination of flawless security measures and the choice of a line of march different from that taken by Harmar and St. Clair fooled the Indians and gave them no openings. The only resistance encountered came from hordes of mosquitoes. By August 20, Wayne was nearing Fort Miami, the British stronghold erected on American territory near Lake Erie.

Wayne had clear instructions about what to do in this situation. Even though it might mean war with Britain, something Washington fervently hoped to avoid, he authorized Wayne to attack this fort if necessary. However, he should only do so if he could guarantee success; an unsuccessful assault would be disastrous. If successful,

Wayne should then escort any British prisoners to the next nearest fort and release them.

Before confronting this delicate situation, Wayne's legion had to march through a belt of windstorm-felled trees that blocked further advance. Hidden amid these trees on the morning of August 20, 1794, were some 400 Indians and 60 Canadian militia. The small number of defenders was a consequence of Indian over-confidence. They did not expect Wayne to advance so rapidly. Leading Wayne's advance was a select squadron of Kentucky Mounted Volunteers numbering about 150 men. Four hundred yards behind them were two companies of regulars followed by the army's main body, who were toiling through the thick woods in a long, strung-out column.[58]

Two Kentucky privates, Sherman Moore and William Steele, volunteered to scout ahead of everyone else. They were literally the point men of their commander in chief's Indian policy and they were about to be killed. The Kentucky cavalry saw them carefully track through an open wood and enter the belt of fallen timber. Amid the downed trees grew lush grass and thick underbrush that limited visibility to a mere twenty yards. As was so typical in this and every other guerrilla war up to and including Vietnam, the first indication that the enemy was present came when an unseen foe shot down the two scouts. Next a rolling volley from the fringes of the trees flayed the entire squadron. Riders toppled from their saddles; horses reared in terror. Then the survivors sighted the enemy: Indian braves seemingly risen from the ground and now running hard at the startled cavalry. Those who remained horsed and those who could rise from beneath their fallen mounts scuttled back in a panic-stricken tangle toward the main army.

They encountered the two regular companies who were acting as Wayne's advance guard. The regulars had little time to prepare. They fired into the routing Kentuckians in an effort to halt their flight. The Kentuckians recoiled briefly, and then surged through the regulars' line. Some of the regulars managed to fire two or three times at the pursuing Indians, but most fell back in disorder. The main column had not yet had time to extricate itself from the forest and to deploy for battle. It seemed as if another disaster was in the making.[59]

Ignoring the plan to await attack behind the fringe of fallen trees, the Indians rushed forward for a quarter mile into more open timber. Here the white man would have all the advantages if he would stand and fight. Already the legion had begun to deploy, but it was not a well-ordered maneuver. On the left, Colonel John Hamtramck hurried his men into the prescribed formation, a two-rank line; but on the right, Brigadier General James Wilkinson extended his men in a single rank covering a much too broad front of eight hundred yards.[60] Furthermore, the routing advance guard and cavalry plunged through the American lines spreading disorder and opening up gaps. If the Indians could follow up their initial success with one more hard blow, victory would be theirs. But the effort was not made because what had transpired had not taken place according to the Indian plan. In fact, only a small number of Indians—Ottawas and Potawatomis, noted for their impetuous ardor—were in contact with Wayne's army. The balance hung back in their defensive positions in the fallen timber. This lack of coordination gave Anthony Wayne the precious few minutes he needed to sort out his command.

Riding with his aide, the young Lieutenant William Henry Harrison, Wayne assessed the situation. He had drilled his legion in careful preparation for this encounter. His tactical method called for his mounted soldiers to work around the Indians' flanks while his infantry attacked their front. Pressured front, flank, and rear, the enemy would break. What Wayne sought, and had practiced in several mock combats, was a battle of annihilation. Now that it came time to put tactical theory to the test, Wayne realized that the Indians' choice of position negated his mounted arm. The tornado-felled trees and thick underbrush made mounted maneuver nearly impossible.

Accordingly, Wayne resolved to win this battle with his infantry alone. Harrison asked the general what he intended to do, and Wayne replied, "Charge the damned rascals with the bayonet!"[61] It was the same tactic that St. Clair had tried two years ago. The difference this time was twofold: the American regulars were much better trained; and the Indians, lacking Little Turtle's sure tactical touch, were fighting in a disjointed fashion. At first, the American assault was equally uncoordinated. A small group of regular dragoons commanded by Captain Robert Campbell draw sabers and charged across the open ground toward the timber belt. Entirely unsupported, Campbell and twelve of his dragoons were shot down.

Then on came the legion infantry. With fixed bayonets they advanced without firing, took losses, and kept coming. At point-blank range they halted, fired a heavy volley of buckshot, and closed on the enemy. Facing the terrifying spectacle of a bayonet charge, outnumbered about two to one, the Indians broke and ran. A survivor recalled: "We were driven by the sharp ends of the guns of the Long Knives, and we threw away our guns and fought with our knives and tomahawks." Remembering Little Turtle's prophecy that unless the Indians talked peace with Wayne, the Great Spirit would hide his face in a cloud, this survivor concluded, "the Great Spirit was in the clouds, and weeping over the folly of his red children."[62]

Wayne's pursuit drove them back to Fort Miami, where, to their dismay, they found their erstwhile British allies had closed the gate against them. The shutting of the gate also closed out the possibility that a new war between England and the United States would begin here. So ended the forty-five-minute battle of Fallen Timbers, which had cost Wayne thirty-three killed and one hundred wounded.[63] The Indians suffered fewer than forty casualties, but among the losses were some of their most valiant chiefs. More importantly, the battle proved to the Indians that British promises of support were hollow.

Over the ensuing days Wayne paraded his legion around the British fort, burned Indian crops and villages, and in general tried to provoke an encounter. The British commander refused the bait and so Wayne marched off to establish a chain of forts to control the territory. It would take another year of sporadic fighting to bring peace, and there would be one last battle fought seventeen years hence in which a certain Major General William Harrison would win a great victory, but Fallen Timbers sealed the fate of the Northwest Indians and opened a vast new territory to American settlers.

Congress responded to Wayne's victory in curious fashion. On December 3, a representative offered resolutions of thanks to Wayne, the regulars, and the Kentucky militia. Such a seemingly simple gesture stimulated divisive argument pitting the growing body of Anti-Federalists against the administration-loyal Federalists. The Anti-Federalists maintained that it was inconsistent with republican principles to honor a mere general and that he and his army had merely done what they had been paid to do. In the end a compromise resulted that pointedly did not mention Wayne but did thank the soldiers. However unsatisfactory to the proud Wayne, the real point of this episode was proof that even at a time of national triumph partisan politics were emerging as a dominant force. George Washington's prestige could partially surmount partisan obstacles, but future commanders in chief would not find it so easy. Henceforth, the ability to manage Congress would be added to the selection of a strategy and the choice of a commanding general as essential duties for the successful prosecution of America's wars.

During the Revolutionary War, George Washington had displayed great strategic ability. His comprehension of the importance of sea power, his decision to resist political appeals to distribute scarce resources in a cordon defense of all rebel territory, and his resolve to avoid risking the main army in battle were events of surpassing importance.[64] His selection of General Nathanael Greene to command in the south reversed the flood tide of the final British offensive and led to victory at Yorktown.

In contrast, from a military standpoint Washington did not shine so brilliantly as president and commander in chief. He made two poor choices in Harmar and St. Clair. Still, he kept Congress and the public united in a resolve to triumph and with his selection of Wayne overcame the consequences of earlier failure. Wayne's campaign proved that the United States could create, maintain, and use a national army against external foes, something it had not been able to do under the Articles of Confederation. The near future saw the suppression of the Whiskey Rebellion and answered the question of whether the central government could compel observance of national laws.

So the young nation prepared for a new century. Wise as they had been, the Founding Fathers had not foreseen important implications stemming from the emergence of partisan politics. No future president would conduct a war in such a relatively apolitical climate, and none would have a stature like Washington's to buffer him from criticism. The emerging political parties shared a republican reliance upon the will of the people. But they suspected one another of trying to subvert the people for political goals. Thus, the people became objects of political competition and not, as the Founding Fathers had envisioned, independent jurists weighing policy by merit. This removed one of the constitutionally intended checks against an executive's taking the nation into war. This at least was clear: less than a decade after the Constitution's ratification, political parties were going to influence America in peace and in war in ways no one had fully anticipated.

PART TWO

JAMES POLK'S

MANIFEST DESTINY

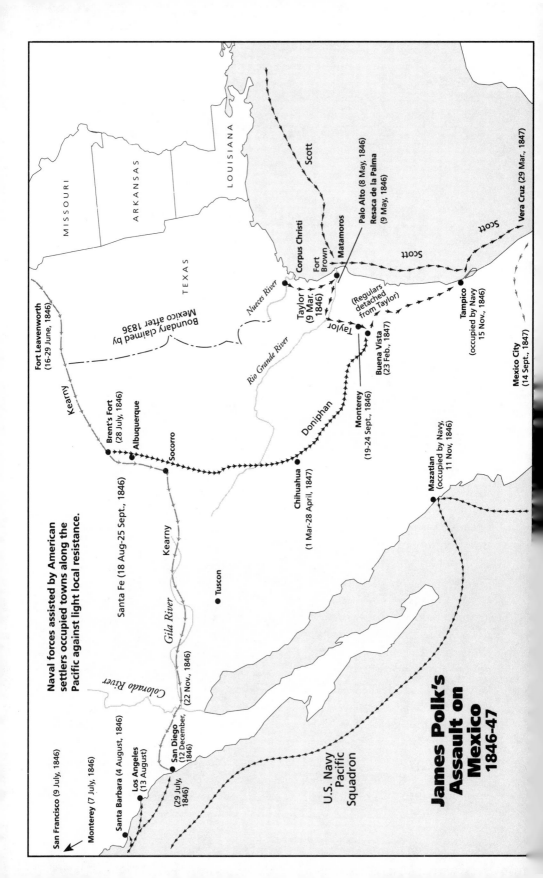

James Polk's Assault on Mexico 1846-47

San Francisco (9 July, 1846)

Monterey (7 July, 1846)

Santa Barbara (4 August, 1846)

Los Angeles (13 August)

San Diego (12 December, 1846)

(29 July, 1846)

Colorado River

Gila River

Tuscon

Kearny

Santa Fe (18 Aug-25 Sept., 1846)

(22 Nov., 1846)

Brent's Fort (28 July, 1846)

Albuquerque

Socorro

Fort Leavenworth (16-29 June, 1846)

Kearny

MISSOURI

ARKANSAS

LOUISIANA

TEXAS

Boundary claimed by Mexico after 1836

Nueces River

Rio Grande River

Corpus Christi

Fort Brown

Matamoros

Palo Alto (8 May, 1846)

Resaca de la Palma (9 May, 1846)

Scott

Taylor (9 Mar. 1846)

Taylor

(Regulars detached from Taylor)

Doniphan

Chihuahua (1 Mar-28 April, 1847)

Monterey (19-24 Sept., 1846)

Buena Vista (23 Feb., 1847)

Tampico (occupied by Navy 15 Nov., 1846)

Scott

Scott

Vera Cruz (29 Mar., 1847)

Mexico City (14 Sept., 1847)

Mazatlan (occupied by Navy, 11 Nov, 1846)

U.S. Navy Pacific Squadron

Naval forces assisted by American settlers occupied towns along the Pacific against light local resistance.

5 ⊂══✕⊷

WAR FOR CONQUEST

"Let the treaty of peace be made at the city of Mexico."

IN SEARCH OF A GENERAL

THE YEAR 1846 FOUND THE UNITED STATES AT THE END OF "THE Thirty Years' Peace," a time during which no foreign enemy had menaced the nation. The peace had been all the more welcome because it was so unexpected. The struggle to consolidate American independence, the War of 1812, had witnessed a dispiriting chain of debacles and defeats climaxing with the British capture of the nation's capital in the summer of 1814. Yet two weeks later, spirited fighting by Maryland militia had blocked a British land thrust against Baltimore, allowing Fort McHenry's defenders to repulse the enemy fleet in a combat celebrated by what would become the nation's anthem. Better still, in January 1815 a motley force commanded by "Old Hickory," Andrew Jackson, had mown down red-coated soldiers—veterans who had defeated Napoleon's vaunted infantry—outside of New Orleans and sent them packing back to their ships. The fact that the battle occurred two weeks after a war-ending treaty had been signed in distant Europe mattered little to the American public. Since news of the peace circulated hard on the heels of Jackson's victory, the war entered popular consciousness as a success earned by American arms.

93

In fact, the War of 1812 had been a draw at best, with the United States achieving none of the objectives for which it went to war. Early war failure was largely a legacy of President Thomas Jefferson's policy that had emphasized peace and economy over military preparedness. The nation entered the war with a militia-based land force and a coast defense system employing small gun-boats. While such a force accorded well with Jefferson's design of preventing military hegemony, reducing expenses, and avoiding foreign entanglements, it proved entirely inadequate to wage war. Consequently, both the regular land forces and the militia suffered repeated, humiliating defeats during the war's first years. Only the glorious single-ship duels, fought and won by the nation's fledgling navy, relieved the pervasive gloom. Fortunately for the United States, as had been the case during the Revolutionary War, North America was a decidedly secondary front for British strategists. Instead, they had to concentrate most of their resources for the death struggle against Napoleon's France, thereby permitting American political and military leaders time to rebound from their blunders to create an efficient military. The late war success of the regular forces lead by young, able officers, most notably General Winfield Scott, contributed to the peace settlement and helped consolidate the notion that America's defense required a professional military.

In 1815, Congress met in Blodgett's Hotel—the Capitol was a burned ruin, a victim of British occupation—and voted to create a peacetime army of ten thousand men. This was a strength nearly three times that established before the war. The subsequent years of peace saw a struggle between those who wanted to dismantle the military on the grounds it was no longer needed and a young Secretary of War named John Calhoun. Calhoun pressed for a variety of modern reform measures, including the expansion of the Military Academy at West Point and the creation of a new position that became known as Commanding General of the Army. Thereafter, West Point became a vital force in maintaining a professional officer corps while the position of the commanding general rectified a serious deficiency in the military chain of command. At the close of "The Thirty Years' Peace," General Winfield Scott occupied this post.

*   *   *

When Mexico severed diplomatic relations with the United States over the pending American annexation of Texas in March 1845, it triggered a chain of events leading to America's first war of foreign conquest. The commander in chief who conducted this war, James K. Polk, had no prior military experience. Polk was a Nashville lawyer and ardent supporter of Andrew Jackson, to whom, along with a favorable marriage, he owed his rise to power. His political oratory had earned him the sobriquet "the Napoleon of the stump." Whether he shared any other characteristics with one of history's great military geniuses remained to be seen. In any event, Polk became both the youngest president to date—he was not quite fifty—and was the first civilian to lead in time of war.

For ten uneasy years Texas had been an independent republic. Back in 1836 Texans had voted for annexation by the United States only to have the proposition rejected by Presidents Jackson and Van Buren. In 1845 Texas tried again, and this time the American Congress assented. President Polk heartily concurred. In his inaugural address he laid out his case for the annexation of Texas. It was purely a matter of state between two independent powers, the United States and Texas. This formulation conveniently overlooked Mexico's historic territorial claims. Sensitive to foreign criticism, Polk explained that foreign countries should view the Texas annexation "not as the conquest of a nation seeking to extend her dominions by arms and violence," but as a peaceful implementation of a contract.[2] It was all quite disingenuous, because one way or another the president intended to expand the nation's frontier south and west. If necessary, he was ready to employ violent force of arms to achieve this goal.

The military establishment he inherited to wreak such violence was quite small. This well accorded with the nation's continued suspicion of a standing army. In his first annual message to Congress, Polk explained that it had never been American policy to maintain a large force in times of peace. Using words that would not have been out of place if spoken in the Continental Congress, he said that standing armies were "contrary to the genius of our free institutions, would impose heavy burdens on the people and be dangerous to public liberty."[3] National defense should rely on citizen soldiers ever ready to heed their country's call in the event of war. In his attitude toward the standing army and reliance upon the militia, Polk also kept faith with the Anti-Federalist views of

Jeffersonian democracy from which his Democratic party claimed its roots. If, on the eve of war, this was somewhat at odds with the dictates of "Manifest Destiny"—the God-given right to expand westward to the Pacific—no one seemed to notice.

The American army of this period was a tight-knit, professional bunch. Its professionalism derived from the full flowering of the Military Academy at West Point, which since 1812 had operated with a four-year curriculum devoted to engineering and military studies. Its graduates filled the army's junior officer ranks and provided high-quality tactical leadership. To recite just a few of their names is to enter the pantheon of Civil War generals: Lee, Grant, Sherman, Jackson, Johnson, Thomas, Longstreet, Bragg. The army's main mission for the past decade had been to assist in the westward settlement of the United States. Indeed, in the last thirty-one years it had not fought a conventional battle. How it would fare in battle against Mexico was an open question. Although the U.S. Navy was undergoing the transition from sail to steam propulsion with consequences no one could completely foresee, since Mexico had no navy to speak of the American navy could reliably be expected to dominate. But it could not be anything more than a useful adjunct to the war on land. In sum, if Polk's military machine was small and untested, at least it was not as unprepared as had been and would be the typical case in American history. Much depended upon the capacities of the lawyer-politician who was its commander in chief.

When the rupture of diplomatic ties with Mexico occurred, the president responded by sending the available regulars of the U.S. Army, commanded by Zachary Taylor, to occupy posts in Texas. Its mission was to stand in readiness should Mexico invade Texas. While Taylor's "Army of Occupation" gathered strength, Polk acted on the diplomatic front. This gesture was akin to, though even less sincere than, Washington's peace initiative with the Indians back in 1792. Polk dispatched John Slidell—the same gentleman whose mission to England on behalf of the Confederate government sixteen years hence would nearly plunge the United States and England into war—to Mexico with a bundle of demands that no Mexican government could accept.

While Slidell performed a very public peace dance, Polk toyed with a covert means toward his goal. Possibly, the Mexican government could be bribed. It would take a hefty payment, somewhere between a half and two million dollars, the president believed.

This was a very considerable sum in the 1840s, so Polk cast about for a means to finance it. He hit upon an act passed in 1806 giving President Jefferson two million dollars for the purchase of Florida. In addition, Polk cited the congressional practice of placing a secret service fund at the discretion of the executive. Armed with such precedents, Polk hoped to convince key congressmen to authorize him funds—and to do so without congressional debate in order to keep it all secret from the public and from foreign governments. Like future presidents who confronted inconvenient legal obstructions to their policy, he was also prepared to invoke executive privilege to hide what he was doing from snooping congressional opponents. In the end this scheme went for naught because Mexico refused Slidell's credentials before any bribe money could be collected. Rebuffed, Polk returned to more direct methods.

At the beginning of 1846, he sent Taylor's army into disputed territory well south of the Nueces River, the traditional border between Texas and Mexico. Polk instructed Taylor to advance aggressively until he neared the town of Matamoros on the Rio Grande. There, for the time being, Taylor was to act defensively. However, if Mexico committed "any open act of hostility toward us," Polk authorized Taylor to begin aggressive action.[4]

Polk possessed a strong streak of self-righteousness. Given that and his secretive nature, it is difficult to know whether he believed his own rhetoric or not. Assessing events, the former "Napoleon of the stump"argued to his Cabinet that efforts to conciliate Mexico had been in vain, that the United States "had forborne until forbearance was no longer either a virtue or patriotic."[5] Henceforth, only firm measures would do. In anticipation of going to Congress with some kind of war message, Polk ordered his staff to assemble the relevant documents to support his case. Then, the inevitable occurred.

Mexican and American soldiers had faced off across the Rio Grande for some three weeks of uneasy peace. They trained artillery at one another, hurled invective across the river, and generally worked themselves into a state of high excitement. When Mexican rancheros, armed bandits only loosely connected with the Mexican army, killed Taylor's quartermaster on the American side of the river, it added fuel to an already inflammable situation. But it took the actions of a remarkably arrogant, incompetent Mexican general to bring the nations to war.

Because of the Byzantine character of contemporary Mexican politics, new governments came and went in rapid succession, making it difficult to craft a coherent policy toward the border dispute with the United States. With no central direction, Mexican field commanders could act pretty much as they pleased. The field commander opposing Taylor, General Pedro de Ampudia, sent Taylor an ultimatum to withdraw from the Rio Grande or face war. Taylor refused. He naturally considered the ultimatum to constitute an "act of open hostility" and, as per instructions, felt free to take countermeasures. Taylor ordered the U.S. Navy to blockade the mouth of the Rio Grande. Shortly thereafter, when a sixteen-hundred-man Mexican cavalry detachment crossed to the American side of the river, Taylor sent a sixty-three-man dragoon patrol to intercept it. The Mexican cavalry bagged the lot, killing American soldiers in the process. Following the skirmish, Taylor sent word to the president that hostilities had commenced.

The news came as no surprise to Polk. Aware that two suspicious armed forces were glowering at each other across the disputed Rio Grande, on May 8, fifteen days after the loss of the dragoon patrol but before he received Taylor's report, he had told his now returned envoy Slidell that it was a mere matter of time before conflict began. In a similar vein, the next afternoon he told his Cabinet that "the danger was imminent."[6] That evening Taylor's dispatch arrived.

Having already assembled the documents supporting his position, it remained only to craft a war message and send it to Congress. This message presented Polk's justification for war. It ignored two salient facts: the combat had occurred on disputed territory; and Slidell had been engaging in coercive diplomacy. Instead, Polk asserted that American blood had been shed upon American soil because of an unprovoked Mexican attack and that Mexico had rebuffed all efforts at a diplomatic solution. What the president wanted of Congress was not quite a declaration of war. Rather, he wanted Congress "to recognize the existence of the war" and to give him the power to prosecute it with vigor.[7]

While newspapers spread the word of "American blood of American soil" in the House of Representatives, the president's disciplined Democratic majority forced through a war bill. Their high-handed tactics prevented the Whig opposition from even examining the official documents that had accompanied Polk's war message. The Democrats limited debate on the war bill to two hours and then consumed more than three-quarters of this time reading selected portions of the bill. In this manner, the House of Representatives, the body intended by the Constitution to reside closest to the people so as best to represent their interest, "debated" the issue of war or peace. By a margin of 174 to 14 the House passed the war bill.

It was not quite so easy in the Senate. To Polk's displeasure, Senator Thomas Hart Benton told him that "19th Century war should not be declared without full discussion."[8] However, by trumpeting the undeniable fact that American soldiers had been killed, the Democrats forced their political opponents into a situation where they either went along with Polk's policies or could be seen as failing to support the embattled troops in a time of emergency. Cowed, the Senate approved of the war bill by a vote of 40 to 2.

One administration opponent called it "the most difficult case for an honest man to give a satisfactory vote upon" that he had ever faced.[9] In the end few opponents voted their conscience for fear of the political cost of appearing to have failed in their patriotic duty. They recalled the unhappy fate of the Federalist party, which had withheld its support for the War of 1812 and had never recovered from the stigma of its dissent. Polk and his fellow Democrats had skillfully fused partisan objectives with national patriotism. They then limited debate and made vital documents inaccessible to the opposition. So the nation entered its first foreign war.

By and large, the public greeted the news enthusiastically. There were some, like Henry David Thoreau, who denounced the war. Thoreau also refused to pay his poll tax, but this had been a recurring habit and so attracted little attention. Thoreau's distillation of his thinking, as written in an essay later known as "Civil Disobedience," would only become well known during future popular protests. In 1846, a handful of pacifists and abolitionists—the latter charging that the war was a disguise for spreading slavery—argued against an unjust war of expansion. Others argued that the war violated republican ideals upon which the nation had been built. But every wave of dissent dashed upon the shoal of patriotism, leaving Polk free to conduct an extended war of conquest.

*   *   *

The day Polk signed the war bill, he faced the unpleasant business of meeting with his general in chief, Winfield Scott. Scott was a certified war hero with a distinguished record dating back to the War of 1812. This in itself did not have to be threatening to a civilian president who knew that he was the nation's first commander in chief lacking military experience and embarking upon war. But Scott had presidential aspirations of his own—and worse, much worse, to James Polk, Scott was a Whig. In the president's view, no baser charge could be leveled against a human being. Still, governed by the rules of seniority, Polk had no choice but to offer Scott command of the army being raised for operations against Mexico. Scott accepted.

The next day they again met and Polk described his war plan. He wanted Taylor's force from Texas to invade Mexico's northern provinces to seize and hold territory. This would give the United States the leverage to dictate a favorable peace. Scott agreed and recommended that the government call for twenty thousand volunteers to supplement the regular army. Polk doubted the necessity for so many men but feared to refuse the veteran's request, being unwilling "to take the responsibility of any failure of the campaign" by refusing Scott what he asked. After Scott departed, the president wrote in his diary that "Scott did not impress me favourably as a military man."[10]

Less than a week later, Polk met with his Secretaries of War and the Navy to explain how he wanted to manage the war. Polk had hoped that Scott would depart immediately to the Rio Grande to take command of the field army and that he would thus be rid of an ongoing need to have to deal with Scott face-to-face. Instead, Scott insisted on staying in Washington for the time being to manage the mobilization. In this action Polk saw dark motives, observing in his diary that Scott was guilty of "constantly talking and not acting" in order to embarrass the president.[11] Thoroughly annoyed, Polk hit upon a plan to outflank his general in chief. He told his secretaries that henceforth they should personally supervise all military matters, "even of detail," and not confide in their subordinates. Moreover, Polk insisted that he be kept "constantly advised of every important step."[12] In modern parlance, Polk wanted to "micromanage" his war without regard to his chief military leader.

Polk's suspicions about his top general seemed confirmed when one of his minions produced a private letter written by Scott that charged that the president's motive in raising new regiments was to provide patronage positions for western Democrats. Polk noted in his diary that evening: "... after seeing this letter I can have no confidence in Gen'l Scott's disposition to carry out the views of the administration."[13] Accordingly, Polk ceased communicating directly with Scott altogether.

At first this breakdown in communications had no impact on the three American offensives that began the war. The commanders of two of those offensives were operating under orders received before the war began and were thus oblivious to the rupture in the chain of command back in Washington. The president's war aims were simple: "to acquire for the U.S. California, New Mexico, and perhaps some others of the Northern Provinces of Mexico."[14] He had already sent orders to the navy's Pacific Squadron to occupy ports in upper California once hostilities began. On the day Congress recognized a state of war with Mexico, Polk attended to New Mexico. He ordered a small force of regular cavalry, the 1st Dragoons, commanded by Colonel Stephen Kearny, to ride from Fort Leavenworth, Kansas Territory, to Santa Fe to secure New Mexico. If possible, this force was then to continue to California. The idea was largely Polk's own, and his motive was to be in possession of this territory when peace came. In the event, Kearny conducted a memorable two-month march across desolate country and arrived in Santa Fe in mid-August. There he split his force, sending a detachment of Missouri Volunteers under Colonel Alexander Doniphan to pacify hostile Indians in southern New Mexico, while he himself continued on toward California.

By the narrowest, success crowned both columns. Kearny reached California, where he found the Pacific towns had indeed been occupied by U.S. naval forces supported by local American settlers. Meanwhile, Doniphan invaded northern Mexico and then marched east to cooperate with Taylor. Doniphan's entire march, beginning at Fort Leavenworth and ending at the Gulf of Mexico, covered 3,500 miles, marking it as the most remarkable march in American military history.

The third element in the opening American offensive involved Zachary Taylor's army on the Rio Grande. After sending his dispatch to Washington reporting that hostilities had commenced, Taylor sized up his situation. A strong Mexican force had crossed to the northern side of the Rio Grande, and after an abortive assault against Taylor's Gulf Coast base, had occupied a position threatening Taylor's line of communications. Taylor marched to clear them out. On May 8, 1846, he encountered a 6,000-man

Mexican army stretched out in a mile-long double line blocking the road. Taylor's army—2,288 men, all the soldiers an aggressive government willing to risk war had been able to send to the point of first decision—had been training for this moment for nine months but was untried in combat. More than four in ten of them were foreign born, primarily German and Irish. Their West Point—trained junior officers, U. S. Grant, Kirby Smith, George Sykes, and John Sedgwick—men who were to go on and display much talent in positions of far greater authority fifteen years hence—had instilled pride and professionalism. Still, they themselves were new to war. Honest Sam Grant spoke for many when he recalled forty years after the event his emotions on battle's eve: ". . . for myself, a young second-lieutenant who had never heard a hostile gun before, I felt sorry that I had enlisted."[15]

The subsequent battle of Palo Alto was the first conventional battle fought by American Soldiers since Andrew Jackson had defended New Orleans against the British thirty-one years earlier. Fortunately for the American cause, a gifted battlefield leader commanded them. Seated sidesaddle on his horse, Old Whitey, Zach Taylor arranged a chaw of tobacco in his cheek and deployed his men. When the opponents were some seven hundred yards apart, the rival artilleries opened fire. Included in the American gun line was Ringgold's battery of "flying artillery." Back in 1940 a farseeing Secretary of War had sent American officers to Europe to study artillery weapons and tactics. The result had been the development of a light artillery arm, the so-called flying artillery, capable of rapid battlefield maneuver. Captain Samuel Ringgold had enthusiastically endorsed the light artillery doctrine of rapid fire and movement and trained his battery relentlessly. The field of Palo Alto validated his efforts.

Within the first few minutes of combat it quickly became apparent that the American batteries were superior. Not only were they well served, they also fired high-explosive shells that when accurately sighted killed at long range. The Mexican artillery fired solid cannonballs that were much less lethal. Realizing he would be bested if this unequal duel continued, the Mexican commander ordered his cavalry to close on the Americans. Firing shotgunlike blasts of iron projectiles called canister, the American guns repulsed the first charges. When the Mexican cavalry moved to turn Taylor's right flank, he shifted the regulars of the 5th U.S. Infantry into the chaparral to oppose them. The 5th formed square and withstood the shock of the cavalry charge. Ringgold advanced his artillery aggressively and "gained a favorable position to play upon them and poured in so destructive a fire that they were thrown into confusion."[16] Again Ringgold advanced his guns to rake the retiring cavalry. Taylor sustained his intrepid artilleryman by advancing his entire force. Taking advantage of a dense shroud of smoke from the burning grassland, another American battery on the opposite flank rapidly moved to within three hundred yards of the unsuspecting enemy and opened a destructive fire that broke the Mexican army. Taylor's army held the field and had inflicted some seven hundred Mexican losses while suffering only nine killed and forty-seven wounded. But among the killed was Sam Ringgold, and the Mexicans still blocked the road to Taylor's base.

The next day a second battle took place. Still possessing a three-to-one manpower superiority, the Mexicans defended a position behind the Resaca de la Palma, an empty watercourse of what had once been a channel of the Rio Grande. Again Taylor deployed his army and sent forward his "flying artillery" in hopes of winning by long-range bombardment. But the tangled chaparral largely negated the artillery's effectiveness. Accordingly, Taylor ordered his men to close on the enemy. In the van charged a small force of U.S. cavalry commanded by Captain Charles May. "Wait Charley, until I draw fire," said a nearby American artillery commander. The U.S. battery fired, the Mexicans returned the fire, and May charged. His troopers pierced the Mexican center only to encounter a second, supporting enemy line. A brief melee swirled around the Mexican artillery and then May's troopers fled back toward the American line. Highly aroused, Taylor turned to an infantry colonel and ordered, "Take those guns and by God keep them!"[17]

This the U.S. regulars did. The Mexican commander had placed an eight-gun battery to sweep the center of the field and cut up any charging column. But, as an American participant related, he "did not know then that American soldiers would charge right up to the cannon's mouth."[18] The American infantry closed so rapidly that the opposing battery managed to fire only two rounds before contact. However, the defenders clung tenaciously to their ground and the battle degenerated into a soldiers' brawl. The arrival of an American battery broke the enemy's spirit and sent the Mexicans routing to the rear. From the American lines came "a deafening shout of triumph" as the pursuit began, with "dragoons, Artillery and Infantry in one mass at full run, yelling at every step," until the enemy was driven back over the Rio Grande.[19]

In spite of advice from his young West Pointers to acquire bridge materials before the campaign began, Second Lieutenant George G. Meade recalled, "the old gentleman would never listen."[20] So Taylor was unable to continue the pursuit over the Rio Grande. It was the not uncommon story of victory partially squandered by failure to prepare for the next step. Still, the battles elated Taylor. He sent a dispatch to Washington reporting: "Our victory has been complete."[21]

The twin American victories at Palo Alto and Resaca de la Palma were a source of immense pride to the regular army officers because they had won before the arrival of the detested volunteers. The victories proved that on the battlefield the American army was clearly superior to its opponent. The U.S. artillery provided a tactical trump card to which the Mexicans had to answer. The U.S. infantry showed itself to be much more motivated than the hapless Mexican peasants dragged from their villages to fight for a frequently changing central government to which they felt no allegiance. The battles proved the old adage that there are no bad soldiers, only bad leaders. They also advanced Zach Taylor halfway to the White House.

Strategically, Doniphan, Kearny, the navy, and Old Rough and Ready had accomplished most of Polk's war aims. It only remained to convince the Mexican political leadership to accept the American victory.

TO THE HALLS OF MONTEZUMA

Polk had planned on "a brisk and a short" war.[22] When it did not end after Taylor's initial victories, the consequences of the Polk-Scott feud began to be felt. The president faced an enormous workload, which he did not share with Scott. By trying to do everything himself, Polk began to alienate members of his core support in the Democratic party. After several days of unwelcome advice, Polk testily told a prominent Democrat, "I hoped my friends in Congress and elsewhere would suffer me to conduct the War with Mexico as I thought proper, and not plan the campaign for me."[23]

The unceasing bombardment of office seekers drained the president. He spent long hours dispensing patronage, selecting people to fill positions ranging from a lowly army paymaster to a major general in the militia. But he could not give everyone all they asked, and when he failed to appoint some congressional Democrats to coveted war positions they turned on their leader. Polk complained about Congress with sentiments that would recur in the 1900s: "They create offices by their own votes and then seek to fill them themselves."[24]

Another strain on Polk stemmed from slow communications with the field. A correspondence required about two months to complete the trip from Washington to the Rio Grande and back. Thus, weeks would go by during which Polk would hear no news from the front. This required patience, which is often not a bad thing in matters of war, and also deterred excessive executive meddling, but the waiting took a toll.

Preoccupied by decisions large and small, Polk sent Taylor only general instructions. However, Scott, in his position as general in chief, also sent orders to Taylor. Scott tried to interpret Polk's desires, which was difficult since the two were not on speaking terms. Consequently, Scott's instructions often contradicted or confused the orders Taylor received from Polk himself. One of the consequences of Polk's failure to define clearly a chain of command was that much that should have been done was not done. It was the common soldier who suffered from the resultant maladministration. Volunteers from the Midwest and south poured into Taylor's base camp, which was not properly prepared to receive them, and died in droves. During the buildup period, some fifteen hundred of Taylor's men—about one in every eight—died from disease.

When autumn found Taylor still in camp, the public and the press became impatient. Newspapers labeled Old Rough and Ready "General Delay." Always sensitive to criticism—people were beginning to say he had brought on this war to ensure his own reelection—Polk himself grew anxious. Then, on Sunday evening, October 11, 1846, Secretary of War Marcy brought news to the White House that Taylor had left his base and marched to Monterrey, where he had won another victory. It had been a grueling, hard-fought engagement featuring house-to-house fighting. At battle's end Taylor had arranged a truce with his Mexican opponent. This infuriated Polk. Privately he railed against his general, claiming that Taylor had the enemy in his power, should have captured the entire lot, and then pushed on and ended the war. Publicly, he held his tongue because Scott had proclaimed Taylor's achievement "three glorious days" and it was in this light that the nation reflected upon Monterrey.

Neither Taylor's victory nor Scott's patriotic response to it did anything to alter Polk's mistrust of his senior generals. He already believed that Scott, a confirmed Whig, intended a sabotage his plans. Now Taylor's string of victories marked him as a rising national hero and a possible political opponent as well. Equally bad, following an unbroken string of American victories, Mexico showed no willingness to negotiate. Consequently, the president considered what to do next. Many advised a policy of "masterly inactivity" by holding the existing line until Mexico sued for peace. Alternatively, Taylor could advance farther into Mexico and perhaps a second force could land on the Mexican coast. Here was a strategic decision of the highest order.

For counsel the commander in chief relied upon Thomas Hart Benton. Benton was one of the giants in a Senate populated by men of surpassing talent. Polk deferentially called him "colonel" and Benton maintained to all who would listen that he was senior to every other officer in the army. This was technically correct, for back in the War of 1812 Benton had employed his silver orator's tongue first to gain election as colonel of a Tennessee volunteer regiment and then appointment as lieutenant colonel in a regular army unit. But he had never seen combat, excepting a memorable pistol-firing, knife-wielding brawl against Andrew Jackson that left Jackson nearly dead with a serious gunshot wound, Benton's coat burned by the blast of Jackson's pistol, and Benton's body punctured by five stab wounds when Jackson's friends pitched in to avenge their fallen leader.

At Benton's suggestion, back in August Polk had begun seriously to examine a plan to land on the Mexican coast near Vera Cruz. Climate was the controlling issue. *Vomitto* the natives called it, yellow fever to the gringos, and it would kill off an invading army more surely than bullets unless the landing took place during the healthy winter months. So Polk began collecting information bearing on a possible landing at Vera Cruz. Whether the landing would be a first stage in a march on Mexico City remained an open question.

Simultaneously, Polk was growing dissatisfied with the performance of many regular army officers. As future presidents would find out, years of peace had produced a sizable body of hide-bound, slothful older officers unable to respond to wartime demands. Some, observed Polk, "required to have a coal of fire put on their backs to make them move promptly."[25] Increasingly, Polk found that he had to attend to military details or they would be left undone. He also began to appreciate that command of a field army required an officer willing to exercise initiative and that this was an all too rare talent. Old Zach Taylor did not seem to have it. He willingly obeyed orders but was reluctant to assume responsibility and offered no strategic suggestions. In Polk's view, this made him a good subordinate but "unfit for the chief command."[26]

The officer with whom Polk should have been consulting was, of course, the army's general in chief, Winfield Scott. But Polk still believed Scott belonged to a group of officers who opposed the administration to such an extent that they were indifferent about the success of the country's military operations. Since Polk could not yet replace Scott, for the time being he decided to continue to "observe his course" but to avoid consulting with him.[27] So, in the White House was the amazing spectacle of the president poring over sketches of possible landing beaches near Vera Cruz and planning troop movements without assistance from Scott or any other important military officer.

At last in late October, after close consultation with Benton, Polk sent his plans to Scott. Scott returned a professional military critique that rejected the idea that Taylor continue south to Mexico City and supported the Vera Cruz project.[28] Moreover, Scott requested this command for himself. Polk labeled Scott's criticisms as founded purely in politics with the intent to embarrass the administration. But his attitude did not address a looming problem. The president had to prepare a budget message for Congress and this depended upon the number of soldiers and sailors deemed necessary to win the war. In turn, this number depended upon future strategy. If Polk decided merely to hold what had already been gained, then a lesser number would suffice; if he desired an offensive against Vera Cruz, then a much larger force was needed. Polk and Benton pondered all of this. Benton urged "a rapid crushing" movement from Vera Cruz to Mexico City. to support this plan, Benton observed that inactivity would only worsen the Democrats' declining political fortunes. Thus did partisan politics influence vital decisions regarding the war. Benton elaborated, saying Americans "were a go-ahead people, and that our only policy either to obtain a peace or save ourselves was to press the war boldly."[29]

Three days later Benton made another proposal pertaining to high strategy. He suggested that Polk use his power to appoint a lieutenant general who would outrank Taylor and Scott. Benton's dislike of Taylor dated back to the war against the Seminole Indians. On Christmas Day 1837, the then Colonel Taylor had placed his Missouri Volunteers in the front line with his regulars in support. When the Seminoles shot up the Missourians, the folks back home expressed deep outrage. Missouri Senator Benton charged that Taylor had sacrificed the volunteers to preserve his precious regulars. Benton had not forgotten this experience. Accordingly, he told Polk that the lieutenant general should be a man of "talents and resources" able to conduct vigorously a military campaign and possessing the requisite political acumen to negotiate a satisfactory peace. Of course this officer should be a trustworthy Democrat, and he, Thomas Hart Benton, would accept the position if offered. To his Cabinet and to his diary, Polk confided that politics never mingled in his conduct of the war. However, in November 1846, he began maneuvering to make Benton a lieutenant general.

By mid-month Polk also decided to launch an expedition to take Vera Cruz. What happened next would be determined according to circumstances, but he personally favored a march on Mexico City. The problem was selecting a commander. Since he suspected Taylor's ambitions, and his plan for Benton would take time, for the present there remained only Scott. Stern necessity seemed to require his selection. Benton and Polk agreed that they had "to use the instruments which the law had given."[30] Accordingly, Polk summoned Scott to his office.

Polk toyed with his general in chief by describing the proposed expedition while emphasizing the need for mutual trust between the expedition's commander and the president. His talk reduced Scott to fawning obsequiousness. Scott pledged to show his gratitude by his conduct in the field. Then, for the first time in the war, Polk and his top military man engaged in "free and open" conversation regarding strategy.[31]

While Scott briefly rose in presidential esteem, Taylor sank even further. The Secretary of War had been meddling in Taylor's dispositions, and the crusty general responded with a strong letter of complaint. In this letter Polk saw the long hand of presidential aspiration: "It is perfectly manifest that Gen'l Taylor is very hostile to the administration and seeks a cause of quarrel with it."[32] Describing Taylor as "narrow minded" and "a bigotted partisan," the president concluded that he was unfit for any command higher than a regiment.[33]

On November 23, 1846, the Secretary of War issued orders to Scott governing his conduct in Mexico. In spite of the administration's distrust, they were commendably broad: "It is not proposed to control your operations by definite and positive instructions, but you are left to prosecute them as your judgment ... shall dictate."[34] Events proved that this fredom was crucial since communications between Scott in Mexico and Polk in Washington took so long. Winfield Scott was the last American general to assume field command without the possibility of close meddling from the president.

This is not to say that Polk's influence went unfelt. His insistence upon a level of secrecy regarding Scott's expedition set the stage for confusion and quarrel between Scott and Taylor. Although Scott was to draw a substantial body of men from Taylor, Polk refused to permit Scott to send advance warning. Few generals readily yield troops to someone else's command, and Taylor was no exception. Unaware of the Vera Cruz plan, Taylor had in mind his own campaign—for which he would need every available soldier. Scott believed that "many of the wiseacres at Washington" agreed with Taylor. Given all of this, Scott concluded that "instead of a friend in the President, I had, in him, an enemy more to be dreaded than Santa Ana and all his hosts."[35]

At the end of 1846, Polk asked Congress to create a new rank of general officer to command all the forces in the field. The rationale he gave was transparent. The "efficient organization" of the army required such an officer.[36] Since the army already had a general in chief, everyone recognized that what the president had in mind was the creation of a position that would enable him to appoint a trusted Democrat to run the war. In the end the proposal fell afoul of warring factions within the Democratic party in a debate that had nothing to do with Benton's fitness for command and everything to do with the widening sectional feud over the extension of slavery to new territories.

When Scott learned to Polk's request, it confirmed his fears. Scott dreaded "fire upon the rear" from the Polk administration, and would later write that "party madness and malice" nearly thwarted his entire campaign.[37] As he embarked upon the United State's first saltwater invasion of a hostile coast, a poisonous cloud enveloped both the relationship between Scott and his chief subordinate, Taylor, and the one between Scott and the president.

*   *   *

Polk's annual message, presented to Congress on December 8, 1846, contained a comprehensive defense of his Mexican policy. It also charged his critics with failing to understand the conflict's "origin and true character." Their dissent was dangerous, "a more effectual means could not have been devised to encourage the enemy and protract the war . . . and thus give them 'aid and comfort.' "[38] Polk had a majority in both houses of Congress. Instead of patriotically sustaining the administration, Congress seemed more concerned with maneuvering for the next presidential election and debating the issue of slavery than with vigorously prosecuting the war. For three months his proposed military bill hung fire. Echoing Washington's complaint that "factions glow like coalpits," Polk observed: ". . . faction rules the hour, while principle & patriotism is forgotten."[39] Enduring increasing public criticism, deserted by his party, saddled with generals he did not trust, Polk began counting the days until his term ended and he could be relieved of the burden of leadership.

In mid-January Polk learned about some Mexican peace overtures. His Secretary of State advised that if actual negotiations began, as a gesture of goodwill the naval blockade of Vera Cruz should be lifted. It was a situation much like that Lyndon Johnson would confront when he considered bombing pauses against North Vietnam. Peace would solve all, but unlike Johnson, Polk concluded that negotiations might be an enemy ploy. If he relaxed pressure and lifted the blockade, Mexico could rearm. However beleaguered, he ordered "the most energetic crushing movement of our arms upon Mexico." Polk was certain that if he had a general "who would lay aside the technical rules of war" learned from books, Santa Ana and his army would be destroyed in a short time.[40]

On March 20, 1847, Polk heard rumors concerning Santa Ana—and they were frightening. Apparently a general had laid aside the technical rules of war, but unfortunately that general was the Mexican commander. Santa Ana had delivered a surprise blow against

Taylor and a horrible battle ensued with heavy losses on both sides. As Polk waited for hard news, anxiety nearly overcame him. For the first time since the war's start, something akin to panic struck. He railed against his generals, did what he could to hasten reinforcements toward Mexico, and waited in painful suspense. The army's safety, and perhaps the war's outcome, depended upon his field commanders.

Finally, on April 1, he received Taylor's dispatches describing the battle of Buena Vista. It transpired that because Polk had failed to adhere to any regular sense of a military chain of command, Scott and Taylor had failed to coordinate strategy. Consequently, Taylor had advanced his army in a strategically useless direction when he should have been consolidating his position in order to detach forces for Scott's invasion at Vera Cruz. Furthermore, he had allowed his army to become scattered and vulnerable. No American was overly worried, because the Mexican strategy clearly necessitated a concentration to defend their capital. However, politics influenced Mexican maneuvers just as much as they did those of the Americans. Hoping to elevate his standing by an overwhelming victory, General Santa Ana force-marched his army across two hundred miles of desert and mountain to attack Taylor. It was logistically impossible, his army suffered terrible privation, yet he arrived on the field near the hacienda of Buena Vista with fifteen thousand men to face an American force numbering five thousand mostly green troops.

Santa Ana's initial assaults routed several regiments of American volunteers. One demoralized soldier encountered a female camp follower and claimed that the army was cut to pieces and whipped. She snapped at him: "You damned son of a bitch, there ain't Mexicans enough in Mexico to whip old Taylor."[41] So overwhelming did the Mexican attack appear that by the time Taylor arrived on the field his chief subordinate reported: "General, we are whipped." Taylor replied, "That is for me to determine," and proceeded to conduct the hardest fight of the Mexican War. Since he lacked his prize regular infantry—they had been sent to join Scott—Taylor relied upon his artillery and the Mississippi Rifles, commanded by a West Point–educated officer, Jefferson Davis, to win the battle.

Davis led his men forward to check the Mexican advance. They repulsed the heretofore victorious Mexicans until Taylor brought up additional forces. Taylor ordered Davis to hold his position and departed for another threatened sector. This Davis did. His regiment would be the only American unit not to turn its back on the enemy this day. Meanwhile, astride Old Whitey, his leg hooked over the pommel of his saddle, Taylor's calm, conspicuous presence at the battle's center electrified his army. The general ignored two bullets that tore through his coat. Occasionally he rose on his stirrups to shout encouragement, and his volunteers responded by rallying to fight on.

The battle's crisis came when Santa Ana committed his reserves to storm the American position. On the left a Mexican column drove three volunteer regiments back on confusion. On the right another fresh force advanced into a yawning void and seemed about to win the battle. Suddenly, Jefferson Davis's command appeared to confront Santa Ana's charging host. Facing some two thousand enemy cavalry who emerged from a ravine, Davis arranged his own regiment and an adjacent unit of Indiana Volunteers into an inverted V-shaped formation with artillery commanded by a Captain Braxton Bragg at the apex. Although painfully wounded, Davis rode along his line to steady his men and order them to wait until the cavalry drew close. When the Mexican lancers drew within seventy yards, rifle and musket fire assailed their flanks while Bragg's guns shattered their front. Hit from two sides, the surviving Mexican cavalry broke and ran. Supported by Bragg, Davis advanced and crushed all opposition.[42]

The American victory at Buena Vista had less impact on the war's outcome—Scott's invasion at Vera Cruz had already shifted the strategic center south—than on the fate of three key participants. Zachary Taylor had been careless preparing for battle, failed to scout adequately, and underestimated his enemy. But his superlative display of physical and moral courage redeemed all, and this, his fourth successive victory and last Mexican battle, cemented his presidential fortune. The battle propelled Colonel Jefferson Davis along a star-crossed path that also ended at a presidential mansion. Davis's fate would intertwine with that of Braxton Bragg, who on this day also displayed fine leadership and won Davis's undying admiration. In time, Davis would appoint Bragg to the most important command position in the Confederate army. And so it would be said that because at Buena Vista Davis gained faith in his own military judgment, and Bragg first achieved renown, that the "Confederacy died from the V at Buena Vista."

*　　*　　*

Nine days after Polk learned the details of Taylor's victory, a telegraphic dispatch from the office of the *Baltimore Sun* arrived that announced that the "crushing movement" Polk had ordered had been crowned with initial success. Winfield Scott's army had captured Vera Cruz. To accomplish this Scott had organized the largest amphilbious invasion since the invention of gunpowder. He had performed with thoroughgoing efficiency, attending with care to the myriad details that make an invasion of a hostile coast so difficult. For the first and only time Polk entered something positive in his diary regarding Scott: "This was joyful news."[43] As Polk reflected, he attributed battlefield success not to the generals but to the rank and file. "The truth is," he observed, "our troops . . . will obtain victories wherever they meet the enemy. This [they] would do if they were without officers to command them higher in rank than Lieutenants."[44] Because of the soldiers' good conduct, henceforth there would be no repetition of the doubts experienced before Buena Vista. Polk was certain about final success.

Success was much less certain to his field general. Along with Andrew Jackson and Jacob Brown, Winfield Scott had been one of the generals whose tactical acumen helped stave off the worst consequences of the strategic bankruptcy of the War of 1812. Since that time he had only commanded in one other conflict, the Second Seminole War in 1836. During that guerrilla-style war, which proved a graveyard for military reputations, Scott showed no particular ability. By virtue of seniority, he became the Commanding General of the Army in 1841, but in that position his greatest concern had been coping with the Indians as the frontier pushed west. In sum, Scott had won a fine reputation as a tactician thirty-three years before. Now he had to serve as a strategic operating under his commander in chief's simple directive to crush his enemy.

Two major factors influenced his decision making. His command was composed of fewer than 14,000 men, of whom 5,741 were regulars. He knew he could expect few reinforcements and that his regulars were virtually irreplaceable. Unlike Taylor, he had to avoid costly battles. Yet he also had to move inland quickly, before the onset of yellow fever. He balanced these factors and decided he had just enough time to avoid the certain heavy losses that would ensue from a storm of the city, and instead lay methodical siege to Vera Cruz. Then he knew he had to hurry.

Scott devised a strategy that was Napoleonic in its brilliant simplicity: "To compel a people . . . to sue for peace, it is absolutely necessary . . . to strike, effectively, at the vitals of the nation." In Scott's view, Mexico's vitals were the Halls of Montezuma themselves, Mexico City. He marched with a force that never exceeded ten thousand men, and advanced with the knowledge that somewhere ahead he would encounter a much more numerous enemy. He refused to weary his army and divide his forces chasing scattered Mexican detachments or to be distracted by secondary objectives: "I played for the big stakes. Keeping the army massed and the mind fixed upon the capital, I meant to content myself with beating whatever force that might stand directly in the way of that conquest—being morally sure that all smaller objects would soon follow that crowning event."[45]

Once he advanced to capture the enemy's capital he would be separated from his base by two hundred miles of guerrilla-infested mountain roads and a fever coast. It was an audacious plan, and upon hearing of it, no less a strategist than the great Wellington pronounced it doomed: "Scott is lost . . . He can't take the city, and he can't fall back upon his base."[46]

In Washington, Polk supported Scott's campaign by making his own sound strategic choices. Although he expressed no satisfaction over Scott's conduct during the advance on Mexico City, when confronting a decision on where to send reinforcements, Polk opted to reinforce success by supporting Scott rather than strengthening Taylor, who was stationary in northern Mexico. The president even proved somewhat flexible when he doled out a coveted appointment to brigadier general. Rather than promote a favored friend, he allowed himself to be swayed by public opinion, which supported a Mississippi colonel who had behaved most gallantly at Monterrey and Buena Vista. Thus did Jefferson Davis become a general.

Polk also began to appreciate the political value of announcing war news in advance of the newspapers. Ships carried military and press dispatches from Mexico to U.S. ports. Then a combination of regular mail and telegraph—the telegraph system did not yet link many cities—brought the news to Washington. Newspapers relied upon express riders to hasten dispatches north, and these riders usually arrived in advance of the regular U.S. mail. Polk demanded that a government express be established in Alabama to close a gap in communications and gain a day on the regular mail. In this way he hoped to receive news from the front at least as soon as the newspapers.

In spite of the president's improved manipulation of the news, and the undeniable fact that most of the war news was good, Polk's political opponents continued to criticize in the pages of partisan newspapers. Furthermore, the press seemed uncannily able to learn administration secrets and publish them. Polk complained that newspapers' articles "against their own Government and in favour of the enemy, have done more to prevent a peace than all the armies of the enemy." In the president's view, they were committing "moral treason."[47]

During the war's second year, the commander in chief did make two potentially very damaging decisions. Like Napoleon, Polk believed that war should support war. Accordingly, he authorized his field generals to draw supplies from the enemy without paying for them and to levy contributions on the Mexican population. He justified this action on several grounds. The president cited what he called the "laws of war," which bestowed certain rights, including this one, upon the conqueror. The Mexicans had already "shown themselves to be wholly incapable of appreciating" previous American a "forbearance and liberality."[48] In Polk's view, forced contributions would provide another pressure point on the Mexicans and thus shorten the war. Finally, and not least important to a politician trying to spare the electorate the pain of war, it would help defray the army's expenses, thereby lessening the nation's war debt.

Fortunately, Polk allowed Taylor and Scott discretion to ignore this policy if they believed local conditions inappropriate. Taylor, occupying an exceedingly poor region of Mexico, declined because of the paucity of local resources. Scott, at the end of a tenuous line of supply already subject to guerrilla interdiction, wisely chose to continue to pay for supplies rather than obey Polk's preference and further inflame local hostility.

Polk made his second questionable decision in anticipation of Scott's eventual triumph. He sent one Nicholas Trist, Thomas Jefferson's grandson-in-law, to Mexico to negotiate a peace treaty. Polk empowered Trist with considerable authority, including the option to terminate military operations and arrange a truce. Originally the president had intended that his man Benton would be in the field and thus able to manage the war and negotiate a peace. But the power he would give Benton he would not give Scott. Trist's presence angered Scott. That general bitterly wrote Polk that he had to respect Trist's judgment on purely military matters as if it were the president's own judgment. Scott said that while he would cheerfully obey any direct order from the president, he would not "obey the orders of the chief clerk [Trist] of the State Department."[49]

From a military standpoint Scott had a valid complaint. He was five months into a delicate campaign against the enemy's main army, which outnumbered him considerably and was protected by elaborate fortifications. His own army stood at the end of a very insecure line of supply, and now, to complicate further his situation, here was the State Department's chief clerk with the power to interrupt Scott's combinations.

None of this mattered to Polk. Scott's complaint was merely one more display of hostility toward the administration. He decided to relieve Scott from command. He only hesitated as to the best time to do this. The "fire from the rear" that Scott had so feared was growing heavier.

While Polk plotted against his general in chief, Scott led his army through the mountains toward Mexico City. Employing the superb reconnaissance skills of his staff, and in particular those of an engineering officer named Robert E. Lee, Scott outflanked successive Mexican defensive positions. He won an easy first battle on the outskirts of Mexico City but then confronted strong fortifications at a place called Churubusco that blocked entry into the city. In the ensuing battle the Mexicans fought as never before. From the shelter of a thick-walled church and a massive stone convent they poured fire into the American ranks. When the day ended, Scott's army held the field but at the frightful price of 155 killed and 876 wounded. Then, Scott surprisingly paused. "Intelligent neutrals and some American residents" had told him that to pursue into the capital would drive the Mexican government away, "scatter the elements of peace, excite a spirit of national desperation, and thus indefinitely postpone the hope of accommodation."[50] Mindful that his mission was "to conquer a peace," he accepted Santa Ana's proposal for an armistice and halted his offensive. He faced a situation much like the one another victorious American army faced 140 years later in Kuwait, as it too was in full career but chose to stop for many of the same reasons that influenced Scott.

After two weeks, talks collapsed. Reinforced to some eight thousand men, but still outnumbered by about two to one, Scott sent his army across Mexico City's western plain toward a dominating height on which perched the Castle of Chapultepec. Serving as an outwork for the castle was a range of low stone buildings, known as El Molino del Rey, which Scott mistakenly believed housed a cannon foundry. On September 8, 1847, a picked five-hundred-man storming party spearheaded the assault against this position. The defenders waited until the Americans closed to within seventy yards and then opened a heavy musketry fire thickened by cannon fire. A participant described that although the fire "cut us up considerably . . . still no one thought of retreating. On the brigade went, but the enemy was in such force that the fire was continuous, like the roll of drums. Our men could not stand it and gave way." The Americans rallied and tried again only to fail. It required a third assault to capture El Molino del Rey. Of forty officers in the assault brigade, only half remained unhit. Recalls a survivor; "It was a dearly-bought victory on our side. We gained all we attempted, but oh we shall think of the cost as long as we live."[51]

A week later Scott sent the army against Chapultepec itself. Showing fierce determination, his men braved heavy Mexican fire from the ramparts, crossed into the moat, positioned their scaling ladders, and climbed to victory. On September 14 Mexico City surrendered. Scott had achieved a memorable series of triumphs, but the resultant collapse of the Mexican government left no one with whom to negotiate a peace.

*   *   *

By the end of 1847, Polk confronted a situation akin to the one that President George Bush faced in the aftermath of the war against Iraq. Polk heard political and public criticism about a president who could not gain his objective despite his generals' battlefield successes. In his third annual message to Congress, he squarely addressed the outstanding strategic question:

> *Our arms having been everywhere victorious, having subjected to our military occupation a large portion of the enemy's country, including his capital, and negotiations for peace having failed, the important questions arise, in what manner the war ought to be prosecuted and what should be our future policy.*[52]

One strategy being discussed in Washington recommended that the Americans withdraw to a handful of key posts and then wait until the Mexicans came to their senses. It was remarkably like the so-called enclave strategy promoted by certain opponents of President Lyndon Johnson's Vietnam War policy. Polk rebutted the 1847 version of this strategy by arguing that a passive defense would allow Mexican guerrillas to chose the time and place for hit-and-run raids. They could slip between American posts to steal from and murder the inhabitants. They could mass in secret and assault isolated American posts. Even if repulsed, the enemy could simply withdraw into remote interior regions or even across borders, where he would be safe from pursuit and able to refit for another offensive. It would be costly in blood and treasure and would not work. Just like George Washington, who had pondered similar problems in devising a strategy against the Indians, Polk showed a very keen appreciation of guerrilla warfare.

Rejecting a static defensive, Polk explained his choice for a forceful continuation of the war. He bluntly advocated the extension of U.S. civil rule to territory occupied by the army as preliminary step toward permanent acquisition. Without apology he stated that this should be done to coerce Mexico to accept America's "just terms of peace."[53] He worried that Trist's continued presence in Mexico impeded his strategy by encouraging the Mexican government to believe that the United States was overly anxious for peace. After some deliberation, he decided to recall his envoy.

Polk's conundrum would be confronted by future commanders in chief. Public opinion, freely expressed in a democracy, could demand peace negotiations. An enemy could interpret this as a sign of weakness and use this insight to modify his strategy. Thus it would be in the distant future when Communist statesmen relied upon American domestic political forces when conceiving their military and diplomatic strategy for capturing South Vietnam. So it was in 1847 when the possibility that Whig political pressure would force Polk to accept more lenient terms convinced some Mexican politicians to prolong negotiations. Some clung to the hope that if Polk's party failed in the 1848 election a new administration might make an easier peace. In the near future the principal hope of the Confederate government, as it analyzed Lincoln's forthcoming bid for reelection, would rest on the same line of thinking. At the end of 1847, so splintered was the Mexican government that it was unable to exploit the possibilities inherent in a war leader's running for reelection. Instead a political change occurred in Mexico itself.

After a rocky beginning, that State Department clerk Nicholas Trist and Scott had gotten on famously. It helped that Trist had liberally interpreted his initial set of instructions from the president, and exercising his own judgment had refused to heed Polk's order recalling him. Instead, after the fall of Mexico City, he reopened negotiations when a newly elected Mexican regime finally emerged. More startling, his efforts led to a treaty, signed at the Mexican village of Guadalupe Hidalgo.

When news of the treaty reached Washington in February 1848, Polk found himself in a most delicate position. Of course he felt betrayed, since Trist had disobeyed his recall order. Worse, the president was convinced that Trist had become a tool of General Scott. Yet the treaty itself, although flawed—expansionists claimed it gave Mexico too much, war critics said it took too much—was within the guidelines of Polk's instructions. Polk understood that given this fact it would look back to reject the treaty. Such an action would throw new negotiations to the next administration, which very well might be a Whig administration. Finally, the president knew that the nation was war-weary. So, in the end, he swallowed his pride and submitted the treaty to Congress. Even then he worried that it might not be ratified:

> *The truth is the approaching Presidential election absorbs every other consideration, and Senators act as if there was no country and no public interests to take care of. The factions are all at work, and votes are controlled, even upon a vital question of peace or war, by the supposed effect upon the public mind.*[54]

In the event, ratification proceeded relatively smoothly. A year and a day after Scott's landing at Vera Cruz, the Senate approved a modified version of the treaty. This left the president one last war-related issue to address: how big a military establishment to retain now that the nation was again at peace. Polk recommended that all of the units raised for the war, regular and volunteer alike, be discharged. Opponents argued that the new territory required a bigger army. Polk rejected this view. Echoing the debate during the Revolution, he said it was simply wrong to create a large standing army in times of peace. Some 70 percent of the force that fought the war had been militia and volunteers. The volunteers had been the key, since they fought without the constitutional scruples that inhibited a president's employment of militia. The war seemed to prove that the nation could retain a small standing army and rely upon a flood of patriotic volunteers as an efficient instrument to accomplish national objectives.

Before the Senate met to ponder the treaty, Polk had enjoyed one last victory. Sixteen days after the signing of the peace treaty, Scott received a letter announcing his relief and requesting his presence before a military court of inquiry. As one of his most devoted officers, Robert E. Lee, bitterly remarked, the general had been turned out as an "old horse to die."[55] Although the subsequent inquiry collapsed for lack of evidence, it did serve to thwart Scott's presidential ambitions for 1848.

So James K. Polk's war of conquest ended in triumph. It had been a costly affair, depleting the Treasury of more than $100 million and causing the deaths of 13,780 American soldiers. Sensitive to criticism that he had caused an unjust war, Polk had tried to run it on the cheap. Consequently, the field armies lacked adequate logistical support, which increased sickness and disease, and had to campaign without adequate manpower. A legacy of Polk's leadership was that in every significant battle the Mexicans substantially outnumbered the Americans. Polk's mistrust of his generals made military coordination difficult, which also contributed to this state of affairs.

Nonetheless, through his actions the country gained "an immense empire" including modern-day Arizona, New Mexico, Utah, Nevada, California, portions of Colorado and Wyoming, and the Texas border on the Rio Grande. Polk predicted that within twenty years this empire would generate an immeasurable wealth.[56] The discovery of gold in California the next year proved him overly pessimistic.

Polk had performed the commander in chief's twin wartime tasks in an unusual manner. From the start, because he had a very clear idea about what he was fighting he understood what constituted victory. He arrived at the winning strategy, invasion and march upon Mexico City, only after the miscalculated, costly campaign across the Rio Grande. When Santa Ana launched his surprise counteroffensive against Taylor that culminated in the battle of Buena Vista, Polk momentarily lost confidence. But when the American forces won that battle in spite of Taylor's mistaken dispositions, he realized before his military men that the Mexicans were incapable of defeating the American regulars and volunteers.

Thereafter, Polk confidently pursued a consistent strategy that brought victory.

Regarding his second responsibility, choosing a commander to execute his strategy, Polk's conduct was also most singular. Thomas Hart Benton observed that Polk had "wanted a small war, just large enough to require a treaty of peace, and not large enough to make military reputations, dangerous for the presidency."[57] Polk began the war detesting his Whig general in chief. At first, he had some confidence in Taylor, but quickly he turned against that general as well. Consequently, he planned operations in the near absence of professional military advice. Then, with great reluctance he had to entrust those plans to two generals whom he believed unworthy. Even while Scott departed for the front Polk schemed to supplant him. As soon as Scott captured Mexico City he relieved him. In victory, he thanked the soldiers and the bureaucrats who staffed the Department of War, but uttered not one word of appreciation for Taylor or Scott.

Given this behavior, why had Taylor and Scott achieved Polk's strategic goals? First, both generals served patriotically, putting nation before politics. Second, they were able officers. Taylor was a good battlefield general who showed particular skill at fusing his regular and volunteer components into a highly motivated whole. Scott was one of America's great strategists. Unlike most future American generals, who relied upon superior forces to wage a war of attrition, he did not pursue a direct approach. Instead, he substituted maneuver for combat and aimed, by capturing Mexico City, to prove to his enemy the futility of prolonging the war. Scott was particularly good at selecting qualified young officers for important positions and then relying upon their judgment. When he hosted a celebratory dinner following the capture of Mexico City, Scott explained the fundamental basis of his campaign's success: without the "science of the Military Academy . . . this army, multiplied by four, could not have entered the capital of Mexico."[58] Another factor had an immense bearing on the war's outcome. The enemy was fatally handicapped by an absence of skilled general officers. The Mexican soldier usually fought bravely. The leadership he received from his officers was atrocious.

The United States' third great war was both a historical watershed and a harbinger of future wars. The conflict had been the nation's first foreign war. Polk drew a lesson for the still-young nation: the war had "fully developed the capacity of republican governments to prosecute successfully a just and necessary foreign war with all the vigor usually attributed to more arbitrary forms of government."[59] Moreover, as the president proudly boasted, the nation had passed through more than two years of war "with the business of the country uninterrupted."[60] Unlike European nations, who faced wars in which invaders very much interrupted business, the United States—protected by a vast ocean moat and endowed with colossal natural resources—had fought this war without disturbing the great majority of its population. In contrast to its two prior wars against England, once mobilized, the United States enjoyed a potential superior military strength over its foe. Whether this superiority, coupled with the relative ease and comfort with which it fought, would encourage future wars remained to be seen.

Writing in the *New York Tribune*, Horace Greeley worried that it might be so. Greeley tried to extract lessons from an aggressive war of conquest and asked: "Shall not our People be cured of a passion for that Glory which only idiots or demons can so verily prize and exult in? ... O let us resolve henceforth to treat as a public enemy the man who dare propose the sending of a single regiment, on any pretext beyond the limits of our own country!"[61]

A final legacy of the Mexican War involved the three Americans who had featured most prominently: Polk, Scott, and Taylor. A driven man to start with, Polk had worked unceasingly during his term, redoubling his efforts during the war. It quite probably killed him. He died a mere four months after voluntarily leaving office. He was the nation's most successful war leader, yet he is all but forgotten.

Passed over by his party in 1848, Winfield Scott received the Whig nomination for president in 1852 only to suffer defeat at the hands of his onetime subordinate in Mexico, Franklin Pierce. He continued into his dotage as general in chief of the army. The year 1861 would find him helping an inexperienced president plan to suppress a civil War. Scott would also recognize that his advancing age and physical infirmity dictated the passing of the baton to a younger man. He selected his most able subordinate from his Mexican days, only to have that officer, his fellow Virginian Robert E. Lee, rebuff him.

Only Zachary Taylor immediately benefited from the war. To Polk's mortification and Scott's displeasure, Taylor received the

Whig nomination for president in 1848. Old Rough and Ready won without even bothering to campaign.

The war had displayed many modern features. That erstwhile lieutenant general, Senator Thomas Benton, observed that the American volunteer soldier had exhibited such energy and strength that henceforth the United States could mobilize large armies with undreamed-of speed and efficiency. Benton predicted that the telegraph would "summon the patriotic host" and the railroad would carry soldiers to the battlefield. He concluded that the war's lessons could be reduced to two simple principles: "accumulation of masses, and the system of incessant attacks." Benton believed that his vision applied to a defensive war fought against foreign invaders. He envisioned invading armies "shot like pigeons on their roost" by rifle-armed volunteer soldiers.[62] Benton accurately described the future, missing only that his prophecy would apply to Americans fighting fellow Americans.

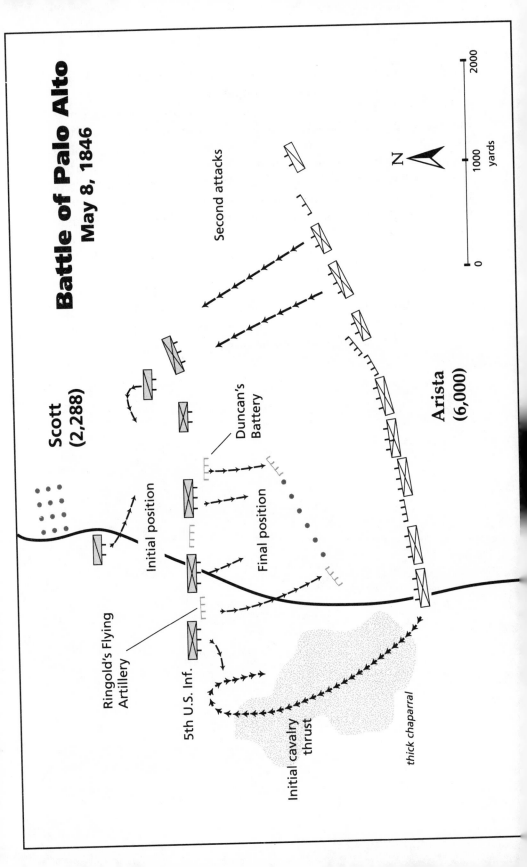

Battle of Palo Alto
May 8, 1846

Scott (2,288)

Arista (6,000)

Second attacks

Ringold's Flying Artillery

5th U.S. Inf.

Initial position

Final position

Duncan's Battery

Initial cavalry thrust

thick chaparral

N

0   1000   2000
yards

PART THREE

JEFFERSON DAVIS'S

LOST CAUSE

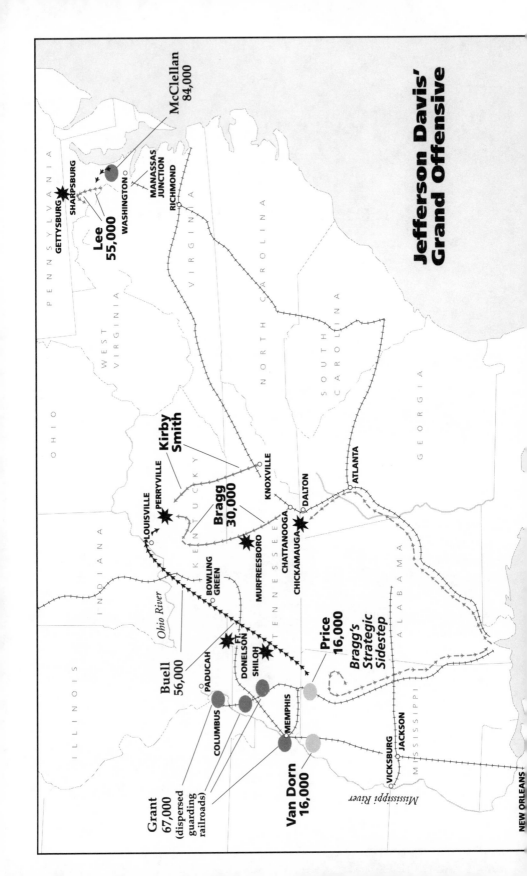

**Jefferson Davis'
Grand Offensive**

6

WAR BETWEEN THE STATES

"We feel that our cause is just and holy; we protest solemnly in the face of mankind that we desire peace at any sacrifice save that of honor and independence; we seek no conquest . . . all we ask is to be let alone."

JEFFERSON DAVIS, 1861[1]

"THE MAN AND THE HOUR"

THE UNITED STATES ARMY OF THE 1830S TESTED A MAN'S CHARACTER, revealing much. Most officers served in small frontier garrisons where boredom and isolation reigned supreme. Some became indolent, others fell to drink. Lieutenant Jefferson Davis fell to feuding. His temperament was such that when challenged, he simply could not back down. He responded to verbal attacks with heat and temper, and at one point escalated a petty disagreement with a superior officer into a near duel. Only a friend's intervention dissuaded him, and only then because the friend pointed out that it would be unwise to kill a man whom the lieutenant hoped would become his father-in-law. For this superior officer was Zachary Taylor and Davis had fallen in love with his daughter. Thirty years later he would recall his dispute with Taylor and explain that he was right in principle, only "impolitic" in asserting it.[2]

Prospects for promotion were so poor in the frontier army—a West Point graduate could anticipate a wait of more than fifty years before becoming a colonel—that it is unsurprising that Davis resigned his commission after four and a half years of service. He took up the life of a planter on his older brother's plantation in

Mississippi. There his twenty-one-year-old new bride, Zachary Taylor's daughter, died of a fever that almost claimed Davis himself. He responded to this tragedy with a stoical, iron application of self-control. He became a recluse, seldom leaving the confines of his plantation. To old acquaintances the change was dramatic; henceforth he appeared mirthless and cold.

A new acquaintance, a seventeen-year-old woman, met Davis as he began to emerge from his shell of sorrow. She wrote to her mother describing his winning manners, his "peculiarly sweet" voice, and a face that was both young and old. She continued: "He impresses me as a remarkable kind of man, but of uncertain temper, and has a way of taking for granted that everybody agrees with him when he expresses an opinion."[3] This young woman had penetrated Davis's character in one short afternoon. Offended by his assertiveness, she also saw in him many admirable characteristics, Varina Howell would become his second wife.

National events renewed Davis's interest in life. He and his beloved older brother Joseph would read recent congressional debates and discuss the opinions of the nation's statesmen. In 1846, at the age of thirty-eight, Davis shared Polk's Democratic party's victory when Mississippi sent him to the House of Representatives. In Congress, Davis quickly showed that unlike many politicians, he believed what he said. After explaining his premises he simply could not comprehend how anyone could reason differently.[4] Because of his easy passage into politics—Joseph had paved the way for him—he had not acquired the essential political skills of negotiation and accommodation. In a typical encounter, a fellow congressman offered to support one of Davis's pet projects if Davis, in turn, would support his. Davis indignantly replied: "Sir, I make no terms, I accept no compromises." Davis continued by saying it was self-evident that his project was worthy, and he "defied the gentleman" to vote against it.[5]

Exhibiting a capacity to become swallowed by paperwork, Davis served an undistinguished term. Soon the conflict with Mexico commanded his attention. On this, as with everything else, he had no doubt. In a letter to a Vicksburg newspaper he urged that a peace treaty should be forged from the mouths of American cannon at the gates of Mexico City.

Swept up by such patriotic rhetoric, a newly mustered infantry regiment elected Davis to lead them to war. This was the celebrated 1st Mississippi Volunteers. Davis accepted the appointment, and before leaving Washington he managed to both convince President Polk and overcome the opposition of General Scott in order to equip his unit with a rifle that was the latest in American shoulder arms technology. Taking the field, Colonel Davis led his riflemen from the front in their first battle, a house-to-house combat in the streets of Monterrey. Although this was the first time he had ever been under enemy fire, he impressed fellow officers with his gallantry. So it was again at Buena Vista, where he conspicuously rode along his line to steady his men. An admiring observer reported that his actions could "infuse courage into the bosom of a coward."[6] Buena Vista earned Davis a national reputation. The America press promoted him as a hero second only to Zach Taylor himself. Propelled back into politics, he filled an empty Senate seat from Mississippi and emerged at the forefront of the great issue of the day, the extension of slavery into the vast new territories won as a result of the war.

It was an issue that generated great passion, and Davis's exceeded most. Because of West Point and his subsequent army duty Davis had escaped the narrow parochialism typical of many southern politicians. Still, he shared their belief that regardless of northern promises not to intervene where slavery already existed, the rising abolition party would take hold in the North and change everything, including the Constitution. Thus would be undone the South's immense investment in slavery, its way of life, and its very social order. From 1848 on, Davis warned that unless the South maintained equal representation with the North in Congress, self-preservation would dictate secession. Over time, he assumed John Calhoun's mantle as the foremost champion of southern rights.

He also expanded his bureaucratic experience. During his second Senate term he became chairman of the Military Affairs Committee. In 1853 he served a four-year term as Secretary of War during which he proved an innovative reformer. He improved the soldier's lot by raising pay and providing better living conditions. With his Mexican experience in mind, he introduced the latest technology to the army. He attended to national strategy by building coastal fortifications and extending the military road net. When faced with Indian problems on the frontier, he, like George Washington, resisted the prevailing strategy of scattering soldiers in small garrisons. Instead, he recommended concentrating the army along rail and steamboat lines as a mobile reserve capable of responding to Indian threats. He managed sums amounting to nearly a third of the entire government's operating budget with thrift and efficiency. Then and thereafter he was recognized as a topnotch Secretary of War.

Davis accomplished this by long stints of hard work. He felt responsible for everything that took place in the department, and therefore delegated very little. Sometimes he seemed to take refuge in routine paperwork, preferring the constancy of rules and regulations to the uncertainty of human interaction. He had yet to acquire suppleness, tact, and finesse. Still intolerant of criticism, he repeatedly told his wife, "I cannot bear to be suspected or complained of, or misconstrued after explanation."[7] When civil war seemed imminent, and Mississippi chose him to command her troops, Davis disagreed with those who predicted a short and easy war. He foresaw a dreadful calamity. Davis had been a fire-eater before Abraham Lincoln's election, but the prospect of civil war made him gloomy and depressed. Fifty-three years old in 1861, he suffered from a variety of ailments—fever, neuralgia, an inflamed eye, poor digestion, insomnia—that stress exacerbated. On the eve of the first meeting of the seceded states, he told a delegate that he wanted neither to be president nor general in chief, although he thought it likely that the latter post would be offered. In accordance with his strict concept of duty, he left his fate in the hands of the Montgomery delegates.

The unwelcome news found him tending his roses on his Mississippi plantation. His wife relates that while reading the telegram announcing he had been elected president of the Confederate States of America, "he looked so grieved that I feared some evil had befallen our family. After a few minutes' painful silence he told me, as a man might speak of a sentence of death."[8]

Davis arrived in Montgomery, Alabama, to popular acclaim. William Yancey introduced him with the words "the man and the hour have met," and it seemed to be only the truth, given his West Point education, Mexican War service, and performance while Secretary of War. In the eyes of most southerners Jefferson Davis possessed surpassing qualifications for the task at hand. Davis, in turn, understood that the Confederacy's bid for independence rested upon the leadership of its president and commander in chief. Amid the giddy pace of events in the new nation's jubilant first spring, he applied himself to the twin mandates of serving as a strategic architect and finding leaders to execute his scheme.

VICTORY AND DISCORD

On February 4, 1861, delegates from the six seceded states gathered in Montgomery, Alabama, to create a new and better nation. Like the first American revolution, this second one had been determined by a small political elite. State legislatures selected 854 delegates to state secession conventions. Six hundred and ninety seven of these hand-picked delegates voted for secession and by so doing committed millions of people to war. One of their first tasks was to mobilize the people's loyalty, and one of the ways they did this was to model the new nation's constitution on the original.

To begin they selected Howell Cobb of Georgia to preside over their convention. Cobb was anything but a fire-eater. His moderate views placed him squarely in the middle between the red-hot South Carolinians and those who only hesitantly supported withdrawal from the Union. Delegates divided over whether the South's bid for freedom was a revolution against the North or a conservative effort to maintain the original intent of the Constitution. How they answered this question had a great deal to do with how the war would be prosecuted. A revolution was open to novel and pragmatic approaches. A war based on conservative ideology was not. Cobb shared, along with Jefferson Davis and certain other southern leaders, a self-image grounded firmly in the belief that the South, not the North, remained true to the Founding Fathers' ideals. It was an attitude fraught with enormous strategic consequence because it meant that from the Montgomery Convention on, a conservative view predominated.

Steeped in the legalisms of constitutional debate, the delegates sought to refine the tried and true. Their product differed from the original Constitution only in its explicit recognition of slavery and state sovereignty, its establishment of a single six-year presidential term, and its inclusion of a line item veto for the executive. Their actions caused a prominent Richmond newspaper editor to boast that the South waged war "to revive conservative ideas rather than to run into new and rash experiments."[9]

It was the South's misfortune to base her bid for independence upon a conservative philosophy at a time when warfare was undergoing revolutionary change. Quite simply, the Civil War marked a transition from limited to total war. The neat distinction between the civil and the military no longer applied. The process of mobilizing, supplying, and transporting thousands of men distorted all aspects off the economy. Historic patterns of production and consumption altered beyond recognition. Armies drew into their ranks factory workers and farmers, including those whose special talents—rail workers, iron smiths, wagon and harness makers—produced the sinews of war. Their absence from productive society caused huge changes in wages and profits. On the consumption side, armies were like open maws, receiving money, food, munitions, clothes, and always demanding more. When supplies did not arrive, the armies took from the area around their camps, leaving desolation and blight where there had been plenty.

Modern war demanded centralized efficiency and a subordination of everything to the war effort. In the heady days of 1861, no one could anticipate all of this. But the North had sufficient resources to buffer against misstep and muddle. The South's margin for error was wafer thin.

*   *   *

In the spring of 1861, President Davis delivered to Congress a clear articulation of his country's strategic goal: "... all we ask is to be let alone."[10] This statement implied that initially the South would refrain from offensive action, waging instead a defensive war. It was one of the commander in chief's most important strategic decisions and, on the face of it, was totally out of character. He had won his military reputation in Mexico by bold maneuver. Vigorous attack on his political foes characterized his congressional style. Yet he restrained his aggressive instincts for what he believed the nation's benefit and devised a strategy he styled the "offensive-defensive." The defensive portion of this strategy relied upon positioning troops to repel Yankee thrusts. The offensive portion involved waiting for, or maneuvering to create, an enemy blunder and then exploiting it by a hard blow.[11] It would have to be a land-based strategy, because from the inland rivers to the high seas the Confederacy had few naval resources beyond some extremely able officers.

The band of brothers composing the professional sailors of the U.S. Navy—as tight a fraternity as their West Point brethren—split apart when war came. Officers who together had fought the Mexicans and shared lonely vigils on distant oceanic stations now opposed one another. In contrast to the army, mobilization for war did not dilute the naval talent pool. The South had few naval postings and so could appoint sailors of great ability to the few available commands. Davis employed talented, resolute administrators for the top positions, including Secretary of the Navy Stephen Mallory and the resourceful Matthew Fontaine Maury, nominally the chief of the Submarine Battery Service. Maury would show what a hard-driving, resourceful officer could accomplish in the face of a poverty of resources. His innovations—submarines, mines (which sank some thirty-one Federal blockaders), and torpedoes— foreshadowed the future of naval warfare.

Because the South lacked an industrial base, it could not hope to compete with the Federal Navy. The most Confederate naval strategy could strive to accomplish was to defend its own coast while engaging in the traditional American underdog naval strategy of mounting privateering operations against the enemy's merchant fleet. While this latter would be enormously successful—it destroyed scores of vessels and drove the American merchant marine under the protection of foreign flags, a position of inferiority from which it has not recovered to this day—it could not win the war. The Rebel navy could serve as a useful adjunct, but strategy had to hinge upon infantry regiments supported by cavalry and guns.

So Davis's offensive-defensive was a land strategy and it did not exactly conform with the ideas of General Pierre Gustave Toutant-Beauregard. Beauregard had been a soldier since age sixteen. Of Louisiana Creole stock, he was a West Point graduate and Mexican War veteran who used his training and experience to good purpose at Charleston harbor. Celebrated thereafter as "the hero of Fort Summer," admired by partisans as a reincarnation of one of Napoleon's marshals, he arrived in Virginia to assume field command and quickly showed himself to be a man of great imagination. During the first weeks of July 1861, he sent his aide to Richmond to describe his concept for uniting the Confederate forces in Virginia and attacking the Union forces along the Potomac. Jefferson Davis resisted the pull for what he viewed as a premature offensive and rejected Beaurgard's plan.

In contrast, one hundred miles to the north, Abraham Lincoln lacked the military experience to comprehend the dangers of launching an offensive with an underprepared military. Swayed by public and press demands, he sent the Union army south into Virginia toward one of those small rail hubs that were to feature so prominently in this war, the world's first where mechanical instead of equine power supplied the soldiers.

The ensuing battle near Manassas Junction featured a Union flanking move over Bull Run that gained initial success but ultimately ran out of steam because of the combination of its soldiers' rawness, its officers' inexperience, and the arrival of Confederate reserves via train from the Shenandoah Valley. During the action, Beauregard handled the army's tactical operations while General Joseph E. Johnston facilitated the flow of reinforcements that turned the tide of battle. In the end the Yankees broke rather badly, fled all the way back to Washington, and the South gained the first great victory of the war.

Davis was present at the battle's end. At a postbattle conference he urged pursuit, but was persuaded to wait until the morning. Then he wrote and signed a telegram to Richmond announcing the "glorious victory," and by so doing ruffled the feathers of General Beauregard. Beauregard saw in this action an attempt by Davis to claim credit when the credit should be his. Indeed, there was something to Beauregard's intuition. Describing the battle to friends in Richmond, Davis exaggerated his role to such an extent that one of his closest colleagues felt compelled to emphasize that Beauregard's leadership also had had something to do with the outcome.[12] Even Davis's approval, a week later, of a congressional resolution honoring Beauregard and Johnston for their victory failed to relieve Beauregard of a suspicion that he was dealing "with an ambitious man."[13] It boiled down to a matter of conflicting personalities. Davis was proud and controlled, Beauregard proud and pompous. Their personalities clashed and it was a harbinger of things to come.

The Battle of First Manassas had many consequences, small and large. The most significant arose from what on the surface seemed to be the smallest of issues, and thereafter grew like a cancer to weaken forever after Confederate war-making ability. A few days after the battle, an officer appeared to Joe Johnston's headquarters carrying orders signed by Robert E. Lee. Johnston exploded. Not only did Johnston believe that he outranked Lee, he also considered himself the "ranking General of the Confederate Army," and lost no time asserting vigorously this opinion to the War Department in Richmond. While the issue of rank was somewhat hazy— it had to do with rank in the old federal army, among other things— on balance the facts clearly supported Johnston. Indeed, Johnston's strict construction of military law was a type of argument that Jefferson Davis, a master of rules and laws, should have applauded. Instead, when he read Johnston's letter of protest, the president scrawled "insubordinate" on the bottom.[14]

Davis had found Johnston's tone challenging, which was probably enough to stimulate his wrath. But unbeknownst to Johnston, Davis had recently made a major decision regarding the Confederate high command. Exercising presidential prerogative, he had nominated five officers to fill a newly created rank of full general.[15] Looking to the time when separate field armies would combine, the president wanted to avoid the problems at Manassas where Beauregard and Johnston had had to debate rank and improvise a command structure. Davis had long entertained deep doubts about the wisdom of promotion based on seniority and had tried to eliminate it during his service as U.S. Secretary of War. Now, as Confederate commander in chief, Davis played fast and loose with the rules of seniority in order to create the command hierarchy he desired.

The venerable adjutant general, Samuel Cooper, headed the list. No one expected him to take field command and no one quarreled with his choice. The next four officers on Davis's list were his old friend Albert Sidney Johnston, Lee, Joseph Johnston, and Beauregard. Sidney Johnston, Lee, and Joe Johnston were the three most eminent career officers in the nation prior to the war's outbreak. Beauregard, by virtue of his victories at Fort Sumter and First Manassas, also clearly deserved high rank. But Davis's list badly rankled Joe Johnston. Back in 1851, Joe Johnston had described himself as desiring promotion "more than any man in the army."[16] His behavior in the coming weeks showed he had not changed.

Joe Johnston had served on Winfield Scott's staff during the Mexican War, where he undoubtedly learned a thing or two about civil-military discord. He put his experience to good use after learning that he was fourth on Davis's list. He employed loaded language in a letter accusing Davis of "trampling" on his own and Congress's rights. He reminded Davis that he had ranked A. S. Johnston and Lee in the old army and by God he should still rank them.

Of course this was too much for Jefferson Davis. He replied angrily that Johnston's arguments was one-sided and "its insinuations as unfounded as they are unbecoming," and by so saying

widened the breach to insurmountable dimensions.[17] Before this
feud Davis had signed his letters to Johnston "Your friend." Likewise, the two men's wives had been very close. Henceforth, with
both men feeling full of wounded dignity, all communications
would be stiff, cold, and difficult. Their wives established rival
Richmond salons from which they sniped at one another and at
the menfolk. Johnston-Davis antipathy became common gossip.
The tragedy for Davis and Johnston and for the cause for which
they fought was that success required their wholehearted cooperation. Instead, on grounds with which he should have been utterly
familiar, Davis stumbled badly.

In the midst of all of this, newspaper editors and some politicians asked why, after First Manassas, the army had failed to pursue
and destroy the defeated Yankees. In fact, the raw Confederate
soldiers, enlisted men and officers alike, had been as undone by
their victory as their defeated foe. Adding to the debate was
Beauregard's public complaint that lack of logistical support had
prevented him from advancing to take advantage of the victory.
Since the officer charged with providing logistical support was a
Davis appointee, the president's critics seized upon this to attack
the administration. Davis displayed rare patience and wrote
Beauregard a conciliatory letter that said in essence that the battle
reflected creditably upon every participant and no good could
come from further dispute. The Creole replied with a Davis-like
statement that he accused no one of error, but merely stated facts.

Surrounded by such petty disharmony, Davis traveled to
Manassas Junction to meet with his Virginia field commanders and
address larger issues of war strategy. Beauregard had another
grand plan, which proposed uniting forces from distant areas in
order to take the offensive across the Potomac. "Old Bory," as his
men affectionately called him, was willing to cede territory elsewhere to concentrate resources and gain victory in Virginia. Underlying his strategic notion was the belief that after victory in
Virginia the South could recapture whatever had been abandoned.

Before First Manassas he had made a similar suggestion, and he
would advance versions of this strategy for the remainder of the
war. Then and evermore it was difficult for Davis to appreciate the
merits of Beauregard's strategy, coming, as it did, from a man he
had grown to detest. The president agreed that inaction was unwise, but emphasized that he had to look to the defense of the
whole nation. To cede one inch of Confederate soil was politically

difficult. More important, at this stage in the conflict Davis showed himself unwilling to stake his country's future on a military gamble.

Rebuffed over future plans, Beauregard returned to refighting battles past. Rejecting Davis's proposal to dispute no longer First Manassas, "Old Bory" submitted his formal battle report. It claimed that Davis had overruled him and thereby prevented him from conducting a campaign to liberate Maryland and capture Washington. It left the clear impression that had Beauregard's ideas been followed, First Manassas could have led to a war-ending campaign. The rupture between the two men was complete and would persist until their deaths, which was another great pity for the South since Beauregard was the one general who possessed the breadth of vision to devise Napoleonic master strokes that just might have won the war.

The situation in Virginia in 1861 was all very reminiscent of the bickering between the Continental Congress and Washington's army. It clearly pointed to a future that would demand of the commander in chief an ability to soothe the exceptionally touchy feelings displayed by so many southern generals. An impartial observer might have resolved matters fairly easily. Instead, it became clear that the president and his two generals were prideful people who quite simply were developing a dislike for one another.[18] So the battle of First Manassas yielded an unproductive victory—and worse, placed the commander in chief at odds with two of his top four field commanders.

THE SINEWS OF WAR

When he first arrived in Richmond, an admiring newspaperman commented that the mantle of George Washington sat gracefully upon Davis's shoulders. As had been true in Washington's case, the task confronting Davis and his government was stupendous. In the beginning the commander in chief commanded a nation lacking everything it most needed. The Confederacy had no army or navy, few shipyards or arsenals, little manufacturing capacity, and a limited railway system. Davis had no foreign service to conduct international relations and no internal revenue service to levy and collect taxes. In sum, the South lacked the resources to make war.

What it had in abundance was cotton, and many southerners believed that this one thing was enough.

They called it "King Cotton." During his Senate days, when he had threatened disunion if the political balance was not maintained, Davis had placed the weight of "King Cotton" on the scales of debate. He described cotton as the great staple required by the industrial world. It was a belief stoked by the 1855 publication of *Cotton Is King*, a statistical book that seemed to prove that the industrialized world could not thrive without cotton. The South supplied at least 85 percent of the cotton Europe consumed. Soon everyone from stump speakers to senators throughout the South spread the word: "Cotton is king." Once war came, this belief led naturally to the conclusion that the power of cotton could be employed to coerce England and France to intervene in the war. Davis and other southern strategic thinkers well knew that France's recognition and intervention in the first War for Independence had been necessary for victory. One promising path to southern victory in this second War for Independence was to use King Cotton as the lever to force a similar chain of events.

London Times correspondent William Howard Russell was in Charleston shortly after the surrender of Fort Sumter. Meeting with that city's leaders, he was struck by their absolute confidence in the King Cotton doctrine. One member of the Charleston Club told him: "We know John Bull very well. He will make a great fuss about non-interference at first, but when he begins to want cotton he'll come off his perch."[19] It was a message Russell heard throughout his travels in the South during the war's first months and one held by the Confederate president's closest confidants. Secretary of War Judah Benjamin told Russell that when an interruption in the cotton trade occurred, England would abandon its "coyness" about acknowledging a slave power and intervene.[20]

How to utilize cotton as a weapon was a vital strategic decision. Reflecting his nation's confidence, believing he had been dealt a strong coercive hand, and burdened by numerous pressing problems, the commander in chief left this decision up to Congress and his Cabinet. Congress examined the proposition and saw a choice. Either the South could embargo its own cotton to hasten the happy day when foreign recognition occurred, or it could admit the heavy hand of government into commerce regulation, blockade running, loans, debts, and the like, and ship its cotton overseas. For a cause predicated upon freedom from central government, this was no choice at all. Thus the politicians opted for a cotton embargo and resolved to wait until it took effect. It was a decision endorsed by Davis and it proved wildly popular. The *Charleston Mercury* exulted that embargo would either bring foreign recognition or cause every English and French cotton factory to go bankrupt. The tighter the blockade, the sooner intervention would come. Throughout the South it became a patriotic duty to prevent cotton from being exported. This was all done with great enthusiasm and it proved a great mistake.

The King Cotton strategy ignored certain facts that proved critical. First of all, in recent years the British cotton industry had begun to decline in importance in relation to the overall British economy. Second, it was overwhelmingly concentrated in one area of England, which meant it had limited representation in Parliament and thus limited influence upon British policy. In addition, once the embargo began, other cotton-producing regions, such as Egypt and India, proved eager and capable of increasing production to replace imports from America. Finally, Europe had just imported a bumper cotton harvest in 1861.

Then there were the real costs a foreign government had to consider if it went to war against the United States. For Britain these costs included loss of investment in the United States, potential loss of Canada, certain losses in its merchant marine, and the human and material expense of conducting a war.

Southern strategists could and should have been aware of all this. But believers in King Cotton closed their minds to such analysis. Jefferson Davis, although alerted by advisers of the merit of shipping cotton immediately overseas as a basis for credit, was too preoccupied with purely military matters to give it great thought. In contrast, Abraham Lincoln, in his first annual message, clearly analyzed the situation and concluded that it would be too expensive for the British government to go to war with the United States over cotton.[21]

The president did not advance his cause when he dispatched a first diplomatic mission to Europe to seek recognition and commercial treaties. It was led by William Yancey, the man who had introduced the new president to the crowd back in Montgomery. Internationally recognized as a champion of slavery, Yancey had long been urging the resumption of the slave trade so every adult person in the South could afford at least one slave. Given the strong antislavery sentiment in England and France, it was an amazingly inept appointment.

By the spring of 1862 most southerners, including the commander in chief, still believed in King Cotton, but the absolute need for foreign supplies caused a policy reversal. The South required rifles, artillery, powder, and all of the war supplies produced by the manufacturing world, and the only thing it had to exchange was cotton. The new plan called for running a small amount of cotton through the blockade but not enough to upset the basic equation. England would still have to intervene, it would just take a little longer than originally expected. This thinking, too, proved fallacious. Although the cotton embargo did bite hard at one crucial juncture, on balance it had a limited impact. The *London Times* concluded, with some amazement, that "outside of Lancashire it would not be known that anything had occurred to injure the national trade."[22] Not until mid-1863 did the Confederate government embark upon a sensible program to trade its cotton. Adopted two years earlier, it might have made all the difference.

Davis entered office as leader of a nation with a staple products economy that had to sell to foreign markets and had to import manufactured necessities. If the economy was to support the war effort, crops had to be harvested, shipped to Europe, and sold for cash. The cash could then purchase the modern arms and armaments required to fight. So, the government's task at hand should have been designing laws to regulate commerce and organizing blockade-running operations to ship cotton on every available vessel before the jaws of the Union blockade clamped down. These tasks, in turn, implied creating a foreign exchange reserve and floating a foreign loan to bridge expenses until trade began to flow. In the final analysis, all of this was linked to cotton. Davis accepted a policy that, instead of serving as a lever to trigger foreign intervention, proved counterproductive. The failure to ship cotton was an enormous strategic error.

*   *   *

Jefferson Davis was well versed in the classics. In 1861, before the consequences of the ill-conceived cotton embargo were yet realized and while Davis toiled to establish a government in its permanent capital at Richmond, he might have usually contemplated Marcus

Cicero's words calling taxes "the sinews of the state." While there were several alternative paths to ultimate victory—the cotton embargo, foreign intervention, battlefield triumph—all required the South to build a strong infrastructure to support war. In the war's early months, one of Davis's key subordinates was making decisions, overlooked at the time, that proved of great importance in determining how strong the South could become.

War finance was and remains a testing experience, demanding sophisticated understanding of how an economy operates. The new administration had to anticipate the South's economic, monetary, and fiscal requirements while creating the machinery for a new treasury. This made Davis's choice of Secretary of the Treasury critical. He would be the president's chief subordinate charged with guiding the nation's economy and wielding whatever economic weapons the nation could muster. Yet the man selected was neither Davis's first choice nor his choice at all. The appointment of Christopher Gustavus Memminger was pushed upon him by the South Carolina delegation once Davis's preferred candidate proved unavailable. Davis did not know Memminger personally, but accepted the assertion that Memminger possessed "a high reputation for knowledge of finance."[23]

Born in Germany, Memminger arrived an orphan in Charleston at age two. By age fifteen his talents attracted the attention of a former South Carolina governor, who sent him to college. Trained as a lawyer, Memminger became a citizen and joined the state bar. Thereafter, he had long experience as a director of a South Carolina bank and during the 1850s was a member and later chairman of the state's House Ways and Means Committee. To Davis, who had little knowledge of financial matters, these surely seemed impressive credentials.

During the Confederacy's first months. Memminger repeatedly warned about the bad state of Confederate finances. In December 1861, he told Davis that either expenses had to be reduced, a certifiable impossibility with mobilization under way, or measures had to be taken to raise revenues. Memminger did not see how more could be done with treasury notes, and Davis agreed. Already a flood of paper money was devaluing the currency, yet with so much else to worry about, Davis paid little heed.

Amazingly, for a nation locked in a death struggle, the major effort to finance that struggle, the Tax Act of August 19, 1861, was a onetime event. Not only did it fail to raise the monies anticipated, for the twenty subsequent months the tax was not repeated. So Memminger committed the nation to a program of deficit financing without fiscal revenues. It proved disastrous. As Robert Toombs, Davis's first choice for Secretary of the treasury, reflected in 1863: "The first great error was in attempting to carry on a great and expensive war solely on credit—without taxation. This is the first attempt of the kind ever made by civilized people. The result of the experiment will hardly invite its repetition."[24]

When addressing the newly convened First Congress of the Confederate States in February 1862, Davis said little regarding financial matters, omitting even to mention taxation. Not until the following fall did Memminger inform him of the need for a tax to be imposed annually as the basis for the treasury's credit. Finally in January 1863, Davis recognized the importance of fiscal policy and the need for taxes: "The increasing public debt, the great augmentation in the volume of the currency . . . the want of revenue from a taxation adequate to support the public credit, all unite in admonishing us" on the need for "energetic and wise legislation."[25] The president observed that given that families were willing to sacrifice their precious sons to the cause, it was inconceivable that they would not contribute part of their income. He was confident that the people were willing to pay the taxes necessary to maintain public credit and to support the government. But Davis left it to the legislators to prepare a tax plan.

Slowly, propelled by a skyrocketing inflation, politicians came to recognize the importance of Davis's 1863 message. But still the narrow legalisms so beloved by many ardent secessionists, the legacy of years of constitutional examination to justify maintenance of the "peculiar institution" foiled a rational policy. Instead of straining every nerve to achieve victory, political leaders spent a great deal of time and effort debating the government's role in mobilizing the nation for war. Strict constructionists argued that since the Confederate constitution did not permit property taxes without a census-based apportionment—and they refused to recognize the validity of the last federal census of 1860—neither real estate nor slaves, the basis of southern wealth, could be taxed. So the planter class, which included about 40 percent of Congress, managed to evade direct taxes designed to support the government founded for their special benefit.

The fiscal challenges confronting the Confederacy were not unique. In the preceding sixty years the United States had addressed the twin questions of who should provide a sound currency and how the government should raise revenues. Southern leaders were aware of historical mistakes and solutions. During the War of 1812, the United States had faced a situation remarkably similar to that which the South confronted in 1861. Then, a foe possessing overwhelming naval force had blockaded the coast and attacked vulnerable ports. Shipborne trade had nearly ceased, thus eliminating the central government's chief revenue source, customs dues. While bulky staple goods could not be shipped overseas and earn foreign exchange, blockade-runners brought in expensive luxuries that depleted stocks of hard currency. Madison's government had borrowed huge sums and tried to use treasury notes as currency. All of this, coupled with military setbacks, opened the floodgates to an irredeemable paper currency and a resultant massive inflation. The venerated Calhoun had derived sound economic conclusions from the War of 1812, but his descendants ignored his writings.

Jefferson Davis knew better than to base an economy upon tariffs. As recently as 1857, he had participated in a congressional debate on the tariff system. He asserted that import duties taxed the consumer while failing to fill the public treasury. He urged that the burdens of government fall upon property via a direct tax on wealth. Yet when the Confederate Congress tried to solve its fiscal problems, it turned away from direct taxation—the path of success according to the historical experience—and continued an inefficient though politically convenient tariff system.

The South had the economic and human resources, had they been wisely mobilized, to have fought a lengthy war of attrition. In the absence of such leadership, the belief in private rights over public interests and a fear of central authority resolved into a narrow parochialism. A skilled politician might have overcome this. Instead, the combination of inept administration leadership and the selfishness of the planter class severed the nation's military muscle during the Confederacy's infancy. By the time southern leaders realized their error, the wound had crippled.

*   *   *

By design of the Founding Fathers, an American commander in chief's relations with Congress are vitally important. George Washington's enormous prestige buffered him from much congressional criticism. James Polk had enjoyed an enormous Democratic majority, but even this had not completely shielded him. Jefferson Davis's situation was both like and different from that of his predecessors. The Confederate constitution's idea of a single six-year presidential term was to encourage executive independence and the pursuit of the national interest, unswayed by electoral considerations. However, the absence of a two-party system undid many of these theoretical advantages. Because there were no party affiliations, there was no congressional faction naturally supportive of Davis, no group who promoted administration programs as its own. In a one-party system, politics in the Confederacy was a matter of personalities rather than issues. In addition, during the decades preceding the war southern politicians had perfected the role of critic, proposing little meaningful legislation while condemning northern proposals. They had become professional adversaries and they continued this behavior in the Confederate Congress.

Those who disliked Davis, an easy group to join given his unbending personality, could and did criticize freely without the responsibility of suggesting alternative policies. Davis's well-known sensitivity to criticism made him an easy target for personal attack. Because he refused to lower himself by personal politicking, Davis found it very difficult to enlist the congressional support necessary to conduct the war. After the war, an acquaintance observed, "No man could receive a delegation of Congressmen, or any company of persons who had advice to give, or suggestions to make, with such a well-bred grace, with a politeness so studied as to be almost sarcastic, with a manner that so plainly gave the idea that his company talked to a post."[26]

In public encounters Davis's sense of decorum dominated and gave him a cold-seeming appearance. Time and again both the well-intentioned and the critics departed meetings with Davis feeling scorned and angry. It was simply beyond Davis's nature to be friendly and conciliatory toward public visitors. This inability stood in marked contrast to his private behavior when ensconced in the comfort of his "snuggery," his private book-lined office retreat. There he repeatedly charmed visitors over cigars and a glass.

The Second Confederate Congress, assembled in May 1864, mirrored the behavior of the Second Continental Congress. In both cases the first congresses had featured devoted patriots while the second ones featured many who represented much narrower special interests. By 1864 the Confederacy's setbacks were undeniable and voters had responded by picking men who opposed the target of opportunity, Jefferson Davis. Addressing unpopular conscription and exemption measures, congressmen called Davis a burgeoning dictator, referring to him as "King Jeff the First." Still, this congress finally passed effective conscription and taxation policies and all but nationalized foreign trade. But it was too late. Battlefield casualties and desertion exceeded conscription; the fundamental public confidence needed to maintain a monetary system had ebbed; too many blockade-running ports had been closed.

During Davis's four-year tenure Congress overrode a veto only once, and that on a minor matter. Likewise, it eventually approved all of the president's major legislation. These important successes aside, Jefferson Davis never succeeded in mobilizing Congress so the executive and the legislative branches pulled in harness. This failure had much to do with the fact that the army went into battle poorly armed, ill-fed, and clad in rags.

In a revolution bred in states' rights doctrine, the role of the state governor also assumed high significance. Unfortunately for the commander in chief, as early as the last month of 1861, his Attorney General observed that certain governors were "giving trouble ... & not acting in harmony with the Administration."[27] He predicted things would get worse, which is indeed what happened.

During the difficult first month of 1862, one contentious issue was firearms. Throughout the country a shortage of weapons was near crippling, yet many governors requested that arms sent out of their states be promptly returned for state defense. This caused Davis to remark to intimates that if the states were to interfere with central authority in this manner, conduct of the war "was an impossibility," the South should make terms, and those leaders with "halters around our necks" had best flee immediately.[28]

Few governors behaved more singularly than Georgia's Joe Brown. Brown responded to Richmond's conscription act with hot words, saying it "was subversive of [Georgia's] sovereignty, and at war with all the principles for the support of which Georgia entered into his revolution."[29] In 1863, when Davis issued a proclamation urging planters to sow their fields with food crops to feed the starving armies, Brown saw this too as a violation of revolutionary principle and urged his people to plant their fields from fencerow to fencerow in cotton.

Not only were Confederate governors inclined to cast a dubious eye on central authority, it also turned out they had the legal basis to do so. In the spring of 1863, Robert E. Lee's army experienced an alarming hemorrhage of deserters from its North Carolina regiments. Lee complained to the North Carolina governor, who cooperated by ordering his state militia to arrest the shirkers. All this was well and good until the Chief Justice of the State Supreme Court overruled him, explaining that the governor had no authority to enforce Confederate laws. Still, in the final analysis, when Richmond forced such extreme measures as conscription, impressment, suspension of the habeas corpus, regulation of blockade running, and taxation in kind, Confederate governors fumed, protested, but generally complied.

The Confederate Congress and Confederate governors did much less than they might have to help their commander in chief build a strong war machine. Davis, in turn, neither a man of high finance nor a true politician, failed to attend adequately to the economic and political dimensions inherent in his role as commander in chief in a democracy. He was a soldier first and foremost, and it was because of his military acumen that he had been chosen to lead the nation. In the coming months it appeared to the world that the South had chosen wisely because Davis brought his national tantalizingly close to the military victories that would have meant independence.

7 ⟝⟞

TO LOSE A WAR

"I have sacrificed so much for the cause of the Confederacy."
JEFFERSON DAVIS, 1865

"Tis been said I should apply to the United States for a pardon, but repentance must precede the right of pardon, and I have not repented. Remembering as I must all which has been suffered, all which has been lost, yet I say, if I were to do over agin, I would again do just as I did in 1861."

JEFFERSON DAVIS, 1884

DEATH OF A FRIEND

THE AUTUMN OF 1861 BROUGHT PROMISE OF BATTLE AND BLOODSHED once the forces mustering throughout the South and the North collided. The prevailing strategic focus was on Virginia, an inevitable consequence of the closeness of the rival capitals. Union volunteers swarmed to Washington, marching to the drumbeat of the popular press demanding a war-ending advance on Richmond. In keeping with Davis's notion of the offensive-defensive, Confederate volunteers gathered around the Confederate capital to resist this advance. Although Virginia commanded great attention and a disproportionate amount of southern resources, nothing significant would happen here until winter passed. Meanwhile, the war spanned the continent, and out west one of Jefferson Davis's personal appointments and friends was committing strategic mayhem.

The original northern strategic plan, formulated by aging but still astute Winfield Scott, envisioned the Mississippi River as a corridor of invasion to bisect the Confederacy. Key to the Mississippi was the border state of Kentucky, which maintained an uneasy neutrality as forces massed just over its borders, north and south. Kentucky had to be handled very, very gingerly, but for the moment it well served Confederate interests by blocking the Mississippi and shielding Tennessee from any Union thrust. Ultimately, both sides needed Kentucky and both believed that whichever side crossed Kentucky's borders first would drive the state into the opposite camp.

Major General Leonidas Polk appreciated much of this. He had graduated from West Point in 1827, went on furlough, and decided to discard the uniform of a warrior for that of an Episcopal minister. Since that time he had neither studied war nor seen a battle. When Polk offered his services to the Confederacy in 1861, his friend the president assigned him the defense of the Mississippi River. Polk was a popular man who hailed from this region and he knew, and was known by, most of the key figures whose cooperation was essential if the mission were to be accomplished. Moreover, Davis intended the command to be temporary until a higher ranking officer arrived. However, for the moment he placed a man who had never even held the rank of second lieutenant in charge of one of the key sectors in the entire Confederacy.

While cognizant of the implications of Kentucky's neutrality, the bishop-general began receiving ominous reports about a Yankee buildup in southern Illinois. A little-known officer named U.S. Grant commanded this buildup, and Polk worried that it foreshadowed an enemy advance into Kentucky. Consequently, he decided to preempt the enemy move by occupying the high bluffs at Columbus, Kentucky, from where his guns could control the river. On September 3, 1861, employing "the plenary powers delegated to me by the President," he invaded the neutral ground.[1] Foreseeing disaster, the Confederate Secretary of War tried to order him to withdraw immediately only to be overruled by the president himself, who telegraphed Polk that "the necessity justifies the action."[2] It proved a mistake because the Yankees had more resources to bring to bear than did Polk. Grant countered Polk's move by rapidly occupying Paducah, and soon thereafter other

Federal forces marched over the Ohio River into the Bluegrass State. Suddenly unshielded, the Confederacy lay vulnerable from the Mississippi River east to the mountains.

This was the situation the commander in chief faced when he sent the man he considered the nation's ablest officer, Albert Sidney Johnston, to assume command in the west. During the Mexican War, Sidney Johnston's quick-thinking reaction to a dangerous confrontation had probably saved the lives of both Davis and Johnston. Thereafter, Davis's admiration knew no bounds. The outbreak of the Civil War found Johnston posted in California. The Confederate president could barely contain his impatience for his old friend to return. When Sidney Johnston arrived in Richmond, Davis did not appreciate the extent of the problems that Johnston would confront in his new command, indeed, one of the virtues of assigning the trusted Johnston was that he would relieve the president from having to deal with the west. As 1861 drew to a close, Johnston seemed to have provided just the tonic the western Confederacy required.

Johnston boldly advanced his small army to Bowling Green, Kentucky, and by so doing frightened his opponents into inactivity. It was all a colossal bluff that gave false reassurance to Confederate leaders, a bluff that Johnston knew would collapse when the Yankees found an aggressive fighting general. Johnston sent his aide to Richmond to request help, urging Davis to abandon peripheral regions to concentrate every available man in Virginia and Tennessee. This was the same plea made by Beauregard, only now it was coming from Davis's most admired friend. With the might of the Union massing around the South's land and sea border, Davis petulantly rejected Johnston's proposal, asking, "Where am I to get arms and men?"[3]

Sidney Johnston stretched his forces to the breaking point as he tried to form a defensive arc covering the crucial Tennessee border. In the third week of January 1862, he sent Richmond an urgent dispatch: "All the resources of the Confederacy are now needed for the defense of Tennessee."[4] It was too late. Two weeks later, just as Johnston had feared, the North found the determined officer who was willing to take risks. Grant advanced to capture Forts Henry and Donelson, the twin pillars that guarded western Tennessee, and thereby opened the way to the Confederate heartland.

As his fragile defense collapsed and Johnston withdrew south, critics assailed his cession of territory. A friend advised Johnston to defend himself in the papers, and the general replied, "What the people want is a battle and a victory."[5] In Richmond, the Tennessee congressional delegation asked the president to remove Johnston, saying he was "no general." Davis replied that if Johnston was not a general, "we had better give up the war, for we have no general."[6]

At this time of crisis, another old friend emerged with a plan that showed that the South did indeed have able strategic thinkers. Major General Braxton Bragg, Davis's old comrade from Buena Vista, served in a backwater command comprising Alabama and western Florida. From that vantage point he offered the Secretary of War a strategic analysis. The Confederate forces were too scattered. Bragg recommended that secondary points be abandoned, troops ruthlessly stripped from garrison duty in order to concentrate at the point of decision. That point was on Sidney Johnston's front. Bragg was certain: "We have the right men, and the crisis upon us demands they should be in the right places."[7] Defeat and disaster found Davis willing to attempt that which heretofore had been impossible. He approved Bragg's plan.

Ironically, it fell to Sidney Johnston's second in command, General Beauregard, to implement the plan. "Old Bory" ably masterminded a concentration of men from five different independent commands, from places as far distant as Mobile and New Orleans, to join Johnston in western Tennessee.[8] From there Johnston intended to strike Grant's army, currently encamped around a small frame building known as Shiloh Church.

*   *   *

The first week of April 1862 was one of near-unbearable suspense for the commander in chief. He wanted to travel west to be with his friend but instead had to remain in Richmond, against which a massive Union army was slowly advancing. He anticipated good news from Tennessee, telling friends that after Johnston's victory the future would brighten. To Johnston himself he sent an eve-of-battle telegram saying, "I anticipate victory."[9] Davis understood that Johnston's plan hinged upon two factors: surprise; and striking before a second Union army commanded by General Don Carlos Buell united with Grant's army.

Amazingly, the Rebel host achieved the first of these preconditions. Although plagued by poor roads, faulty staff work, and the troubles associated with supervising a green army's first advance, Johnston's army finally reached Grant's picket line in front of the Tennessee River. There Johnston's subordinates lost their nerve as Beauregard and several other generals urged a retreat. They explained that the army was behind schedule, that the soldiers had been heedlessly test-firing their muskets close to the enemy's camps, that surely surprise was impossible. Johnston rejected this advice. Although he did not know it, the enemy generals remained unaware of the pending blow. Placing his trust in the "iron dice of battle," he ordered the assault to go in. Mounting his horse on the morning on April 6, he remarked to his staff, "Tonight we will water our horses in the Tennessee River."[10]

It was not to be. Although the surprise assault swept the Union troops from their camps, poor tactics coupled with inexperience allowed Grant to hold on by the narrowest. By nightfall the Confederates had advanced almost to the Tennessee, but there they faltered, exhausted, hungry, and badly disorganized. To darken matters further, Buell's fresh Union soldiers reached the field at dusk. Worse, the Rebels found themselves deprived of their leader. Sidney Johnston was dead, the victim of rifle fire and his own style of front line leadership.

In Richmond, no news from Tennessee arrived. The president considered this a very bad sign, believing that if his friend were alive he would have heard something. When confirmation of Johnston's death came he broke down and wept. The nation had strained mightily to concentrate force in Tennessee and not only had that force failed, but Jefferson Davis's most trusted subordinate and admired friend had fallen along with eleven thousand other dead and wounded young Confederate men. With the clarity of hindsight, the president later observed, "When Sidney Johnston fell, it was the turning point of our fate; for we had no other to take up his work in the West."[11]

Any replacement would have found it difficult to measure up to Johnston in the grief-stricken mind of the commander in chief. The detested Beauregard, who replaced Johnston, would have to provide near-flawless performance to regain the president's trust. Instead, in the ensuing weeks Beauregard yielded western Tennessee. To Davis it seemed that "Old Bory's" retreat undid the victory that was there for the grasping when Johnston fell. He concluded that the withdrawal was precipitous and the general

unequal to the task at hand. When Beauregard left his army because of poor health, and did so without asking permission or
notifying the commander in chief, Davis replaced him with Braxton Bragg. It was one of the few times he relieved a field commander, and it cemented the Creole's dislike for the president.
Beauregard called Davis "demented or a traitor," characterizing
him as "that living specimen of gall & hatred."[12]

In truth, at Shiloh, Beauregard had neither planned well nor
exhibited any particular battlefield genius. Worse, he had failed to
keep Richmond informed about developments. But such conduct
was hardly unique to Beauregard. Other generals would lose battles and retain their commands, notably Lee in western Virginia
and Bragg repeatedly. Beauregard had to answer to a different
standard, and the president was only too happy to be rid of him.
Although Beauregard would hatch grand plans from time to time,
and perform well in minor assignments, for all intents and purposes he was out of the war.

THE GRAND OFFENSIVE

The spring of 1862 witnessed one setback after another, and critics
lost no time in assailing the commander in chief's strategy.
Uncharacteristically, the president replied to one critic, acknowledging "the error of my attempt to defend all the frontier."[13] Yet
whenever the Confederate government urged manpower concen-
trations, it provoked howls of protest from local leaders who lost
their defenders and thus felt naked before Federal might.[14] Moreover, experience so far showed that territory lost could not be
recaptured, which caused a depletion of resources the nation
could ill afford. Consequently, the president still wanted to hold
as much territory as possible.[15] Many asked, was not the best way
to defend to take the fight to the enemy's soil? Davis responded
that he, too, understood the theoretical advantages of the offensive, but to date the Confederacy simply lacked the resources to
support such a strategy.

It was a strategic conundrum: a long defensive line stretched
thin could be broken by the superior enemy most anywhere; to
abandon territory to concentrate risked losing valuable assets forever. Indeed, this is what had taken place at the South's greatest
city. Stripped of its defenders for the grand stroke at Shiloh, New

Orleans fell to an aggressive Federal fleet in the dismal spring of 1862. Looking at the strategic map, Davis saw that Tennessee remained vulnerable from the Mississippi to the Alleghenies. Crisis also came from the south, where there was little to prevent the enemy fleet from sailing upstream from New Orleans. In the president's mind, most threatening of all was the Federal host preparing to march on Richmond.

Before Shiloh, Davis had summoned his Virginia commander, Joe Johnston, to a conference during which the entire Cabinet participated in a long session devoted to Johnston's plans for the impending spring campaign of 1862. Secretary of the Navy Stephen Mallory observed that Davis had an "uncontrollable tendency to digression" that wasted everyone's time by prolonging Cabinet meetings, and this meeting highlighted the problem.[16] The issue requiring resolution was one of simple arithmetic: in Washington, the Union army was growing bigger, faster than was the Confederate army at Manassas Junction. Soon a mighty blow was sure to be delivered. Before that happened something should be done. At great length Davis quizzed Johnston about what that something should be. Typically, the Cabinet had to endure detailed discussion of such arcane matters as how to shift heavy siege guns from the forts along the Potomac back to secure Confederate lines. These were hardly matters requiring the presence of the Secretary of the Treasury and the Postmaster General.[17]

Indeed, throughout the war Davis immersed himself in bureaucratic minutiae to the neglect of more important matters. While failing to delegate, he simultaneously occupied his Cabinet members' time by meeting with most of them daily and staging formal Cabinet meetings that ran up to five hours two or three times a week. In this case, not only did the conference occupy the Cabinet's valuable time, but by meeting's end the two principals, Davis and Johnston, had come to very different ideas about what had been agreed upon. Seven hours spent examining if, when, and how Johnston should retreat led, as events shortly proved, to disagreement and mistrust.

When, on March 10, 1862, Davis learned that Johnston had begun to retreat from his camps near the old First Manassas field, his surprise bordered on shock and nearly shattered his waning confidence in this general. He had neither expected a withdrawal so soon nor anticipated that Johnston, who was not being hard-pressed by the enemy, would precipitously abandon enormous supply depots. Yet, with surprising patience, Davis watched Johnston continue to withdraw over the ensuing weeks. By early May, confronting an imposing army commanded by the woefully misnamed "young Napoleon," Major General George B. McClellan, Johnston had retired all the way to the Richmond suburbs.

Davis's Cabinet began to question Johnston's maneuvers and recommended giving Johnston specific orders about how to conduct the capital's defense. Davis refused. While he understood the commander in chief's responsibility to include strategic planning, he believed, like George Washington, that a field general possessed the clearest understanding of a tactical situation. "It would not be safe," he said, "to undertake to control military operations by advice from the capital."[18] It was a philosophy Davis clung to throughout his tenure as commander in chief.

This refusal to meddle took great resolution given the situation, with one Johnston dead in Tennessee, the Mississippi River Valley threatened, and the other Johnston here at Richmond seemingly unable to resist the Union juggernaut. Staring disaster in the face, Davis sought solace in religion. Never before particularly devout, he began regularly to attend Episcopal services and was baptized. It did little to relieve his anxiety. He sent his family away from Richmond and ordered his possessions at the Executive Mansion packed. It seemed that the Confederacy was about played out.

Finally, on the last day of May 1862, Johnston delivered a counterstroke. As had been his habit—he believed that Union spies had thoroughly infiltrated the Confederate War Department—he did so without informing the president.[19] Davis heard the sounds of firing and rode to the front to find out what was happening. The resultant battle of Seven Pines was a confused, bungling affair that might have revealed Joe Johnston to be a less than able field commander, except that something happened that superseded the importance of the battle itself. A Union bullet grievously wounded Johnston and concern for his life shielded him from criticism. Moreover, with McClellan's enormous army still poised just outside Richmond, Davis had to find a new commander to lead the army. He chose Robert E. Lee.

They had known one another at West Point, but had not been friends. During the Mexican War, Lee displayed great skill and emerged as Winfield Scott's favorite. While Secretary of War, Davis had observed Lee's competent performance as superintendent of West Point. When Virginia seceded, Davis immediately asked about

Lee. Turning down Scott's offer to command the United States Army, Lee came to Richmond, where he performed ably as adviser during the First Manassas campaign. The Virginian then headed into the western mountains, where, under trying circumstances, he failed dismally in an autumn campaign. Lee's failure brought derisive criticism from the Richmond papers. He was "Granny Lee," "Spades Lee" (for his predilection for entrenching), and "Evacuating Lee." Through it all Davis steadfastly supported him.

As the 1862 campaign began, the Confederate Congress had responded to crisis by giving Davis authority to place a military man in the position of Secretary of War. Everyone assumed that he would appoint Lee. When the president declined, Congress tried a different approach by preparing legislation creating one commanding general for the entire army. Again Congress expected that Lee would occupy this position. Believing that the position usurped his constitutional rights as commander in chief, even though the Federal government had utilized such a position for more than thirty years, Davis vetoed the bill. So strongly did he oppose the bill that his wife, an ever faithful reflector of her husband's inner thoughts, attacked a family friend who had supported the bill, saying "if I were Mr. Davis, I would die or be hung before I would submit to the humiliation."[20]

Instead, Davis appointed Lee to an anomalous position as military adviser. Lee reluctantly accepted. Like most military men of his time he preferred field command to staff duties. A different man could have made much of this potentially extremely influential position. This Lee did not do, preferring to attend more to routine army bureaucratic matters than to operational decisions and strategic planning.[21] But it proved an important time, because Davis saw Lee's unshakable resolve. Asked to brief the Cabinet about the next best position to take should Richmond fall, Lee gave a military engineer's assessment. Then, with high emotion, he said "Richmond must not be given up—it shall not be given up."[22]

Just as this period gave Davis time to assess Lee, so the Virginian, in turn, saw firsthand how Joe Johnston and Beauregard fell afoul of executive wrath. Lee concluded that the best way to get along with his commander in chief was to avoid challenging him and his friends, to distance himself from the press and politics, and to keep Davis informed about military operations. The day after assuming command of the Rebel army in Richmond, he applied these principles when he asked Davis what he thought should be done. This deference, so different from the attitudes of Joe Johnson and Beauregard, did much to endear Lee to the president.

As Lee analyzed the situation he saw both peril and opportunity. The Union army stood athwart the Chickahominy River, just east of the capital. Heavy rains had reduced the country lanes that served as roads in this area to near bogs. Additional rains following Johnston's wounding gave Lee invaluable time to prepare while keeping his foe divided by the swollen Chickahominy. Yet sometime the rains would end and if McClellan was allowed to advance by his preferred siegelike tactics, the Confederates could not stop him. Accordingly, Lee resolved to strike before McClellan brought his overwhelming force to bear. But it would take time to prepare this blow. Resisting the considerable pressure to do something immediately, Davis made a surpassing decision to give Lee the time he needed.

The president did this because even before he saw Lee commit his army to battle, it was clear that he trusted his general. A staffer wrote in his diary about Davis's visit to headquarters:

> *The relations between General Lee and Mr. Davis are very friendly. The general is ever willing to receive the suggestions of the President, while the President exhibits the greatest confidence in General Lee's experience and ability, and does not hamper him with executive interference.*[23]

A key element of Lee's strategy, implemented with Davis's full approval, entailed summoning Stonewall Jackson and his men to Richmond in order to attack the Union army in flank. The fact that Jackson still held a field command was another example of Davis's policy, excepting Beauregard, of supporting a field general through thick and thin. In the previous winter, the president had studied Jackson's recent failed campaign in Virginia's western mountains and concluded that Jackson was "utterly incompetent."[24] But Davis's supportive policy stood him in good stead when Jackson followed setback with his dazzling Valley Campaign that established him as one of the war's great generals. And now Jackson was coming to help save the capital in further repayment of Davis's trust.

The great Confederate counteroffensive on June 26, 1862, involved a colossal gamble that exposed Richmond to certain capture if McClellan saw his chance. Davis understood the risk, and so high were the stakes that it tried even his stoical self-control. When the attack began, soldier Davis could not restrain himself and rode to the front to see firsthand what was taking place. He and his entourage attracted enemy shell fire and the attention of General Lee. Spurring up to Davis, Lee bowed politely and inquired: "Mr. President, am I in command here?"

"Yes," Davis replied.

"Then I forbid you to stand here . . . Any exposure of a life like yours is wrong. And this is useless exposure."[25]

Davis answered that he would set an example of obedience to orders and comply with Lee's request, but in fact he merely moved out of sight of Lee but not out of view of the Union artillery. It was the first time he had been under enemy fire since his Mexican War days, and it was the riskiest moment of his presidency.[26] The day did not pass smoothly, as Confederate coordination proved lacking. Instead of taking an isolated Federal corps in flank and destroying it, a series of disjoined charges ensued. The enemy resisted until nightfall and fell back to an even stronger position. Lee resolved to try again the next day.

Ultimately the orders of a commander in chief are manifest on the battlefield where units assemble and individual soldiers enter combat. No unit had traveled farther to participate in this battle than Company E, the Lone Star Guards, of the 4th Texas Regiment. Nearly a year before, the Lone Star Guards had departed Waco for Virginia while the band played "The Girl I Left Behind Me." Brigaded with sister Texas regiments, as well as one from Georgia, the Lone Star Guards were about to enter their first large battle at Gaines's Mill in the late afternoon of June 27.

During the day so far, Lee's combinations had failed to drive the Yankees from a strong position on the crest of a plateau overlooking a marshy ravine known as Boatswain's Swamp. The flanking attack conducted by Stonewall Jackson had miscarried; three frontal charges delivered by A. P. Hill's vaunted Light Division had been repulsed by the triple-tiered Union defense. The battle hung in the balance. Lee summoned Brigadier General John B. Hood and told him that another frontal charge was required, that the enemy must be dislodged.

"Can you break this line?" Lee asked.

"I will try, sir," Hood replied.[27]

Hood advanced his brigade eight hundred yards across a plain while eighteen well-served Federal artillery pieces fired from the heights. He saw that the supporting brigade on his right had paused to return the enemy fire and then been unable to resume its advance. There was a resultant dangerous gap in the Rebel line. Hood spurred to the 4th Texas. The men knew him because he had been their first colonel. Reminding them that he had pledged to lead them in their "first big fight," he told them not to fire until reaching the enemy and ordered "Forward, quick, march" to close the gap and charge the plateau. In the regiment's ranks was twenty-six-year-old Bennett Wood. He recalled the assault:

> We moved steadily down as open, gentle slope . . . receiving shot and shell from two or three lines of infantry and two lines of artillery . . . Oh, the slaughter as we charged! We understood why Gen. Hood wanted us to go to the enemy without firing, for in piles all around us were other Confederates, who stop[ping] to load their guns, lay dead and dying. When we reached the creek we soon flushed our game. We pushed them back . . . and on we went, yelling, shooting, seeing men fall and die, up up to the top of that murderous hill.[28]

Hood had boasted that he "could double-quick the Fourth of Texas to the gates of Hell" without disrupting the unit.[29] Gaines's Mill proved his contention. Aided by the 18th Georgia, the 4th broke through successive infantry lines and stormed the cannon, captured fourteen guns, repulsed a cavalry counterattack at forty yards' range, and created the first breach in a heretofore impregnable position. One in four participants in the two assault brigades fell during the attack. No unit was worse hit than the 4th Texas. All of its field officers were either killed or wounded. Company E, the Lone Star Guards, charged with forty-seven men and lost five killed and fourteen wounded, but this was less than the percentage loss of the regiment as a whole. At Gaines's Mill, the unit's first "big fight," barely half the men remained unhit by day's end.[30] Bennett Wood received a minié ball below the eye but lived. Hearing that his brother had been shot down, he got a lantern and searched for him that night.

> I found Jake Smiley hunting his brother . . . Jake had borrowed Gen. Hood's horse, on which he carried his two dead brothers . . .

I looked where I had left James Robertson shot through the hips
. . . and found him dead. Next morning I heard that my brother
was at the field hospital with a shattered knee. I found him with
his leg amputated. I was sent with him to Richmond and remained
with him till his death from blood poison on the 22nd of July.[31]

Bennett Wood returned to fight in numerous additional battles and would be wounded at Gettysburg and again in the Wilderness. His conduct was typical of the entire brigade. Examining the Gaines's Mill field, Lee observed that "the men that carried this position were soldiers indeed."[32] Henceforth, the Texas Brigade would be renowned as the South's foremost shock unit. Its fame spread overseas. When news of the battle reached England, admiring newspapers showed cartoons of the Texans "struggling to the front" as they charged a Union line.

By the time Bennett Wood's brother died, Lee's offensive, the Seven Days' Battle, had ended and the general had justified Davis's confidence. The Army of Northern Virginia had delivered blow after blow, hounding McClellan from Richmond's gates back to a mere toehold on the James River. Then and thereafter both Davis and Lee believed a great deal more could have been done. In the future Lee would often discover his enemy's weak point or divine an error in his foe's plan, but never again would he find the entire enemy in retreat across his front, vulnerable to annihilation. Lee's offensive had been greatly hampered by near-catastrophic staff work. So poorly had Lee's staff operated that none of the battles began until late afternoon, there was little coordination among columns marching on adjacent roads, and there was little knowledge of Union dispositions even though the battles occurred in areas where every civilian was a potential spy.

Victory, then, was bittersweet, both for what could have been but was not, and because it cost the South some 20,141 casualties. The ranks of the fallen included the South's best fighting men, the ardent physically fit volunteers who had rushed to defend the nation's capital. A disproportionate number of the slain were officers: intelligent, martial-minded men who had entered service in 1861 and fallen leading reckless charges. Had more survived, the severe shortage of general officers in 1863 and 1864 would not have been so devastating. This, then, was the price for "constitutional liberty."

Still, it was a dramatic string of victories that both delivered

Richmond and established a psychological ascendancy over the Army of the Potomac that endured until hard-bitten U. S. Grant, who cared not one whit for his enemy's supposed mastery, took the field in Virginia in 1864. With victory, Davis's mood shifted full circle. He believed that with a few more men the war might end in a matter of weeks, that European recognition might be forthcoming. Because of Lee, all seemed possible. The president's customary determination returned, not to depart until after Lee's surrender three years hence.

*   *   *

When Lee saved Richmond from McClellan's threat from the east, his job was merely half done. Another Federal army under John Pope was marching on the capital from the north. Applying the offensive-defensive, and taking yet another colossal risk that the president fully endorsed, Lee detached Stonewall Jackson and sent him to "suppress" Pope. It was a gamble because McClellan's hundred-thousand-man army remained in camp a mere day's march from Richmond. He could resume his offensive, and if he did, could capture the capital before Jackson could return. But Davis agreed with Lee that to do nothing was an even greater gamble; the Federal vise would tighten until it squeezed the very life out of the Confederacy. So Jackson went against Pope, fought a portion of the Yankee army at the appropriately named Slaughter Mountain, and taught the Union general caution. Always eager to reinforce success, Lee first sent Jackson more men, and then turned his back entirely on McClellan, confident that the "Little Napoleon" was a defeated general intent only on withdrawal. Although Lee's maneuvers denuded the capital of its defenders, again Davis approved.

During the summer of 1862, in an audacious Second Manassas campaign featuring Stonewall Jackson at his best, Lee badly defeated Pope and drove him back to the fortifications surrounding Washington. Davis's offensive-defensive and his selection of Lee had been vindicated only to expose a new challenge. Twice the Army of Northern Virginia had thoroughly defeated a Yankee invasion but been unable to prevent the enemy from withdrawing behind Washington's invulnerable fortifications from where they could refit and try again. No Rebel completely realized it yet, but Virginia was a strategic dead end. The best the South could hope

The Battle of Trenton. After a bold nocturnal march on December 26, 1776, Washington's men attacked the surprised Hessians at Trenton. American artillery swept Trenton's streets and compelled the Hessian surrender. (Author's private collection)

George Washington Rallying the Troops at the Battle of Princeton. Washington rode between the lines and recklessly exposed himself to enemy fire to check his men's retreat. Confidence restored, the Americans shattered Cornwallis's rear guard at Princeton on January 3, 1777. (Author's private collection)

George Washington's Entrance into New York City Following the British Evacuation, November 25, 1783. The image of a triumphant general receiving lavish public acclaim exactly matched the fears of the ardent anti-militarists. (Library of Congress)

Wayne's Legion and General Anthony Wayne. With the selection of Anthony Wayne, Washington found a general capable of instilling discipline in the young United States Army. The Battle of Fallen Timbers put Wayne's training to a severe test. (Center for Military History)

President James K. Polk.
In the final analysis,
America's most success-
ful wartime commander
in chief. (Library of
Congress)

U.S. Soldiers of the
Mexican-American War.
The battlefield
performances of the
tough American
regulars vindicated
those who supported a
standing army. (Center
for Military History)

"The Issue Joined." This period political cartoon, showing an indignant Polk (left of center) taking exception to Senator Daniel Webster's public attacks on his expansionist policies, underscores the war's controversial origins. Polk says, "If you say the Mexican War is a War of my own making, you tell a falshood!" Webster retorts, "I did say it & say it again!" (Library of Congress)

General Zachary Taylor. The imperturbable Taylor led American forces to the opening victories of the Mexican-American War. (Library of Congress)

Storming of Chapultepec. In the face of gallant resistance, Scott's army breached the defenses of Mexico City at Chapultepec on September 1, 1847. (Library of Congress)

General Winfield Scott Entering Mexico City. Scott's brilliant campaign climaxed in the capture of the enemy capital. This feat still left Polk with the problem of how to end the war. (Library of Congress)

Jefferson Davis's Inaugural, 1861. William Yancey introduced Davis to Montgomery, Alabama with the words "the man and the hour have met." (Library of Congress)

President Jefferson Davis. Jefferson Davis made an impression upon those he met. Different first-time acquaintances describe him: "pale, thin, and wiry"; "a piercing but kindly eye, and a gamy, chivalric bearing"; "prim and smooth-looking, with a precise manner, a stiff, soldierly carriage"; and "an austerity at first forbidding." According to Varina Davis, this is the only wartime photo of her husband. (National Archives)

General Albert Sidney Johnston. Davis's favorite general, about whom Davis said, "If Sidney Johnston is no general, then we have got none." (National Archives)

General Leonidas Polk.
Another Davis friend.
Bishop Polk's impetuous
advance into Kentucky
began a disastrous chain of
events climaxing in Sidney
Johnston's death at Shiloh.
(Tennessee State Library)

Battle of Gaines's Mill. Davis's selection of Lee to replace the fallen Joe
Johnston led to the Confederate assault at Gaines's Mill. When Lee took
command, he was 55 years old. He earned his place in military history in
just under three years of generalship. In comparison, Marlborough had
had supreme command for ten years; Wellington for seven; Napoleon for
19. (Library of Congress)

Secretary of War Judah Benjamin. Davis had great difficulty in delegating responsibility. Consequently, his Secretaries of War had trouble performing their jobs. Benjamin's loyal support for his commander in chief caused him to rise greatly in Davis's esteem. (National Archives)

Jefferson Davis Just After the War. Wasting diseases in his younger years gave Davis a permanently gaunt look. Continuing poor health contributed to his difficult personality. In 1863 a British visitor was struck by Davis's emaciated, wrinkled face. Here, the war's strain is apparent. (National Archives)

Battle of the Bulge, 1944. German soldiers charge past a ruined American mechanized column. The U.S. lost over 75,000 men in its greatest European battle, and the nation did not flinch. (National Archives)

Truman Campaigning in 1948. While campaigning in Omaha, Truman leapt from his car to lead veterans of his WWI battery in parade, underscoring the popular value of military service for a commander in chief. (National Archives)

The Battle of Dien Bien Phu. Few people appreciated the extent of
Eisenhower's commitment to Vietnam. French air crews at Dien Bien
Phu surrounded by U.S.-supplied aircraft. (U.S. Military History Institute)

***Mobility and
Firepower.***
The helicopter
encouraged
American plan-
ners to believe the
war had a "techni-
cal" solution.
(Department of
Defense)

President Lyndon B. Johnson and His Advisers. Johnson (on far right) faces his Secretary of State Dean Rusk. On his left is Secretary of Defense Robert McNamara. It is 1967, the last year the United States sought to win the war. (Lyndon B. Johnson Library)

The Commander in Chief and His General. Johnson believed that Westmoreland was the man to win the war. (Lyndon B. Johnson Library)

Superbly Camouflaged Surface to Air Missile Sites. On July 24, 1965, a surface to air missile downed its first victim. Thereafter, the SAMs became a key component in the ever-strengthening North Vietnamese air defense network, destroying in 1965 11 planes; 1966, 31; 1967, 96; and in 1972 during the Linebacker Operations, 49. (Military Archive and Research Service)

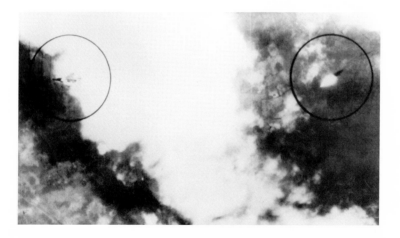

Near Miss. In the view of many pilots, including Commander James Stockdale, Washington's interference with tactical details took "very expensive and highly capable airplanes right by the power plant to the bomb the privy—which the Vietnamese had of course figured out was the place to put their guns." Johnson tolerated restrictive rules of engagement, which meant that planes could not attack SAM sites until the missiles fired first. Here, a SAM narrowly misses a U.S. fighter-bomber. (Military Archive and Research Service)

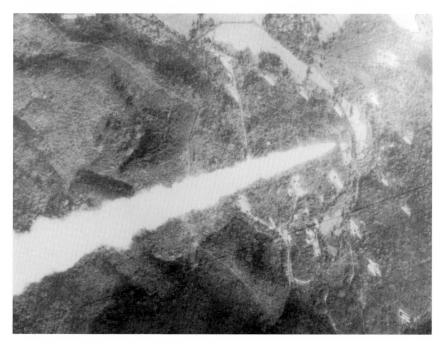

Revenge. Even after the lifting of many restrictions, pilots still found the North Vietnamese a tough foe. A just-fired American missile pushes toward a SAM launcher. (Military Archive and Research Service)

Cam Ranh Bay, 1966. The president receives a warm welcome during his brief visit to the troops in Vietnam. (Lyndon B. Johnson Library)

Tet, 1968. The extent and severity of the Tet Offensive caught everyone by surprise. No place was secure. Installations at Saigon's Tan Son Nhut Air Base catch fire after Viet Cong shelling. (Department of Defense)

Khe Sanh, 1968. The military and the commander in chief feared that the worst was still to come. Johnson examines a topo map of Khe Sanh in the White House basement. (Lyndon B. Johnson Library)

President George Bush and General Norman Schwarzkopf in Saudi Arabia at Thanksgiving, 1990. Learning from the Vietnam experience, the commander in chief gave his general the resources he said were needed to fight the war. (Department of Defense)

Bombed Iraqui Aircraft Shelters. In the open terrain of the Arabian Peninsula, air power could dominate. Precision strikes penetrated enemy aircraft shelters. The Iraqis played a shell game with their shelters, so whether these actually housed planes is unknown.
(Department of Defense)

The Highway of Death. Televised scenes of destruction alarmed the image-sensitive American war leaders. (Department of Defense)

Liberated Kuwait. The allies enter just-liberated Kuwait City. Whether this constituted victory remains an open question. (Department of Defense)

to accomplish here was what had already taken place, and it was not enough. So the nation's strategic thinkers cast about for a new plan.

The late summer of 1862 witnessed the South's first, and last, multiarmy offensive of the war. Three advances, including two incursions into enemy territory, took place. In the east, Lee invaded Maryland. In western Tennessee, two small Confederate forces maneuvered against Grant as a support for the main drive featuring an invasion of Kentucky. Lee's effort fit well with Davis's strategy of the offensive-defensive. The Virginian had just thrashed two Union generals and their commands and the situation seemed ripe to carry the conflict into enemy territory. Lee's was a spontaneous offensive born both of opportunity and of need. He could not feed his army in war-ravaged northern Virginia and had to march somewhere. Maryland seemed to offer food, new recruits, and possibly something more. The effort in the west was somewhat different.

Richmond housed a powerful, articulate Kentucky lobby that had long maintained that the Bluegrass State merely awaited the arrival of a liberating Confederate army to overthrow the Yankee yoke. The idea appealed to Braxton Bragg, who commanded the largest Rebel army in the west, because currently a superior enemy army stymied any advance from his base in northern Mississippi. By shifting to Chattanooga, Bragg could sidestep this foe, strike into Kentucky to gain the enemy rear, cut the Federal line of communications, and encounter and defeat the enemy in detail.[33] It was an ambitious and well-conceived plan that Davis heartily approved. The president then made an administrative decision that seriously impaired success.

It seemed like such a small thing, an administrative refinement adjusting departmental boundaries to improve overall efficiency. However, Davis took this step without informing Bragg. Consequently, when Bragg arrived at Chattanooga, having successfully stolen a march on the opposing Union general, he expected to join hands with Kirby Smith's small army operating in east Tennessee. Given that Bragg planned to pass through Smith's domain, success clearly required close coordination. However, because of the new boundaries, Bragg was uncertain whether he had the authority to issue orders to Smith. Smith, in turn, jealousy defended his command prerogatives within his department. This was an issue that required resolution by a higher commander, and the only higher commander was Davis. But he failed to delineate clearly a chain of command.

Nonetheless, at first it seemed like all would proceed smoothly. Smith volunteered to serve under Bragg and the two met in Chattanooga to plan future movements. Three days later, Smith had second thoughts. He began the great invasion on his own and somehow over the ensuing weeks never managed to link up with Bragg.

In the beginning of September 1862, Smith's impetuosity appeared to presage splendid success. From the Mississippi to the Potomac, Rebel armies held the initiative as they advanced against the enemy. The dazzling prospect of southern independence never shone more brilliantly, and it was to Davis's credit that this was so. He had provided the overall strategic direction for this offensive. A year earlier he had resisted Beauregard's proposals for this kind of gamble. One year wiser, Davis showed he had grown with the job. The commander in chief awaited news, confident that victory was near.

*   *   *

Europe too, closely watched the unfolding Confederate offensive, and in England the watching was particularly acute because the cotton shortage, which the South had anticipated would occur a year earlier, had arrived. Each month of 1862, the leanest cotton year in England during the entire war, the famine worsened. It also coincided with the arrival in England of a twenty-seven-year-old southern journalist named Henry Hotze. Dispatched by the Confederate government, Hotze's mission was to impress the public mind with the Confederacy's ability to maintain its independence. Hotze succeeded famously. Better than any southern diplomat, he penetrated public and political opinion and wrote deftly, with a lightness of touch certain to appeal to an English readership. His effort won many converts to the Rebel viewpoint and went far toward preparing England for action.

Prime Minister Viscount Palmerston carefully assessed the war's flow—Lee had just evicted the Federals from Virginia—and judged political currents at home as unrest among unemployed workers in the manufacturing districts increased. When summer passed toward autumn the British government seriously considered recognizing the South. Much as the French government had watched the American rebels outfight the British, the British government watched the Confederate offensive, and particularly Lee's advance, with high glee. In September, Foreign Minister Lord Russell predicted to the prime minister that in the next month "the hour will be ripe for the Cabinet" to discuss intervention. Palmerston responded that the Federals had received "a very complete smashing" and it seemed "that still greater disasters await them."[34] The prime minster proposed that after Lee won the expected victory, England and France should end the conflict by mediating a peace based on the existence of an independent South.

The impetuous Chancellor of the Exchequer, William Gladstone, spoke for many when he addressed an audience in early October 1862, saying, "Jefferson Davis and other leaders of the South have made an army; they are making . . . a navy; and they have made what is more than either—they have made a nation."[35]

In the war's first year, the British foreign minister had told Confederate diplomats that "the fortune of arms" would dictate how England responded to the conflict in North America. One year later everything hinged upon the Confederate offensive.

*   *   *

The sweeping advance, so hopefully undertaken, failed. In the nation's single bloodiest day, Lee fought a drawn battle at Sharpsburg along the banks of Antietam Creek. In northern Mississippi, two bullheaded commanders delivered ill-coordinated blows that only briefly impeded Grant's preparations for an attack down the Mississippi River. Worst of all, in Kentucky, Bragg flubbed a great chance.

After skillfully interposing his army between the Union army and its base at Louisville, Bragg confronted a decision. Had he advanced on Louisville, the city would have fallen, the vital artery of the Ohio River lost to the North. Perhaps, just perhaps, a further advance north would have cut the United States in two. This would have taken place at a time of terrifying Federal failure in the east with results incalculable. For a few shining hours Bragg grasped potential victory. Davis's offensive-defensive had given the South this chance but it all depended upon the field general. Bragg hesitated, declined battle, and permitted the Federals to pass his front and gain Louisville. When the Federals regrouped to begin their own offensive, Bragg fought a poorly conducted engagement at Perryville on October 7, 1862, and then retreated. By Christmas he had lost not only Kentucky but much of Tennessee as well.

In light of the failure of the grand offensive, Davis candidly told Congress that the South had entered "the darkest and most dangerous period yet."[36] As soon as the first fragmentary reports of Lee's setback reached England, all plans for meditation, recognition, or forcing the blockade were put on hold. Lincoln's Emancipation Proclamation, delivered in the aftermath of Lee's failure in Maryland, provided the final blow. Observing that the slavery question had always been a difficulty obstructing recognition of the South, Palmerston canceled a meeting devoted to planning for intervention. Britain never came so close to intervention again, and so terminated one of the possible paths to southern independence.

THE DISASTERS OF 1863

Davis's departmental system had sought to rationalize an exceedingly difficult multipart problem comprising the South's enormous extent of threatened territory and the limitations of communications and logistics. The system witnessed a major test during Bragg's invasion of Kentucky and proved too inflexible. With no central direction from Richmond, it relied upon voluntary copperation between officers of equal rank. This was more than most southern generals were prepared to give.

The president learned something important from the experience. He realized that his offensive-defensive required some form of mobile defense. He explained it to one of his generals: "We can not hope at all points to meet the enemy with a force equal to his own, and must find our security in the concentration and rapid movement of troops."[37] Although he would have denied it strenuously, the commander in chief had hit upon the Beauregard approach. To facilitate the transfer of forces, during the winter of 1862–1863, he created four major regional commands: the Trans-Mississippi; the West; the Atlantic Coast; and Lee's command in Virginia and North Carolina. He had invented what future military men would call theater commands, a sophisticated concept still used by modern armies.

In Davis's time, each department embraced a logical strategic theater and, by utilizing the railroad, each was mutually supportable. When a Federal assault began, troops from a quiet sector could move by rail to an adjacent sector, freeing those troops, in turn, to move to the aid of the threatened sector. Davis had seen this pipeline approach work during Bragg's invasion of Kentucky and utilized its principle for the remainder of the war. Having addressed the administrative aspects of high strategy, the president turned to personnel matters, and they proved nearly insolvable.

The fallout from Bragg's failed invasion of Kentucky had divided the Army of Tennessee into warring factions and produced great criticism of Bragg's leadership. He was "either stark mad or utterly incompetent," claimed the Kentucky lobby.[38] In an effort to soothe all concerned, Davis summoned critics to Richmond, heard them out, and decided to retain Bragg in command in hopes that his friend had learned from his mistakes. Bragg himself complained that his invasion had suffered from a lack of unified command. The various armies had operated under their respective department commanders without unity of purpose. Showing an unexpected capacity for change, the president swallowed hard and appointed Joe Johnston to the new supercommand, the Department of the West. He intended Johnston to provide the coordination that had been absent in the recent campaign.

Following his battlefield wound, Johnston had spent six months convalescing. During this time he observed the galling sight of his replacement, Robert E. Lee, leading his former command to glory. Disgruntled, he became a regular guest at Richmond dinners and parties hosted by a political group whose only glue was opposition to the commander in chief. Varina Davis heard about Johnston's backbiting and reported to her husband. The president understood that Johnston was no friend but, unwilling to go outside the limits imposed by seniority, found no alternative leader.[39] So when Johnston's health returned, Davis selected him for a post widely regarded as the second most important in the entire Confederacy.

The Department of the West covered the entire area between the Appalachians and the Mississippi River. Within this area Johnston enjoyed complete strategical, tactical, and logistical authority, yet the general still found the assignment overly limiting. He complained that the Mississippi was a departmental boundary that made no strategic sense. Defense of the river required close cooperation between Confederate armies on both riverbanks. Moreover, he asserted, coordinating the two major Confederate field armies within his department would be impossible since one was in Tennessee and the other at Vicksburg. Johnston maintained that they were too far apart for mutual support. He took his case to the Secretary of War, who could only smile and explain that while he agreed with Johnston, the boundary came from the president and nothing could be done.

So here it was. At an absolutely pivotal point in the war as 1862 drew to a close, Davis chose a general to take command in the decisive theater whom he distrusted and disliked, who returned these feelings in spades, and who forcefully doubted the job could be done. Davis expected Johnston to take field command whenever the general deemed it necessary. Johnston, on the other hand, saw his role as purely advisory to the two existing field commanders. Again Davis had failed to make his expectations clear.

Traveling west to his new assignment, Johnston quickly saw his fear confirmed regarding the coordination of forces across the Mississippi River boundary. Both he and the Secretary of War urged the commander west of the river, Lieutenant General Theophilus H. Holmes, to assist the commander at Vicksburg. Holmes understood that the people west of the Mississippi had grown weary of serving as the eastern Confederacy's recruiting ground while their own homes fell to the Yankees. Accordingly, he told Richmond that a movement to Vicksburg would abandon Arkansas, expose Little Rock to the invader, and therefore he must decline. It was the typical limited vision of a detached general who did not want to exacerbate his own very real troubles by sending scarce resources to meet some distant threat.[40] It was up to the higher authority in Richmond to assess all threats and allocate resources accordingly. This Davis failed to do. Instead, he deferred to Holmes and by so doing undercut, in Johnston's mind, Johnston's ability to perform his job.[41]

In addition, a bureaucratic policy that required Johnston's field commanders to send their reports directly to Richmond instead of to Johnston himself caused a problem. It satisfied Davis's craving for frequent reports but meant that Johnston knew less about what was going on than did the authorities in Richmond. All of this prompted Johnston to wonder if he had been chosen as a scapegoat for impending failure.

The president recognized that the situation in the Department of the West remained serious, and so he undertook a personal mission west to coordinate strategy and heal frayed feelings. Accompanied by Johnston, the commander in chief arrived at a small Tennessee town named Murfreesboro in December 1862, where he found the irascible Braxton Bragg still thoroughly embroiled in a feud with his principal subordinates, most notably Leonidas Polk. Troubled by the command dissension, Davis found solace in Bragg's obvious administrative ability. He observe a thrilling army review, spoke with various generals, and concluded that this army was sound and could defend its territory. Such a defense seemed unlikely any time soon because Bragg predicted that his opponent would remain passive through the winter.

In contrast, dispatches from Vicksburg were most alarming. Grant was on the move again and the defending Confederate general doubted his ability to stop him. Davis considered sending help from Tennessee. Both Bragg and Johnston dissented, the latter arguing that reinforcements would not arrive in time. Unswayed, Davis ordered a strong eight-thousand-man division from Murfreesboro to Vicksburg.[42] He had seldom so meddled and this intervention proved unfortunate. He had just appointed a reluctant Johnston to theater command and then overridden him within his first week of service. By undermining Johnston again, Davis had undermined the unity of command he had hoped to achieve by appointing Johnston in the first place. Worse, so thin was the Confederate margin for error that this decision upset everything. Quite simply, an executive mistake concerning the deployment of a mere division could and did unhinge the defense of a vast region.

After the division departed, and Davis himself moved on, Abraham Lincoln prodded the Union army to advance upon Murfreesboro. Responding with soldierly resolve. Bragg delivered a powerful surprise assault that rocked the foe. During the battle of Murfreesboro decisive victory hung in the balance. Had an extra division been available, a great victory would have been won. Instead, Bragg retreated again, relinquishing central Tennessee, territory the South would never regain. Meanwhile, his detached division reached Vicksburg, where they were welcome but proved unnecessary to defeat the immediate Union thrust. The entire episode gave Joe Johnston some small satisfaction since he had predicted just this outcome.

Having interceded in Tennessee, the president continued his

journey west to Vicksburg, where he also hoped to harmonize the Confederate command structure. Vicksburg was the key to controlling the Mississippi River. It was one of the places the South needed to hold if it were to endure. Commanding there was Lieutenant General John Pemberton, a Pennsylvania-born officer whose brothers fought for the Union and whose birth state made him the focus of suspicion among many.[43] Events would show that Pemberton's determination to prove his southern loyalty made him a bit inflexible. The president received a hint of this when, a day after departing Pemberton's headquarters, he received a carping letter from Pemberton complaining that Joe Johnston was superseding him in command. Pemberton acknowledged that Johnston had yet to prohibit any of his maneuvers, but the mere fact that Pemberton had to clear his moves with Johnston rankled.[44] Davis had just invested time and travel to resolve command disputes, an effort with typical results described by an acquaintance as "composing quarrels which are not composed."[45] In both Tennessee and in Mississippi he had failed.

*   *   *

The president returned to Richmond to shepherd through Congress his legislative program for 1863. It squarely addressed the three greatest Confederate needs: supplies, manpower, and money. He wanted power to impress supplies for the army, to increase the number of soldiers through better management of conscription and exemption, and to raise money through more stringent tax laws. To get any of this he needed to persuade Congress. Suasion was not one of Jefferson Davis's talents, yet he came close to success. By the end of March, Congress passed the Act to Regulate Impressments. Touching the raw nerves of states' rights, the act allowed the central government to seize private property— livestock, produce, wagons, and much more—for the army's use. So manifest was the need that few protested.

Manpower proved more difficult, yet by September a second draft law went into effect that took men aged thirty-five to forty-five and cancelled substitutions in that age group. Congress proved less willing to modify the twenty-slave exemption. Few issues generated more heat. The first draft law had permitted one exemption for each twenty slaves, the idea being that some white men had to remain on the plantation to oversee the work and guard against insurrection. Popular with the planting class, it was hugely unpopular with everyone else, giving rise to complaints about a "rich man's war, poor man's fight." But the planter class had a firm influence on Congress, so while the slave exemption law was improved, it still failed to meet the dictates of national emergency.

Regarding money Davis failed entirely. Congress passed a complicated tax bill that seemed to tax most logical sources of revenue except land, slaves, and cotton. The problem was, of course, that these three items represented the great bulk of southern wealth. Because Davis could not convince Congress, because southern congressmen put parochial interest above national welfare, the South's economy and its menfolk in arms would have to make do. In the late spring of 1863, it seemed that the nation would have to make do with considerably less, because a Federal offensive threatened to separate all of the valuable, resource-laden country west of the Mississippi River from the Confederate heartland.

*   *   *

In the first week of April, Grant began marching his army downriver on the west bank of the Mississippi in order to bypass the heavy Confederate batteries at Vicksburg that interdicted the river. Again the administrative boundary on the river caused a lack of Confederate coordination on both sides of the waterway and seriously impaired Pemberton's response. Unopposed on the west bank, Grant recrossed to the river's east side to sever Vicksburg's communications with the outside world. His skillful maneuvers confused Pemberton, who remained in Vicksburg with his army. Meanwhile Johnston arrived to establish his headquarters in Jackson, Mississippi, some forty miles east of Vicksburg. Here was the crisis for which Davis had placed Johnston in command of the western theater. If Johnston and Pemberton coordinated their efforts, Grant's army stood hugely vulnerable.

Now the mistake of having Pemberton report to Richmond instead of directly to Johnston became evident. Through no fault of his own, Johnston remained ignorant of Grant's whereabouts for days after Grant returned to the great river's east side. When he finally received accurate reports, he ordered Pemberton to march east and attack Grant. It was the right response, defeated before it was attempted due to the consequences of Davis's inability to clearly define a command structure. Pemberton doubted that the recently arrived Johnston correctly understood the situation. The commander in chief had told him that he, not Johnston, was ultimately responsible for Vicksburg's defense. Consequently, instead of obeying Johnston's order, Pemberton did what he thought best. He marched out of Vicksburg in search of Grant's line of supply and by so doing lost the campaign. Worse still, he lost his entire army.

Johnston had told him that above all else, he should not allow his army to be forced back to Vicksburg because if surrounded there, he would lose both the town and his troops. Far better, said Johnston, to save his men. Learning of Pemberton's maneuvers, he ordered Pemberton to evacuate Vicksburg "if it is not too late." Pemberton disagreed. Sensitive to doubts about his loyalty, Pemberton considered Vicksburg his sacred trust—"the most important point in the Confederacy"—and he would not abandon it.[46] While Pemberton vainly sought Grant's line of supply—in fact, it was nonexistent since Grant, somewhat like Scott at Vera Cruz, had made the bold decision to abandon his supply line—the Union general interposed his army between Johnston and Pemberton. Then Grant turned on Pemberton and drove him back to Vicksburg, where he laid siege to the town.

When Davis learned what had taken place he contemplated two plans to retrieve the situation. He hoped that enough reinforcements could reach Johnston so that general could fight his way to Vicksburg's relief. There was one other alternative. Lee had just won a smashing victory over the Army of the Potomac at Chancellorsville. He had accomplished this while a sizable portion of his army under Lieutenant General James Longstreet was absent on detached duty. Given this, it was quite possible for Lee to continue to hold his ground against a shaken foe who would require some time to prepare a new attack, while sending a large force to Johnston for the relief of Vicksburg. It was a strategic decision of immense consequence, and accordingly Davis summoned his most trusted general to Richmond to learn his opinion.

Lee arrived in Richmond on May 15, 1863, the day Grant turned his army west to attack Vicksburg from the rear. For the past week the Virginian had been exchanging telegrams with the War Department regarding the possibility of sending men west. Lee firmly opposed the idea, bluntly saying: ". . . it becomes a question between Virginia and the Mississippi."[47] Lee believed sending a detachment from his Army of Northern Virginia would not only jeopardize Richmond's safety but might not arrive in time, and anyway, the terrible Mississippi summer climate would force Grant to withdraw. He clung to this view in his talk with Davis and during a subsequent Cabinet meeting. Yet he acknowledged that something drastic had to be done and therefore proposed a second invasion of the North. It might or might not relieve the pressure in the west, but in the past Lincoln had shown a special sensitivity to threats to his capital by summoning troops to its defense. Moreover, there was the chance that a victory gained north of the Potomac would actually lead to Washington's fall and foreign intervention. Davis and his Cabinet reflected upon all of this and upon the fact that since Lee had taken command in Virginia he had never lost a battle. With one exception, they endorsed his plan.

That exception was the Postmaster General, John Reagan, who believed a great error was in the process of happening. A self-made lawyer and politician from Texas, the forceful Reagan had overcome enormous obstacles to create a postal service that accomplished something that had never been done before nor would be done again. Instead of operating at a deficit, his postal service made a clean profit. While this hardly qualified him to comment on matters of high strategy, Reagan was unique among Cabinet members since he was the only one to hail from the far side of the Mississippi. This gave him a special knowledge of the consequences of losing all control of the Mississippi River and all contact with the resource-rich Trans-Mississippi. Reagan thought the loss of Vicksburg would be a fatal blow.

He proposed a sham campaign across the Potomac full of noisy preparation and loose talk about capturing Washington. Aided by this deception, Lee would go on the defensive and send Longstreet's corps west to operate against Grant. By the time Lincoln realized that an invasion of the North was a bluff, it would be too late. When opponents argued that Lee's proposed invasion would force Grant to retreat, Reagan countered that Grant was committed—he would either capture Vicksburg or be destroyed in the effort.[48]

Lee's plan or Reagan's plan? The Cabinet, after a day-long deliberation, voted five to one in favor of Lee. Distraught, unable to sleep, Reagan arose at dawn to ask the president to call another meeting to reconsider. Davis obliged; after all, he shared the

Texans's special concern for this, his home region. After further talk, the Cabinet voted again, and again it was five to one. Lee would invade Pennsylvania.

*   *   *

When Lee returned to Virginia after Gettysburg, he wrote to Davis offering to resign. Lee had heard and read criticism of his campaign and it bothered him. He was an even harsher self-critic, writing, "I cannot even accomplish what I myself desire. How can I fulfil the expectations of others?" He thanked Davis for his "uniform kindness and consideration," adding that the president had done everything in his power to support Lee's operations. With uncharacteristic emotion, Lee signed his letter "very respectfully and truly yours."[49]

Three days later Davis wrote back. Lee, above all, had been his anchor through trying times. The general's letter shocked and unsettled the president. Davis began by observing that the nation seemed to be recovering from its depression following the fall of Vicksburg. Fortitude would earn ultimate success. The criticism Lee faced was something utterly familiar to the commander in chief. Davis noted that nothing requires more patience "than to bear the criticism of the ignorant." Then Davis addressed the principal question, the issue of Lee's relief:

> But suppose, my dear friend, that I were to admit . . . the points which you present, where am I to find that new commander who is to possess the grater ability which you believe to be required? . . .
>
> My sight is not sufficiently penetrating to discover such hidden merit, if it exists . . . To ask me to substitute you by some one in my judgment more fit to command . . . is to demand an impossibility.
>
> It only remains for me to hope that you will take all possible care of yourself . . . and that the Lord will preserve you for the important duties devolved upon you in the struggle of our suffering country for the independence . . .[50]

This letter is a mirror to Jefferson Davis's soul. Lee had always behaved deferentially toward the commander in chief. The Virginian served loyally without criticism. Davis returned loyalty in full measure. He was ready to stand shoulder to shoulder in the last ditch to defend supportive subordinates. Davis willingly overlooked that fact that Lee had decimated his army in bungled maneuvers at Gettysburg.

His handling of Joe Johnston stood in marked contrast. In Mississippi, Johnston had faced insurmountable odds, but this Davis refused to acknowledge. A few days after the starved city surrendered, an assistant remarked to Davis that Vicksburg had fallen for lack of provisions. Angrily, the president retorted, "Yes, from want of provisions inside, and a general outside who wouldn't fight."[51]

Also in contrast to his conduct toward Johnston was the president's attitude toward a general who would fight hard but seemed to have a knack for turning victory into defeat. Months ago Davis understood Union strategy to comprise two major offensives: one against Richmond and one to control the Mississippi River.[52] He did not yet appreciate that the Federals had the strength to mount a third offensive against Chattanooga. Chattanooga was another of the places the South had to hold if it were to triumph. It had unmatched strategic and logistical possibilities that reduced to the fact it was a gateway north and south. Defending Chattanooga was Braxton Bragg and his Army of Tennessee.

Each time Braxton Bragg fought a battle the results failed to match expectations and serious dissension among his officer corps resulted. Repeatedly Davis had been told about the command problems in this army. But he had visited Bragg's army and found no evidence of any problem. He had sent Joe Johnston to assess Bragg's fitness for command and that general had returned a glowing report.[53] Still concerned in the early spring of 1863, the president dispatched a trusted aide who returned a quite different verdict: "There is nobody competent to the command of the Western Army."[54] The president acknowledged that Bragg's army had lost confidence in him and that this attitude jeopardized future success. Davis believed that "an officer who loses the confidence of his troops should have his position changed." He also claimed to adhere to the dictate that "success is the test of merit."[55] Yet twice he retained Bragg because he could see no alternative, and in the fall of 1863, the South's last hope for military victory hinged upon this general.

Doing what might have been done before Gettysburg, Lee had finally allowed troops to depart Virginia to reinforce Bragg in Tennessee.[56] There they joined troops concentrated from all over the South as the Confederate States of America summoned strength for one last offensive. Bragg employed them in a great, shattering, and fearfully bloody battle at Chickamauga in the third week of September 1863. The battle featured the most successful infantry charge of the war when soldiers from the Army of Northern Virginia advanced shoulder to shoulder with men from the Army of Tennessee in a pulverizing blow that pierced the Federal center, routed half the Union army, and drove the remnants back to Chattanooga.

Then Bragg inexplicably hesitated and fumbled the South's last offensive opportunity. He simply did not know what to do with his victory, and his indecision promoted anew the terrible command dissension within his army. While the Lincoln administration reacted to the crisis by rapidly dispatching some thirty-seven thousand reinforcements to help hold Chattanooga, the South could send but one, the commander in chief himself.

Davis traveled west into a tangled plot to unseat Bragg from command.[57] In truth, balky subordinates had greatly impeded Bragg's conduct at Chickamauga and in previous battles. More than a year earlier Bragg had requested changes among his corps commanders, referring to several as "incumbrances."[58] The problem was that one of those incumbrances was Davis's good friend, General Polk. When Davis had bristled at this proposal, Bragg backed down, leaving the bishop-warrior in command—to the army's great detriment. So lax had been Polk's leadership during the recent campaign that Bragg had finally relieved him. Fuming, Polk plotted revenge.

While Polk wrote to Lee, imploring him to come command the Army of Tennessee, Bragg's chief lieutenants wrote directly to the president. They also asked for a new general to lead the Army of Tennessee.[59] On his way to Bragg's headquarters, Davis stopped to visit Polk, who venomously poured out his criticism of his former commander. This was immensely trying for the president, who was attempting to soothe troubled waters while supporting both friends, Polk and Bragg. Reaching Chattanooga, Davis sought resolution in an exceptionally clumsy manner. In an "unprecedented scene," he convened a meeting and polled the key commanders of the Army of Tennessee regarding Bragg's fitness for command.[60] While the humiliated Bragg sat crouched in his chair, they responded as one: Bragg had mishandled the army and thrown away the victory of Chickamauga.

Undeterred, Davis stood by his friend, retaining him in command. After all, he could reflect that Bragg had won an important success, reversed the tide in Tennessee, and now had the enemy army besieged in Chattanooga. It was an entirely too optimistic assessment, for again personal loyalty impaired the commander in chief's judgment.

The Army of Tennessee had performed magnificently in battle after battle. Finally, much frayed by eighteen months of command dissension, it snapped. Some seven weeks after Davis's visit, the Union army in Chattanooga—now led by Lincoln's reliable troubleshooter, U. S. Grant—made an improbable frontal charge against Confederate entrenchments on Missionary Ridge. To everyone's surprise, Bragg's army routed. Even Bragg could not survive such a disaster, and manfully he submitted his resignation.

The president endured it all with remarkable fortitude. His Secretary of the Navy marveled at how Davis could:

> *listen to the announcement of defeat, while expecting victory . . . or to whispers that old friends were becoming cold or hostile, without exhibiting the slightest evidence of feeling beyond the change of color . . . he presented . . . the appearance of a man wearied and worn by care and labor, listening to something that he knew all about.*[61]

Bragg's resignation placed Jefferson Davis in another difficult bind. Inevitably, he turned to Lee, asking the Virginian if he would come to Georgia to take command of the Army of Tennessee. Lee was reluctantly willing, but cited a variety of obstacles, and instead suggested Beauregard.[62] Davis pondered: if not Lee, then whom? Again, the choice reduced to Joe Johnston and Beauregard. Beauregard remained a pariah; Johnston was barely better tolerated. That autumn, one of Davis's confidants had told his wife: ". . . the president detests Joe Johnston for all the trouble he has given him. And General Joe returns the compliment with compound interest."[63] Once again overcoming his personal antipathy, Davis appointed Johnston. His choice was wildly popular with the soldiers in the Army of Tennessee. Whether it was the correct one would be determined by the penultimate campaign of 1864.

THE LAST GREAT CHANCE

In the war's fourth year, the president responded to crisis in characteristic fashion by working even harder and thereby exemplifying the determination he believed was the key to ultimate victory. With his Secretary of War in poor health, he took on additional burdens, often acting as Secretary of War and general in chief. He personally issued orders organizing militia reserves, supervised important troop movements, managed the dense of Mississippi against a Yankee raiding column, and intervened in decision making regarding the naval defense of Mobile Bay. His minuscule staff had further dwindled as his young aides felt compelled to join the ranks as the nation's fortunes waned. By the summer of 1864 he retained the service of only two advisers. In addition to everything else, he still faced the time-consuming task of handling applicants for promotion and transfer as well as a host of civil petitions. A War Department clerk estimated that these petitions alone took nine-tenths of the president's time. It was a staggering workload, but a sacrifice Jefferson Davis willingly undertook because there remained one last great chance.

In January of 1864, a Georgia newspaper wrote about the upcoming presidential election in the North and predicted that the "battle-fields of 1864 will hold the polls." It recommended southern bullets as "the best ballot" against Lincoln's reelection.[64] Indeed, by this fourth year of war so daunting were the physical forces arrayed against the Confederacy that a change of Federal commander in chief was the last hope.

Jefferson Davis was well aware of the election's importance. Numerous politicians and military men, including General Lee, had long ago recognized a link between public support for the war among the people of the North and the likelihood of southern victory. When Lee launched his 1862 invasion of Maryland, he paused to write the president about the strategic value of a peace initiative coming just before the fall congressional elections.[65] But nine days later came Sharpsburg and retreat, so Lee's proposal went for nought. Again, on the eve of the Gettysburg campaign, Lee wrote to Davis about the desirability of promoting the northern peace party, but once more battlefield defeat ended such speculation.[66] In 1864 many concurred that the pending military campaign would shape November's presidential election.

Everyone recognized that if reelected, Lincoln would relentlessly continue the war for at least another four years. Alternatively, his defeat would signal northern war weariness and open the way for a negotiated peace that recognized southern independence. A Confederate senator from Georgia described the situation succinctly: the election "is the event which must determine the issue of peace or war, and with it, the destinies of both countries." He concluded that the South could "control" the election through military maneuver.[67] So Davis confronted a final, climactic challenge in which politics and military matters were thoroughly intermingled.

He possessed certain assets the value of which were difficult to measure. The peace movement in the North had grown in proportion to the length of the butcher's bill. Lincoln's repeated calls for more men—in February 1864 he ordered another draft that raised the number called within the past six months to 500,000, and in July would require 500,000 more—were meeting increased resistance. In the U.S. Congress, Democrats asserted that after three years of war, victory was no closer, civil liberties were under assault by a tyrant president, the national economy was in shambles because of war debt, and restoration of the Union was an unobtainable dream. Southerners read northern newspaper accounts of such talk and wondered about the depth of the peace sentiment.

Davis also knew that in many regions, but particularly in the Northwest, antiwar sentiment had coalesced into the formation of secret societies, the largest of which was known as the Knights of the Golden Circle. Replete with secret handshakes, passwords, and the like, these groups, known as "copperheads," were in contact with Confederate agents, and their numbers were estimated at 490,000. Davis was not overly impressed by such estimates, rightly judging their numbers exaggerated. Still, he decided to promote the Copperhead movement by sending agents and money north to stir up trouble while dispatching others through the blockade to Canada, where they would work to encourage antiwar sentiment. These were decidedly limited measures. Some suggested that a "peace offensive" complete with armistice proposals, offers to negotiate, and the like would force Lincoln into a stark, hard-line military position and thereby allow northern Democrats the chance to gain support. Such an effort required a shrewd appraisal of popular sentiment—if it failed it could undermine Confederate morale—and a deft political touch. These were not outstanding Davis attributes. He believed that the only way to obtain favorable terms was to "continue until the enemy is beaten out of his vain confidence in our subjugation. Then, and not till then, will it be possible to treat for peace."[68]

Davis had always been more comfortable with military rather than political affairs, and consequently he focused on the military portion of the 1864 equation. He had a variety of options to choose from. Lee, renouncing the offensive-defensive, urged an early spring offensive to derange Federal plans.[69] Likewise, General Longstreet proposed an invasion of Kentucky to preempt the anticipated Federal spring offensive in the west. Such a spoiling attack, Longstreet explained, would "break up the enemy's arrangements early, and throw him back, he will not be able to recover his position nor his morale until the Presidential election is over, and we shall then have a new President to treat with."[70] The president rejected Longstreet's bold scheme—in truth it was probably logistically impossible—and decided to continue with the more conventional offensive-defensive. Lee would do what he had done since taking over in Virginia: he would parry enemy thrusts and look for an opportunity to strike. The navy would try to expand its commerce-raiding activities to emphasize to New England Yankees, with burnt timber and plundered cargo, the war's cost. The remaining Confederate ports would fortify and resist, the Trans-Mississippi would have to take care of itself, which left the Army of Tennessee and Joseph Johnston. Johnston would have to perform in Georgia as Lee did in Virginia.

On the eve of the 1864 campaign, Vice President Stephens made it crystal clear for Johnston and every other Rebel what the coming campaign was all about: ". . . if our officials civil & military make no blunders and only hold our own for ten weeks . . . Lincoln may be beaten."[71]

*   *   *

For ten weeks and more Stephens's prophecy seemed solid. Facing staggering odds—Lee had accurately informed Davis that this campaign was so important to the fate of the Lincoln administration that the North would strain every nerve to support it—Lee maneuvered masterfully.[72] He inflicted enormous losses upon Grant's army and retreated back to Richmond. There he held hard, dug in behind fortifications the like of which would not be seen again until World War I. Virginia had once again proven a strategic dead end for the Army of the Potomac. Lincoln's political opponents saw stalemate, observing that Grant had merely returned to the ground upon which McClellan had stood two years previously.

In Georgia, Johnston too conducted a well-conceived campaign. Outnumbered at least five to three, he so slowed William T. Sherman's army that it advanced only one hundred miles in seventy-four days. Like Lee, Johnston fell back on fortifications surrounding his base at Atlanta. Here it appeared he had stalemated Sherman's farther advance.

In the coming weeks the price of gold in the North soared to record levels, a sure indicator of the lack of faith in the future. No less sage a politician than Abraham Lincoln foresaw defeat. He wrote: "This morning, as for some days past, it seems exceedingly probable that this Administration will not be reelected."[73] Voicing the opinion of many, the Richmond *Sentinel* concluded that the war had reached its decisive stage. Explaining that in the North the election hung in the balance, it urged Confederate soldiers to greater exertion because "a success at this time" would supersede in political importance "half a dozen military achievements last year or next."[74]

As the electioneering in the North neared its climax, Jefferson Davis examined the strategic chessboard. Lee had done the expected; that is, he had performed prodigies to check Grant's juggernaut. But to Davis's eyes, Johnston too had done the expected. He had retreated and retreated until now he stood on the last natural barrier, the Chattahoochee River, between Sherman and Atlanta. And there was no certainty that he would stop here. In the second week of July, Davis welcomed Georgia Senator Benjamin Hill, who had just returned from a visit to Johnston. Hill had been understandably concerned about Sherman's inexorable advance toward Atlanta. He felt considerable relief when, at the end of June, Johnston acknowledged that he could hold his position above the Chattahoochee River for two months. Ten days later Hill relayed this welcome news to the president. Grimly, Davis showed the senator a telegram just received from Johnston announcing his abandonment of the Chattahoochee line.[75]

As far back as May, the commander in chief had pondered removing Johnston from command. He observed: "It is very easy to remove the General, but where will you find the man to fill the place.?"[76] In July, before addressing this question, he gave Johnston a last chance. He telegraphed a clear request asking him to describe his intentions. Davis demanded, would Johnston hold Atlanta? Johnston made a typical noncommittal reply that hinted he might abandon the city in order to maneuver more freely. To Davis this was the same old story and it was unacceptable. While considering what to do he sent his military adviser, Braxton Bragg—somehow he had found a place for his old friend and somehow continued to trust his judgment—to Atlanta to assess the situation. Bragg reported that he saw no evidence that Johnston intended any dramatic change in the future. In Bragg's opinion the only remedy was offensive operations.

The acknowledged southern master of offensive operations was Robert E. Lee. With the rival armies in Virginia bogged down in static trench warfare, there was again a chance to send Lee to command the Army of Tennessee. Perhaps outside of Atlanta, Lee could do what he had done outside of Richmond back in the glory days of 1862. In the event, Davis did not avail himself of his best general's talents. Instead, he chose an officer who displayed an unsurpassed commitment to offensive warfare, but without concomitant tactical finesse, John Bell Hood.

Hood had come a long way since his 4th Texas had broken the Yankee position at Gaines's Mill. It seemed as if he paid for each step with his own blood. While recuperating from yet another wound—he had lost a leg and sacrificed use of an arm for the cause—Hood had spent the winter of 1864 in Richmond. He expertly cultivated Davis's esteem by playing to the president's vanity. During a discussion of the balky generals serving in the west, Hood invited Davis to take command himself, adding he would "follow you to the death."[77] Such talk helped Hood earn his next appointment as corps commander under Joe Johnston and unofficial spy with a direct link to Davis. During Johnston's campaign, Hood wrote confidential letters about operations in north Georgia that always expressed his enthusiasm for the offensive. At the same time, Davis received reports from Johnston explaining why an offensive was impossible. Believing an offensive necessary, believing that Johnston would abandon Atlanta, the president consulted Lee about appointing Hood to command.

Lee replied carefully. The Virginian had a soldier's love for Hood and for his old Texas outfit. Lee acknowledged Hood's gallantry and zeal for the attack. But he did not unreservedly endorse Davis's choice, commenting that Hood's capacity for army command was unproven. In spite of Lee's lukewarm support, Davis appointed Hood. The president had few options. The only other ranking lieutenant general serving with the Army of Tennessee had consistently displayed an unwillingness to assume the top command.[78] An outsider would stir jealousy in this, the most strife-ridden of armies, and would be unfamiliar with the situation. In Davis's mind there was simply no time to spare for a new man to acquaint himself with the Army of Tennessee's position. A change had to be made before Johnston lost all, and therefore it had to be Hood. Events proved it to be a terrible decision.

Hood proceeded to launch a series of fierce attacks that shattered his own Army of Tennessee. In eight days he absorbed more losses than had Johnston during the proceeding seventy-four. By September 1, Hood abandoned Atlanta, and this gave Lincoln the decisive edge in the November election. None of this was by any means inevitable. Sherman was at the end of a precarious single-rail supply route and had butted up against Atlanta's impregnable fortifications. A skilled defensive general like Johnston might have stalled him there for a long time, much as Lee stalled Grant outside of Petersburg and Richmond. Johnston later claimed that this was his strategy. However, if it was, he never explained it to his commander in chief. In the event, the absence of mutual trust undid the campaign and terminated the South's last chance for independence.

*   *   *

During the Confederacy's final collapse in the spring of 1865, Jefferson Davis descended from admirable determination to bloody-minded fatalism: "The war came, and now it must go on till the last man of this generation falls in his tracks, and his children seize his musket and fight our battle."[79] Before his final flight from Richmond, he gave his wife a pistol, instructed her how to use it, and told her to force her assailants to kill her rather than submit to capture. When he bade her farewell, he said he did "not expect to survive the destruction of constitutional liberty."[80]

Recalling the success of southern partisans against the British, he urged widespread guerrilla war. Fortunately, southern communications had been nearly severed and few heard his plea. Years later, in a rare admission of error, he all but called this idea a mistake. Robert E. Lee, not Davis, set the pattern for capitulation and thereby saved the nation from further horrors. When Grant's relentless pursuit ended all hope of formal resistance, some of

Lee's young aides advocated taking to the mountains to wage guerrilla war. Lee rejected this idea, saying the time had come to make peace. Such was Lee's stature that other Rebel generals followed suit. After Lee's surrender at Appomattox, Davis existed in a near-fantasy world, making plans, calling for redoubled effort. He met up with his old nemesis, Joe Johnston, who commanded the largest remaining Confederate army east of the Mississippi. Plotting future combinations, Davis exclaimed: ". . . we can whip the enemy yet, if our people will turn out." Johnston replied, "It would be the greatest of human crimes" to continue the war.[81]

At last, reduced to flight with a small band of followers, Davis too was ready to quit. He wrote his wife: "I have prayed to our Heavenly Father to give me wisdom and fortitude equal to the demands of the position in which Providence has placed me. I have sacrificed so much for the cause of the Confederacy." He explained that he could give no more; he would not sacrifice his family. He concluded: "My wife and my Children—How are they to be saved from degradation or want is now my care."[82]

It would be some time before he could discharge this care. In the wake of Lincoln's assassination, northern leaders were in no mood to make a soft peace. Union soldiers had marched to war hearing the refrain of a popular tune, "We'll hang Jeff Davis to a sour apple tree." After Federal forces captured him, he was not hanged. Instead, they imprisoned him in conditions of varying severity. For five days in May 1865, his captors placed leg irons on him, which, besides causing personal humiliation, did much to promote a burgeoning aura of martyrdom. By August, under the attentive care of a physician, Davis began a slow recovery from the psychological and physical stresses that had worn him to a near-cadaverous state. After 720 days the Federal government freed Davis. The electrifying news spread across the South: "The President has been baled."

Davis went to Canada in self-imposed exile and traveled to Europe, where prominent statesmen lionized him. Near penury, living off the kindness of friends, he returned to the United States to try to restore his fortune and instead met failure and debt. At last, eleven years after the war's end, he settled in Mississippi to begin work on a book. He did not seek "an 'opportune time' for publication," he cautioned his publisher, rather he wanted an opportunity "to vindicate our cause."[83] The resultant manuscript demonstrated that, among many southerners, Jefferson Davis could not dismiss painful memories of the past. He devoted fifteen chapters to a relentlessly legalistic examination of Constitutional Law, castigated the North for its unlawful "war of subjugation," and in 1,279 pages never admitted that either he or his cause was ever wrong. His conclusion was utterly characteristic of the man. He wrote that the results of the war showed secession "to be impracticable," but that "did not prove it to be wrong."[84]

*   *   *

It is fitting that Davis's legacy proved as complex, as contradictory, as the cause for which he struggled. No one ever doubted his devotion. One acquaintance spoke for all when he wrote, "Mr. Davis believed in the justice of the South's cause . . . He had absolutely no doubt of the right of a State to go out of the Union when the terms of the Union were violated."[85] The North forgave this unreconstructed Rebel before many people in the South were ready to do so.

As soon as the war ended, Davis served as a convenient lightning rod attracting all the blame for failure. In April 1865, a former Davis political ally complained: "Mr. Davis never had any policy; he drifted, from the beginning to the end of the war."[86] He emerged as the most vilified Confederate, damned by his former generals, contemporary writers, and subsequent historians for failing to devise and execute a winning strategy. Trying to make sense of the terrible losing sacrifice, southern hagiography began to depict Davis as the martyr, the gallant, doomed leader of the "Lost Cause." In spite of this effort criticism continued into the 1880s, when the likes of Joe Johnston wrote that the South lost "because its executive head never gathered and wielded its great strength."[87] The critical examination of each of Davis's decisions proceeded unabated through modern times. Because, like the patriots of 1776, the South could win by simply not losing, critics recognized that every Davis decision impinging upon the Confederacy's durability was worthy of analysis.

Questions and contradictions swirled around this man. How could he display great administrative competence when serving as U.S. Secretary of War and then fail as Confederate commander in chief to ensure that the South's military forces received adequate material support? A man who had once ably managed an enormous Federal budget was ultimately responsible for a bankrupt

Confederate treasury that went far toward defeating the Rebel cause by both depleting civilian morale and demoralizing the army. No less a figure than Robert E. Lee concluded that "insufficiency of food and non-payment of the troops" impaired morale more than anything else.[88] Even before Gettysburg, a high-ranking assistant observed that Davis had no "broad policy . . . of finance, strategy, or supply."[89]

Many of the South's difficulties stemmed from Davis's personality. He remained the man the young Varina Davis had first observed, a man whom one of his Secretaries of War described as "the most difficult man to get along with he had ever seen."[90] He needed to forge a strategic consensus, but as his Secretary of the Navy observed, Davis "rarely satisfied or convinced" skeptics "simply because in his manner and language there was just an indescribable something" that alienated.[91] Davis responded admirably to setback and defeat by applying himself with redoubled effort. Such hard work and personal attention to every detail had worked well for him when he was Secretary of War, just as it had worked well for many earlier presidents. But by 1860 the country was entering a more modern era where one-man management was impossible and counterproductive. A perceptive Richmond bureaucrat provides a second explanation accounting for the contrast between Davis's early success and later failure. He observed that Davis was well suited for running an established government, "but he is probably not equal to the role he is now called upon to play."[92] Davis could meet the challenges of a settled, powerful government, but a newly created government required special attributes, notably flexibility. This was beyond Davis's unbending nature.

Ultimately, the South's real hope for either foreign intervention or for a prolonged conflict yielding northern war weariness had to be military success. Success, in turn, depended upon how well the commander in chief discharged the dual mandate of developing a winning strategy and finding generals to implement it.

Davis did articulate a cogent strategy, the offensive-defensive. He failed to find leaders to execute his own interpretation of what this meant. Long after the war it became apparent that two schools of strategic thought arose among his generals. There was the Davis-Lee approach that sought to maintain the war until the enemy gave up. It worked. Lee was able to defend Richmond until the war was irretrievably lost elsewhere. The alternative approach found its principal advocates in Joe Johnston, Beauregard, and Bragg. Inspired by Napoleon, these generals maneuvered, often backward in retreat, until their opponent revealed his intentions and overstretched his supply line. Then would come the Napoleonic counterstroke, the decisive war-winning offensive. Whether this interpretation of the offfensive-defensive could have triumphed is problematical. Bragg lacked the ability to implement it. Johnston always found reason to postpone the decisive stroke. Except perhaps at Shiloh, Beauregard never had the opportunity.

Davis's greatest failure was not appointing a general in chief who could insist that the president's strategy be carried out. A competent, trusted Secretary of War would have helped, but Davis could not tolerate anyone performing this job except himself. In sharp contrast to his steadfast support for field generals, he appointed six different Secretaries of War during his tenure.[93] Likewise, Davis resisted even the notion that the country needed a general in chief. Instead, he also undertook this duty and it was simply too much. Even dear friends perceived Davis's error. Leonidas Polk confided that the cause would benefit greatly if Davis "would lean a little less upon his own understanding" and recognize that "there were some minds in the land from whom he might obtain counsel worth having."[94] Nowhere was his failure more evident than in the way the competing Virginia and Western interests buffeted him. Davis badly needed a general in chief of the stature of U.S. Grant—or later, George C. Marshall—to allocate appropriate resources to the different war theaters. The only man possessing such stature was Robert E. Lee.

When Davis appointed Lee to command the field army outside Richmond, he did not intend for Lee to relinquish his former job as chief adviser to the president.[95] Indeed, Lee's son noted that Lee continued to advise Davis about overall Confederate troop movements "at all times."[96] Lee had unmatched opportunities to influence the president. His operations in Virginia demonstrated he possessed the highest strategic capacity. But he never articulated the principles underlying his success nor sought to have them applied to the Confederacy at large. His advice was most often that of a theater commander, not that of a strategist concerned with the overall war effort.

Repeatedly Lee confined his thinking to troop dispositions that affected his own situation in Virginia. In this he was no different from his predecessor, Joe Johnston. In the fall of 1861 Johnston had said "success here . . . saves everything; defeat here loses all."[97]

Lee heartily concurred. Beginning in the fall of 1862, he decided that the main Federal effort would occur on his front and asked if the Army of Tennessee could defend Richmond while he invaded Maryland. He broached the topic again in December even while a great Federal offensive was about to open in Tennessee. The following spring, when Grant massed on the Mississippi and the Union army in Tennessee gathered strength to renew its advance, Lee reiterated that "Virginia is to be the theatre of action."[98]

Following his defeat at Gettysburg, Lee's every instinct was to try conclusions with the Army of the Potomac immediately again. Only reluctantly did he permit the westward departure of Longstreet's corps. No sooner had Longstreet left than Lee bombarded Davis with requests for his return. By September 25, three days after the great Rebel victory at Chickamauga, Lee had already written four times asking for his recall.[99] In 1864, when Sherman had massed three departmental armies against Joe Johnston in Georgia, Lee could only see the threat in Virginia. He said, ". . . the great effort of the enemy in this campaign will be made in Virginia."[100] Thus he urged that Johnston take the offensive in order to relieve pressure in Virginia.

So daunting were the odds that Lee confronted in Virginia that he simply had little time to ponder events elsewhere. When he did, he lacked sufficient knowledge to make sound assessments. He himself said that he derived most of what he knew from the public papers, hardly a sound basis from which to make decisive strategic choices.[101] In sum, Lee consistently asked for reinforcements from other Confederate commands while rejecting appeals that he detach any of his own troops. Davis, in turn, refused to strip the west in favor of the east or to enforce a request, with the one exception of Longstreet's transfer following Gettysburg, that Lee send men west. Thus the South failed to exploit one of its great strategic advantages, its interior lines. Instead of using this advantage to mass men on one front or the other in what admittedly would have been a colossal strategic gamble, Davis distributed men evenly east and west. This ensured ultimate defeat. The Army of Northern Virginia and the Army of Tennessee received enough men to slow the Union advance—in effect, to prolong the war for years. But they did not have the strength to follow up a battlefield victory, to pursue a defeated foe, to fight an offensive, war-winning campaign.

Ultimately, this meant it would be a war of attrition, and if the

North stuck to the task, only it could win that war. A British observer understood this. Confederate valor, the triumph of the few
against the many, awed him. But he accurately noted that the
system fed on itself. Indeed, during Lee's first four months as
commander, June to September 1862, the Army of Northern Virginia lost nearly fifty thousand casualties.[102] On the eve of the
Gettysburg campaign, Lee comprehended the grim truth, telling
Davis that southern manpower resources were constantly diminish-
ing while the enemy's steadily increased.[103] By 1864, as Beauregard
remarked, there "were no more troops to concentrate."[104]

In intriguing contrast to Davis's conduct as commander in chief
is the performance of his great rival, Abraham Lincoln. In the
broadest sense, both commanders equally discharged the responsibility of articulating a grand strategy: Davis wrote, "we just want
to be left alone"; Lincoln, "a house divided against itself cannot
endure." Where they differed was in their selection of field generals to carry out their strategy.

After Sidney Johnston's death, Davis had to find someone to
assume the great command in the west, and he perceived he could
only choose Joe Johnston or Beauregard. During the crisis on the
Mississippi, he lamented to his brother that a fully capable general
was "a rare product" and each generation might produce but one.
However, in this war "there is need for half a dozen."[105]
Beauregard was probably not a fully capable commander in the
sense Davis understood. However, he certainly was among the
South's top strategists. Yet the commander in chief allowed his
personal prejudice to block this fourth-ranking Confederate from
meaningful service during the final three years of the war.

Here was an important difference between the two leaders.
Lincoln bent his personality to get along with his generals, explaining his toleration of a general's snub with the comment that
he would hold the general's horse if that would advance the cause.
Davis, the aristocrat, could never have said such a thing. Instead,
small quarrels with important generals and politicians developed
into significant faults in the bedrock of southern leadership.

Once Davis chose a general, he stood by him through thick
and thin. Lincoln, in contrast, removed in rapid succession five
commanders of the Army of the Potomac following their defeats.
Better than Davis, Lincoln recognized talent. Confederate Chief
of Ordnance Josiah Gorgas noted that Davis was "an indifferent
judge of men," too often guided by prejudice.[106] Lincoln could

accurately appraise men even at a distance. When many clamored for Grant's relief, Lincoln responded, "I can't spare this man; he fights."[107]

Lincoln, with his background as a country lawyer, hardly possessed the experience Davis acquired at West Point. Yet in so many ways Lincoln overmatched the Confederate president. Lincoln, the civilian, better recognized the importance of unity of command than did Davis, the military man. Lincoln understood that if all the Union forces worked together, the South did not have enough strength to resist. In typical homey fashion he explained, "If someone cannot skin, at least he can hold a leg." To achieve this cooperation he tried four different commanding generals of all the armies; Scott, McClellan, Henry W. Halleck, and Grant. The first three failed him. Scott, after supplying his plan, proved too old to execute it. McClellan was too cautious, Halleck unwilling to assume the awesome responsibility. Finally Lincoln found Grant, his killer-arithmetician to whom the South had no answer.

Lincoln was at least as ignorant about public finance as Davis, yet he managed a treasury that nourished the Federal war effort. Unlike Davis, Lincoln displayed masterful political talents. He was a pragmatist who never lost sight of his goal to preserve the Union. Abolition was a political consideration that Lincoln assessed in relation to how it advanced victory. He fought to restore the Union—preferably without slavery, but with it if necessary. He exercised power ruthlessly toward this end.

Davis and Lee shared a remarkable understanding that achieved much, but not until 1865 did Lee assume his place as general in chief. Together they made a superb civil-military team but, contrary to some historians' claims, the war witnessed one better.[108] Lincoln and Grant also enjoyed a special rapport, but unlike Davis, Lincoln entrusted his foremost general with direction of the entire war effort. Unlike Lee, Grant willingly undertook this enormous burden. This guaranteed a unity of purpose in which the entire northern military machine worked toward a common goal.

Finally, in assessing Davis's performance one must recognize a fundamental fact of the Confederacy. So fragile were southern chances of victory that virtually no significant mistake could be made. A veritable cottage industry has grown up around the issue of why the South lost the war. Writers point out that indeed, the southern economy could have been placed upon a much sounder base. Cotton diplomacy could have been performed more ably.

The railroads could have been maintained had not skilled workers been conscripted to serve as mere infantry. Better generals than Bragg and J. E. Johnston might have been found. In other words, there are prescriptions for southern success, available with hindsight, that assert that, had a complete set of correct decisions been made in the South could have achieved independence. In the final analysis, this prescription hinges upon a consistent competency extending across all important branches of Davis's government and including all important field commands. In other words, it is a prescription requiring a state of perfection no civilization has yet attained.

Jefferson Davis was the first American commander in chief to fail in war. By war's end fully half of all Southern white men of prime military age were dead or maimed. They had done their duty. Their government had proved lacking. The words of an aging Confederate veteran perhaps best conclude Davis's tragedy. Attending a reunion a quarter of a century after the war, the ex-sergeant heard the request from the podium that a southern mother wished to hear the Rebel yell one more time. He responded:

> *The young men and youths who composed this unearthly music were lusty, jolly, clear-voiced, hardened soldiers, full of courage, and proud to march in rags, barefoot, dirty and hungry . . . Alas! now many of them are decrepit from ailment and age, and although we will never grow old enough to cease being proud of the record of the Confederate soldier . . . we can never again, even at your bidding, dear, dear mother, produce the Rebel yell. Never again; never, never, never.*[109]

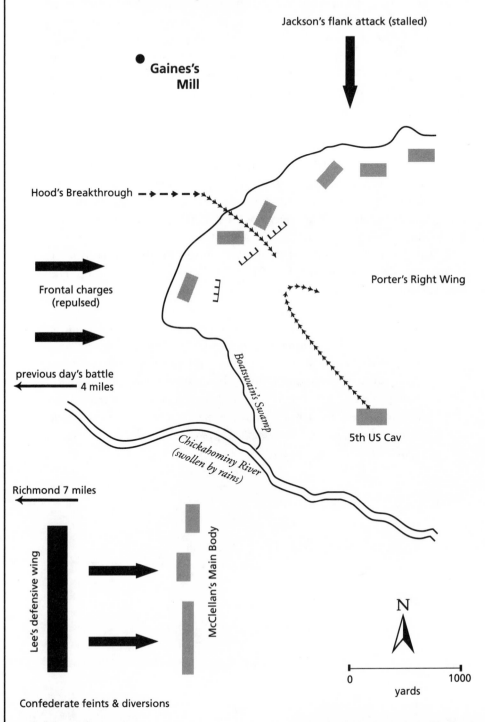

Battle of Gaines's Mill
June 27, 1862

Jackson's flank attack (stalled)

● Gaines's
  Mill

Hood's Breakthrough

Frontal charges
(repulsed)

previous day's battle
4 miles

Boatswain's Swamp

Porter's Right Wing

5th US Cav

Chickahominy River
(swollen by rains)

Richmond 7 miles

Lee's defensive wing

McClellan's Main Body

N

0   1000
        yards

Confederate feints & diversions

PART FOUR

LYNDON JOHNSON'S

STRATEGY FOR DEFEAT

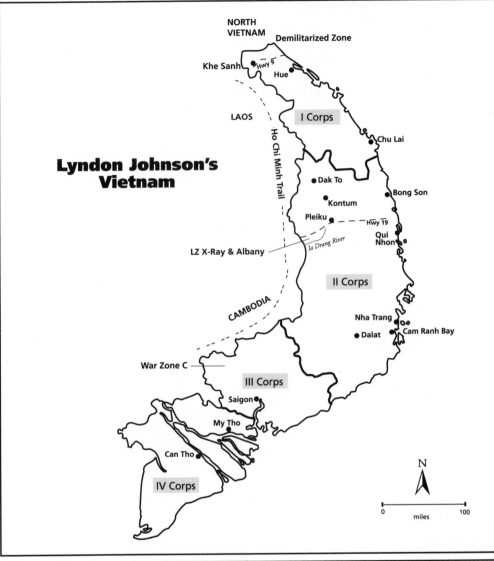

NORTH
VIETNAM

Demilitarized Zone

Khe Sanh Hwy 9
Hue

LAOS

I Corps

Chu Lai

Lyndon Johnson's Vietnam

Dak To

Kontum

Bong Son

Pleiku Hwy 19

LZ X-Ray & Albany Ia Drang River

Qui Nhon

II Corps

CAMBODIA

Nha Trang

Cam Ranh Bay

Dalat

War Zone C

III Corps

Saigon

My Tho

Can Tho

IV Corps

N

0   miles   100

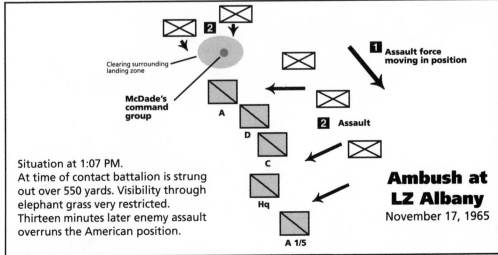

2

Clearing surrounding
landing zone

1 Assault force
moving in position

McDade's
command
group

A

2 Assault

D

C

Hq

A 1/5

Situation at 1:07 PM.
At time of contact battalion is strung
out over 550 yards. Visibility through
elephant grass very restricted.
Thirteen minutes later enemy assault
overruns the American position.

Ambush at LZ Albany
November 17, 1965

8 ⟦⟧

FROM HAVANA HARBOR
TO THE GULF OF TONKIN

"I won't let those Air Force generals bomb the smallest out-house north of the 17th parallel without checking with me."

LYNDON JOHNSON, 1965[1]

A CENTURY OF BATTLE

PRESIDENT WILLIAM MCKINLEY UNDERSTOOD WAR, HAVING ENLISTED AS a private at the age of seventeen, served for four years in some of the Civil War's bloodiest battles, and risen on merit alone to the rank of brevet major. Like many veterans, he concluded his service after acquiring a horror of war, and this attitude continued through to the time he became commander in chief in 1897.

For two years the plight of Cuba had attracted American attention. Cuban rebels were fighting a desperate struggle against Spanish rule. Stirred by the era's rampant "yellow journalism," most American politicians viewed the conflict with a mixture of sympathy and acquisitiveness. Sympathy because the Cuban people's fight was not unlike the American War of Independence, acquisitiveness because here was a fine chance to obtain naval bases in the Caribbean. Opposed to war with Spain, McKinley sought a diplomatic solution even though this was an exceedingly unpopular approach.

Simultaneously, a rising young politician from a socially prominent family, Theodore Roosevelt, strained every nerve to push the nation toward war. With tensions already high, Roosevelt—in his capacity as Assistant Secretary of the Navy—addressed the Naval War College, taking as his text George Washington's maxim "To be prepared for war is the most effectual means to promote peace." He delivered a bloody-minded speech that encouraged further those who favored war.

At last McKinley found himself unable to resist the nation's passion when the battleship *Maine* blew up in Havana Harbor. Amid congressional and public cries for revenge, McKinley struggled to preserve peace, becoming seamed and haggard in the process, turning to narcotics for refuge in sleep. Leaders in his own Republican party demanded action, with one senator threatening "... if he doesn't do something Congress will exercise the [war-declaring] power."[2]

Another Civil War veteran, the commanding general of the army, General Nelson A. Miles, strongly disapproved of the war hysteria being promoted by the yellow journalist tactics of William Hearst and his fellow publishers. Miles had seen combat up close, having won the Medal of Honor for his spectacular front line conduct during the Battle of Chancellorsville in the Civil War. He knew that the rush toward war overlooked the fact that the military was ill-prepared. It lacked everything from smokeless powder—an American invention possessed in ample quantities by the enemy—to an adequate medical corps, a necessity for operations along Cuba's fever coast. Miles had been unsuccessfully advocating an expanded, modern army. A congressional coalition combining traditional opposition to a standing army and a powerful political lobby who favored the National Guard (with its ready receipt of patronage positions) rebuffed the general. Consequently, Congress limited by law the size of the standing army of 1898 to 25,000 men while tolerating a peacetime War Department that had ballooned to a clerical force of 1,366—twice the number engaged at the height of the Civil War.

Congress persisted in the naive notion that the country could spring to arms overnight, remembering the patriotic minutemen of 1775 and the flood of volunteers of 1861 and forgetting all else. Indeed, when McKinley issued a call for 125,000 volunteers, over one million responded. However, as had been the case in previous wars, the lack of logistical preparation condemned too many to death at the grossly unsanitary and undersupplied mobilization camps.

Although dragged unwillingly into war, McKinley proved a shrewd commander in chief. So popular was the war that he had little trouble retaining public support. He successfully oversaw the development of a war-winning strategy and generally selected able men to lead American forces to victory. However, like Polk, he worried that the war might create political heroes, and so chose General William Shafter, an aging, obese officer, to lead the army to Cuba rather than the dashing Miles, whom he believed had presidential ambitions and suspected was a Democrat. To direct the war effort McKinley installed the latest communications technology. He created a White House Operating Room that was a prototype of the modern military command and control center. It featured telephone and telegraphic links to subordinates and maps bristling with colored pins displaying friendly and enemy positions. Recently developed submarine cable allowed him, for the first time in history, to direct operations at sea by instantaneously sending messages to naval officers in distant, foreign harbors.

Technology proved a mixed blessing. Stimulated by an anxious message from one of his admirals, McKinley ordered the Cuban invasion force to sea long before it had made adequate preparations. On the other hand, when Shafter balked after winning a bloody battle, the president cabled him to stand firm: "What you went to Santiago for was the Spanish army. If you allow it to evacuate with its arms you must meet it somewhere else." McKinley concluded with a stern chastisement of Shafter's conduct: "This is not war."[3] The president's admirable decision to leave operational control in the hands of the military also worked unevenly. It promoted subordinate initiative, yet his simple directive to his naval and land commanders to "cooperate' in Cuba was ingenuous and led to an uncoordinated, unnecessarily costly campaign against Santiago.

Concluded in less than four months, the "splendid little war" against Spain changed the nation forever. McKinley wisely used the conflict to heal scars from the Civil War by putting General Fitzhugh Lee, Robert E. Lee's nephew, in charge of a major volunteer formation, and likewise offered command to the former Confederate cavalier "Fighting Joe" Wheeler. The healing proved so successful that Wheeler wore his national uniform when buried, prompting a Confederate veteran to speculate on the look on Stonewall Jackson's face when "Fighting Joe" entered heaven in a blue uniform!

McKinley's war also completed the work begun by Polk. Manifest Destiny had taken Polk to the shores of the Pacific. The war with

Spain extended American hegemony to Guam and the Philippines. The navy soon built bases, including one at Pearl Harbor, to protect its newly elongated line of communications. The coming century would test whether this line could be held against the other emerging Pacific power, Japan.

The United States emerged from the war a world power with far-flung overseas possessions and a new stake in international affairs. Few then living appreciated the implications of America's vault onto the world stage, a position that would require repeated martial performances, and a role that would be resisted by millions of Americans in generations to come.

*   *   *

The last commander in chief to be directly touched by the Civil War, Woodrow Wilson, shared McKinley's hatred of war. Growing up in the South during the final years of the Confederacy and during the humiliation of Reconstruction, he acquired a bitter resentment of military affairs. In 1916, with World War I in its third year, he based American relations on the philosophy of "neutrality in thought and deed." Placards asking "Who keeps us out of war?" encouraged the public to reelect him to a second term. As the first president to appear alone before the Senate since George Washington's failed attempt to use that body as a British-style Privy Council, Wilson employed the occasion to say the conflict must end with the belligerents meeting as equals. He concluded that for peace to endure "it must be a peace without victory."[4] Then came the onslaught of German unrestricted submarine warfare. Just as the sinking of the *Maine* had prodded a reluctant McKinley to war, so the torpedoing of American vessels forced Wilson's hand.

On April 2, 1917, this peaceful man of great eloquence told Congress that German actions represented "warfare against mankind" and required the United States to respond. He said, "There is one choice we cannot make, we are incapable of making; we will not choose the path of submission." America should enter the war in the interest of ultimate world peace, to make the world "safe for democracy."[5] Congress agreed and declared war. John Joseph Pershing was a veteran of the Indian and the Spanish-American wars. He had advanced by dint of his hard work rather than intellectual capacity. He was a silent, grim-faced man; news that his wife and three small daughters had burned to death in a fire on a military post only exacerbated his cold nature. During his failed efforts to catch Pancho Villa along the Mexican border, Pershing exhibited one great characteristic: he obeyed orders. Because of this, Wilson chose him over another senior officer to command the United States Army in France. Then paradoxically, after selecting an obedient general, Wilson delegated to Pershing enormous responsibility to pursue the war as he saw fit. Giving the general broad authority was in keeping with Wilson's command style. Ill at ease with military matters, Wilson tried to have subordinates make the decisions that heretofore had been made by the president. Wilson neither studied war maps in the White House Cabinet Room nor conferred with the appropriate deputies on military matters.

Simultaneously, he concentrated more power through his Selective Service law and espionage bill than had ever been possessed by previous commanders in chief. Cognizant that the war's attrition required a colossal manpower, recalling bloody draft opposition in Lincoln's time, and fearful of German-American, Irish-American, and Socialist dissent, the commander in chief used a combination of strict laws and rigorous enforcement to make antiwar opposition illegal. It was no mean feat given his own leadership of the neutrality movement during the previous years. Although he failed to obtain specific powers of press censorship, multitudinous wartime legislation provided ample authority to meet the same end. Nearly all of the war news that appeared in the press came through his administration's Bureau of Public Information.

The expeditionary force that Pershing took to France suffered the typical inadequacies. Three years of European trench warfare had demonstrated the salient importance of certain weapons. Nonetheless, the regular American army totally lacked hand grenades and trench mortars, possessed insufficient machine guns, automatic rifles, and field artillery, and was well behind world standards in aircraft design and battlefield signaling. On the other hand, following the Spanish-American War, Congress and the country had overcome its fears that an army general staff was a step toward militarism. Consequently, in 1917 a professional staff was available to help solve the immense problems associated with national mobilization.

Wilson's broad instructions to Pershing merely ordered him to cooperate with the allies. Beyond that, Wilson pledged his full support to Pershing and lived up to his word. In the general's mind, the most important part of his orders was the paragraph specifying that the Americans were to fight as a distinct entity rather than as a component of the French or British armies. Complying with this turned out to be nearly as difficult as fighting the Germans because the allies were desperate for manpower. Ravaged by yet another failed offensive, the French army was in mutiny. Although still retaining its morale, the British forces were also sadly depleted. Consequently, the allies welcomed the Americans as an inexhaustible supply of cannon fodder and did everything possible to resist the formation of a separate American army.

Arriving in France 139 years after Rochambeau had come to America, Pershing used the Frenchman's example—Rochambeau had always cooperated with Washington while retaining a separate command—to preserve American autonomy. In so doing he fulfilled Wilson's order and salved American pride, but only at the cost of unnecessary battlefield losses. American doughboys had to learn at high cost the survival lessons that were second nature to European veterans.[6]

While showing little interest in land warfare, Wilson paid much more attention to the war at sea. In April 1917, the month the United States declared war, England was in danger of strangulation from the German U-boat blockade. One in four merchantmen sailing from British ports was lost to German submarines that month. Wilson understood that unless the sea lanes remained open, all else was moot. Anticipating the likelihood of war, he had sent Rear Admiral William Sims to England to coordinate operations with the Admiralty. Sims proved an inspired selection. The American admiral found his British counterpart despondent over the submarine losses but unwilling to try something different. Sims saw that a convoy system was the answer to the submarine menace, found a group of experienced junior British admirals who agreed, and through skilled diplomacy convinced the hidebound senior British leadership to give convoys a try. The first trial convoy arrived without loss. The next day the Admiralty thoroughly endorsed the concept and thereby pulled England back from the brink of defeat. "You are responsible for this," the prime minister told Sims, and Wilson, in turn, was responsible for sending Sims to England.[7]

Thereafter, the scholarly Wilson keenly focused on the nature of the postwar world. He enunciated his celebrated fourteen-point program for a permanent peace. Once the war ended, after 50,585

American servicemen had died and 205,690 had been wounded, he eagerly participated in the postwar world restructuring designed to eliminate points of conflict and promote national and ethnic aspirations. The forum to resolve future disputes would be Wilson's cherished League of Nations. Wilson campaigned tirelessly on behalf of this ideal. Cautioned to slow down because of weak health, he responded that as commander in chief he had sent American soldiers to battle and now, "If I don't do all in my power to put that treaty into effect, I will be a slacker and never able to look those boys in the eye."[8] So he exerted himself and ruined his health in the process. A debilitating stroke rendered him a shallow husk of a man for the last fifteen months of his second term. So consumed had he been in promoting his vision that he failed to keep abreast of public mood. He did not comprehend that so effective had been his wartime propaganda at lashing up hatreds and suspicions against foreigners that the American people had little interest in further entanglement in international affairs.

Wilson had done well in appointing Sims and selecting Pershing for the two major commands. He successfully mobilized congressional and public support for the war. However, one of the consequences of his noninvolvement in military affairs during the war was a great reduction in American influence at the postwar Paris Peace Conference and during the framing of the Versailles Treaty. In pursuit of lasting peace, Wilson abandoned part of his duty as commander in chief and thereby helped pave the way for World War II.

*   *   *

More than any other president, with the possible exception of McKinley, Franklin D. Roosevelt had a background that prepared him to serve as commander in chief during war. At age thirty-one he became Wilson's Assistant Secretary of the Navy, a post once held by his cousin Teddy, from whom he learned much. During World War I it was a position of real responsibility that Roosevelt used to contribute positively toward the allied war effort. Among many projects, Roosevelt pushed the great North Sea mine barrage that worked splendidly to confine the German fleet and its submarines to coastal waters. He went to France in 1918 and saw firsthand "blood running from the wounded . . . men coughing out their gassed lungs . . . the dead in the mud."[9]

He became president at a time when traditional American isolationism was again resurgent. So in 1935 he proclaimed that the nation's primary purpose was "to avoid being drawn into war." In 1940 he assured the public, "I have said this before, but I shall say it again and again and again: Your boys are not going to be sent into any foreign wars."[10]

Five days after the European War began, on September 6, 1939, Roosevelt organized the so-called Atlantic neutrality patrol. He intended this pacifistic-sounding name to fool the German military and the American people. The patrol's exploits were both numerous and secret, and Roosevelt controlled them personally using the most modern communications technology. The "neutrality patrol" was anything but, and greatly aided the Royal Navy. It shadowed German ships and reported their locations. In one typical affair, American warships pursued the 32,000-ton German vessel *Columbus* outbound from Vera Cruz for six days until delivering it into the waiting guns of a British destroyer four hundred miles off the New Jersey coast. The world, including the American public, only heard that an American cruiser accidentally happened on the scene just in time to pull German survivors from the water. As the Chief of Naval Operations explained to a subordinate: ". . . we do not desire you to make public the details of the work of our . . . patrol."[11]

But the commander in chief's real objective was not to help the British intercept the occasional German merchantman but to contain the German U-boat menace. He told his Cabinet that he wanted to patrol "from New Foundland down to South America and if some submarines . . . try to interrupt an Americana flag and our Navy sinks them it's just too bad."[12] When Hitler initially forbid his U-boats from operating in the western Atlantic, Roosevelt had to turn to other means to support the British. So came a succession of measures that were decidedly unneutral but accorded with the president's understanding of geopolitical reality. He swapped fifty destroyers in exchange for certain Caribbean base rights at a time when the British desperately needed them to keep open her sea lanes. He gradually pushed antisubmarine patrols farther out into the Atlantic, and—following his election to an unprecedented third term—managed the passage of the renowned Lend-Lease Act at a time when Britain was near absolute insolvency. More than anyone else, including British leaders, Roosevelt believed "the outcome of this struggle is going to be decided in the Atlantic and unless Hitler can win there he cannot win anywhere in the world in the end."[13] Well before the Japanese attack on Pearl Harbor, Roosevelt bent his will toward persuading the isolationist-minded public and Congress as well as some of his top military advisers that these were wise actions, that Britain's survival was essential to American security.

After his 1940 reelection, the military began final planning for America's entrance into the war. The Chief of Naval Operations, Admiral Harold Stark, codified Roosevelt's strategic inclinations in something called "Plan Dog." It described how the country would fight a two-ocean war. Most naval assets would be sent to the Atlantic, where they would lead a "strong offensive." Eventually an American expeditionary force would spearhead a war-winning assault against the Axis powers on the Continent. Meanwhile, American forces would remain on the defensive in the Pacific. The "Europe first" strategy articulated in Plan Dog provided the fundamental basis for American operations in World War II. It was one of Roosevelt's two most significant contributions toward winning the war, and coming, as it did, a full year before Pearl Harbor, at a time of still-profound American isolationism, it was "political dynamite."[14] Roosevelt orally approved Plan Dog, avoided a written commitment in order to remain off the record, and thereby discharged one of the two mandates of the commander in chief by selecting a war-winning strategy.

A year later, when Japan attacked and Germany conveniently declared war against the United States—surely the most colossal and most easily avoided strategic error committed by the onetime Austrian corporal—Roosevelt set to his second task, that of finding the leaders to execute his strategy. He already had General George C. Marshall, having been impressed by this gifted officer, elevating him over his seniors, and appointing him Army Chief of Staff in 1939. During the week following Pearl Harbor, he summoned Admiral Ernest J. King, formerly the Atlantic Fleet commander, to Washington to name him Commander in Chief of the U.S. Fleet. Few people liked King, but many respected him for his intelligence and decisiveness. King had so impressed the president that Roosevelt overcame personal loyalty to his friend Admiral Stark to clear the way for King's ascension to the top.

Then Roosevelt created a new administrative body, the Joint Chiefs of Staff, where King and Marshall could compete. This technique of playing one strong-willed man against another was a hallmark of Roosevelt's administrative style. In Marshall and King, Roosevelt had two brilliant, determined officers, one for the army and one for the navy. Underneath them, Roosevelt also picked the key officers to see the war through to victory; "Hap" Arnold, who invented the American air force; Chester Nimitz, who led the fleet in the Pacific; and Dwight Eisenhower.

Criticism of Roosevelt's wartime leadership revolves around the notion that he completely focused on the destruction of the enemy and ignored the consequent postwar geopolitical balance. His lack of foresight, so critics claim, sacrificed eastern Europe and China to communism, while his abandonment, in the interest of expediency, of the ideals espoused in his Atlantic charter positioned America on the side of French imperialism in Vietnam.[15] However, when assessing Roosevelt's performance as commander in chief, it is vital to recall that the defeat of Germany alone required four years of unrelenting pressure from three enormously powerful nations. Victory could come only if Russia, the United Kingdom, and the United States held firm in their allied resolve. More than Stalin or Churchill, Roosevelt preserved this fragile coalition, and for this reason alone he must be considered a great commander in chief.

*   *   *

When the United States concluded World War II it possessed unmatched military power. In the wake of Japan's surrender, President Harry S. Truman used some of this power to send American soldiers to occupy a strange and little-known country on the Asian mainland. Free of Japanese domination, Korea was newly adrift without government or political order. It possessed little strategic value to the United States outside of the fact that without American intervention the Soviet Union would dominate its restructuring. So it was that the two great postwar powers divided unhappy Korea along its 38th Parallel. Five years later, before the dawn of June 25, 1950, the North Korean People's Army launched a surprise invasion across the border. Cold War rivalry had erupted in open conflict.

Truman was at home in Independence, Missouri, when his Secretary of State telephoned him with news of the invasion. The president decided that the United Nations Security Council should be asked to convene immediately to consider what to do, and hastened back to Washington to meet with his political and military advisers. He learned that although American advisers had been training the South Korean military, there were no U.S. combat formations present in Korea, that American forces in the Far East were weak, and that no general plan for defending Korea existed. In spite of this, everyone recommended that a line against worldwide Communist aggression should be drawn somewhere and that the best place to start was in Korea. It was the president's decision to make. Of paramount importance to Truman was the knowledge that unchallenged aggression had led to World War II. He judged that a similar failure to defend Korea would lead to a third world war. Therefore, Truman broadly interpreted the Security Council's request that members "render every assistance" in restoring the 38th Parallel boundary by ordering his Pacific commander, General Douglas MacArthur, to use air and naval power against the invaders.[16] From this flowed a subsequent decision to commit ground forces.

The president believed the Soviet Union to be the real aggressor in Korea. Once having made this determination, the commander in chief confronted the novel concern of how a nuclear-equipped Russia would respond to the United States' intervention. For the next forty-odd years, this anxiety about a Russian reaction to the employment of American force dominated the military strategy of the American commander in chief. In 1950, in order to avoid a war against Russia, Truman ordered that fighting be limited to the Korean peninsula and instructed MacArthur to avoid provocative steps that might lead to Russian or Chinese participation. Symbolic of his concept of limited war was the term he used to describe the fighting: the conflict in Korea was a "police action." Moreover, he declined to ask Congress for a formal declaration of war. Thus the Korean War became a historical first. Never before had the nation engaged in such large-scale fighting without employing its entire military might and without declaring war.

Initially, the commitment of ill-equipped American soldiers failed to halt the Communist drive. North Korean infantry and armor pressed the South Korean and American forces back into the southeast corner of the peninsula around the port of Pusan. Then, in an inspired stroke, MacArthur conducted an amphibious envelopment deep in the enemy rear at In'chon in mid-September 1950 and severed the North Korean line of supply. Spearheaded by American infantry and Marine units, the allies drove the North Koreans back across the 38th Parallel. Suddenly, the possibility of a traditional victory seemed close. Although the United Nations mandate of restoring the border had been fulfilled, Truman decided that the long-standing objective of reunifying Korea was within his grasp. He ordered MacArthur to pursue the enemy north across the 38th Parallel toward the Chinese border. By the last week in October the United Nations forces were on the verge of occupying all of North Korea. The president's remaining concern was Chinese intervention. He asked MacArthur what was its likelihood, and the general replied, "Very little."[17] Furthermore, MacArthur said that if the Chinese tried to challenge United Nations forces, American airpower would slaughter them. Reassured, Truman waited for victory.

Instead came the massive, surprise Chinese counteroffensive that drove the U.N. forces back across the 38th Parallel. MacArthur pleaded for the authority and strength to retaliate by blockading the Chinese coast, bombing and shelling Communist China's war industries, and other aggressive measures designed to take the fight to the enemy. After lengthy analysis, Truman concluded that the preservation of allied unity—it was unlikely that many allies would support a war against China—and the need to limit the risk of Russian involvement—Russia and China had recently revealed the existence of a mutual defense treaty—outweighed the benefits of MacArthur's proposals. He resolved that the appropriate strategy in Korea was to fight a limited war using a carefully calculated measure of American force to achieve something far less than the destruction and surrender of the enemy. Henceforth, the U.S. objective was to forge a political settlement by accepting an armistice. There would be no attempt at military victory, no grand alliance of the type that six years earlier had relentlessly pressed forward until overwhelming the Axis powers. Thwarting the enemy invasion was enough.[18]

After bitter fighting during which the Chinese captured Seoul and then lost it to a mid-March 1951 allied counterattack, the battle lines stabilized roughly along the original border. For two more long years the ground war witnessed periodic eruptions of bloody fighting as one side or the other tried to gain a tactical advantage to influence ongoing peace talks. In the air, restrictions against bombing the north end of the Yalu bridges forced American pilots to fly easily predictable paths through violent anti-aircraft fire while under attack from enemy jets that flew from base sanctuaries deemed off-limits to U.S. bombing. Finally, on July 27, 1953, the military armistice agreement at Panmunjom ended the fighting. A total of 142,091 American servicemen had been killed, wounded, missing, or captured to establish a boundary between North and South Korea that differed very little from that which existed before the war had begun. It was a bewildering outcome to many Americans.

The Korean War witnessed the rise of Communist China to great power status. Simultaneously, it established the American precedent of fighting a war with constraints on both how much power the nation would employ and how that power could be used. Additional constraints appeared even more likely since in 1952 American scientists exploded the world's first thermonuclear device and the Soviet Union followed suit the next year. Henceforth, presidents assumed an unprecedented responsibility. The threat of nuclear attack meant, for the first time, that peacetime presidents daily confronted life-and-death decisions that previous commanders in chief had faced only in wartime.

Among many consequences to flow from Truman's decision to resist Communist aggression in Korea was the simultaneous assumption of the burden of helping France defend Vietnam against a Communist insurgency. Within two days of the North Korean strike across the 38th Parallel, Truman ordered more than a doubling of military aid to the French and decided to send a military mission to Vietnam.[19] Largely overlooked at the time, it propelled the nation farther along a path leading to a rendezvous with defeat.

COMMAND DECISIONS

When President James Polk sent Zach Taylor's army to the disputed Rio Grande, the commander in chief expected and welcomed a military encounter with Mexico. In 1964, when U.S. warships steamed into the Gulf of Tonkin off the North Vietnamese coast, no high-ranking American official, let alone President Lyndon B. Johnson, anticipated armed conflict. Although the American military had been training the South Vietnamese since the mid-1950s, and by 1964 there were some 23,000 advisers in the South (118 of whom died that year), few people conceived that the nation was already at war. By design the naval patrols were provocative, and they served specific military purposes intended to constrain North Vietnam's ability to support its Viet Cong allies in the South, but the idea that North Vietnam, whose ragtag "fleet" had a limited offensive capability residing in a hand-ful of motor torpedo and motor gunboats, would attack the world's most powerful navy on the high seas was too improbable to enter-tain.[20] However, strategic assessments of the naval balance of power, made in secure, distant comfort, can seem irrelevant to a captain on the bridge of a vessel under threat. So it was on the afternoon of August 2, 1964.

On that day the captain of the U.S. destroyer *Maddox* became increasingly alarmed as lookouts and radar identified numerous North Vietnamese boats stalking his ship. When three of them closed rapidly, the *Maddox* fired warning shots. Undeterred, they closed the range. The command imperative for self-defense took over and the captain ordered his main battery to open fire. The hostile boats sped through this barrage and launched torpedoes. The *Maddox* dodged the torpedoes, one of which crossed two hun-dred yards astern, and raked a passing enemy boat with gunfire. Hard hit, her commander killed at his battle station, this boat and her two consorts pulled away. Likewise, the *Maddox* withdrew. The entire encounter had taken twenty-two minutes. The action ended when U.S. naval aircraft launched from a nearby aircraft carrier led by Commander James B. Stockdale responded to the *Maddox*'s distress call, blasted the already wounded enemy boat, and left it dead in the water and on fire.

As a naval battle, this had been decidedly small potatoes; one eighty-three-foot enemy boat sunk, another damaged. The only battle damage inflicted on the United States was one machine gun round that deflected off the *Maddox*'s fire director pedestal and lodged in an ammunition-handling compartment below, from which it would be extracted to become a museum curio back in Washington, D.C.[21] The engagement rose in significance not because of what had actu-ally transpired but because of what was to come.

In Washington, the president and his top advisers thought hard about the incident and chose forbearance. So extreme was the mismatch between the two navies that the encounter seemed illogi-cal and therefore inexplicable. They concluded that perhaps the attack had resulted from the actions of some rogue North Vietnamese naval officer. Regardless, the United States would not back away; the freedom of the seas seemed to be at stake. Accord-ingly, Johnson ordered the patrols in the Gulf of Tonkin resumed.

Two days later the *Maddox*, reinforced by another destroyer, re-turned to the same waters. The previous night South Vietnamese naval craft had raided along this coast as part of an ongoing series of American-assisted operations designed to harass the North. Given these raids, and the earlier attack against the *Maddox*, everyone could be expected to be edgy. Sure enough, during daylight hours the *Maddox* reported that enemy boats seemed to be again shadowing the destroyer. At 8:41 that evening, in heavy seas and poor visibility, the *Maddox*'s radar picked up a surface contact forty-two miles ahead in the area the two destroyers intended to patrol. The American ships turned away only to have the unidentified vessels change course to intercept. The Americans altered course again and the radar contacts drifted out of range.

Some thirty minutes later both destroyers picked up three or four contacts approaching rapidly from astern. Soon thereafter, another contact about ten thousand yards distant appeared from a different direction. When this contact neared to seven thousand yards, both destroyers opened fire. The ensuing four-hour engagement would become exceptionally controversial; complete with enemy torpedo sightings unverified by sonar detection, U.S. naval aircraft strafing apparent enemy boats while other planes, including one piloted again by Stockdale, reported no sightings. On balance the evidence indicates that on this night, as had occurred two days previously, North Vietnamese naval vessels attacked American ships on the high seas. What is certain is that this was the conclusion reached by everyone up the chain of command.[22]

Following a lunchtime briefing on August 4, during which his highest officials unanimously recommended retaliation, Lyndon Johnson authorized air strikes against North Vietnam. Commander Stockdale, who led navy jets on this raid, later recalled that this was one of the few times combat officers had the latitude to prepare the mission as they thought fit.[23] Thereafter, systems analysts in the Pentagon interfered in nearly every tactical decision, including the number of planes, type of munitions carried by the planes, and route to and from targets. These were even more onerous restrictions than those applied to the pilots who had attacked the Yalu River bridges in Korea. Such decisions made the difference between pilot survival or shootdown, and in the future the aviators would become increasingly frustrated that a faceless bureaucracy controlled their fate. The first raids were not subject to such control and they successfully struck a petroleum depot, naval bases, and boats in harbor.

Even with full tactical control against a surprised and unprepared enemy, the strikes were not without danger. Antiaircraft fire shot down two planes, killing one pilot and forcing another, Lieutenant (j.g.) Everett Alvarez, Jr., to bail out. Captured on the ground, Alvarez became the first American pilot to suffer at the ungentle hands of the North Vietnamese. For the next eight and one-half years, until his release in 1973, he endured physical and mental torture. Alvarez could not know that he would be the first of many, nor could anyone else anticipate all that would flow from these initial actions in the Tonkin Gulf. Before the next year was over, Lyndon Johnson and the American people would find themselves in a war in Vietnam.

*   *   *

From the earliest days of his political life Johnson believed in a strong military "to fulfill our moral obligations to the world."[24] He also believed the country had to select carefully the times and places to engage. When the fate of Dien Bien Phu hung in the balance in 1954, Johnson had helped mold congressional opposition to American intervention on behalf of the French. "No more Koreas with the United States furnishing 90% of the manpower," he had said. However, after Dien Bien Phu fell, Johnson displayed the politician's zeal to take advantage of the rival party's setbacks when he criticized Eisenhower's policy of nonintervention.[25]

Six years later, Vice President Johnson visited South Vietnam for the first time. He reported to the commander in chief that he had learned much more than he had expected and had no doubt about what needed to be done: "The battle against Communism must be joined in Southeast Asia." He told President John F. Kennedy that failure to do so would surrender the Pacific to the Communists and the next line of defense would begin on the California coast. He predicted that in the future the United States would have to decide whether to commit major forces or abandon the effort in Vietnam.[26]

It is easier to make aggressive recommendations when you are not the man in charge, but Johnson's report to his boss is notable on three accounts: he believed in the "Domino Theory," the notion that if South Vietnam passed into Communist hands the remaining countries in Southeast Asia would topple like a row of dominoes; he believed the nation needed to make a major effort to avoid that dire outcome; and he understood that it might require American foot soldiers to fight on the Asian mainland. Kennedy shared Johnson's views, and in addition had his own reasons to escalate the U.S. effort in Vietnam.[27]

Kennedy had examined the future, and one of the major strategic challenges he foresaw was coping with Communist-inspired wars of national liberation. They provided both threat and opportunity. Defeating some Communist guerrillas would be a satisfying rebound from his recent run of foreign policy setbacks, in particular the Bay of Pigs fiasco and an embarrassing confrontation with Soviet Premier Nikita Khrushchev in Vienna. Accordingly, Kennedy promoted something called the Special Group (Counterinsurgency) intended to ensure that government agencies recognized the dangers posed by insurgency and trained the military to defeat guerrillas. Heretofore, the twin topics of nuclear warfare and conventional war in Europe had dominated American strategic thinking. Trying to reorient toward guerrilla warfare proved difficult. The great sea of bureaucratic inertia formed a wide gulf between Kennedy's plan and its execution. Although the Special Group served successfully as a consciousness-raising device—soon there was a veritable government-wide fad featuring plans and programs devoted to counterinsurgency—the real effect was minimal. Since Kennedy wanted counterinsurgency training to be a promotion requirement for all generals, the war colleges and military schools offered a variety of special classes. In 1962 alone, some fifty thousand officers and civilians participated in this Pentagon growth industry by attending counterinsurgency training, a ticket-punching exercise of trifling value.[28] Events would soon show that little practical strategic thinking had taken place.

Frustrated by continued problems in Vietnam, Kennedy proceeded to approve a United States–South Vietnam partnership. He called for greater American military support contingent upon South Vietnamese President Ngo Dinh Diem's acceptance of performance criteria. In other words, if Diem ended government-wide corruption and took meaningful steps toward democratic reform, the United States would reward him with ever more aid. Given Kennedy's familiarity with the "aid without influence" problems during the 1950s, when the South Vietnamese eagerly accepted aid and just as enthusiastically resisted reform, this was remarkably naive. The real result of Kennedy's diplomacy was that American prestige became increasingly associated with the fate of the shaky South Vietnamese government.

Kennedy dispatched a constant stream of American experts to Vietnam to assess progress. Typical was the fall 1963 visit by Marine General Victor Krulak and the State Department's Joseph Mendenhall. Krulak listened to military men in the field, Mendenhall to civilians stationed in the cities. Krulak reported that the political crisis was a temporary phenomenon and otherwise matters were progressing satisfactorily. In contrast, Mendenhall reported that the root causes of the political crisis lay in the very nature of the Diem regime. Perplexed, Kennedy asked, "Did you two gentlemen visit the same country?"[29]

So it continued into October with the Pentagon waxing optimistic about the military situation while the State Department grew ever more pessimistic about political affairs. It was their joint failure to perceive that in this war the military and the political were inseparable. Then the assassin's shot rang out in Dallas and Lyndon Johnson became commander in chief.

*   *   *

Four days after becoming president, Johnson made his first important decision regarding Vietnam. He believed it his duty to continue the popular fallen leader's programs. Accordingly, he signed a Vietnam policy document stating that he intended to persevere with Kennedy's policy.[30] What he did not realize was that he had signed onto an ongoing and mistaken estimate of the nature of the Vietnam conflict. The document, which spelled out American strategy, and said that the central U.S. objective was to assist the South Vietnamese "to win their contest against the externally directed and supported communist conspiracy."[31] In fact, most of the guerrillas, the Viet Cong, were South Vietnamese. They received material support from the North, but North Vietnam was an "external" source only because of a ten-year-old artificial division of Vietnam into two countries, a division imposed by agreement of the Great Powers in Geneva in 1954. The conflict was a civil war. By describing it otherwise, and basing decisions upon this flawed description, Johnson placed the American effort in Southeast Asia on unsound strategic underpinnings.

Like Harry Truman, Johnson had an international outlook that had been molded by World War II. He saw the consequences of appeasement and believed that had the Western democracies stood up to aggression war might have been avoided. To him,

Vietnam in 1963 was an analogous situation.[32] He saw communism on the march with its strategic pincers about to engulf South Vietnam. Peking, bellicose and boastful, taunted the United States by calling it a "paper tiger," promoted "wars of national liberation," and seemed to mastermind the Communist surge with help from its allies in Indonesia, Vietnam, and Korea.[33] Russia was a fellow traveler, using its immense resources to aid and abet the drive. To halt aggression, to prevent the strategic debacle predicted by the Domino Theory, to uphold Kennedy's commitment, to avoid the nightmare criticism that he was the coward who abandoned an ally, Johnson determined that the first domino, South Vietnam, would stand firm.[34]

STRATEGIC CHOICES

Less than a year later, in response to the August 1964 North Vietnamese attack against the destroyer *Maddox* in the Gulf of Tonkin, Johnson asked Congress for the authority "to take all necessary measures to repel an armed attack against the forces of the United States and to prevent further aggression."[35] By a Senate vote of 88 to 2 and a unanimous House vote the so-called Gulf of Tonkin Resolution passed. For the next two years the commander in chief cited this resolution as the legal basis for his actions in Vietnam. Curiously, having launched retaliatory air strikes against the North, and having received overwhelming bipartisan political support, in the late summer of 1964 the president grew cautious.

There was one more naval encounter in the Tonkin Gulf in mid-September, and then Johnson ordered an end to the destroyer patrols off the North Vietnamese coast. The commander in chief in the Pacific argued that American failure to assert its freedom of the seas would send the wrong message to Hanoi. The Pacific Fleet commander howled that cessation of these patrols would convince China that the United States was indeed a "paper tiger." From Saigon, General William C. Westmoreland urged that the patrols continue. To their joint disgust, the president ended the operations anyway. He was an inherently cautious man who, in his own words, liked to have all his ammunition ready before bringing up his guns, and he was not ready for expanded action in Vietnam just yet. First he had to defeat a political challenge from a hard-line Republican military booster named Barry Goldwater.

As the election campaign progressed, Johnson found it made good politics to maintain a sharp contrast between himself and Goldwater. Like Wilson's promises before World War I, and Franklin Roosevelt's 1940 pledge not to send Americans into a foreign war, Johnson proclaimed that he was "not about to send American boys 9 or 10,000 miles away from home to do what Asian boys ought to be doing for themselves."[36] Initially true to his word, Johnson again forbade retaliation when just before the election a Viet Cong mortar attack on Bienhoa air base destroyed U.S. bombers and killed four American servicemen. Likewise, after his landslide victory over Goldwater he did not respond overtly to a terrorist bomb that exploded on Christmas Eve in a Saigon hotel, killing two Americans and wounding many more. To the military this seemed inconsistent: the attack in the Tonkin Gulf had neither injured nor killed any Americans yet the commander in chief had ordered retaliatory bombing. Subsequent Viet Cong actions in the South did harm American servicemen and the president did nothing. Military men worried what this would portend. Keen-eyed observers in North Vietnam did not fail to note that regardless of American bluster—the Gulf of Tonkin's promise of "all necessary measures" to repel attacks—there had been no follow-up reprisals. They concluded that domestic political concerns influenced the American commander in chief's strategic thinking.

In fact, after his electoral triumph Johnson was hard at work trying to devise a Vietnam strategy and he quite simply had not made up his mind what to do. He worried about taking any "tall dives" into a Vietnam commitment.[37] This anxiety prompted him to do what he always did when on the cusp of a decision; he picked the brains of his closest advisers.

They were the "Kennedy gang," the Cabinet officers Johnson inherited from his predecessor. Later, the president would confess that one of his greatest mistakes was not firing them all—with the notable exception of Dean Rusk, who not coincidentally was a fellow southerner—since they had little loyalty to him.[38] Just now, Johnson listened attentively to State Department Counselor Walt Rostow's theory on how to combat an insurgency such as that taking place in Vietnam. Rostow postulated that the limited and gradual application of military power, coupled with economic and political pressure, against a nation supporting an insurgency would convince that nation to cease its support. This line of reasoning was eminently logical to Johnson. It was much like the type of political persuasion he had successfully employed in the Senate. He said he could 'filibuster" Ho Chi Minh, meeting Ho's enormous initial resistance with "a steady whittling away" that would cause Ho to hurry "to get it over with."[39]

The idea that Ho Chi Minh could be "filibustered" would have amazed anyone who had carefully studied that iron-willed leader. Equally unfortunate, not only did Rostow's theory promulgate the misconception that the nation supporting the insurgency, North Vietnam, was somehow distinct from the greater whole that was Vietnam, it advocated a restrained use of power that Hanoi's leaders would come to view as an encouraging sign of American weakness. All of this would become clearer, although a careful examination of Vietnam's history of struggle against foreigners could have provided the foresight that the commander in chief desperately needed just now, and a comparison of Rostow's theory with Korean War negotiating experience would not have been inappropriate.

By the beginning of 1965 some 23,700 American advisers and support troops were on the ground in Vietnam, and although the frequency of Viet Cong terrorist operations had increased, fewer than 50 Americans had been killed. However, even while the Viet Cong steadily expanded their control over the hinterland, South Vietnamese authorities had fallen into a self-consuming frenzy of coup plotting.[40] Johnson's advisers were divided about what to make of this. A few said that a stable, reform-minded South Vietnamese government had to emerge before anything else. The majority, including the top military men, reasoned that aggression from the North was the primary problem. It was a critical strategic distinction dictating the path of U.S. intervention. If the emphasis was on internal instability, then the conflict could be viewed as a civil war in which competition for peasant support from the Vietnamese people would prove decisive. If otherwise, then all South Vietnam had to do was to provide a "platform" upon which American armed forces would defeat the North Vietnamese.[41]

No prior commander in chief had so thoroughly premeditated a decision to go to war. Lyndon Johnson employed a vast information-collection and analysis bureaucracy to undergird his contemplation. He listened to the government's most experienced civilian and military thinkers.[42] They concluded that the current drift of events was leading to a disastrous defeat and that the appropriate response was "to use our military power . . . to force a change of Communist policy."[43] The president concurred. If the Viet Cong struck again, the commander in chief would respond in kind by ordering the bombing of North Vietnam.

Too often in the past American servicemen had suffered during a war's early stages because of inadequate prewar preparation. Consequently, National Security Adviser McGeorge Bundy and Secretary of Defense Robert McNamara pressed Johnson for a firm, clear statement that the United States had embarked upon a new policy so they could make appropriate military and budgetary plans. Johnson refused. He claimed he did not want to overly alarm Peking and Moscow by a sudden announcement of change, but in the back of his mind was the uncomfortable memory of his recent election promises not to escalate the fighting and his worries that if too much political attention focused on Vietnam it would undermine his domestic agenda.

The decision to begin the bombing—Operation Rolling Thunder, it would be called—unleashed a flood that swept toward an even more momentous decision point regarding the commitment of American ground forces. The decision not to acknowledge the change in policy gave birth to suspicions that the commander in chief was being less than candid with the American people regarding the war in Vietnam.

*   *   *

In February 1965, Viet Cong attacks around Pleiku killed nine Americans and injured nearly one hundred more. In private discussion Johnson angrily commented, "We have kept our gun over the mantel and our shells in the cupboard . . . And what was the result? They are killing our men while they sleep in the night. I can't ask our American soldiers out there to continue to fight with one hand tied behind their backs."[44] So he sent U.S. warplanes against four North Vietnamese targets. Poor weather prevented three of the missions. When the military men wanted to return the next day to take out the three remaining targets, Johnson declined. Citing the fact that the Soviet premier was visiting Hanoi just then, the commander in chief explained that he did not want to provoke the Soviets and give the impression that the Untied States had begun a sustained air offensive.

Within days, another Viet Cong bomb blew up an enlisted men's barracks, killing 23 Americans. Johnson again examined retaliatory options. The military men wanted to bomb two barracks and a key bridge, while some of the president's civilian advisers wanted to delay action until the Soviet premier had departed Asia. To satisfy this concern, Johnson deleted the bridge target before authorizing the strike. When he did approve another bombing raid following a deadly Viet Cong mortar attack that killed 9 and wounded 107 U.S. servicemen, the president hastened to add publicly that the response was measured, appropriate, and that the United States had no desire for a wider war.

All of this was a very peculiar way to utilize airpower, and it frustrated the military men enormously. Their concept of air operations derived from World War II, when air fleets pulverized military and economic targets in Europe and Japan. There had been virtually no constraints, and hundreds of thousands of civilians had died beneath the rain of high explosives, firebombs, and ultimately atomic weapons. It proved hard for the airpower enthusiasts to accept all of the factors that Johnson insisted should enter the calculus of target selection. Indeed, the idea of "tit for tat" retaliation had never been part of any country's strategic bombing doctrine.

The beginning of Rolling Thunder on March 2, 1965, likewise did not conform to the military's idea of how to utilize airpower. It started as an eight-week program of graduated military pressure limited to selected targets in the southern third of North Vietnam for the purposes of signaling U.S. resolve and raising the morale of the South Vietnamese in the hope that this would somehow enhance the stability of the South Vietnamese government. It involved relatively few airplanes and it infuriated Admiral U.S. Grant Sharp, the officer charged with its conduct. In conjunction with air force officers, Sharp had identified ninety-four key targets in North Vietnam. He advocated a blitz attack to destroy them. Moreover, Sharp knew that if North Vietnam had a vulnerable spot it was the port of Haiphong.[45]

North Vietnam imported about 85 percent of its required warfighting material, everything from bullets for the incomparable Kalashnikov AK-47 assault rifle to SA-2 surface-to-air missiles (SAMs), through Haiphong. Reconnaissance aircraft clearly showed Soviet and Soviet Bloc freighters occupying every berth in the harbor and unloading war supplies twenty-four hours a day. It was an obvious strategic chokepoint fully appreciated by American strategists but the commander in chief deemed it off-limits.[46] Johnson forbade bombing, mining, or naval blockade of Haiphong. Not until President Richard Nixon authorized mining was the torrent of war material that poured though Haiphong halted. A one-day mining operation in 1972 closed Haiphong Harbor completely. Not until the U.S. Navy swept the mines a year later following a so-called truce did ships dare to enter the harbor.

In 1965 and afterward, Johnson confronted the same questions regarding Russian intentions that Truman had addressed in Korea. He weighed the expected gains resulting from attacks on Haiphong against the likely Soviet response. The Kremlin, as well as Peking, enthusiastically voiced support for "wars of National Liberation," and Johnson considered that perhaps this indicated a strategic change from Khrushchev's policy of "peaceful coexistence." Khrushchev himself had been deposed. Only twice since the Bolshevik Revolution had power changed hands in Russia, and each time chaotic disruption ensued. Just now Russia was a wild card. Johnson also had to assess the global strategic implications of a strike against Haiphong. American intelligence had begun to appreciate the extent of the rupture between China and Russia. But recently the Chinese foreign secretary had visited Moscow, perhaps indicating that the rupture was narrowing. If mining closed Haiphong, the only alternative would be to send Soviet supplies via Chinese rail lines. Heretofore, the Chinese had displayed solid reluctance to cooperate with the Russians. So Johnson had to consider the distinct possibility that hard strikes against North Vietnam might drive the two Communist giants back together, and this would represent a strategic defeat at least as great as that resulting from the loss of Vietnam.

A second option, pressed upon the commander in chief by his military leaders, involved bombing transportation chokepoint—briges, rail junctions, and the like—in Hanoi, Haiphong, and along the Chinese border. When Johnson deliberated upon this strategy, the specter of Korea, where Chinese "volunteers" had launched a surprise offensive that led to a lengthy war of attrition, haunted him. But it would not be like Korea this time, it would be much worse—because China had recently exploded its first atomic weapon and thus had nuclear power to back up its 2.5-million-man army. During early 1965, the Joint Chiefs of Staff told the president that there was a fair chance the Peking would commit some soldiers to the fight if the United States struck decisively through the air against North Vietnam.

When pondering plans for an aggressive offensive, the president also asked what would happen if a Soviet freighter struck a mine, suffered casualties, or even sank? Soviet leaders could apply pressure at some point of U.S. vulnerability such as Berlin, or even send minesweepers to clear the shipping lanes. Everyone had seen how a similar confrontation in the waters off Cuba had brought the world to the brink of nuclear holocaust a little over two years before. Johnson speculated on the likelihood that "some damn fool will drop some TNT down the smokestack of a Russian freighter in Haiphong, or some plane will get lost and dump its bombs over China, and we're in World War III."[47] He decided it was too much to risk.[48]

Last, one other important factor influenced Johnson's decision on how to conduct the air war. Many of his top civilian advisers believed it important to limit the war's violence and thereby give North Vietnam an opportunity to explore negotiations without complete loss of face. A proud man himself, Johnson appreciated this logic.[49] These advisers conceived of the unstruck targets around Hanoi and Haiphong as hostage to future U.S. action and thus a check on North Vietnamese aggressiveness.[50] Consequently, the president order the Pentagon to establish "Prohibited Areas" off-limits to U.S. warplanes and two "Restricted Areas"—a thirty-by-ten-mile area around Hanoi and a ten-by-four-mile area around Haiphong—where only very limited raids could take place. Because the combination of prohibited and restricted areas covered virtually every important target, Rolling Thunder had to attack targets of decidedly secondary importance. The president accepted this, decreeing during his weekly review of Rolling Thunder that he would allow planes to rebomb targets, while adding, "I don't wanna run out of targets and I don't wanna go to Hanoi."[51] The resultant limited effectiveness made Rolling Thunder an easy target for criticism by the emerging school of doubters and critics.

Even in the areas where Johnson permitted the planes to fly, the target-selection process for Rolling Thunder was unlike anything in previous U.S. military experience. The Joint Chiefs received target recommendations from Admiral Sharp. The Chiefs endorsed or deleted targets and passed on recommendations to the Secretary of Defense. Before McNamara read this paper, several layers of civilian "experts"—the secretary's systems analysts as well as members of the State Department—annotated the recommendations.

Then the commander in chief consulted with his closest advisers during his Tuesday luncheons and made the final target selections, often complete with number of sorties allowed, munitions carried, and flight paths. Once the recommendations left the offices of the Joint Chiefs, no military man had any input into the decision-making process.

It was a mistaken idea taken to absurd lengths. It was an example of how tactical meddling by the commander in chief could be counterproductive. It was a policy that needlessly killed American pilots. Although military men understood this, no military man stood up to protest effectively. Instead, complaints passed routinely up the chain of command and were ignored.[52]

So the pattern was set. For the remainder of its history, the bombing of the North was a major focus of Johnson's attention. He devoted an incredible amount of time and energy trying to manipulate Rolling Thunder to achieve diverse political goals. His meddling reflected his own uncertainty. One moment he was interested in peace on "any honorable basis," saying, "I don't want to bomb those places, I really don't," complaining that "bomb, bomb, bomb" was all his generals knew.[53] The next he was full of determination, observing that there were "plenty more targets" and "we got to find 'em and kill 'em." Over time, he permitted more targets to be struck, but never in a systematic or all-inclusive manner. This restraint permitted the North Vietnamese to relocate important assets to locations where they rightly anticipated bombing would always be forbidden.

Lyndon Johnson was at ease with political strategizing, familiar with the art of congressional compromise. The dictates of power politics in an international arena overwhelmed him. The constant stream of high-ranking civilian and military experts he dispatched to Vietnam to assess the situation gave little help.

He complained: "They tell me it's terrible, but not what to do about it."[54]

*   *   *

From 1965 to 1968 the air war continued, fought in extraordinary fashion.[55] Pilots had to watch helplessly while the North Vietnamese completed surface-to-air missile (SAM) sites and stockpiled missiles. In the days following the first shootdown of an American plane by a SAM missile, it was not the operational commanders who planned countermeasures. Instead, in an amazing example of inappropriate micromanagement, officials devoted an entire Cabinet meeting in Washington to the subject of which SAM sites to attack.[56] For some time thereafter, rules of engagement specified that only after the missiles had fired first could U.S. aircraft attack the sites. Consequently, the enemy was able to disperse them throughout a fortified air defense network that grew to become the most dangerous in military history. So it was also with the enemy's MiG fighters. The MiGs flew from bases around Hanoi that were off-limits to American strikes. Thus, instead of destroying them on the ground, pilots had to permit the MiGs to take off before they could fight them.

In sum, as Admiral Sharp explained, U.S. restraint permitted war material to reach Haiphong "from external sources through routes immune from attack" and allowed the enemy "to then disperse and store this material in politically assured sanctuaries from which it could easily be infiltrated into South Vietnam."[57] The Secretary of Defense failed to understand this. To him, it made little difference if a rifle was interdicted in Haiphong or in Laos, it was merely a matter of effort and expense. It made a great deal of difference to the pilots who expended the effort and faced the ultimate cost of loss of life.[58] For them, the rules of engagement combined with frequent poor weather to take away many fighting advantages and to put enormous strain on their missions:

> *Whether you stayed above the clouds, went below them, or tried to hide inside them, you were in for trouble.*
>
> *If you stay on top on the way to the target you can look for Migs, but you cannot see the ground for that extra double check on your approach, nor can you see the Sams as they kick up a boiling cauldron of dust when they leap from their launch sites. If you can't see them on the way up when they are relatively slow . . . you are in trouble, for by the time they come bursting up through the undercast, accelerated and guiding on course for you, your chances of evading them are slim. If you duck just under the clouds you have a better visual shot at the Sams and better visual navigation, but you give both the Sam people and the ground gunners a perfect silhouette of your force against the cloud backdrop at the same time telegraphing your exact altitude for both sighting and fuzing purposes. If you go far below the clouds, up goes the fuel consumption and up goes the exposure to smaller*

guns on the ground . . . It was a tough decision that constantly faced fighter commanders going north.[59]

Human loss greatly pained Lyndon Johnson. However, he had little appreciation of the link between the fighting constraints he forced upon American pilots and their subsequent deaths.

*   *   *

While Johnson awaited results from Operation Rolling Thunder, a second element of his strategy emerged. In part, he had begun the bombing to outflank conservative criticism that he was too soft on communism.[60] Then, on March 24, 1965, the first "teach-in" against the war occurred at the University of Michigan. Domestic protest against the bombing mobilized with startling suddenness. Initially the president doubted the significance of such protests, telling an aide, "Don't pay any attention to what those little shits on the campuses do."[61] When Gallup polls indicated a dramatic increase in peace sentiment, the president began to take heed.

To answer his liberal critics, and to assure that Hanoi clearly understood that he preferred peace, in April he spoke at John Hopkins University, urging North Vietnam to negotiate a diplomatic settlement and promising lavish developmental aid—he would turn the Mekong Delta region into an Asian TVA, he said—following the peace. His speech was part of a two-fisted strategy: one fist held military power; the other, peace proposals. He believed that whenever he increased military pressure he had simultaneously to make diplomatic overtures. It was a strategy in marked contrast to the Communist approach of dictating peace from behind the barrel of a gun. It contradicted the military maxim, expressed by Napoleon, to wage war "energetically and with severity" since that was the only way to make it shorter and less inhuman.[62] However well intentioned—and the president himself doubted the speech's efficacy, asking confidants why the North should negotiate when U.S. pressure had just begun—the speech undermined one of the major purposes of Rolling Thunder, the demonstration of U.S. resolve.[63]

The Ambassador to South Vietnam, Maxwell Taylor, had cautioned against this type of diplomacy, explaining that Hanoi had not yet realized the extent of American determination. He warned that Hanoi's fear of bombing strikes seemed to be offset by its calculation that bombing restraints and peace overtures were indicative of "US desire to find a face-saving solution that would permit US disengagement."[64] Hanoi's rejection of Johnson's olive branch fulfilled Taylor's prophecy.

To the president's dismay, the North seemed unresponsive to the bombing campaign, or if it responded it was through military escalation. Two days after Rolling Thunder began, a Viet Cong bomb detonated in a bar, killing two Americans. Such incidents continued. The service family viewing stand at a softball game, bars frequented by Americans, and barracks where servicemen slept were all targets. Terrorist attacks culminated with the explosion of a 250-pound bomb outside the U.S. embassy, which killed two and wounded forty-eight Americans. In the field, South Vietnam army units continued to get battered while Intelligence reported heavier infiltration coming down the Ho Chi Minh Trail. The CIA told the president that American effort had failed to alter the essential equation of power in South Vietnam.[65] By June, the commandeer in chief demanded that his Secretary of State explain the seeming ineffectiveness of the bombing campaign. Dean Rusk replied, "We never thought it would bring them running." Glumly, Johnson rejoined, "They think they are winning. We think they are winning."[66] Because of this perception, Lyndon Johnson reluctantly turned to confront another major strategic issue, a dread decision whether to send American soldiers to fight on the ground in Asia.

9 ⟱

GROUND WAR IN ASIA

"No one starts a war . . . without first being clear in his mind what he intends to achieve by that war and how he intends to conduct it."

KARL VON CLAUSEWITZ, 1827[1]

UPPING THE ANTE

THROUGHOUT HIS POLITICAL LIFE, LYNDON JOHNSON HAD SHOWN A BRIL-liant capacity to reconcile competing goals. Try as he might, he could not do the same now. He felt hemmed in by his limited choices, telling his wife in early March, "I can't get out. I can't finish it with what I have got. So what the Hell can I do?"[2] Before sending "Johnson City boys" to Vietnam he wanted to know that the war could be won.[3] But the internal logic of past decisions pushed inexorably toward new commitments.[4]

The current strategy of persuading the North to negotiate hinged upon the bombing campaign. Many of the planes flying the missions used bases in South Vietnam, and those bases required protection. Unlike other imponderables, this was a military reality that could be precisely understood. During their war against the French, the Communist guerrillas had displayed an uncanny ability to infiltrate well-defended bases in order to destroy planes on the ground. Their recent attacks against Da Nang and Bien Hoa proved they had not lost this ability. To defend the staging areas for Rolling Thunder, Westmoreland asked for two more Marine battalions. On the surface this seemed a small and reasonable request. However, back at the beginning of the year, Maxwell Taylor had informed the commander in chief what such a request portended.

Taylor explained that Westmoreland's comprehensive study of the requirements to secure U.S. bases in Vietnam demonstrated it would take "the startling requirement" of thirty-four battalions. He described the calculation in language a civilian could easily understand: to secure any given point from Viet Cong mortar fire, a defender had to secure an area of roughly sixteen square miles. To man such an extensive perimeter meant that a single large airfield would require six battalions. Worse, Taylor predicted that the additional commitment of U.S. combat forces would be offset by the likelihood that the South Vietnamese would let the Americans fight their war. The South Vietnamese possessed the manpower and basic skills to win, he explained, but they lacked motivation. More U.S. troops would merely erode motivation further and encourage the South Vietnamese to unload missions on the United States. Taylor concluded, "Intervention with ground combat forces would at best buy time and would lead to ever increasing commitments until, like the French, we would be occupying an essentially hostile foreign country."[5] Taylor had well served his president; events proved his forecast all too accurate.

Simultaneously, General Westmoreland too had a duty to perform. Charged with helping the bombing campaign, he personally inspected the key base at Da Nang. He saw that the Marine engineers building a position atop Hill 327 were isolated and vulnerable. The security of the airfield itself was porous, and for this reason he had asked for reinforcements.[6] He wanted more than just additional manpower; he wanted the tactical freedom to allow the Marines to patrol aggressively. Indeed, the alternative idea— that the Marines should merely defend passively by hunkering down in their foxholes and trenches to serve as sitting ducks for enemy bombardment—went against Marine tradition, good military doctrine, and every instinct instilled in the American fighting man from private to general.[7] The military chain of command functioned properly by candidly conveying to the president the need for tactical freedom while explaining that it "will open a new phase of combat" and substantially alter "the methods of conducting the war."[8]

Sending more Marines was Lyndon Johnson's decision to make. His analysis of Russian and Chinese intentions told him that if he sent ground forces to Vietnam, he would have to impose con-straints greater than those under which Americans had fought in Korea. Instead, he might have chosen a more favorable field and pulled out of Vietnam at this point, citing the prevailing South Vietnamese political instability, inefficiency, and corruption as a rationale. Johnson had the rare advantages of having just won a landslide election and enjoyed a huge majority in the Senate and House of Representatives. The public had voted for him largely because he was a military moderate. He could have ended America's commitment to Vietnam at low political cost, and this is exactly what a handful of advisers, including Vice President Hubert Humphrey, recommended. Trusted troubleshooter Clark Clifford told him to avoid an open-ended troop commitment that could become a "quagmire," to accept a less than perfect negotiated settlement because there was no realistic chance of ultimate vic-tory. The nation would "learn to live with" a compromise.[9] "I suspect," wrote General Westmoreland with the advantage of hind-sight, "few in the world would have faulted us at that point had we thrown up our hands in despair."

Johnson chose to up the ante. He sent the two Marine battalions and additional support troops, thus raising the total commitment to forty thousand, and shortly thereafter, in the first week of April 1965, approved a change in their mission to permit them to initi-ate combat.[10] Henceforth, as Westmoreland later wrote, "the time when we could have withdrawn with some grace and honor had passed."[11]

Simultaneously, Johnson insisted that an effort be made to avoid the impression that there was either a large buildup under way or any fundamental change in the U.S. mission. The president could and did tell himself that he made the decision both to avoid pub-licity in order to keep Hanoi from demanding that Peking and Moscow match the American effort, and to provide Ho Chi Minh with face-saving cover once Ho saw reason and gave up the fight. But surely something else influenced him as well.

All presidents experience difficulty in peacetime, and even more so in times of armed conflict, in separating the national interest from their own political interests. In the late spring of 1965 Lyndon Johnson was within reach of achieving his lifelong ambi-tion. He called it a "golden time" with a huge Democratic majority in Congress and "the right President."[12] He wanted congressional attention to focus on his domestic social agenda, the Great Society programs, that he expected would be his historical legacy. Congressional passage was so close he "could see and almost touch [his] youthful dream of improving life for more people . . . than any other political leader, including FDR . . . I was determined to keep the war from shattering that dream." Johnson knew that many conservative congressional leaders, particularly southerners who held key committee positions, would seize any pretext to derail measures intended to help poor minorities. "I knew the Congress as I know Lady Bird," he recalled, "and I knew the day it exploded into a major debate on the war, that day would be the beginning of the end of the Great Society."[13]

So, when a reporter asked if there were any circumstances under which a large number of Americans might become involved in fighting, Johnson answered that the U.S. purpose remained "to advise and to assist" the South Vietnamese in resisting aggression.[14] He spoke vaguely about the future and failed to mention his recent decision approving the Marines' combat mission and a 150 percent increase in U.S. combat forces. He ordered Taylor not to explain the whole program just yet, but rather to announce individual deployments as the troops arrived in Vietnam. He instructed Westmoreland to manage the buildup "at lowest key possible."[15]

Westmoreland obeyed, but then and thereafter the president's evasiveness caused him enormous difficulty. Military headquarters in Saigon already had experienced some problems with the press. Westmoreland's predecessor had been well known for his rosy claims of progress, statements undercut by the reports of field officers and journalists. Tension between the press and the military had always been present during prior wars, but in Vietnam a new breed of reporters who realized they could enhance their careers by discrediting authority exacerbated the problem.

Then, somehow the newly arriving troops did not quite get the word to maintain a low profile. The Marines landed on Vietnam's coast in full battle gear complete with tanks and artillery, looking as if they were restaging the Iwo Jima invasion.[16] In keeping with orders from Washington, a military spokesman claimed that they had an exclusively defensive mission. When reporters accompanied them on missions and saw they were not sitting passively in their foxholes but rather were aggressively searching for the enemy, they again queried officials in Saigon and Washington about the Marines' mission. Finally, two months after the president's decision, a government public relations official confirmed the change.

An indignant storm of protest ensued, typified by a *New York Times* editorial: "The American people were told by a minor State Department official yesterday that, in effect, they were in a land war on the continent of Asia."[17]

"Historically, American confidence in its commander in chief stemmed from reciprocal trust. Lyndon Johnson broke faith with the American people and gave birth to a disastrous credibility gap.

*   *   *

Back in March, disappointed with the lack of results from Rolling Thunder, the president had dispatched the U.S. Army Chief of Staff, General Harold K. Johnson, to Vietnam. His departing advice was quintessential Lyndon Johnson: "You generals have all been educated at the taxpayer's expense, and you're not giving me any ideas and any solutions for this damn little pissant country." He did not need ten generals to come in and tell him ten times to bomb. He needed answers. As the general prepared to depart, the president thrust his index finger against his chest and said, "You get things bubbling, General."[18] Shortly thereafter, Johnson made his intentions even clearer. Bluntly, he told the Joint Chiefs to come up with measures to "kill more VC." In the mind of any American military man, the U.S. military was a killing machine par excellence. Given the resources, if the commander in chief wanted to kill more Viet Cong, the U.S. Army could oblige.

Accordingly, General Westmoreland began asking for further substantial reinforcements.[19] McNamara encouraged him with the words not to "worry about the economy of the country, the availability of forces, or public or Congressional attitudes."[20] However, there was a manpower limit constraining what Westmoreland could ask for. For domestic political reasons, the president did not want to call up the Reserves. This was most awkward because, ever since the end of World War II, American military strategy had been based on the idea that any significant conflict would involve the Reserves. Army Chief of Staff General Johnson recognized that a terrible blunder was taking place and resolved to resign in protest. He rehearsed in his mind what he would tell the president:

> *You have refused to tell the country they cannot fight a war without mobilization; you have required me to send men into battle with little hope of their ultimate victory; and you have forced us*

in the military to violate almost every one of the principles of war in Vietnam. Therefore I resign and will hold a press conference after I walk out your door.

In the event, as had occurred when aviation officers chose duty over protest and accepted the constraints on Rolling Thunder, General Johnson changed his mind at the last minute in the belief that he could do more for his country by working from within than protesting from without. At the end of his life he related that his reluctance to protest effectively, this "lapse in moral courage," was his greatest regret.[21]

The future would show that the decision not to call the Reserves at a time when the army was rapidly expanding was one of Johnson's worst mistakes. It overstretched the leadership pool. In lieu of the trained Reserves, Officer Candidate Schools churned out 3,500 graduates per month. In comparison, West Point produced 500 officers per year. This hasty process meant the premature promotion of unqualified men to the noncommissioned and junior officer ranks. In any war these are the men who lead tactical operations. In the small unit engagements typical of the Vietnam War, the lack of qualified leadership was particularly punishing. While Johnson's decision needlessly killed American soldiers, it also had a tremendous impact on public reaction to the war. Had the Reserves been summoned there would have either been massive protest—an unlikely response, given the nation's historic patriotic response when a president enters a war—or the entire country would have been forcibly engaged in the conflict.[22] By calling upon only dedicated volunteers and unfortunate draftees, the balance of the country, with no personal stake in the war, could go about its business untouched by what took place in Vietnam's remote jungles. Johnson's attempt to shield the majority of the nation from war's ugliness would backfire badly.

In the short term, Westmoreland's staff calculated the largest number it could request in the absence of a Reserve call-up and arrived at a half million men. This figure became the basis for Westmoreland's estimate of the "minimum essential forces" he needed to fight the war. It was a backward way to arrive at such an important figure. Instead of the military mission determining the number of troops, the reverse occurred. Westmoreland's estimate also assumed that Rolling Thunder would cause North Vietnam to end its support for the Viet Cong. He plainly said that if the bombing was unsuccessful or was slow to take effect, he would need more men.[23] In the general zeal to do something, most everyone overlooked Westmoreland's careful hedge.

In the critical spring of 1965 in both Washington and Saigon, all the attention focusing on how many troops to send and how to provide them impeded careful thought about what to do with them. To date the best definition of overall objective anyone had come up was "over time ... to break the will" of the enemy "by depriving them of victory."[24] McNamara and the top generals said this would require one or two years. This was a remarkable definition of victory and at odds with the French experience. The Communists had been fighting for more than twenty-five years, which surely indicated they possessed formidable will. The idea that one or two years after American intervention they would collapse was most optimistic.

Even while sending substantial reinforcements to Westmoreland, Johnson continued to grope about seeking reassurance that he had chosen wisely. He telephoned the man he considered his best military adviser, General Dwight D. Eisenhower. Plaintively, he asked, "Do you really think we can beat the Viet Cong?"[25] Eisenhower replied that it was hard to say given the lack of good intelligence about the enemy. Then Johnson read disturbing reports from the director of the Central Intelligence Agency, who predicted dire consequences if American ground forces entered Vietnam.[26] The Communist would meet American escalation with increased assistance from North Vietnam. Air strikes on the planned basis would not injure their ability to persevere. On the ground the enemy would avoid large-scale battles and revert to guerrilla war, and wait for domestic opposition to the war to take its toll.[27]

All of this and more worried Johnson as he conducted one last searching strategic analysis during July 1965. Throughout these meetings none of his skeptical advisers told the president to his face that sending American ground forces to Vietnam would be a mistake. In contrast, there were many stalwart partisans of intervention, including number-crunching Secretary of Defense McNamara, a man widely considered most brilliant.

McNamara liked to quantify otherwise complex, messy human interactions. He had been told that a successful antiguerrilla campaign required a ten-to-one numerical manpower superiority and the elimination of outside assistance for the guerrillas. In 1965 the idea that a ten-to-one superiority could defeat a guerrilla movement enjoyed considerable intellectual currency within the American military community. In fact, it was based on the rather thin reed of a recent British success against the Malaysian guerrillas. McNamara fastened onto this formula for victory. He explained to Johnson that the military objective was to reach a favorable settlement by demonstrating to the enemy that the odds were against a Communist victory. Currently the odds of South Vietnamese to enemy were about three-to-one and declining, and because of this "unfavorable" ratio the Viet Cong were winning.[28] This was terribly erroneous analysis. It entirely overlooked political and social factors—most important, South Vietnamese government instability and corruption. It ignored why a Vietnamese peasant served as a skilled, motivated fighter for the National Liberation Front's Viet Cong and as a reluctant draftee for the army of the Republic of South Vietnam. So blinded, it was easy for McNamara to say that the United States had the capacity to win by changing the force ratio, by adding Americans troops to the equation.

Looking at the likely enemy response, McNamara predicted that more North Vietnamese divisions would infiltrate and this would cause heavy fighting, costing the United States 500 deaths per month. McNamara acknowledged that no one knew what the enemy would do when confronted with 175,000 Americans. They might revert to guerrilla war and avoid combat in a repetition of their tactics against the French, but it was doubtful the Viet Cong could maintain morale after such a "set-back." The chairman of the Joint Chiefs of Staff, General Earle G. Wheeler, added the reassurance that aggressive American tactics would force the Communists "to fight somewhere," and in such fights there could be no doubt about the outcome.[29]

Johnson responded to this presentation by asking cogent questions. Why did the situation require another 100,000 Americans and what would they accomplish? He clearly wanted to limit the troop commitment to the lowest number possible.[30]

Wheeler answered that Westmoreland believed that with the additional forces the allies could hold the present position and possibly reclaim some contested areas. Here was a modest answer predicting an outcome well shoot of victory.[31] No one seemed to notice.

The president focused on the high-stakes poker game he saw evolving, asking again, "What makes you think if we put in 100,000 men Ho Chi Minh won't put in another 100,000?"

Confident in American firepower, General Wheeler replied as had MacArthur when asked about the consequences of Chinese intervention in Korea: "This means greater bodies of men—which will allow us to cream them."

"What if Ho kept sending more men?" the commander in chief persisted.

The chairman replied that he would be "foolhardy" to do so because it would make the North vulnerable to invasion. Here Wheeler overlooked the fact that the United States had already publicly renounced any intent to invade the North. If North Vietnam took the United States at its word—and it already had ample evidence that America intended to fight this war with enormous restraints—then matching the American buildup would be a risk-free proposition.

Having been told that Vietnam would ultimately require another half million Americans for a fight lasting five years (no one now stood on the earlier claim that the war would take one or two years) Johnson recalled a recent speech in which Ho Chi Minh announced the Communists were prepared to fight for twenty years. What, he asked the Army Chief of Staff, did he make of it?

General Johnson replied, "I believe it."

The president had sought and would continue to seek the advice of able men in and out of government. In his memoirs he overstated the degree of consensus surrounding all his Vietnam decisions, but he also candidly acknowledged that in the end the decision was his. He searched his soul and found that his sworn oath to defend the nation resonated loudly. The president summarized what he had heard and gave a clear distillation of why he thought the nation had to fight in Vietnam: "The situation is deteriorating. Even though we now have eighty to ninety thousand men there, the situation is not very safe." He rejected getting out because national honor and credibility were at stake. He rejected a defensive "hunker up" approach because no one thought this would ultimately win. On the other end of the spectrum, he rejected massive mobilization because it would cost billions and Hanoi could get matching commitments from Peking and Moscow. He rejected the employment of massive strategic airpower "to bring the enemy to his knees" because it might bring on World War III. He chose to send ground forces—"to put in our big stack now"—because it met the present emergency, and it would "give the commanders the men they say they need."[32] The victory vision had receded; America would go to war to stabilize a deteriorating situation.

On July 28, 1965, Lyndon Johnson announced to the nation:

> *I have asked the commanding general, General Westmoreland, what more he needs to meet this mounting aggression. He has told me. We will meet his needs. I have today ordered to Vietnam the Air Mobile Division and certain other forces.*[33]

In less than four months, eager but inexperienced American soldiers would fight North Vietnamese regulars in the first pitched battle of a new war.

ATTRITION IN THE IA DRANG

No American soldiers had ever traveled so far from home to fight a war. Although many were draftees, they were proud to serve their country, to emulate the patriotism shown by their fathers in World War II and their older brothers in Korea. President John F. Kennedy's clarion call to "pay any price, bear any burden, meet any hardship" in the defense of freedom had stirred them. Lyndon Johnson's belief that freedom was on the line meant their patriotism would be tested in Vietnam. Although they possessed the world's most formidable mix of high technology and firepower, they went to war as had their fathers, sailing across the Pacific aboard troopships that had plied these same waters in the war against Japan. In distant Saigon, no one awaited the arrival of these soldiers of the 1st Cavalry Division, the "Air Cav," more eagerly than the field commander, General William C. Westmoreland.

Fifty years old on June 20, 1964, when he assumed command of the U.S. military effort in Vietnam, Westmoreland possessed an impeccable background. Born in South Carolina, he attended The Citadel, the Military College of South Carolina, for one year before receiving an appointment to the U.S. Military Academy. At West Point he had been chosen as first captain and regimental commander of the corps and won the coveted Pershing Trophy for leadership. In World War II he served in both combat and staff positions, winning the Legion of Merit for his able handling of the artillery at Kasserine Pass and later a Bronze Star for his conduct fording the Rhine at Remagen. Maxwell Taylor identified him as a comer in 1943, and one year after the war Westmoreland joined the paratroop "mafia," that group of paratroop generals who were on the ascendant in the postwar army, by attending jump school. Backed by Taylor, his paratroop patron, "Westy," as his colleagues called him, received the plum job of commanding the only paratroop unit that fought in Korea. After Korea he served in key Pentagon staff positions, attended the Harvard Business School, returned to West Point as superintendent, and then commanded an airborne corps that was the heart of the U.S. strategic reserve. His combination of combat and staff experience marked him as an ideal choice for Vietnam, and he was one of three officers President Johnson had considered for the job.[34] His background, including his service as deputy commander in Vietnam, McNamara's strong endorsement, and perhaps the fact that he was southern-born brought him the job.[35]

Although South Vietnam had received training from American advisers and lavish aid for more than a decade, upon assuming command Westmoreland quickly concluded that "almost everything had to be started from zero."[36] By mid-1965, he had accomplished much, but the challenge remained daunting. When the president decided to send ground forces to Vietnam, Westmoreland had to plan for an entirely new war. It did not help that even as major reinforcements were in transit, he had to cope with renewed political upheaval in Saigon.

In spite of the obvious mounting Communist threat, many of the Army of South Vietnam's (ARVN) best units were not employed in combating Communist inroads. Instead they and their leaders participated enthusiastically in the safer and more rewarding coup d'états that characterized South Vietnamese politics for the first year and a half of Westmoreland's tenure. Consequently, Johnson's general had to devote much time and effort trying to pilot among the tangled reefs of Vietnamese politics. On June 19, 1965, yet another government, this one headed by General Nguyen Van Thieu, took over. Although it proved more enduring, it too had little popular appeal. The need to square away matters with the new government while simultaneously absorbing a huge influx of American soldiers underscored the fact that Westmoreland's job was a colossal civil-military undertaking.

Just as Jefferson Davis had been besieged by petition seekers with demands that had to be addressed, so Westmoreland's flood of visitors took up an immense amount of his time. A typical day included meeting with everyone from a sergeant who had distinguished himself in a firefight, a visiting congressman, a prominent French reporter, the Australian ambassador, and the head of the Vietnamese government. It left precious few hours for attending to the business of devising a strategy to fight the war. America's most complex military operation to date had been the invasion of Normandy. According to its commander, General Eisenhower, Westmoreland's task was more complex.[37] Eisenhower explained that he had enjoyed a simple directive: invade Europe and march on Germany. Twenty years later, Westmoreland's orders were much less straightforward.

Westmoreland had found time to study likely enemy strategy. He expected it to follow the precepts developed by Mao Tse-tung and comprise three phases. In phase one the insurgents sought to control the population through acts of intimidation and terrorism. Next, they formed regular military units and selectively attacked isolated government units while simultaneously intensifying guerrilla activities. In phase three, the war-winning phase, the regular military units undertook conventional military tactics to defeat the government's large units and to control terrain objectives. The Vietnamese had successfully employed this doctrine against the French, and Westmoreland had every reason to believe they would follow it again against the Americans.

In the summer of 1965, the Communists were well into second-phase operations. Instead of hitting and running in classic guerrilla style, the Viet Cong were standing and fighting in pitched battle. More ominously, more often than not they were winning these battles. In spite of Rolling Thunder bombings, entire divisions of North Vietnamese were successfully infiltrating the South.

After the event there would be much said and written about Washington's interference with the military. However, once Westmoreland accepted that his operations had to be confined within South Vietnam's borders, he enjoyed the traditional American command prerogative of devising his own strategy.[38] First he had to concentrate on developing logistical bases to support the influx of American troops. During the Civil War, Federal troops had become accustomed to receiving a variety of comforts that a munificent government provided for its citizen soldiers. It began a tradition that continued through Vietnam, only more so. In place of Civil War–era canned oysters, cheeses, rubber blankets, and canvas tents came steak, ice cream, laundry facilities, and rest-

and-recreation centers. Many soldiers later commented on the incongruity of leaving a hot landing zone, where enemy fire clanged off and through their helicopters as casualties mounted, and returning to a base camp where their comrades lazed in newly built swimming pools, cans of beer clutched in their hands. For a hundred years the U.S. Army had gone to war with an ever-lengthening logistical tail, and in Vietnam that tail would require most of 1966 to construct.

Once it was in place, Westmoreland's plan called for driving the main force enemy units away from the population centers. While military units secured the cleared areas through a combination of outposts and patrols, civilian agencies protected by South Vietnamese soldiers could begin to restore government control. It would be a ticklish business because the elusive enemy operated from decades-old sanctuaries hidden in Vietnam's jungles and mountains. As long as they were able to emerge to terrorize the people, there was little chance to defeat the insurgency. Accordingly, Americans would operate from their own secure bases on search-and-destroy missions in an effort to find and eliminate the enemy's base camps. Hopefully, these operations would force the enemy to join battle where superior U.S. firepower would destroy them. In the war's last phase, American forces would enter sustained ground combat to eliminate or push the Communists over the border. By this time the South Vietnamese military should be large enough and well enough trained to combat any remaining guerrillas.[39]

The battlefield strategy Westmoreland chose, search-and-destroy operations, was the same approach the ARVN had ben failing at for years. In Westmoreland's mind, it was a failure of execution, not strategy. American forces would win out because of their superior resources. Meanwhile, these search-and-destroy operations became a focus of antiwar protest. The term sounded brutal because it was, because war remained a brutal business. Westmoreland failed to appreciate that candidly describing something as what it was could be such a propaganda error. He, like most American military men, failed to understand that this war was being fought on three fronts: in the field, in capitals throughout the world, and in the United States.[40] Not until 1968, when it was too late, did the head of Voice of America tell him, "General, you are your own worst enemy to perpetuate a term that has been so distorted."[41]

Part and parcel of Westmoreland's strategy was the idea of pitting American forces against the enemy's big units. In broadest terms this involved conventional warfare of the type fought in America's most recent wars. Largely absent from Westmoreland's thinking was the old counterinsurgency war, the battle against the guerrillas.[42] This was an important strategic shift brought about by the arrival of U.S. infantry. Their presence changed the American command focus to an emphasis on the big battle, a battle in which the United States could excel since its unmatched mobility and firepower provided a tremendous tactical edge. Westmoreland planned for such battles to occur in the hinterland, thus minimizing both civilian losses and American contact with the xenophobic Vietnamese. It left the South Vietnamese military the job of rooting out guerrillas from urban areas, a task they were presumably better able to handle.

This strategy had many consequences. One perhaps foreseeable problem was that inevitably attention focused on the big unit battles. American officers appreciated that glory and promotion resulted from these big battles. The American press covered operations involving American soldiers to the exclusion of South Vietnamese efforts. Although South Vietnamese casualties consistently exceeded U.S. losses, the American fighting man in Vietnam and the people back home received the impression that it was American boys who were doing all of the fighting while the South Vietnamese did little or nothing. An adviser named Norman Schwarzkopf recalled that American officers began disparaging the South Vietnamese, saying: "None of them are fighters. None of them are worth a damn."[43] Westmoreland recognized that Americans were in Vietnam not to do the job for the South Vietnamese but rather to enable them to do it themselves someday. But because his strategy consciously shielded ARVN units from encounters with main force enemy units, many of them did not develop the combat skills they would need.[44]

Another flaw in Westmoreland's strategy was that he lacked the manpower both to pacify the countryside and deal with enemy main force units who could always escape over the border to refit and who could rely upon a constant influx of fresh manpower from the North. Even if he defeated the enemy in conventional battle, they could revert to guerrilla warfare, where political and social factors would weigh as heavily as military might. Westmoreland lacked the vision to anticipate what lay beyond the initial big battles, but his was an understandable error because in the summer of 1965 it was the threat of the newly arriving North Vietnamese units that most concerned him. These units could win the war right now, before enough U.S. forces arrived to stop them, thus rendering all future planning irrelevant. Westmoreland's plan to deal with them revealed that however much national leaders spoke of Vietnam as a different kind of war, his own war-fighting notions remained rooted in World War II.

The Central Highlands of South Vietnam comprised a 5,400-square-mile area in the northern third of the country. Sparsely populated, primarily by primitive Montagnard tribesmen, it was a forbidding and desolate land. Westmoreland believe it a strategic key. Should the Communists attack from their Cambodian sanctuaries through the Central Highlands to the sea, South Vietnam would be cut in two. The only significant road to penetrate the highlands was Highway 19. General Westmoreland thought that just as the highlands were key to the country, Highway 19 was the key to the highlands. He declared, "Highway 19 must be kept open." He planned to use the newly arrived Air Cavalry for this mission. If the enemy decided to contest the cavalry, so much the better, because "this is as good terrain as any" on which to engage.[45] The troopers assigned to fight in the central Highlands might have disputed their general's assessment.

The first battles America fought in wars past—Washington's debacles around New York City, Queenston Heights, and Kasserine Pass, among many—had not been happy affairs. Perhaps mindful of this, Westmoreland's superior had sent the less than helpful warning "that there would be grave political implications involved if sizable U.S. forces are committed for the first time and suffer a defeat."[46] However, none of America's first battles had been fought on terrain like that in the Central Highlands. The neat pastures of Long Island, the rolling hills along Bull Run, the rocky heights of Kasserine Pass, none were as foreign as the trackless jungle of towering elephant grass, scrub bush, and stunted trees surrounding the Special Forces camp at Plei Me and the jungle in the nearby Ia Drang Valley. Intelligence reported three North Vietnamese army regiments, about six thousand men, had moved into this area to capture Plei Me. Westmoreland sent the Air Cavalry Division to find and fight them. Instead, the North Vietnamese found the Americans.

In late October 1965 Westmoreland ordered an Air Cav brigade west toward Cambodia in hopes of intercepting the elusive enemy before they retired over the border.[47] The divisional commander, in turn, having received the simple orders to find and kill the enemy, ordered his men on a series of fruitless search-and-destroy missions during the first weeks of November. On November 13, a brigade commander decided to shift the scene of operations into the Ia Drang Valley, historically an enemy stronghold. The 1st Battalion, 7th Cavalry, commanded by Lieutenant Colonel Harold Moore, received the mission. Because the best available landing zone, a hundred-yard cleared area, could accommodate only a limited number of helicopters, the initial assault force was less than a company. Thus, Johnson's July decision to dispatch ground forces to Vietnam led to this, a helicopter landing by fewer than eighty American soldiers into a place named Landing Zone X-Ray, where took place the first major encounter between the American and North Vietnamese armies.

As the first Air Cav troopers fanned out to secure the open area of Landing Zone X-Ray, unbeknownst to them, from the nearby heights of the Chu Pong Massif an aggressive North Vietnamese officer was awaiting their arrival: "We had a very strong position . . . We were ready, had prepared for you and expected you to come. The only question was when."[48] So began a race, with the American helicopters shuttling the rest of Moore's battalion into X-Ray while the regulars of the 33rd Regiment, People's Army, came boiling off the heights to surround and attack them. Moore's 450-man unit traced its lineage back to the ill-fated 7th cavalry commanded by Custer at the Battle of the Little Bighorn. As they prepared to defend a position ringed by scrub brush and tall trees, covered with five-foot-high elephant grass, and dotted with huge termite hills that provided excellent firing positions for hostile automatic weapons, they did not know they were facing a foe who outnumbered them five to one. Then the battle began and it seemed that they might share Custer's fate.

However, unlike Custer's men, these troopers had several advantages. They were a close-knit outfit with numerous veteran sergeants and officers, including a colonel who had fought in both World War II and Korea. The battalion had trained long and hard in the newly invented air mobile tactics, which meant it was practiced in the difficult art of summoning close-in fire support from helicopter gunships and fixed-wing aircraft. It was this fire support that made the difference in the ensuing engagement.

As soon as his men contacted enemy forces, Moore made several key decisions that gave his force the best tactical chance possible.

His men pushed out from the cleared area to try to secure as broad a perimeter as possible to enable the helicopters to bring in the balance of his battalion. It worked, but at a cost. An overly aggressive company became disordered while chasing enemy scouts during the initial encounters. One of its platoons found itself isolated and surrounded. For the remainder of the day and throughout the long night, it fought a lonely battle, held together by a gallant sergeant and aided by artillery fire that literally exploded in the Americans' faces. Relieved after a nearly twenty-four-hour ordeal, the twenty-nine-man platoon took stock and found it had lost nine dead and thirteen wounded.

Meanwhile, the balance of the battalion contracted its perimeter under repeated enemy assaults. Both sides displayed incredible valor as fighting occurred at point-blank range. But try as they might, the North Vietnamese could not penetrate the curtain of steel that surrounded Landing Zone X-Ray. During the forty-hour battle, U.S. artillery fired more than 33,000 rounds. Aerial artillery contributed 3,756 rockets. Air force fighter-bombers launched strikes every fifteen minutes to pound the enemy with napalm, cluster-bomb units, and high explosives. As Colonel Moore recalled, the difference between him and the opposing colonel was "that I had major fire support and he didn't."[49]

For the first time since Dien Bien Phu, a North Vietnamese division had entered battle. Pitted against the unprecedented firepower of the U.S. Army, it suffered terrible casualties in this battle, including at least 600 killed. For the remainder of the war, although they tried repeatedly, the North Vietnamese and Viet Cong never overran an American unit in a defended perimeter tied in with firepower. Moore's command lost 79 killed and 121 wounded, a casualty rate of 40 percent and reminiscent of the Civil War.

The results from Landing Zone X-Ray, and in particular the advantageous kill ratio, elated General Westmoreland. The action seemed to justify fully his big-battle strategy. Visiting the weary troopers, the general told them that they had distinguished themselves in the most difficult battle to date. Moore's leadership "tremendously impressed" him.[50] All in all it was a heady moment, giving every indication that the American war machine could ultimately triumph here just as it had in most every war in the nation's history.

A sour note occurred when Westmoreland went to a hospital to talk with wounded troopers. Here he heard about surprise, heavy loses, and ambush. This was not what he had been told when visiting the brigade headquarters and he began to suspect something was amiss. Returning to his headquarters, the general found his suspicions confirmed when he read an anxious telegram from Secretary of Defense McNamara quoting press headlines about ambush and retreat. However successful, the combat at Landing Zone X-Ray had been only one part of an ongoing action. The next phase had brought a startling disaster.

After the unsuccessful Communist attacks against X-Ray, the enemy commander ordered his men to break contact and withdraw. The American response previewed the frustrating nature of nearly every engagement in Vietnam: once the enemy retreated, the ground, regardless of how much American blood had been spilled to purchase it, became valueless. So the Americans departed X-Ray as well. The division commander directed one battalion, the 2/7 Cavalry, to march overland across the Ia Drang Valley toward another landing zone, named Albany. To move a unit on foot was a questionable decision in a division having 435 helicopters, particularly considering that the troopers were worn out, having been awake for most of the previous thirty-six hours.

Although the 2/7 Cavalry was a sister battalion to Moore's unit, it was an Air Cav battalion in name only. It had been hastily assembled from disparate units in order to fill out the division just before it went overseas. The battalion sergeant major recalled that precisely one helicopter ride at Fort Benning constituted its entire air mobile training. Its commanding officer, Lieutenant Colonel Bob McDade, was a three-war veteran, but he had been in charge of the 2/7 for only three weeks and had not yet gotten a good feel for his unit.[51]

As it set out for Albany, a woeful lack of intelligence hampered the battalion's march. McDade later complained, "We really didn't know a goddamned thing ... We had no idea what to expect out there."[52] McDade concluded that his mission was merely a route march to a certain clearing where he would establish a landing zone. Confident that it would be a mere walk in the sun, he declined an offer for firing data that would have given his unit quick and accurate artillery support. Departing X-Ray, where the largest battle of the war had just taken place, and entering what could only be conceived of as enemy territory, the unit marched in battalion column, a formation suitable for quickly traversing ground but inappropriate for maneuvering when in contact with the enemy. An hour or so into the march, amid signs of the recent passage of enemy soldiers, the column passed some Montagnard huts and an officer ordered them set afire. The North Vietnamese, watching the march from adjacent heights, hardly needed this signal to pinpoint the location of the American column.

The 2/7 became strung out as the tired troopers struggled in hot weather over difficult terrain. Visibly drooping, most were happy when the column staggered to a halt. The stop occurred because just as the leading platoon neared the objective, it captured two enemy soldiers. McDade spent an inexplicable thirty minutes interrogating them and then compounded this error by summoning all of his company officers to the front of the column for a meeting. Behind him, strung out over a 550-yard distance, the toiling troopers collapsed in the tall elephant grass surrounded by thick vegetation. Here they lay idle, smoking cigarettes and dozing. More than an hour after taking the two prisoners, the van started moving again into the clearing that was Landing Zone Albany. The men at the front heard Vietnamese voices. Some mortar rounds exploded nearby, followed by small arms fire from the trees surrounding Albany. It was 1:15 P.M., November 17. The most savage one-day battle of the entire war had begun.

The North Vietnamese commander took advantage of the lengthy American halt to create an improvised L-shaped ambush. The base of the L confronted the American van around the clearing while its long axis paralleled the right of the U.S. column. North Vietnamese units quickly marched the length of the column, a mere hundred yards away from the unsuspecting troopers, and then turned to assault the column in flank. Had there been any flank security this maneuver would have been impossible. Instead, the troopers' first warning came when bullets from an unseen enemy began tearing into their ranks.

Automatic weapons fire flailed McDade's command group and drove them to cover. One company officer ignored it and ran back to his unit, which he managed to form into a defensive perimeter. The remaining officers did not see their units for the next sixteen hours. From snipers' positions in the trees and brush-covered termite hills, the North Vietnamese poured fire into the exposed troopers trapped in the grass below. The result was a massacre. In the first ten minutes key soldiers—platoon leaders, sergeants, radio operators—died, leaving the survivors huddled and leaderless. None of the surviving American commanders had any idea what was happening. Amid deafening noise the troopers hit the dirt, their world reduced to a table-sized area surrounded by thick grass. So limited was visibility that one unsuspecting enemy machine gunner set up his weapon three feet from a trooper, who proceeded to kill him with a full magazine to the face. Seemingly from every direction the scything fire of enemy machine guns cut the grass like lawn mowers. The wild return fire against the unseen enemy, coupled with misdirected air strikes that dropped napalm on friend and foe alike, inflicted further losses. "All afternoon," recalled one survivor, "there was smoke, artillery, screaming, moaning, fear, bullets, blood, and little yellow men running around screeching with glee when they found one of us alive, or screaming and moaning with fear when they ran into a grenade or a bullet."[53]

Nightfall brought further horrors. The North Vietnamese began shelling the stricken American battalion while sending in patrols to finish off the survivors: "Every few minutes I heard some guy start screaming 'No no no please,' and then a burst of bullets."[54] It was a scene reminiscent of St. Clair's battle against the Wabash Indians and one unlike anything Americans had experienced since the end of the Indian Wars.

At dawn the enemy withdrew and the survivors began the grim task of policing the field. They found North Vietnamese and American bodies intermingled. They saw the bodies of several obviously wounded troopers with bound hands, having been executed with a shot to the head. In total, McDade's command, which had begun the fight with some 450 men, suffered 155 killed and 124 wounded.

It was while talking with some of these latter the next day that General Westmoreland began to suspect that something untoward had happened out in the Ia Drang. After receiving McNamara's telegram, he ordered a full investigation and even sent a planeload of reporters to the scene so they, too, could learn exactly what had taken place. Reporters heard from the survivors' lips a story of surprise, ambush, and carnage. They they heard the military briefers, who, aware of the pressure from Washington concerning the "ambush" and "retreat," argued semantics about a "meeting engagement" and a "strategic movement." The exercise did little to restore mutual confidence.

The next day, more fully informed about the action himself, Westmoreland explained the battle to reporters. He reminded them that he had resisted censorship but that the types of reports they had just submitted were "distorting the picture at home and lowering the morale of the people" and his own troops. Equally bad, it was "providing comfort" to the enemy and informing him of "our mistakes and vulnerabilities."[55] The next edition of the *New York Times* dutifully quoted Westmoreland's claim that the action in the Ia Drang had been "an unprecedented victory." However, to undermine military reports it then contrasted the division commander's comment that McDade's battalion "might not have been ambushed" with eyewitness accounts, and concluded: ". . . it was evident that the battalion had been ambushed."[56] The more compliant *Washington Post* headlined "BIG IADRANG VICTORY HELD TURNING POINT" and explained that after the battle some cavalry had marched east, others southeast, and others had been removed by helicopter; thus: "It was not a retreat, but a strategic movement."[57]

Whereas Westmoreland's intercession with the press did change the next day's headlines, similar review and analysis did not occur within the 1st Cavalry Division. The brigade commander whose men fought at Albany had failed to provide clear orders for the movement to the landing zone. He compounded this omission by not notifying his superior in timely fashion when trouble occurred, thus delaying the arrival of reinforcements who might have saved the situation. Nonetheless, he remained in command. McDade, who had received his appointment as a favor from his superior officer, remained protected by that superior and also continued in command. Key records pertaining to the fight at Albany "disappeared."[58]

While the battered North Vietnamese retired to nearby sanctuaries in Cambodia, both sides recoiled from the shock of combat to assess the implications of the Ia Drang campaign. At the small unit level, the battles at X-Ray and Albany proved that American soldiers would fight this war with valor equal to that displayed by Americans in wars past. In partial recognition of their heroism, President Johnson would award the division with a Presidential Unit Citation. Because the 1st Cavalry Division displayed such formidable hard-fighting resolution, henceforth it carried the nickname "the First Team."

The campaign also seemed to vindicate the novel air mobile tactic. From Westmoreland's perspective, the campaign had thwarted a major North Vietnamese offensive. He looked at the campaign's statistics and saw a kill ratio, the centerpiece of his attrition strategy, of better than twelve to one. Ignoring the facts that in spite of the American mobility advantage the enemy had retained tactical initiative, beginning and breaking off contact when they chose, and that throughout the engagements maneuvers had been hampered by an inability to locate the enemy, Westmoreland concluded that faced with more defeats like this the North would desist. In the future, North Vietnamese leaders would say that they had provoked the battle in order to assess American combat methods.[59] Indeed, Hanoi published a tactical guide based upon American characteristics exhibited during this campaign. In addition, North Vietnamese strategists gleaned lessons quite different from Westmoreland's conclusions. Their army's indoctrination had stressed the importance of men, not weapons and equipment, as the decisive element in a "People's war." By their lights, their men had stood toe to toe with an enemy backed by a modern, high-tech arsenal. Veteran leaders disseminated lessons learned about how to fight the helicopters. Never again would major units be so vulnerable to the air mobile tactics of vertical envelopment. After the Ia Drang, although disappointed that American intervention delayed the victory that had been so tantalizingly close at the beginning of the year, Communist leaders prepared a new strategy. Confident of success, they did not even bother to keep it a secret. The North Vietnamese premier told a French journalist: "Americans do not like long, inconclusive wars—and this is going to be a long, inconclusive war."[60]

On the American side, two key leaders also concluded that the fighting in the Ia Drang presaged a long contest. In the battle's aftermath, President Johnson ordered his Secretary of Defense to go to Vietnam to receive a firsthand battle report. McNamara listened while Colonel Moore described the action. Moore stressed that the well-disciplined enemy had displayed a near-suicidal determination not seen since the Communist human wave attacks of the Korean War. Impressed and sobered, McNamara told reporters, "It will be a long war."[61]

Although pleased with the battle's overall results, General Westmoreland also informed his superiors that everyone "must be prepared for a long war" requiring more U.S. forces.[62] Down the chain of command came a query from the president, asking, would the reinforcements Westmoreland wanted be enough to persuade the enemy to desist? Westmoreland replied: "No." He hoped to establish an equilibrium in 1965 and gain the initiative the following year. But much depended on how many more men the North sent. If North Vietnam committed more men to the fight, the general told his commander in chief that he would need more men as well. Months ago, the president had asked his top military adviser, General Wheeler, what would happen if Ho Chi Minh matched the American buildup. Wheeler had replied, "We will cream them." Now the first big battle was over and the president's field commander was telling him something very different.

Although the Americans had inflicted terrible casualties in a tactical battlefield triumph, Johnson's decision to forbid overt military operations in Cambodia and Laos meant there could be no battlefield pursuit. Thus, Westmoreland could not convert tactical success into a strategic outcome. The conflict in the Ia Drang convinced most American leaders from Washington to Saigon that Westmoreland's strategy would yield success. After all, the United States had never lost a war, and it stretched credulity to imagine that a small, weak country like North Vietnam could defeat the world's mightiest nation. No American appreciated that by accepting the constraint to limit the ground fighting to South Vietnam, Westmoreland had adopted the strategic defensive.

Von Clausewitz observed that the strategic defensive embodies "the idea of waiting," adding "The idea implies . . . that the situation . . . may improve."[63] As 1965 drew to a close, the outstanding question became whether Westmoreland could demonstrate such improvement before the American people grew weary of waiting.

10 ⊨⊶

THE TEST OF WILLS

"Our country has no capability to defeat you on the battle-field. But war is not decided by weapons so much as by national will. Once the American people understand this war, they will have no interest in pursuing it. They will be made to understand this. We will win this war on the streets of New York."

A NORTH VIETNAMESE INTERROGATOR
TO AN AMERICAN POW, 1966[1]

SIGNALS OF DISTRESS

AT THE BEGINNING OF 1966, ADMIRAL SHARP HAD BEGUN TO UNDER-stand that Vietnam was becoming a test of wills, observing, "It appears that the very foundation of the enemy's morale and resultant tenacity stands squarely on the belief that our patience will run out before his."[2] Referring to a long, inconclusive, eighteenth-century European war, General George Marshall once observed that unlike other peoples, Americans would not tolerate a Seven Years War. Lyndon Johnson also well understood that Americans lacked patience, and it worried him.

Beginning with the Ia Drang campaign in 1965, the increased tempo of military operations brought a lengthening casualty list. How the American people would react to battlefield losses was an open question. Already the president sensed a flaw in his strategy, telling his close advisers, "The weakest chink in our armor is American public opinion. Our people won't stand firm in the face of heavy losses, and they can bring down the government."[3] In the Civil War and again in World War II, Americans had stood firm while their military absorbed heavy losses. In those wars, the commander in chief had articulated a clear vision of why the fight

245

was necessary. Johnson likewise "was hammering away" on television, in private meetings, and in every available forum "to win the war of words," to explain why Vietnam was vital to the public's security.[4] He failed to comprehend that his effort to buffer the public from the war's reality—by simultaneously pursuing his Great Society, by refusing to mobilize the Reserves, by concealing plans for increasing Westmoreland's manpower—undermined this effort. His own duplicity contributed greatly to the moral ambiguity surrounding the war and to the public's resultant lack of patience.

Confronting the dismal possibility that American will would prove insufficient, he reacted—as had Jefferson Davis—by redoubling his own effort. Every night he tried "to put myself in the shoes of Ho Chi Minh" in order to understand the impact of American policy upon the enemy leader.[5] But it was futile, he admitted; he neither knew Ho nor understood his customs and beliefs. Yet all he needed to know was that Ho Chi Minh had fought against great odds and endured great sacrifice for more than forty years in a battle to control Vietnam. He was unlikely to give up the struggle now. Failing to realize this, the only choice Johnson perceived he had was to send more men when Westmoreland asked for reinforcements, while exhorting his military to "nail the coonskin to the wall." Stubbornly he escalated the war, persisting, like Dickens's Mr. Micawber, in hopes that something would turn up.

He did not coldly send Americans to battle, but instead took his responsibility as commander in chief very personally. "There's not a mother in the world who cares more about [her boys] than I do," he said, "because I have two hundred thousand of them over there."[6] Their fate preyed upon him. Ever more frequently he complained, "God, we have to find a way to end this war."[7]

One possible way to end the war had to do with the bombing of North Vietnam. Rolling Thunder's purpose had been to demonstrate U.S. resolve and then to limit infiltration. It had apparently done neither. Grasping at straws, the president began to listen to those who said that perhaps stopping the bombing would convince Hanoi to negotiate. Discussing the possibility of a bombing pause in late 1965, Johnson asked McNamara if the Joint Chiefs of Staff should be consulted. McNamara said no, he knew exactly what the chiefs would say and they would be totally opposed. McNamara explained, "They see this as total military problem. Nothing will change their view."[8] He advised Johnson to make up his mind and then McNamara could handle the chiefs. The secretary's recommendation to avoid talking with his military men about something that assuredly had important military ramifications was reminiscent of James Polk's planning the invasion of Mexico without consulting Winfield Scott.

Unlike Polk, in this instance Johnson did consult with his foremost military adviser. He telephoned General Wheeler only to have McNamara's opinion confirmed when Wheeler claimed that a bombing pause would undo all that had been accomplished. McNamara said that was "baloney." Johnson disagreed, understanding that a pause incurred military risks. But his diplomats said there could be no talking while the bombing went on. So he weighed the military risks against the faint hope of meaningful negotiation, and ordered the pause.

Many times in the coming months Johnson would return to this curious idea that somehow halting an ineffective bombing campaign would signal to the enemy his desire for peace and prompt North Vietnam to negotiate. He did so in spite of ominous warnings from his field officers. None the less, he insisted upon periodic halts, timing these "pauses" for Christmas, Tet—the Vietnamese celebration of the lunar new year—and Buddha's birthday. None yielded the desired objective. When the North Vietnamese did not budge, the president reluctantly resumed the bombing.[9]

His entire public life had involved careful navigation among the shoals of extremism, as when he guided his native South between the demands for immediate, full-scale integration and the conflicting calls for "segregation now and forever." Influenced by that experience, he had chosen a war strategy of gradualism and restraint. Now he was caught between the military's request for escalation and his civilian advisers' claims that escalation had not worked. Public sentiment mirrored the schism within the government, with hawks urging a "win or get out" policy and doves marching in ever-increasing throngs to a tune of "get out" regardless. Buffeted from right and left, he tried to maintain a temperate, middle course that pleased no one and offered no promise of ultimate success. Inexorably, the president was losing the support of the American people.

Simultaneously, North Vietnam correctly read such gestures as the bombing pauses as further signs of U.S. timidity and self-doubt. As Westmoreland later put it: "... the signals we were sending were the signals of our own distress."[10]

*   *   *

The signals also distressed the Joint Chiefs of Staff. Highly attuned to White House mood as the White House became more pessimistic, the Joint Chiefs, in turn, became more defensive in their justification for current strategy. The historical, and seldom comfortable, executive-military relationship during times of war became more abrasive to the detriment of good communication and good planning. Civilians, led by McNamara, believed the military had a one-dimensional response, more firepower, to any of Vietnam's problems. The strategic advice proffered by these "doves" became ever more focused on avoiding defeat rather than taking decisive action to achieve victory. In turn, the Joint Chiefs found civilian "interference," the restrictions on how to fight the war, ever more irksome. This left the hapless Westmoreland to get along as best he could.

Further hampering the general was a near-Byzantine chain of command.[11] Unity of command is a long-established military principle. At the end of World War II, General Marshall commanded over eight million men in a global conflict. He did so from a newly built Pentagon housing eight subordinates at the undersecretary level. Marshall was Roosevelt's direct agent charged with winning the war. In 1965, a one-million-man army required fifty bureaucrats at the undersecretary level. Here was a formidable barrier between the field general and the man at the top. Furthermore, unlike the theater commanders of World War II, Westmoreland had commanded responsibility only for operations within the borders of South Vietnam. Admiral Sharp, in Hawaii, commanded the air operations against the North; an entirely different command supervised the B-52 bombers that were to prove such a useful weapon; the State Department oversaw the American ambassadors assigned to Southeast Asia; and the South Vietnamese maintained their own entirely separate command organization.

In addition to requiring an extraordinary amount of time merely shuffling paper among them all in an effort to coordinate strategy and tactics, this chain of command impaired communication. By the time a message from Westmoreland went through Sharp's command in Hawaii, to the JCS in the Pentagon with its fifty assorted undersecretaries and the like, through McNamara's office of the Secretary of Defense, through White House aides and advisers, and onto the president's desk, clarity and meaning could be lost. The Continental Congress had allocated scarce funds to establish a courier route to communicate better with General Washington. James Polk had used a new communications technology, the telegraph, to speed reports from the front. In the war against Spain, President William McKinley had built a telephone bank to link the different parts of his government so as to better command the war. But Johnson and Westmoreland learned of each other's desires and intentions only through the distorting filter created by the opinions of others. Partially because he appreciated this, and partially because he was old-fashioned at heart, Johnson turned to an ancient means of obtaining information: he sent lieutenants to the front to assess the situation firsthand.

Unfortunately, these "fact-finding" missions to Vietnam brought the president far less than he would have hoped. A visitor from Washington could hardly take in all of the important military and political events and trends during a whirlwind Saigon visit. In the 1950s, the South Vietnamese had learned how to showcase "progress" to their American visitors. In the 1960s, both they and the American military and political bureaucracy learned to do the same. It was part of the "can do" syndrome, the desire to report "progress" in part because it enhanced one's career. If not willfully misleading, it was also not particularly informative, while giving the visitor the dangerous impression that he understood.

What the commander in chief most wanted to learn was whether America was winning or losing. Finally, he determined to hear it from the horse's mouth, and so in February 1966 he met with Westmoreland for the first time since becoming president. Arriving in Honolulu, Westmoreland found his leader "intense, perturbed, uncertain how to proceed." At one point Johnson earnestly said to him, "General, I have a lot riding on you."[12] The president came away from this first encounter with a very positive impression of his general's talents.[13] It was an attitude reinforced in August when Johnson invited Westmoreland to his Texas ranch. The president felt more at ease with his general, having become convinced that Westmoreland did not suffer from the MacArthur disease of harboring political ambitions. The general, on the other hand, did not want to become embroiled in the domestic political turmoil caused by the war and wanted to decline the invitation. The president insisted; and so, after an absence of a year and a half from the continental United States, the general returned. To Westmoreland's disappointment the visit proved largely social and devoid of important policy discussion. They engaged in one of the president's favorite activities—chasing deer about the ranch in his Lincoln Continental convertible and taking refreshment from the mobile bar mounted in the Secret Service car—but they talked little about the war. However, at one point Johnson asked him directly, are we winning? Will the war end in less than five years?[14] Westmoreland reported progress, but he could not say when it all might end.

Still, Johnson had assessed his general and liked what he found. Thereafter he often confided to his wife his respect, pride, and confidence in his field general.[15] In the coming months he would write Westmoreland fulsome person notes of praise, handwritten birthday greetings, and a condolence letter when the general's mother died.[16] Because he trusted him, Johnson continued to leave the conduct of the ground war largely in his field general's hands.

CONFLICT AND DOUBT

From the Ia Drang campaign Westmoreland and his staff had derived a remarkably accurate summation of enemy combat strategy.[17] They correctly perceived that North Vietnamese units would maneuver so as to threaten widely scattered targets, thereby tying large numbers of allied units to static defensive positions. The Communists would avoid actual battle except to launch occasional surprise attacks and to entice allied forces into attacking prepared positions. From these positions—jungle-covered bunkers, trenches, and spider holes overlooking preregistered killing zones—the North Vietnamese expected to inflict heavy casualties. While regular Communist units fought it out in the jungles and mountains near their border sanctuaries, the Viet Cong would continue classic guerrilla action in the more populated areas. Knowing the enemy strategy was one thing; successfully coping with it was something else.

A 1967 retrospective analysis of combat encounters highlighted the enemy's success. It showed that in four out of five engagements the Communists had the tactical initiative. These engagements involved either enemy-triggered ambush, surprise enemy attacks, or U.S. assaults on prepared enemy positions where the Communists willingly stood and fought.[18] Clearly the Communist counter to overwhelming U.S. mobility and firepower was concealment and fortifications. Because the Communists could strike virtually anywhere at any time, well over half of all allied maneuver battalions, the basic fighting units that would have to win the ground war, were tied down protecting bases, government installations, roads, and the like.[19]

There was little indication that this would change absent the removal of the restraints on Rolling Thunder or prohibitions on movements into Laos and Cambodia. The Joint Chiefs and Westmoreland periodically requested these changes, but they were never forthcoming from the commander in chief.[20] There were two resultant problems with Westmoreland's war of attrition. First, at its best it would take a long time. Second, unless the flow of fresh troops from the North was cut off, it was questionable if it ever could prevail. Westmoreland's war machine could kill vast numbers of enemy soldiers, but the enemy could afford the losses. Before committing ground forces, Johnson had often asked what would prevent the enemy from matching the U.S. buildup, from putting in their "stack" whenever the United States added forces. By the end of 1965, Westmoreland acknowledged that the enemy buildup was twice the rate of his own.[21]

The American people knew little of this. The president's decision to wage war with a minimum disruption of domestic life was initially both publicly and politically popular. To thunderous congressional acclaim, he said in his 1966 State of the Union Address: "Time may require further sacrifices. If so, we will make them. But we will not heed those who will wring it from the hopes of the unfortunate here in a land of plenty. I believe that we can continue the Great Society while we fight in Vietnam."[22]

However, over time, skepticism regarding the military's conduct of the war emerged. It was fed by Robert McNamara's increasing disenchantment. Even while Johnson proudly told the nation it could have guns and butter too, the defense secretary could see little hope of ending the war anytime soon if the military continued along current lines. Yet when he pressed the Joint Chiefs about the lack of progress, all they seemed to suggest was more of the same using ever greater numbers of men. McNamara turned to his systems analysts and they refuted the military position. Employing clever math, the analysts examined the ratio of U.S. troops to the number of enemy killed and factored in the monetary costs.

Thus, they were able to inform McNamara that if Westmoreland received another 100,000 men it would cost the Treasury a small fortune while enemy losses would increase by a mere 70 per week.[23] This meager result would not alter the essential balance of power on the battlefield. As one disgruntled analyst commented to the press, "Essentially we are fighting Vietnam's birthrate."[24]

No war had ever been analyzed in this fashion. Von Clausewitz observed that assessing all the diverse factors bearing upon war is a colossal task calling for intuitive genius. "To master all this complex mass by sheer methodical examination is obviously impossible," the Prussian noted. He concluded that Napoleon was "quite right when he said that Newton himself would quail before the algebraic problems it could pose."[25] But the power of their computers emboldened McNamara's systems analysts to persevere in their mathematical examination of the war.

Their discouraging conclusions reinforced press and public doubts that the war could be won, and caused the president's mood to darken. Johnson spent many sleepless nights agonizing about Vietnam. A nightmare in which one of "his boys" died in combat would awaken him and he would call the White House Situation Room to learn the daily casualty report. If the news was bad "he would come to work the next morning with the features of a haunted man."[26] He understood that Vietnam was like a fungus, spreading to contaminate all it touched, including his cherished Great Society programs. The possibility of defeat began to haunt him and, as had Jefferson Davis, increasingly he turned to religion for solace. Both at home and abroad he desperately wanted to be thought of as the benevolent provider, the man who gave Vietnam health and education programs, "two hundred pound hogs" in place of their scrawny hundred-pounders, vines producing twice as many sweet potatoes as they had before. Instead, he feared he would be remembered as a war leader—or worse, a warmonger.[27] "With a few drinks under his belt," wrote one of his assistants, "he would tell anyone within hearing range that the war would be his downfall."[28]

*   *   *

In Saigon, General Westmoreland did not share his president's despair. He had been caught up in the task at hand and perhaps thrilled and awed by the unprecedented power generated by his forces. As 1966 ended, the number of American servicemen in Vietnam had risen to 385,000, roughly 100,000 more than the total Westmoreland had predicted he would need when planning began back in 1965. Although the American presence had stabilized the situation—there was now little danger the Communists could militarily conquer the South—and the needed logistical bases had been constructed to support the voracious appetite of the American military, the North had countered the U.S. buildup by increasing its own rate of infiltration.

In February 1967, twenty-two American and four South Vietnamese battalions formed a vast horseshoe around War Zone C, an important enemy base area northwest of Saigon. Armored troops belonging to the famous Blackhorse Cavalry swept into the open end of this horseshoe to push the enemy against the steel barrier created by waiting allied soldiers. Although this Operation Junction City killed thousands of enemy soldiers, the majority escaped through what proved an all too porous barrier into Cambodia. American engineering went to work on a massive scale, employing giant bulldozers capable of felling the tallest trees to level the jungle to prevent the enemy from hiding here again. Westmoreland wanted to leave troops behind to prevent the enemy from returning, but he lacked the manpower. Although Junction City damaged the enemy, the Communists reestablished their bases in the nearby sanctuary of Cambodia, and once the Americans departed found they could reenter the blasted and blighted landscape of War Zone C.

The demonstration of American might was both exhilarating and depressing. U.S. forces showed they could do what the French before them could not: they could attack the enemy virtually anywhere in Vietnam. But as Westmoreland told McNamara and his staff in March of 1967, unless there was some way to halt the flow of reinforcements from the North, the war could "go on indefinitely."[29]

*   *   *

If the enemy was successfully coping with U.S. ground action, albeit at enormous human cost, Hanoi was also defeating the United States in the international arena and on the domestic front. The bombing had stimulated the anticipated storm of international protest. So skillful was the Communist conduct of the competition for world opinion that the president never found a satisfactory counter.[30] Likewise at home the bombing caused dissent, and this irked the president terribly. In his opinion the media was just not giving a balanced view. He complained that when the Viet Cong bombed the U.S. embassy it received little media attention, yet when U.S. warplanes bombed a bridge the media portrayed it as an atrocity. So the president labored mightily to reverse his declining support, to persuade important politicians and media figures to back the war.[31] Moreover, he had always believed in bipartisan support for the president, particularly in matters of national security. Instead, he found the members of his own party dividing over the war. With his political support shredding, he complained bitterly, "How can an American Senator or an American newspaperman or an American student tie the hands of our fellow American military men? Are they duped."[32] Had he gone beyond irritation to thoughtful analysis, he might have concluded that this state of affairs stemmed from two factors: his own lack of candor about his Vietnam policy; and the immensely skillful North Vietnamese and Viet Cong manipulation of public opinion. Far better than Johnson, his Communist opponents understood the link among international opinion, American public opinion, and battlefield outcomes.

American impatience with the war manifested itself by a decline in Johnson's popularity in various national polls. In World War II progress could be seen on the maps showing American armies inexorably advancing on Berlin and Tokyo. It was difficult for the American people to assess progress in Vietnam's area war in which there were no front lines. The resultant increasing public protest worried Johnson: "This thing is assuming dangerous proportions, dividing the country and giving our enemies the wrong idea of the will of this country to fight."[33] American soldiers had been sent to Vietnam to defeat the "will" of the enemy. Instead, the commander in chief sensed that the reverse was occurring.

In spite of all criticism, by mid-1967 it seemed that he had made the right decisions, that the sacrifices were paying off and his legacy would be that of a victorious commander in chief. Secretary of Defense McNamara returned from a Saigon visit to report for the first time that the United States was winning.[34] Westmoreland's command had learned to feed the secretary's appetite for numbers. The resultant tremendous churn of statistical indicators—kill ratios, numbers of weapons lost by the South Vietnamese versus number captured from the Viet Cong, territory "pacified"—

showed favorable trends. The president could not know how unsound were many of these measurements. But he did know enough to ask his field general why, given so many reports of heavy Communist losses, the total enemy force had not been reduced. Westmoreland answered that the combination of infiltration and recruitment in the South made up for enemy battle casualties.[35] This should have given the commander in chief pause. If the enemy was losing as badly as field reports claimed, why could they continue to recruit substantial numbers of South Vietnamese for the fight? Instead, Johnson focused not on Westmoreland's assessment of the present but on his prediction for the future. Westmoreland said that he was hopeful that the elusive "crossover point," where enemy losses exceeded their replacement ability, was near.

When Westmoreland returned to the United States in April 1967, he met with the president to discuss the need for more men. Once more the commander in chief inquired, would not the enemy respond with another "stack" of their own? Johnson asked, "Where does it all end?" Westmoreland answered that it now appeared that the crossover point, the long-sought goal of his attrition strategy, had been reached. However, he cautioned, without another 100,000 men the war was likely to go on for another five years. Even with the desired reinforcements, it would last two to three more years. Westmoreland explained that this was so because the enemy's skillful diplomacy had provided him "hope that he can do politically that which he cannot accomplish militarily." To the president's dismay, Westmoreland had no answer to the president's query asking if Hanoi would not follow the Korean model and summon "volunteers" from China to replace losses if their manpower shortage became critical.[36]

Such skepticism emerged only in private. Publicly, the president used the general's visit to buttress his own sagging popularity. Dutifully, Westmoreland castigated antiwar protesters in a public speech and addressed Congress about the war. It backfired badly. A flood of telegrams descended on the White House criticizing both Johnson for using his general as a propaganda tool and Westmoreland for meddling in politics. Many of the messages echoed sentiments expressed during the Revolutionary War. They alluded to "a danger to democracy," to the terrible consequences when generals became involved in politics or the military tried to influence foreign policy.[37] The storm of protest prompted Johnson to assign an aide to research General Washington's relationship with the Continental Congress and the entire history of a serving military officer speaking before Congress. The public's historic doubts about the threat to liberty caused by a standing army had resurfaced in this time of conflict and doubt.

A month after Westmoreland's visit, politics intruded full force upon the commander in chief's thinking. In May 1967, McGeorge Bundy, who had left the government, wrote Johnson that escalation would not bring victory before next year's presidential election. Therefore, he recommended defending policy on a different ground, namely that South Vietnam was becoming ever more self-reliant.[38] In fact, most South Vietnamese troops were only too happy to allow the United States to undertake their burden of national defense.[39] However, Westmoreland's inability to answer satisfactorily several of the president's pointed questions, opposition to escalation from military men who feared that the army in Europe was being gutted to feed the war's manpower demands, political considerations, and his own sense that the attrition war was not working made Johnson determined to refuse Westmoreland's requests for additional reinforcements. Simultaneously, he demanded that attention shift to making the South Vietnamese forces more effective. It was an important strategic redirection. Made earlier, it might have led to a much different outcome.[40]

Heretofore, the task of "pacifying" the countryside had been a sorry distant cousin to Westmoreland's main focus on the big unit war. Shielded by American armed might, South Vietnamese forces performed pacification duties without marked success. Too often graft and corruption ruled. Revitalized by the dynamic presence of Robert Komer, who became the head of the new Civil Operations and Rural Development Support Program, pacification began to make demonstrable gains. It was perhaps these gains that prompted a change in the enemy's strategic planning.

In July 1967, Communist political and military leaders from both the South and the North met in Hanoi. Along with the suddenly effective allied pacification programs, they confronted aggressive American tactics on the battlefield that were inflicting significant losses. Impatient and concerned over these trends, North Vietnamese Defense Minister General Vo Nguyen Giap proposed a general offensive.[41] It would take place during the next lunar new year festival, the Tet holiday, some six months hence, and carry the fighting into previously untouched South Vietnamese urban centers. Giap's decision led to the climactic battles of the American war in Vietnam.

EMBASSY SHOWDOWN

To reassure Congress and the public that the war was indeed being won, in November 1967 Johnson recalled the popular, telegenic Westmoreland to Washington. In a speech he would live to regret, Westmoreland gave a very upbeat talk to the National Press Club that emphasized progress throughout Vietnam and discounted enemy abilities. He said the enemy could fight is large units only along the edge of his sanctuaries, namely along the border. "We have reached an important point when the end begins to come into view."[42] Getting a little carried away, he responded to a reporter's question about previous ill-founded optimism expressed by administration officials with the comment "It is conceivable to me that within two years or less, it will be possible for us to phase down our level of commitment."[43]

A month later Lyndon Johnson himself returned to Vietnam. He had visited the troops for a brief hour the previous year even though historically it was not expected of American commanders in chief to enter a war zone. Not since Abraham Lincoln had poked his head above Fort Stevens' earthworks during Jubal Early's abortive attack on Washington had an American president been at such risk in a combat zone. Both trips to Cam Ranh Bay were security nightmares for William Westmoreland, but the second proved a bracing tonic for the president. At the president's request the general ordered the assembled servicemen to break ranks and gather around. Johnson delivered what Westmoreland described as "an excellent speech," after which the general wished the president and his wife a "Merry Christmas and Happy New Year" on behalf of all of the troops. This brought forth loud applause and cheers that much moved the president. Westmoreland observed that as Johnson departed—he had been in Vietnam for some three hours—he was quite obviously pleased.[44]

Nineteen sixty-seven had been a roller coaster year for the commander in chief. As the year closed, Johnson could reflect with some hope that victory was near. One month later the

Communists' Tet Offensive exploded on the battlefields of Vietnam and on the television sets of a stunned American nation.

It did not come as a complete surprise. As early as August 1967, Westmoreland's intelligence officers had begun to detect signs of a major enemy operational change. By December, enough ominous intelligence had been collected to prompt the president to tell Australian officials about the enemy buildup and warn: "We face dark days ahead."[45] Unfortunately, Johnson did not warn the American public. General Earle Wheeler spoke publicly on December 18, twenty-three years and two days after the surprise German assault in the Ardennes, to say that a similar, desperate Communist thrust might occur in the near future. His warning went largely unheeded. In sum, the highest echelon of American leadership suspected something was up, they just did not know quite what.

In large measure, American uncertainty stemmed from Westmoreland's fixation on the North Vietnamese buildup along the so-called demilitarized zone (DMZ) separating North from South. Years before, Westmoreland had concluded that correct enemy strategy would mass forces against South Vietnam's two northern provinces and overwhelm the allied forces there.[46] By the fall of 1967, this nightmare approached reality as the Marine Corps barrier line defending the DMZ, and in particular a regimental combat base at a place called Khe Sanh, faced a menacing mass of North Vietnamese soldiers. Westmoreland had to respond to this threat. Under the impression that Giap aimed at making Khe Sanh another Dien Bien Phu, he sent large numbers of men northward. Meanwhile, the Communists moved southward in preparation for their nationwide offensive. The result was that by January 1968, enemy pressure had overstretched U.S. resources.

One Communist force moved from its Cambodian sanctuary toward Saigon, a mere thirty miles distant. On the way it used staging bases in the Iron Triangle, bases that supposedly had been cleared by repeated allied search-and-destroy operations. They marched through numerous populated areas, yet no civilians from these supposedly pacified areas reported their passage to the Saigon government. Still, the movement did not go entirely unnoticed.[47]

At the proverbial last minute, on January 10, 1968, one of Westmoreland's able deputies, Lieutenant General Frederick Weyand, telephoned his commander that something unprecedented and dangerous was afoot.[48] In one of his best wartime decisions, Westmoreland reacted by canceling planned operations out on the distant periphery and shifting resources toward the defense of Saigon.[49] Likewise, he tried to convince the South Vietnamese to cancel the coming Tet cease-fire, but President Thieu argued that it would adversely affect the morale of his nation and its soldiers. Thieu's blunder meant the South Vietnamese military would be ill-prepared for the enemy's attack.

In the event, the Americans proved only slightly more ready. Westmoreland did not believe the enemy would commit the sacrilege of attacking during Tet. Ignorant of the historic precedent of 1789, when Vietnamese patriots had chose Tet to attack the occupying Chinese in Vietnam's capital of Hanoi, he thought any action would come before or after the holiday.[50] Still, during the day of January 30, Westmoreland's headquarters ordered a maximum alert with particular attention to the defense of headquarters complexes, logistical installations, airfields, population centers, and billets. These were precisely the enemy's prime targets, but the warning either came too late or was largely ignored.[51]

Heedless of the approaching crisis, South Vietnam prepared to celebrate its lunar new year. The celebration's peak would come the night of January 30. The official South Vietnamese history describes the nation's mood:

> *A relative lull seemed to be prevailing all over South Vietnam . . .*
> *leaves were readily granted the troops for the lunar New Year and*
> *measures were taken by the Administration to give the common*
> *people as normal a Tet as possible . . . The people had forgotten*
> *about the dying war. They wanted to celebrate Tet with as much*
> *fervor as in the old days.*[52]

As revelers swarmed Saigon's streets to greet the new Year of the Monkey, the explosions of thousands of traditional firecrackers rocked the air. Slowly, as some of the sixty-seven thousand Viet Cong committed nationwide to the first assault wave moved from their safe houses into attack position, the sounds of combat replaced the sounds of festival.

The attack's synchronized ferocity surprised everyone from Westmoreland on down. Throughout the country allied forces responded to emergency piled upon crisis. In the Saigon area alone the Communists attacked with fifteen battalions. The map showing reported enemy attacks reminded General Weyand of "a pinball machine, one light after another going on as it was hit."[53] Four thousand Viet Cong, mostly local men and women, assaulted Saigon's urban center. But it was a mere nineteen soldiers belonging to the C-10 City Sapper Battalion who mesmerized the American public's attention with their attack against the U.S. embassy.

The embassy had already been struck by a Viet Cong car bomb in 1965. It then moved to a new location. In 1968 it should have surprised no one that the enemy would try again, but this oversight was just one of many ways the embassy battle served as a microcosm of the entire war. The weapons and explosives the enemy sappers used had been slipped through a hopelessly porous South Vietnamese security cordon around the capital. The nineteen guerrillas mustered in a building owned by a female Viet Cong agent of thirteen years' standing who had often been arrested for subversive activities but whose building was not under surveillance. The attackers received help from an embassy driver Americans had often jokingly said "must be a VC" because he was so smart.

A South Vietnamese policeman saw the Viet Cong driving to the embassy in two vehicles without headlights, but chose to avoid trouble and to do nothing. Nearing the embassy, the attackers encountered a first line of defense, four more police, who fled without firing. Approaching the night gate in the eight-foot-high wall that surrounded the embassy, the Viet Cong encountered two American military policemen. Although attacks had been taking place for more than an hour, so poor was interallied communication that the American MPs had no idea that the Communists had broken the truce. Amid an exchange of gunfire, the MPs backed into the embassy compound, shut the gate, and radioed news that the embassy was under attack.

Out in the streets, the Viet Cong unloaded explosives and blew a three-foot hole in the wall. Exhibiting formidable courage but poor tactics, two enemy officers led the rush through the breach. Alerted by the explosion, the two MPs whirled around and shot down the officers. One shouted on his radio: "They're coming in! They're coming in! Help me! Help me!" It was his last message.

The first American reaction force, a two-man MP jeep patrol, rushed toward the embassy only to die in a hail of fire from the sappers outside the embassy walls. Inside the compound, two Marine guards locked the building's heavy teak doors. Seconds later a rocket grenade smashed through the granite slab on which hung the United States Seal, badly wounding one guard. Backed into the lobby, the surviving guard resolved to sell himself dearly as he awaited the enemy's final assault. It never came.[54] Deprived of leadership, the attackers hesitated and failed to exploit their initial success. Even though they faced only a few surviving Americans inside the embassy building itself, for the remainder of the night the Viet Cong milled about in confusion.

Within fifteen minutes of the opening assault, an Associated Press reporter typed out the first news bulletin announcing the attack. By a twist of fate that was to have immense impact, the quarters housing the American press was near to the embassy. Reporters rushed to the scene of the action, where all was pandemonium. Because the reporters could not see over the compound's walls, they did not know what was going on inside and relied upon the excited comments of the U.S. soldiers gathering around outside. One MP said, "They're in the embassy." Asked for confirmation, a captain responded, "My God, yes . . . we are taking fire from up there . . . keep your head down."

It was enough for the Associated Press to send another bulletin:

> *The Vietcong seized part of the US Embassy . . . Communist commandos penetrated the supposedly attack-proof building in the climax of a combined artillery and guerilla assault that brought limited warfare to Saigon itself.*[55]

The bulletin arrived just before the first-edition deadlines of influential morning newspapers on the U.S. eastern seaboard. Credulous editors hastily rewrote headlines and America awoke to read that the enemy had captured the symbol of U.S. prestige in Vietnam.

Outside the embassy, the American tactical commanders were quite content to await daylight before proceeding to clear the grounds. The American command, including Westmoreland, did not attach any particular significance to one clash among many. As General Weyand recalled, it was hard to make sense of the enemy's multiple thrusts. Only when Washington pushed for action did Westmoreland order a helicopter with a platoon of soldiers aboard to head for the embassy.

The heavy enemy fire that drove off the helicopter confirmed that it was prudent to wait for daylight. Then military policemen forced the gate and easily killed the surviving Viet Cong. As one

American participant recalled the entire episode had been "a piddling platoon action."

Reporters swarmed around the compound and tried to make sense of what had happened. Some disputed the military's claim that no Viet Cong had actually entered the embassy. Too often reporters believed that official pronouncements had been deceptive, and so the Associated Press stood by its claim, although it turned out to be erroneous. It set the stage for one of the most memorable visual images in this, the world's first television war.

General Westmoreland arrived at the just-secured embassy compound dressed, as usual, in an immaculately pressed and starched uniform. He held a hasty press conference. In America, viewers saw a scene of carnage, with dead enemy sappers sprawled atop the debris of battle. In the midst of an embassy apparently under siege, Westmoreland exuded confidence, denied that the Viet Cong had ever penetrated the embassy, and said that the allies were about to resume the offensive.

A *Washington Post* reporter recalls, "The reporters could hardly believe their ears. Westmoreland was standing in the ruins and saying everything was great."[56]

In the United States, the American public, who had read that the Viet Cong had seized the embassy, now heard the general seemingly lie and say they had not. The psychological fallout from the embassy combat shattered the confidence of many in their general and their president.

Westmoreland had no idea that anything was amiss. The demands of the battlefield required his full attention as he coped with enemy attacks against thirty-nine of forty-four provincial capitals, five of the six autonomous cities, a third of the district capitals, and numerous assaults against allied military installations.[57] This left it to Brigadier General John Chaisson, head of his combat operations center, to say what it all meant when he briefed the press on February 3, 1968:

> *It's been a week of surprises. I think the VC surprised us with their attacks . . . We have been faced this week with a real battle. There is no sense in ducking it; there is no sense in hiding it. When you look at figures that are in the magnitude of 1,000 friendly killed in less than five days of fighting, and something of the magnitude of 12,000 of the enemy killed in the same period, you're talking about real fighting.*[58]

Three weeks after the opening assault, the enemy's high command issued orders for its units still in contact around the cities to withdraw. Their attacks had been extremely costly and failed to achieve the expected successes. Only later would they realize the extent of their political victory.

In Washington, shocked by the battle's furor, Johnson braced for worse. Westmoreland maintained that Tet was a diversion for the enemy's main offensive along the demilitarized zone. In particular, he expected the heaviest blow to fall against the beleaguered Marines defending the Khe Sanh Combat Base. Alarmed, believing that the enemy was "putting all of their stack in now," Lyndon Johnson demanded detailed daily information from his military advisers.[59] Just as he had asked in the past if the war was being won or lost, so now he asked, would Khe Sanh become another Dien Bien Phu? Its fate obsessed him during the critical February days. It didn't help when he asked pointed, detailed questions, questions that underscored his growing grasp of military affairs regarding the base's tactical situation and the Army Chief of Staff merely responded that he believed there was an even chance of holding out.[60] In no uncertain terms Johnson told the chairman of the Joint Chiefs, "I don't want any damn Dinbinphoo."[61] It also did not help when Maxwell Taylor, again advising the president closely on military matters, told Johnson that he had serious doubts about both Westmoreland's strategy and his desire to hold Khe Sanh.

Tension increased when Westmoreland responded to Taylor's concerns with the observation that "we are now in a new ball game" against a powerful North Vietnamese force engaging in an all-out offensive.[62] The term "a new ball game" must have discouraged the commander in chief. He had heard about new programs and new starts since U.S. support for the French began in the early 1950s, and now, after much bloody sacrifice, it seemed the situation was back to where it had begun: an enemy offensive threatening to gain a major victory.

To Westmoreland, the situation offered a fine opportunity to inflict substantial damage on the Communists. When his subordinates worried whether Khe Sanh could be defended, Westmoreland reacted decisively, making it absolutely plain that he "wanted no talk that we could not hold it, since we were going to do just that."[63] In Westmoreland's mind, Khe Sanh was a particularly attractive opportunity because so often major U.S. forces had searched in vain for the enemy. Here they were concentrated around Khe Sanh and vulnerable to bombs and shells. During the course of the siege, aircraft alone would average the staggering total of thirteen hundred tons of bombs dropped around the base every day, a cumulative total of five tons of bombs for every enemy soldier in the area. On the debit side, Khe Sanh was of little intrinsic value and its defense required an enormous investment of U.S. manpower, thus necessitating a thinning of the lines somewhere.[64] That somewhere was the rural areas of the three southern corps regions. Pacification programs, one of the presumed paths to victory, or at least to U.S. disengagement, had already been hard hit by the Tet Offensive. The threat around Khe Sanh meant that pacification would be slow to recover.

Maxwell Taylor told Johnson that Khe Sanh could be held, but it was an albatross impairing all American effort. Here was another blow to the president. His most trusted military adviser was telling him that his field general's strategy was deeply flawed. There was so much to consider, and Johnson tried mightily to master it all. Daily he read Westmoreland's cables, reports from the JCS, National Military Command Center summaries, CIA reports, logistics and casualty summaries, an intelligence checklist, and listened to advice from his various secretaries and members of the National Security Council. It was a Herculean effort. To help him make sense of it all, intelligence experts built a scale-model terrain map of Khe Sanh. It pleased Johnson and provided a central focus for situation briefings. It was something concrete to latch onto and helped convince Johnson to disregard Taylor's advice and accept Westmoreland's resolve to hold Khe Sanh. It was the battle his field general clearly wanted to fight. Shortly thereafter, Johnson told the press, "If I had to select a man to lead me into battle in Vietnam, I would want General Westmoreland."[65]

The major post-Tet U.S. operation in Vietnam involved the 1st Cavalry Division (Air Cav) in a drive to open land communications with Khe Sanh. It proved a costly operation as Marines and cavalry drove up Route 9 to "relieve" the embattled combat base. In fact, the North Vietnamese no longer had any designs on the base and had withdrawn substantial forces from the area. Soberly, General Earle Wheeler reported: "Khe Sanh appears to have served the NVA's [North Vietnamese Army's] purpose."[66] Moreover, the base's principal strategic value was negated by the combination of logistical overstretch and political change in Washington.

Westmoreland lacked the resources to pursue his hoped-for invasion; Johnson lacked the standing to approve such a bold expansion of the war. On June 12, 1968, Marine headquarters authorized the abandonment of Khe Sanh.

Although generals and historians would argue ever after about the strategic connection between Khe Sanh and Tet, the plain facts are that on the eve of Tet, Westmoreland's focus was squarely on the north and Khe Sanh. For months his strategy had focused on reinforcing the north in preparation for this battle.[67] He regarded enemy movements elsewhere as an effort to divert allied attention from Khe Sanh and consequently misread the major threat.

RETREAT

Visiting Saigon shortly after Tet, the chairman of the Joint Chiefs told Westmoreland that the newspapers had conveyed the impression that Tet was "the worst calamity since Bull Run."[68] Wheeler himself felt pessimistic, and the explosion near his sleeping quarters of a Viet Cong rocket his first night in Vietnam only darkened his mood. It reinforced the impression he had brought with him: the enemy held the initiative; nowhere, not even here in the heart of the allied defenses, was safe from a surprise enemy strike. Wheeler discussed what to do. Westmoreland promoted concepts based upon the enemy's weakness and the arrival of more American troops. The two generals recognized there was only an even chance that the president would agree to a more aggressive policy. However, Westmoreland failed to persuade Wheeler that Tet had been a great victory.

Instead, Wheeler returned to Washington to advise that the enemy was freely maneuvering in the countryside, recruiting heavily, and recovering rapidly. The all-important pacification program had "suffered a severe setback." Wheeler concluded: "In short, it was a very near thing."[69]

Somewhere between Saigon and Washington, sometime between the Tet Offensive and the end of March, a solid U.S. achievement on the ground metamorphosed into a North Vietnamese strategic victory. There had been a breakdown in the always fragile line of communications between the field general and his commander in chief. In Saigon, Westmoreland did not appreciate that a turning point was at hand. Meanwhile, in Washington, the president's most trusted advisers highlighted the incongruity between Westmoreland's statements of great gains, his request for reinforcements, and Wheeler's pessimistic appraisal.

In Tet's aftermath, Westmoreland had made a very modest request for reinforcements. The Saigon visit of Wheeler changed that. Wheeler encouraged Westmoreland to ask for enough troops to start a country-wide counteroffensive and to invade Cambodia and Laos. This optimal number totaled some 206,000 men. Westmoreland did not know that Wheeler intended to use this total to achieve his own pet dream, the reconstitution of the badly depleted army strategic reserve. Back in Washington, Wheeler presented the figure as one that was needed on an emergency basis for service in Vietnam. When the figure leaked to the press it embarrassed the administration and probably also cost Westmoreland his job. Having himself observed the nightly television images of carnage and destruction, unaware of how the camera misleadingly magnified what was taking place, and now receiving Wheeler's depressing report, Johnson demanded an "A to Z" reassessment of the war.

His only friend, newly appointed Secretary of Defense Clark Clifford—the unrelenting grind of the attrition war had finally shattered McNamara—oversaw the project. Johnson probably did not know that before his appointment Clifford had turned against the war. During the study, Clifford asked for the military victory plan, only to be told that there was no such plan in the traditional sense. Such as it was, the strategy remained to inflict losses until the enemy gave up. After four years of American intervention, there were no signs that the enemy's will was wavering. No one could predict when the Communists would desist. To Clifford's distress, there was no reassurance that sending more men would change anything.[70]

Meanwhile, the commander in chief received a message of a different kind from the American public, or at least from the voters of New Hampshire. In a stunning outcome, dark horse antiwar candidate Eugene McCarthy nearly defeated the incumbent in the New Hampshire primary. In fact, McCarthy's vote total underscored public disapproval of the president's war management from both the right and left. It included for every two voters who wanted out of Vietnam, three antiadministration voters who believed the president should unshackle the military and let them fight. Nation-wide opinion polls showed that for the first time more than half the people considered involvement in Vietnam a mistake.[71] The president tried to stop his slide in public esteem, telling the nation that Hanoi was trying "to win in Washington what it cannot win in Hue or Khe Sanh."[72] But it was too late.

Depressed already by the unexpected violence of Tet and the "request" for another several hundred thousand troops, believing he had been poorly served by many in government and in the Pentagon, the president convened a group he called the "Wise Men." They comprised a virtual roll call of senior advisers who had served presidents all the way back to Truman and Roosevelt: Dean Acheson, McGeorge Bundy, George Ball, Omar Bradley, Maxwell Taylor, and others—all recognized as veteran, sharp-minded public servants. They, along with Clark Clifford, carefully examined U.S. prospects in light of the Tet Offensive. While Generals Bradley and Taylor wanted to persevere, to "do what our military commanders suggest," the majority told Johnson that the U.S. strategy had failed.[73] Even his steady Secretary of State, Dean Rusk, observed that Tet had taken away the nation's hope, adding, "People don't think there is likely to be an end."[74] Although hurt and shocked by his Wise Men's seeming betrayal, Johnson accepted that a change had to be made. Instead of 206,000 men, he sent only a small reinforcement. More important, on March 31, 1968, he spoke to the nation about the future. He began:

> *Good evening, my fellow Americans. Tonight I want to speak to you of peace in Vietnam.*

The war's climactic battle had just occurred, its full results were unknown, and the commander in chief wanted to talk about peace. This was not the determined attitude of Washington after the St. Clair disaster, Davis after Gettysburg, or Roosevelt after Pearl Harbor.

Johnson proceeded to review his previous peace initiatives and give a brief accounting of the Tet Offensive. He could have made a ringing victory claim; instead, he offered an uncertain prophecy of fierce fighting to come. To avoid further suffering, he announced, "I am taking the first step to deescalate the conflict." He ordered a near-total cessation of the bombing and pleaded

with Ho Chi Minh "to respond positively." He continued by out-
lining his achievements—the building of a durable South
Vietnamese government protected by the shield of American military might while simultaneously giving the United States "seven
years of unparalleled prosperity"—and talked about the future direction of the war in which the South Vietnamese would undertake
more of the burden.

Then he elaborated upon how peace would come, giving the
hollow warning that U.S. resolve remained unbroken and the
country would "never accept a fake solution" to the war "and call
it peace." Eloquently, he spoke of America's sacrifice and how "it
has been my fate and my responsibility to be Commander in Chief.
I have lived—daily and nightly—with the cost of this war." Again
he explained that America's purpose was noble and one that three
separate administrations had endorsed. Over the years a single
principle had sustained him, the belief that Vietnam "is vital to
the security of every American."

Then, in his conclusion he shocked the nation. Alluding to
Lincoln's famous warning about a "house divided against itself,"
he spoke about a "division in the American house" that imperiled
everything. He urged all Americans to unify, to strengthen the
country so it could achieve its historic goals. He concluded that
he would lead by example, cast aside partisanship in this year of
national election, and attend solely to "the awesome duties of this
office" by refusing to seek or accept his party's nomination for
another term.[75]

A defeated president was retreating from the field.[76]

*   *   *

In the preceding twenty-five years the American military had frequently been victimized by enemy surprise attacks. Pearl Harbor,
Kasserine Pass, the Battle of the Bulge, and the Chinese intervention along the Yalu River had all caught the American military
unawares. Of all these surprises, only the Tet Offensive achieved
decisive results. Yet, by conventional military calculations, Tet was
an allied victory. At the cost of about 4,000 American casualties
and 4,000 to 8,000 ARVN soldiers killed, the Communists suffered
40,000 to 50,000 battlefield deaths. Most significant, large numbers
of irreplaceable local Viet Cong fighters had died. As predicted by
General Wheeler, the enemy had concentrated and his masses had

been consumed by U.S. firepower. During a visit to the White House after Tet, Westmoreland said, "Militarily, we have never been in a better relative position in South Vietnam."[77] The general was right. If this had been a conventional war, it would have ended in 1968 with a Communist defeat. The way the American public perceived the battle astonished many soldiers in Vietnam. Standing next to enemy corpses stacked like cordwood outside his headquarters, one cavalry officer wondered: "To our complete bewilderment in the weeks that followed, nobody ever publicized this feat of battlefield triumph. Instead, we read that we had been defeated."[78]

Incomplete, inaccurate, and biased press coverage of Tet influenced the public's perception. Even so, the public recognized that a hard kernel of truth had been demonstrated by the enemy's synchronized, ferocious violence; the Communists remained much stronger than American political and military leaders had led them to believe. However imperfectly they understood the details, the public realized that the choice was to escalate again or to seek terms. Jefferson Davis had written: "In all free governments the ability of its executive branch to prosecute a war must largely depend upon public opinion."[79] The Tet Offensive underscored Davis's wisdom.

In 1968, political and military leaders from Johnson and Westmoreland down blamed the press for losing the war. The effort to shift the blame continued for years thereafter as discredited leaders sought to recover prestige. A month before his death, Lyndon Johnson told Westmoreland that he had made a tremendous mistake by not imposing censorship.[80] Such carping obscures the fact that even had the press been fully muzzled, the commander in chief had no viable war-winning strategy. At the time the Communist high command was opting to gamble on a general offensive, top-level American planners had met in Honolulu. The conference's final report stated: "A clear concise statement of US strategy in Vietnam could not be established . . . A war of attrition provides neither economy of force not any foreseeable end to the war."[81] In other words, the country's foremost civilian and military planners simply could not identify anything worthy of being called a strategy.

In mid-1967, the North Vietnamese army numbered about 450,000 men, of whom a mere 70,000 served in Laos and South Vietnam. Each year about 200,000 North Vietnamese men turned eighteen. Simple arithmetic proved that the Communists had the manpower to endure terrible losses for years to come. If Westmoreland's attrition strategy could not kill the enemy fast enough, in spite of amazingly favorable kill ratios of ten to one or better, then the outcome hinged on will. The French war, let alone Vietnam's long history of resistance to the Chinese, clearly demonstrated that the Communist leadership, which had assumed the mantle of stubborn Vietnamese nationalism, would not crack first.

The Tet Offensive was part of an unbroken record forged by the American fighting man from 1965 to 1973 of not losing a single important battle during the Vietnam War. While Tet failed to defeat the U.S. combat soldier, it defeated their general and their political leaders, and it reversed the support of the people back home. Before Tet, American leaders sought some form of victory. After Tet, they sought to withdraw gracefully. If a decisive battle is one in which a world power is overthrown by armed combat, then Tet was one of history's rare decisive battles.

Three months after Tet, American and North Vietnamese negotiators met in Paris to begin peace talks. To date some twenty-one thousand Americans had been killed in Vietnam. American leaders never fully comprehended the masterful Communist negotiating strategy of "fighting and talking, talking and fighting."[82] Because they did not, more Americans would be killed after the "peace talks" opened then before they began.

In July 1968, General William C. Westmoreland became the new Army Chief of Staff. Few doubted that, defeated and discredited, he had been kicked upstairs.[83] His successor, General Creighton Abrams—one of the three officers Johnson had originally considered for the assignment—responded to domestic political pressure by ordering sweeping strategic changes. American tactical aggressiveness gave way to a new mandate to reduce American battlefield losses and to defend high-visibility population centers. Equally important, South Vietnamese troops switched from pacification to mainstream combat, the beginning of the ill-fated "Vietnamization" policy.[84]

On the other side, so badly had Tet hurt the Communists that they would not launch another general offensive until 1972. Then, American airpower proved decisive in defeating it. Three years later South Vietnam was short on war supplies of all types, including most fundamentally ammunition. It was a shortage created by the United States Congress which, after the departure of the last American combat troops, voted to cease all military aid for South Vietnam. Taking advantage of this and the absence of American airpower, a conventional tank-led invasion conquered Vietnam. With the ignominious flight of the last American government representatives from the embassy rooftop, the United States had lost its first war.

*   *   *

The memoirs written by leaders of the American war effort have sought to uncover the root causes of failure. Since it is a rare person indeed who can participate in such a debacle and say, afterward, "I provided poor advice to the commander in chief" or "I designed a flawed strategy and thousands of my countrymen died as a result," most of these memoirs feature blame for someone else. Senior military officers criticized civilian leadership for tying their hands and thus preventing them from "winning" the war. Many civilian leaders, in turn, claimed that the military devised an unsubtle attritional strategy and failed to comprehend the conflict's political dimensions. Last, both blamed the media for undermining the public's will.

The war witnessed a renewal of the historic tension between a civilian government and its military as critics attacked Johnson and his staff for "micromanaging" the war. In his memoirs Westmoreland bitterly complained about civilians who lacked any knowledge of military affairs yet wielded "undue influence" to shackle the professional military man.[85] Indeed, Secretary of Defense McNamara failed to understand that while his beloved systems analysis could be very helpful in making military procurement decisions, it was not conterminous with strategy once war began. Worse, McNamara and his civilian advisers interfered with military tactics, an interference that had lethal consequences for too many American servicemen. On the other hand, while an unconstrained American military could have inflicted additional incalculable damage, this would not have addressed a fundamental strategic flaw for which the commander in chief must be blamed.

Johnson's policy forced the United States to strive to prop up a corrupt and thoroughly unpopular regime that had inherited the wreckage of a French colonial system. The South Vietnamese government perpetuated a stratified class system with a bourgeois elite atop a peasant base. It maintained itself by military power and resisted mass political participation while pitted against an adversary who cloaked himself in the mantle of nationalism and promoted a "People's War." Before committing his nation to war, Johnson had ample evidence that this was so.

Lyndon Johnson's war-fighting strategy was not his greatest error. He selected a field commander whose subsequent performance would have been acceptable given any prior historical set of circumstances. Rather, the error was his decision to begin a war for Vietnam that could not be won at an acceptable price—if it could be won at all.

As memories of the Vietnam War's horrors fade with time, the triumphs of the Gulf War intercede, and a new generation reads theories propounding how the Vietnam War could have been won, it is worth recalling the words of a North Vietnamese officer who acknowledged the terrible losses suffered during Tet: "We had hundreds of thousands killed in this war. We would have sacrificed one or two million more if necessary."[86]

Of the many who reflect upon the leader of America's first defeat, the kindest words come from an old foe. In the summer of 1990, a quarter century after Lyndon Johnson made the decision to send America's sons to war, General Giap mused, "Of course he would have been wiser not to escalate the war. But throughout history, even the most intelligent leaders have not always been masters of their fate.[87] Giap is too kind. In 1965 Johnson was the master of his own fate. As commander in chief he had to determine where his country had the most at stake and the greatest chance to prevail. He chose Vietnam. In 1969 he again explained why:

> *I knew that if I ran out that I'd be the first American President to ignore our commitments, turn tail and run, and leave our allies in the lurch, after all the commitments Eisenhower had made, and all that SEATO had made, and all that the Congress had made, and all that the Tonkin Gulf said, and all the statements that Kennedy had made, and Bobby Kennedy had made, and that everybody had made. I'd be the first American President to put my tail between my legs and run out because I didn't have the courage to stand up.*[88]

Haunted by a fear that he lacked the courage to "stand up," Johnson lacked the courage to resist starting a war. Later, he lacked the courage to cut the losses and withdraw. Throughout, he failed to level with the American people about the extent of the sacrifice needed. In the end, this man with such a shrewd political grasp doubted the people. In time, after an immense sacrifice, the people reciprocated this distrust and drove him from office.

PART FIVE

Presidents Under Fire

11 ☞⊶

VICTORY AND DEFEAT

> *"By God, we've licked the Vietnam syndrome once and for all."*
>
> President Bush, March 1, 1991

> *"The military student does not seek to learn from history the minutia of method and technique. In every age these are decisively influenced by the characteristics of weapons currently available and by means at hand for maneuvering, supplying and controlling combat forces. But research does bring to light those fundamental principles, and their combinations and applications, which in the past, have been productive of success. These principles know no limitation of time."*
>
> Douglas MacArthur, 1935[1]

WAR IN THE PERSIAN GULF

WHEN A WAR ENDS, IT IS NATURAL THAT PARTICIPANTS AND THE PUBLIC will discuss events to reflect upon what it all meant. Such reflection is all the more acute when the war ends in defeat. Inevitably, attention focuses on what might have been. So it was when Confederate veterans gathered to refight lost battles, to explore lost opportunities, to identify those moments when things might have turned out differently. So it has been in recent years regarding Vietnam. The lessons of Vietnam became all the more important when a major presidential contender, Bill Clinton, who had opposed the war in the 1960s and avoided military service on what he said were moral grounds, reiterated in 1992 that he strongly believed American policy had been wrong.

The publisher of the *Wall Street Journal*, Peter R. Kann, spoke for many conservatives when he took exception to Clinton's statement. Kann cited Vietnam's postwar history—the infamous "reeducation camps," the mass exodus of the boat people, the misery of those who remained behind—as evidence that America's cause had been good. Furthermore, he said that the American intervention in Vietnam shielded the rest of Asia from the Communist menace and permitted the eventual development of many Asian free-enterprise economies. In sum, it was an articulate restatement of the Domino Theory and a warning that would-be commander in chief Clinton's misunderstanding of history disqualified him for the job.[2]

Clinton's record contrasted sharply with the meritorious war service of his rival, President George Bush. Moreover, Bush could point to his conduct of the recent Gulf War as a shining example of his own fitness for continuing to serve as commander in chief. In large measure, Bush staked his 1992 reelection bid on the strength of his leadership during the Gulf War. How had he performed? To begin to answer this question requires an understanding of how thoroughly Vietnam's legacy influenced the events of 1990–1991.

Foremost of all the lessons from that war was the military's determination to avoid another conflict that lacked public support. Creighton Abrams, the general who succeeded Westmoreland in Vietnam, went on to become Army Chief of Staff. He set himself the task of restoring the morale and integrity of an army that had just lost the nation's first war. Actually, few military men, and certainly not Abrams, believed that the army had "lost" the war. But Abrams recognized that the army had suffered regardless of who was to blame, and accordingly, this gifted soldier worked to correct the institutional problems that Vietnam had exposed. Above all, he believed that Johnson's failure to summon the Reserves had created a gulf between the army and the people. He resolved that politicians were "not taking us to war again without calling up the reserves."[3]

Therefore, he directed that every active army division would have a National Guard component. Their thorough integration made them indispensable, ensuring that the army divisions could not function without the Reserves. Abrams's goal in implementing his "round out" concept—the term referred to the way the Reserves completed, or rounded out, the regular units—was straightforward: a future commander in chief would be unable to deploy significant numbers of army troops until the Reserves had been summoned. In the admiring words of historian Harry G. Summers, Jr., Abrams seized upon the Reserves as the ideal instrument to restore von Clausewitz's "remarkable trinity"—the connection among the people, the commander and his army, and the government—by "stiffening the congressional backbone and ensuring Congress's active support for wartime operations."[4]

The reality of what Abrams had done became apparent in 1984. At that time, Secretary of Defense Caspar Weinberger articulated six preconditions for the commitment of U.S. forces to battle. One emphasized the salient need for popular and congressional support for the proposed action. In spite of the so-called Weinberger doctrine, during the Persian Gulf confrontation of 1990 Abrams's plan worked imperfectly.[5] It succeeded in getting the Reserves front and center in Saudi Arabia—on the eve of hostilities reserve forces comprised 58 percent of total army strength—yet it did not force Congress to become involved. However, because the Reserves who contributed to Desert Shield came from all parts of the nation, it was clear that when hostilities commenced a broader cross section of the country's homes would be touched than had been the case in Vietnam. The public consequently displayed its traditional patriotism in support of their "boys" overseas, and their zeal did much to persuade wavering politicians to jump aboard the war band wagon.

While President Bush pondered his constitutional duty vis-à-vis Congress, his spokesmen repeatedly cited the statistic that United States forces had been sent abroad some two hundred times with only five formal declarations of war. It followed that in 1990 the president did not need to ask Congress for a formal declaration of war. Besides overlooking Supreme Court Justice Felix Frankfurter's warning—"illegality cannot attain legitimacy through practice"— this specious contention regarding executive war-making authority ignored the fact that the majority of the two hundred incidents involved congressionally authorized and bloodless naval landings to protect citizens. Until Korea and Vietnam, the commander in chief had always asked Congress for a declaration of war before pursuing America's major military conflicts.

By Thanksgiving 1990, a time of uneasy standoff between American troops defending Saudi Arabia and Iraqi forces occupying Kuwait, Bush's standing in the polls was plummeting. He had been unable to explain to the American people why more servicemen might be needed in the Gulf or why a war might be necessary. Bush exhibited Jefferson Davis–like puzzlement over the resultant lack of public support, commenting, "I truly don't understand how anyone could be against the stand we've taken."[6] The commander in chief was certain his policy was in the nation's best interests and emphasized that neither the poll results nor Congress were going to intimidate him. He concluded that legally he did not need congressional approval to proceed. Throughout these months it was Chairman of the Joint Chiefs General Colin Powell, acting in the Abrams tradition, who brought up the issue of public and congressional support as a prerequisite for sending more men to Saudi Arabia. In his mind the Vietnam experience loomed large. He did not want the president to repeat Lyndon Johnson's error.

Finally, when Bush asked for another 150,000 men to reinforce the 230,000 already in the Gulf, congressmen began to protest the executive's high-handed action. Memories of how congressional timidity had allowed Johnson to wage war on the slim pretext of the Tonkin Gulf Resolution influenced them. During a congressional hearing, a senator asked the Secretary of Defense point-blank whether the president needed congressional approval in advance of offensive action against Iraq. The secretary unabashedly replied no. His response stimulated nationwide debate. Even pro-war congressmen recalled the Vietnam experience, and they warned Bush of the danger of going to war without a national consensus. This uproar prodded a reluctant president to include Congress in the war-making decision. At the proverbial last minute, Bush resolved to seek some kind of consensus.

This was reminiscent of 1846, when Senator Thomas Benton had incurred Polk's wrath by demanding debate on the proposed war with Mexico. Benton explained that "Nineteenth Century war should not be declared without full discussion"[7] If the three days of congressional oratory in January 1991 hardly made for "full discussion"—conducted, as they were, in an emotionally charged atmosphere with huge American forces eyeball to eyeball with Iraq and the deadline already imposed by Bush just five days away—at least they were more than had taken place before Johnson sent America to war in Vietnam. And, as it turned out, the congressional resolution authorizing the commander in chief to use force satisfied most that the Constitution had been served.

Whether Congress had been manipulated or persuaded remains an open question. Nonetheless, however much Bush shared Johnson's indifference to constitutional niceties regarding war making, he far outperformed Johnson as a strategic architect. He did this by defining a clear objective. Three days after Iraq's invasion of Kuwait, he stated that "this shall not stand." It was a position from which he did not waver and led to an articulation of national policy objectives that included first and foremost the "complete, and unconditional withdrawal of all Iraqi forces from Kuwait."[8]

The president was less successful in building a chain of command that smoothly translated policy goals into actual military strategy. Bush's narrow but concrete definition of objective pleased military planners. Overlooked was longer range thinking, what to do once "victory" was won. The field general charged with executing Bush's strategy, General H. Norman Schwarzkopf, recalled that as he began to lay out a campaign plan, he did so without guidance from the men at the top. Although no one told him not to destroy Iraq as a nation, he simply assumed "that the United States would continue to need Iraq as a regional counterbalance to Iran."[9] Likewise, in October 1990, a time Schwarzkopf had begun planning for an offensive campaign against Iraq, an American diplomat asked him if he was satisfied that he understood the U.S. strategic objective. the general replied, "No. I'm working in the dark."[10]

Traditional civil-military tensions climaxed within the next two weeks. Schwarzkopf believed he needed substantial reinforcements in order to execute a proper offensive. When one of his aides described his plan to the president, a top presidential adviser interjected, "My God, he's already got all the forces he needs. Why won't he attack."[11] Another compared Schwarzkopf to the overly cautious George McClellan, who had confronted Lee outside of Richmond.

Fortunately, the commander in chief disregarded these sentiments and did not force his general into a premature operation, partially due to the entrance of another traditional American factor into the strategic calculus, the upcoming congressional election. General Powell told Schwarzkopf that the mood in Washington shifted every week, but that everyone was preoccupied with the election and consequently no decision would be made until after that event. Finally, after the November congressional election passed, the president announced that a heavy armored corps would be sent from Germany to give Schwarzkopf the offensive capacity he requested.

Jefferson Davis had given Lee the time he needed to prepare

his counteroffensive against McClellan and then told his general, "I give you the material to be used at your discretion."[12] In 1990 Bush emulated the best of Jefferson Davis.

*   *   *

During the Vietnam War, one of Lyndon Johnson's military advisers had reminded him that a commander in chief always confronts trying periods of uncertainty during which information is sketchy at best. He told Johnson that on the eve of the Normandy Invasion General Dwight D. Eisenhower had described the anxiety as "the interminable wait . . . between the final decision of the high command and the earliest possible determination of success or failure."[13] Johnson failed to learn from this story. Instead, to relieve his strain, he had demanded daily telephone updates from Westmoreland. Modern communications technology gave him and his successors the unprecedented opportunity to meddle. To his great credit President Bush did not avail himself of this capability. Between Christmas Eve 1990 and the last days of the ground war, he did not speak with his field general.

The war ended in apparent triumph. Happily the president announced victory and the end of the Vietnam syndrome. While everyone acknowledged that the military had performed well, slowly a growing suspicion emerged that the job had not been completed, that there was less to the victory than first met the eye. When Iraqi dissidents revolted against Saddam Hussein—a revolt encouraged by allied wartime propaganda—only to be crushed by Saddam's forces, suspicions hardened. The image of a swaggering, strutful Saddam, still atop his war-ravaged nation, played heavily upon the American public's mind when it voted in the 1992 election. In an extraordinary outcome, the public rejected a commander in chief who had recently succeeded on the battlefield.

The complete facts bearing upon the end of the Gulf War will not be released to the public for a very long time, if ever.[14] Certain things are known. In his prewar briefing, Schwarzkopf told his subordinates that one of his objectives was to destroy utterly Iraq's Republican Guard.[15] When the war ended, enough Republican Guards remained intact to crush a revolt among Iraq's Shiites and to preserve Saddam in power. In the war's waning hours, American forces were hounding the surviving Republican Guard formations into a pocket against the

Euphrates River near Basra. Simultaneously, journalists began inter-
viewing pilots who had been attacking Iraqi convoys fleeing from
Kuwait City. These pilots described a veritable turkey shoot along
Highway 6, the so-called Highway of Death. Television pictures
showed images of destruction and carnage along this highway, giving
the impression that it was wanton killing.

Had television covered World War II, it could have readily
shown similar scenes. During the Normandy breakout, Allied
forces drove the retreating Germans through the Falaise Gap.
Harried mercilessly from the air, the defenseless Germans lost
thousands of men and most of their vehicles. Still photos taken
afterward depicted frightful scenes of dead, bloated horses and
men intermingled with ruined or abandoned equipment. In 1944,
the public had little idea of what was taking place on the battlefield, and no one felt any remorse. The enemy was trapped, help-
less, vulnerable, and slaughtered in due course. In 1991, with the
public witnessing the violence almost as it happened, political leaders became squeamish and apparently ended the war.

When Colin Powell apprised Schwarzkopf that the televised
scenes along the Highway of Death were causing the White House
anxiety, Schwarzkopf relates that his reaction was to tell them "to
turn off the damned TV in the [White House's] situation room."[16]
Instead, the war was "turned off," allowing some Republican
Guard units to escape the imperfectly emplaced American cordon.
It was these forces who helped provide a nucleus around which
Saddam rallied his military to preserve his rule.

Perhaps this outcome was a consequence of a lack of forward
thinking that had characterized the war. From the beginning,
when the commander in chief announced that the Iraqi invasion
"would not stand," American planners had been highly focused
on liberating Kuwait. In this they may have violated von
Clausewitz's dictate to avoid taking "the first step without considering the last."[17] The liberation of Kuwait was an agreeable objective
for the military because it was something concrete. For the generation of officers who had served in Vietnam and now led the United
States forces in the Gulf, a concrete objective was a wonderful
contrast to the murky goals of the Vietnam War. In their minds
the battle against the Iraqi invaders would revenge Vietnam, and
so it did. Had this desire to revenge Vietnam, to prove that the
military had recovered from that debacle, not been uppermost,

perhaps military leaders might have advanced a more ambitious strategy. Instead, they apparently accepted the narrower objective of clearing Kuwait, and this task they performed superbly.

While as of 1993 we do not know what strategic advice the military proffered President Bush regarding objectives and definitions of victory, ultimately the president made the critical decisions. As intended by the Founding Fathers, a civilian had served as commander in chief, and the responsibility for what was done, and what was not, was his.

The activities of the media were subordinate in controversy only to the issues of appropriate congressional involvement in war making and whether the Gulf War ended too soon. America beheld startling televised images of an enemy leader holding forth about the justice of his war aims. The public witnessed unprecedented live scenes of an enemy capital under attack as the war began. Completing the circle, television played a huge role in determining when the conflict ended.

Every American commander in chief has been vexed by the fourth estate. James Polk railed against the press for giving "aid and comfort" to the enemy. Since Jefferson Davis resented the press, he told reporters nothing of his plans. In time, the press assumed that he had no plans, no strategic vision, and accordingly flayed him relentlessly. This undoubtedly eroded the South's will to fight. But it was little different in the North, where Abraham Lincoln endured similar, if not greater, hostility. A British visitor who traveled throughout the nation in 1863 sniffed that neither the Richmond nor the New York papers were respectable. He observed that throughout America "Liberty of the press is carried to its fullest extent."[18]

Whereas the press attacked Davis for his lack of plans, it attacked Lyndon Johnson because he kept his plans secret, a secrecy from which emerged the credibility gap. Johnson, in turn, concluded that his failure to impose censorship was a tremendous mistake. Many who conducted the Gulf War shared his view.[19] The American headquarters in the Persian Gulf imposed restrictive rules involving media pools and "escorted" visits to the troops. Usually these escorts limited or denied reporters access to candid conversations with the men in the field. Instead, reporters had to rely on official military briefings.

In the conduct of these briefings the military showed it had learned much from the infamous "five-o'clock follies" that had characterized Saigon press affairs. Acronym-laden, high-tech battle descriptions, accompanied by sanitized video clips, served to confuse and deflect press interrogation. Equally important, the military appreciated the wisdom of having a colorful general available to charm a skeptical press, an idea broached by Lyndon Johnson back in 1967.[20] General Schwarzkopf filled the bill brilliantly. Contributing to his success was the general's resolve to avoid the public disenchantment that had occurred in Vietnam when the people believed they were willfully misled by their leaders. As Schwarzkopf wrote in his memoirs, he was determined to keep faith with the American people by never lying to them.[21]

While restrictions on the press created controversy during the Gulf War, from the administration's standpoint they worked in two regards: by war's end some 85 percent of the public expressed a high confidence level in the military; and, with one exception, there were no significant breaches of military security. Six days before the beginning of the ground war, a front-page *New York Times* article accurately detailed the pending allied plan of attack. Apparently, the Iraqis never read the story. In spite of the much looser press restrictions in Vietnam, such a breach had not occurred in that war. The official army history of the Vietnam War concluded that "a system of voluntary guidelines . . . largely eliminated security problems."[22]

While the surface competition between the press and government during times of war remains unresolved, another characteristic of this relationship becomes apparent. At the bottom line, the press operates as a business. It promotes itself by exaggerating its ability to sway public opinion. The government often perpetuates this idea so that it can say that the public is reacting to the media's portrayal of a situation as opposed to the real situation. It is a symbiotic relationship.

THE LESSONS OF HISTORY

In Vietnam's aftermath, many observers throughout the world believed that the American people had undergone a decisive change. Admiral U. S. Grant Sharp spoke for this group when he speculated that a nation willing to give up after seeing some 57,000 men killed and 300,000 wounded, and investing over $150 billion, was no longer capable of being a world leader. He wondered if

America had lost the will to make the sacrifices needed. It was a concern shared by the older generation, which had come of age during World War II.

In their war, President Franklin D. Roosevelt had worked hard to engage the public's will for the coming struggle. In his second wartime radio "fireside chat," he described the exploits of a B-17 pilot who had distinguished himself in the Philippines. The president related how the pilot had completed his mission despite the loss of three crew members, two engines, the radio and oxygen systems, and how he had downed seven Japanese fighters in the process. Roosevelt pointedly mentioned the small Texas town where the pilot had been born. Ten days later this pilot went to the Boeing plant where the B-17s were built. After the relevant passages of the president's speech had been replayed, eighteen thousand workers heard the pilot express thanks while explaining that lives like his depended upon their workmanship. In one finely calculated speech, Roosevelt ensured that small towns throughout the nation felt involved in the war and that thousands of people engaged in war work understood that their efforts mattered. Such leadership helped the public accept the horrors of a war in which a single battle, the Battle of the Bulge, cost some seventy-five thousand American casualties. Such leadership did much to encourage the people to persevere until victory.

After Vietnam, when many wondered if the American people had lost their will, they did so without fully appreciating the role of the commander in chief. Slowly, the lessons of history showed that Lyndon Johnson had deliberately refrained from mobilizing the American will to fight the war. Still, it remained uncertain whether the American character had undergone a profound transformation. It was an issue at the core of the Gulf War.

The Gulf War answered the question about American will. The outpouring of support for the men and women sent to Saudi Arabia, the hundreds of thousands of packages addressed to "Any Serviceman," revealed that the public had indeed changed since Vietnam, but perhaps in a way no one had anticipated. In this conflict they demonstrated an ability to separate debate about the wisdom of entering a war from concern over the welfare of those who had to fight the battles.

*   *   *

The Gulf War also highlighted the ongoing imperative to ponder past wars in order to prepare for future challenge. Vietnam had taught that lesson as well. Among the flaws exposed during the Vietnam War was the paucity of classical strategic thinking within the military. When military leaders lacked the capacity to provide strategic advice to the commander in chief, the president and his civilian advisers muddled along as best they could.

In perhaps his greatest contribution to the understanding of war, von Clausewitz explained that the "political object is the goal, war is the means of reaching it, and means can never be considered in isolation from their purpose."[23] In 1965 none of Johnson's highest-ranking military men alerted him that he was violating the surpassing military principle of defining clearly the objective before all else. This was symptomatic of a problem that had emerged within the military since 1945.

After World War II, high-ranking officers had concentrated on the conduct of war in a new environment dominated by nuclear weapons. Then, in 1961, President Kennedy had partially refocused attention on the supposedly novel need to fight counterinsurgency warfare. Concurrently, entrance requirements into the expanding and prestigious Pentagon bureaucracy promoted business management over military study and combat leadership. Reflecting these trends, the service academies and war colleges deemphasized the study of military history. All of this left a void in classic strategic education.

Inattention to the campaign lessons of history's Great Captains combined with ignorance of relevant aspects of America's own martial history. In his memoirs, General Westmoreland complained that the experience in Vietnam was novel, that there was no book explaining how to do the job. In fact, the U.S. Army had a long history of counterinsurgency operations, including the wars against the Seminoles, conflicts in the Philippines, Scott's problems with Mexican "bandits," and widespread guerrilla activities during the Civil War. Consider the relevance to Vietnam of a small sampling of words from various Americans who have passed in the previous pages.

From Valley Forge in 1778, Nathanael Greene observed that the Rebel army, inferior in numbers and lacking all material advantages, could not conquer the well-equipped British "at once, but they cannot conquer us at all. The limits of the British government in America are their out-sentinels."[24] So it was in Vietnam. The night belonged to the Viet Cong, while in daylight the allies controlled only the ground they stood on.

Fourteen years later, President Washington wrote about Anthony Wayne's proposed campaign against the Wabash Indians. The conventional strategic temptation to secure settlements from Indian raids involved the construction of forts. Washington warned against this, explaining that they could be attacked "or avoided at the option of the enemy in a covered Country."[25] Vietnam, a "covered country" if ever there was one, proved Washington's point.

During the war against Mexico, some proposed that American forces retire to a certain fortified line and there wait until the enemy ran out of patience and sued for terms. President Polk analyzed this proposal and concluded that "it would not terminate the war. On the contrary, it would encourage Mexico to persevere and tend to protract it indefinitely." Polk proceeded to analyze expertly Mexico's "favorite system of guerrilla warfare."[26] his musings could have applied to the 1965 proposal for an "enclave strategy" for Vietnam.

There were available to Westmoreland, just as there will be available to future generals and presidents, relevant historical lessons. In recognition of this, in 1972 Vice Admiral Stansfield Turner led what can only be called a renaissance in American military thinking. He promoted the study of classic military history as exemplified by the rediscovery of von Clausewitz. By 1981, von Clausewitz's *On War* was on the war college curricula in all three services. As the war against Iraq showed, this rebirth of strategic study came not a moment too soon.

Even assuming that future commanders in chief will have the benefit of a military staff firmly grounded in classic military education, there remains the question of whether presidents will be able to recognize its value. This is a risk inherent in having a civilian serve as commander in chief. A president will have to digest a blizzard of reports and statistics from his government's information-gathering and analysis sections. As he narrows the alternatives, the bureaucracy grinds out facts and figures to support the wisdom of the pending decision. The entire process can dangerously foreclose debate and analysis just when it is most needed.[27]

Complicating matters is the fact that while future commanders in chief confront new information arriving at startling velocity, the human mind's operating capacity has not changed over the course of American history. In Washington's days, the speed with which news traveled allowed him time to ponder the implications of St. Clair's disaster before revising his strategy. Modern decisions about war and peace are made in an emotional atmosphere fueled by a media-promoted sense of crisis. Lyndon Johnson commonly kept three televisions switched on in order to track how the major networks responded to his Vietnam decisions. Today, in an era of highly competitive global communications, the temptation to respond reflexively to fast-breaking news stories is even greater and it impedes calm reflection. A hint at how things have changed is seen in General Schwarzkopf's comment regarding the "damned TV" in the White House situation room. It requires considerable presidential self-assurance to ignore the media clamor. A commander in chief knows that his thoughtful contemplation can easily be portrayed as vacillating indecisiveness.

*   *   *

There is no blueprint specifying how to be a successful commander in chief. In many of his decisions Lyndon Johnson showed he was not a war genius. Yet few of his predecessors had been, and they had managed to win their wars. During his war against Mexico, James Polk railed against his generals, the lack of congressional support for the war, leaks to the press, and hostile unpatriotic journalists. He withheld key documents from congressional scrutiny, citing executive privilege. It was a thoroughly modern performance, in spite of which he won overwhelming victory. key to his success was his unswerving focus on clearly defined objectives.

George Washington, who certainly should have known better, supervised two unsuccessful campaigns against the Wabash Indians. Then, in a third campaign that risked war with Britain, the world's ranking superpower, he too accomplished his objective. Key to his success was patience, his willingness to grant his field commander the time required to prepare for battle.

In contrast to Washington, Johnson could not find a way to conduct a war against the ally of the ranking superpowers of his era. The specter of a broader war with China and Russia constrained him enormously. This, coupled with his decision not to engage the will of the American people, led to a novel experiment in gradualism. Johnson hoped that slowly increasing military pressure would convince the enemy to negotiate and desist. Furthermore, Johnson's instinct for compromise did not serve him well in his capacity as commander in chief. In war, half measures—the compromise solution—are frequently the worst of all alternatives.

By all rights Jefferson Davis should have been a great success as commander in chief. Like Washington, he possessed combat, political, and bureaucratic experience. He shared Polk's iron will and focus on the main objective. Despite all these attributes he failed totally. He was undone by his own personality.

Casting the net wider, examination of the performances of other presidents under fire only underscores the conclusion that there is no formula for success. There are, however, many ways to fail. That said, it must also be reemphasized that when a future president ponders war, his task reduces to certain essentials: he must match national policy with national means to define tangible, obtainable political goals; and he must select military leaders to implement his strategy.

In 1976, The Chief of Staff of the U.S. Army, General Frederick Weyand—the officer who had provided Westmoreland with the timely alert just before the Tet Offensive—observed that the Vietnam experience had reaffirmed the "jealous and proprietary interest" the American people display toward the army. Weyand concluded that the people must be committed to the national objective if the army is to be sent to war. If popular support is lacking, it is futile to fight. Using words that would have heartened the Founding Fathers, Weyand said that in the final analysis the American army is not so much an arm of the commander in chief as it is an arm of the people.[28] Weyand is perhaps overly sanguine about popular control of the military.

In 1951, the U.S. Senate worried that President Harry S. Truman's Korean War would set a new precedent, allowing the commander in chief to begin a war without congressional consent. Its Armed Services Committee concluded that the United States "should never again become involved in a war without the consent of the Congress."[29] Nearly forty years later, and after the undeclared Vietnam War had been fought and lost, the issue arose again in connection with military operations in the Persian Gulf. Certainly Vietnam had taught the necessity to involve the people, but such involvement can be accomplished by both persuasion and manipulation, and the two approaches are dangerously different.

Furthermore, as we have seen, they are easily confounded by commanders in chief who confuse the national interest with their own political agendas.

Civil-military tension will be an ongoing characteristic of the American democratic experiment. Even as this book was being written a front-page newspaper headline reported RUMBLINGS OF DISCORD HEARD IN PENTAGON as a new presidential administration grapples with the military. Using words that would have pleased John and Samuel Adams, a presidential aide announces, "We are coming in and reasserting civilian authority."[30]

The Founding Fathers gave the nation a constitution through which the country could respond to its military needs while retaining civil control. They decided that in the end, the military could be safely restrained as long as the people retained popular control over the government through elections. However, they never envisioned that the country to which they gave life would conduct most of its military operations on foreign soil. They could not imagine an age of immense military spending during times of peace. They did not expect the near exclusion of the congressional voice in war making. They did not foresee a future political system lacking popular control, a system featuring career politicians and an incumbency reelection rate of better than 90 percent.

However, the Founding Fathers did understand human nature, and they constructed a system to ensure that one of humankind's great banes, a military dictatorship, would find enormous difficulty arising in the United States. The lessons of history teach that this is a great gift, one to be cherished and preserved. History may also show that the end of the Cold War is an appropriate time to return to the process devised by the Founding Fathers when they decided that a president should not enter a war until requesting a declaration from Congress. Then, if the people can regain control of the political process, a legitimate popular voice in the decision to go to war will once more be in place.

NOTES

INTRODUCTION

1. Matthew B. Ridgway, *Soldier: The Memoirs of Matthew B. Ridgway* (New York: Harper and Bros., 1956), p. 290.
2. James D. Richardson, ed., *A Compilation of the Messages and Papers of the Presidents 1789–1897*, vol. 1 (Washington: 1898–1908), To Congress, December 12, 1791, p. 113.
3. Lady Bird Johnson, *A White House Diary* (New York: Holt, Rinehart and Winston, 1970), p. 329.
4. Karl von Clausewitz, *On War* (Princeton: Princeton University Press, 1976), pp. 88–89.
5. Harry G. Summers, Jr., *On Strategy II: A Critical Analysis of the Gulf War* (New York: Dell, 1992), p. 46.

CHAPTER 1

1. Worthington C. Ford, ed., *Journals of the Continental Congress 1774–1789*, (Washington: Government Printing office, 1904–1937), vol. 2, p. 96.
2. John C. Fitzpatrick, ed., *The Writings of George Washington*, (Washington: Government Printing Office, 1931–1944, vol. 3, Accep-

tance of Appointment as General and Commander in Chief, June 16, 1775, pp. 292–293.

3. *Writings of George Washington*, vol. 3. To Burwell Bassett, June 19, 1775, pp. 296–298.

4. Peter Force, *American Archives*, 4th ser. (Washington: 1837–1846), vol. 2, p. 1321.

5. *Journals of the Continental Congress*, vol. 2, p. 96. For Washington's formal instructions, see vol. 2, pp. 100–101.

6. *American Archives*, 4th ser., vol. 3, pp. 241–242.

7. *Writings of George Washington*, vol. 3, To the President of Congress, September 21, 1775, pp. 505–513.

8. Edmund Cody Burnett, *Letters of Members of the Continental Congress*, vol. 1 (Washington: Carnegie Institute, 1936), John Adams to Horatio Gates, June 18, 1776, p. 497.

9. *Journals of the Continental Congress*, vol. 5, p. 601.

10. *Writings of George Washington*, vol. 6, To the President of Congress, September 24, 1776, pp. 106–116.

11. *Writings of George Washington*, vol. 6, To the President of Congress, October 4, 1776, pp. 152–156.

12. In light of what was to come, Washington's impressions of Lee are of great interest. See *Writings of George Washington*, vol. 4, To John Augustine Washington, March 31, 1776, p. 451.

13. *The Lee Papers*, vol. 2, 1776–1778 (New York: Collections of the New York Historical Society, 1873), To General Gates, October 14, 1776, pp. 260–262.

14. *The Lee Papers*, vol. 2, To Benjamin Rush, November 20, 1776, pp. 288–289.

15. Cited in Douglas Southall Freeman, *George Washington: A Biography*, (New York: Charles Scribner's Sons, 1948–1957), vol. 4, p. 248, note 109.

16. *Journals of the Continental Congress*, vol. 6, p. 1027.

17. *Writings of George Washington*, vol. 6, To Major Horatio Gates, December 14, 1776, pp. 371–372.

18. *Writings of George Washington*, vol. 6, To John Augustine Washington, December 18, 1776, p. 398.

19. *Writings of George Washington*, vol. 6, To the President of Congress, December 20, 1776, pp. 400–409.

20. Freeman, *George Washington*, vol. 4, p. 321.

21. Ray Thompson, *Washington Along the Delaware* (Fort Washington, Penn.: The Bicentennial Press, 1970), p. 60.

22. Thompson, *Washington Along the Delaware*, p. 62.

23. Cited in Richard M. Ketchum, *The Winter Soldiers*, (Garden City, N.Y.: Doubleday and Company, 1973), pp. 282–283.

24. Cited in Ketchum, *Winter Soldiers*, p. 384.

CHAPTER 2

1. John C. Fitzpatrick, ed., *The Writings of George Washington* (Washington: Government Printing Office, 1931–1944), vol. 4, To Joseph Reed, January 14, 1776, pp. 240–245.
2. For the complete text of the 1689 Bill of Rights, see *The New Encyclopaedia Britannica*, 15th ed., vol. 10 (Chicago: Encyclopaedia Britannica Inc., 1990), Micropaedia, p. 69.
3. Worthington C. Ford, ed., *Journals of the Continental Congress 1774–1789* (Washington: Government Printing Office, 1904–1937), vol. 2, p. 24.
4. Edmund Cody Burnett, *Letters of Members of the Continental Congress*, vol. 1 (Washington: Carnegie Institute, 1936), John Adams to Mrs. Adams, 29 May, 1775, p. 102.
5. Benjamin Franklin, *The Autobiography of Benjamin Franklin* (New Haven: Yale University Press, 1964), p. 226.
6. *Writings of George Washington*, vol. 3, To George William Fairfax, June 10, 1774, pp. 221–226.
7. *Writings of George Washington*, vol. 3, To Byran Fairfax, August 24, 1774, pp. 237–242.
8. *Journals of the Continental Congress*, vol. 2, p. 77.
9. L. H. Butterfield, ed., *The Adams Papers: Series I: Diary and Autobiography of John Adams*, vol. 2 (Cambridge, Mass.: Belknap Press, 1961), pp. 415–418.
10. Burnett, *Letters*, vol. 1, letter 174, June 14, 1775, p. 124.
11. George W. Corner, ed., *The Autobiography of Benjamin Rush* (Westport, Conn.: Greenwood Press, 1948), p. 113. See also: *Writings of George Washington*, vol. 3, Acceptance of Appointment as General and Commander in Chief, June 16, 1775, pp. 292–293.
12. Burnett, *Letters*, vol. 1, Silas Deane to Mrs. Deane, June 16, 1775, p. 126.
13. Burnett, *Letters*, vol. 1, Eliphalet Dyer to Jonathan Trumball, June 16, 1775, p. 128.
14. *Writings of George Washington*, vol. 3, To Burwell Bassett, June 19, 1775, pp. 296–298.
15. Henry A. Cushing, ed., *The Writings of Samuel Adams* (New York: G. P. Putnam's Sons, 1904–1908), vol. 3, p. 230.
16. *Journals of the Continental Congress*, vol. 6, p. 1045.
17. Burnett, *Letters*, vol. 2, William Hooper to Robert Morris, December 28, 1776, pp. 195–196.
18. Burnett, *Letters*, vol. 2, Benjamin Harrison to Robert Morris, December 29, 1776, pp. 196–197.
19. For example, see Richard K. Showman, ed., *The Papers of Nathanael Greene*, vol. 2 (Chapel Hill, N.C.: University of North Carolina Press,

1976), Nathanael Greene to Christopher Greene, January 20, 1777, pp. 8–9.

20. *Writings of George Washington*, vol. 7, p. 61, see note 8.

21. Burnett, *Letters*, vol. 2, The Committee in Philadelphia to George Washington, December 31, 1776, p. 198.

22. Douglas S. Freeman, *George Washington: A Biography* (New York: Charles Scribner's Sons, 1948–1957), vol. 4, p. 359.

23. *Papers of Nathanael Greene*, vol. 2, John Adams to Nathanael Greene, March 9, 1777, pp. 36–40.

24. *Writings of George Washington*, vol. 4, To Joseph Reed, February 1, 1776, p. 301.

25. Burnett, *Letters*, vol. 2, John Adams to Samuel Holden Parsons, August 19, 1776, p. 57.

26. *Writings of Samuel Adams*, vol. 3, Adams to James Warren, June 18, 1777, pp. 373–374.

27. *Writings of George Washington*, vol. 7, To Brigadier Samuel Holden Parsons, Morris Town, April 3, 1777, pp. 354–355.

28. *Journals of the Continental Congress*, vol. 8, p. 528.

29. *Papers of Nathanael Greene*, vol. 2, John Adams to Nathanael Greene, July 7, 1777, pp. 111–113.

30. *Journals of the Continental Congress*, vol. 8, p. 668.

31. *The Adams Papers*, vol. 2, p. 265.

32. L. H. Butterfield, ed., *Letters of Benjamin Rush*, vol. 1 (Princeton, N.J.: Princeton University Press, 1951), pp. 159–61, 182–183, and 184n.

33. Freeman, *George Washington*, vol. 4, p. 545.

34. *Journals of the Continental Congress*, vol. 9, p. 976.

35. Hugh F. Rankin, ed., *Narratives of the American Revolution* (Chicago: Lakeside Press, 1976.), pp. 181–182.

36. Freeman, *George Washington*, vol. 4, pp. 586–587; and Burnett. *Letters*, vol. 2, p. 570.

37. *Writings of George Washington*, vol. 10, To the President of Congress, Valley Forge, December 23, 1777, pp. 192–198.

38. Freeman, *Letters*, vol. 4, p. 587.

39. *Writings of George Washington*, vol. 4, To the President of Congress, February 18, 1776, pp. 335–338.

40. *Writings of George Washington*, vol. 10, p. 411; and vol. 11, p. 164.

41. Cited in William S. Stryker, *The Battle of Monmouth* (Princeton: Princeton University Press, 1927), p. 185.

42. *Journals of the Continental Congress*, vol. 11, p. 684.

43. *Writings of George Washington*, vol. 13, To Benjamin Harrison, Philadelphia, December 30, 1778, pp. 462–468.

44. Freeman, *George Washington*, vol. 6, pp. 102–103.

45. Burnett, *Letters*, vol. 5, The Committee at Headquarters to the President of Congress, May 10, 1780, p. 133.

46. *Writings of George Washington*, vol. 18, To Lund Washington, Morris Town, May 19, 1780, pp. 391–392.

47. *Writings of George Washington*, vol. 18, To Joseph Jones, Morris Town, May 31, 1780, pp. 452–454.

48. See Burnett, *Letters*, vol. 5, Joseph Jones to George Washington, June 19, 1780, p. 227.

49. *Writings of George Washington*, vol. 19, To Fielding Lewis, pp. 129–134.

50. *Writings of George Washington*, vol. 19, To John Augustine Washington, July 6, 1780, pp. 134–137.

51. See *Writings of George Washington*, vol. 21, To Lieutenant Colonel John Laurens, New Windsor, January 30, 1781, pp. 161–162.

52. Henri Doniol, *Histoire de la Participation de la France a L'Establissment des Etats-Unis d'Amerique* (Paris: Imprimerie Nationale, 1842), vol. 5, Rochambeau to Washington, May 11, 1781, p. 460. For the maturation of Rochambeau's thinking, see Rochambeau to Destouches, May 1, 1781, pp. 456–57.

53. Doniol, *Histoire de la Participation*, vol. 5, Rochambeau to de Grasse, May 28, 1781, pp. 475–476.

54. *Writings of George Washington*, vol. 22, To John Mathews, June 7, 1781, pp. 176–177.

55. John C. Fitzpatrick, ed., *The Diaries of George Washington* (Boston: Houghton Mifflin Co., 1925), vol. 2, p. 208.

56. Rochambeau's questions, which are not fully provided in the standard reference (*Writings of George Washington*, vol. 22), are in Doniol, *Histoire de la Participation*, vol. 5, pp. 514–515.

57. See Fitzpatrick, *The Diaries of George Washington*, vol. 2, p. 241.

58. Fitzpatrick, *The Diaries of George Washington*, vol. 2, p. 254.

59. Gilbert Chinard, ed., *George Washington as the French Knew Him* (New York: Greenwood Press, 1940), p. 43.

60. *Writings of George Washington*, vol. 23, To Compte de Grasse, September 25, 1781, pp. 136–139.

61. *Writings of George Washington*, vol. 24, p. 273, note 81.

62. *Writings of George Washington*, vol. 24, To Colonel Lewis Nicola, May 22, 1782, pp. 272–273.

63. Washington's communications with Congress, and the Newburgh Addresses, are in *Journals of the Continental Congress*, vol. 24, pp. 294–305.

64. *Writings of George Washington*, vol. 26, To the Officers of the Army, March 15, 1783, pp. 222–227; see also note 38.

65. *Writings of George Washington*, vol. 27, To James McHenry, December 10, 1783, p. 266.

66. *Journals of the Continental Congress*, vol. 25, p. 818.

67. Letter of Dr. James Tilton, provided in Julian P. Boyd, ed., *The Papers of Thomas Jefferson* (Princeton: Princeton University Press, 1950–1990), vol. 6, p. 407.

68. *Writings of George Washington,* vol. 27, pp. 284–285.
69. *Papers of Thomas Jefferson,* vol. 6, p. 413.

CHAPTER 3

1. Henry P. Johnson, ed., *The Correspondence and Public Papers of John Jay* (New York: G. P. Putnam's Sons, 1890–1893), vol. 3, p. 84.
2. Edmund Cody Burnett, *Letters of Members of the Continental Congress,* vol. 2 (Washington: Carnegie Institute, 1936), John Adams to Samuel Holden Parsons, August 19, 1776, p. 57.
3. Jennings B. Sanders, *Evolution of Executive Departments of the Continental Congress 1774–1789* (Chapel Hill, N.C.: University of North Carolina Press, 1935), p. 20.
4. Burnett, *Letters,* vol. 4, pp. 176–177. The decision to reform is reported in *Journals of the Continental Congress,* vol. 17, p. 791.
5. The "at" instead "of" was an import from England. When Congress later established the Department of War, on August 7, 1789, it changed the title to Secretary of War.
6. Sanders, *Evolution of Executive Departments,* Osgood to Adams, p. 103.
7. For a contemporary summary of this, see Henry A. Cushing, ed., *The Writings of Samuel Adams* (New York: G. P. Putnam's Sons, 1904–1908), vol. 3, Samuel Adams to James Warren, January 7, 1776, pp. 250–254.
8. Richard H. Kohn, *Eagle and Sword: The Federalists and the Creation of the Military Establishment, 1783–1802* (New York: The Free Press, 1975), p. 11.
9. Kohn, *Eagle and Sword,* p. 12.
10. *Writings of George Washington,* vol. 26, "Sentiments on a Peace Establishment," May 2, 1783, pp. 374–398.
11. The Articles of Confederation, from *Annals of America,* vol. 2 (Chicago: Encyclopaedia Britannica, 1976), pp. 557–559.
12. Joseph E. Smith, *History of Pittsfield, Massachusetts* (Boston, 1869), p. 405.
13. Don R. Higginbotham, *The War of American Independence: Military Attitudes, Policies, and Practice, 1763–1789* (New York: Macmillan, 1971), p. 448.
14. *Writings of George Washington,* vol. 13, To Benjamin Harrison, Philadelphia, December 30, 1778, pp. 462–468.
15. Freeman, *George Washington,* vol. 6, p. 114.
16. Alexander Hamilton, John Jay, and James Madison, *The Federalist Papers* (Garden City, N.Y.: Doubleday and Co., 1961), no. 51, p. 160.
17. Harry M. Ward, *The Department of War, 1781–1795* (Pittsburgh: University of Pittsburgh Press, 1962), p. 95.

18. "Let one executive be appointed who dares execute his powers!"—cited in Ward, *The Department of War*, p. 95.

19. Max Farrand, *The Records of the Federal Convention of 1787*, vol. 3 (New Haven: Yale University Press, 1986), p. 421.

20. Support for this tradition comes from Madison, who is said to have been the recipient of Washington's comment, through his Federalist 40, where he paraphrases Washington thus: "With what color of propriety could the force necessary for defense be limited by those who cannot limit the force of offence?"

21. Christopher Collier and James Lincoln, *The Constitutional Convention of 1787* (New York: Reader's Digest Press and Random House, 1986), p. 247.

22. *Writings of George Washington*, vol. 29, pp. 507–508.

23. Kohn, *Eagle and Sword*, p. 81.

24. Kohn, *Eagle and Sword*, p. 82.

25. As a contemporary document, *The Federalist Papers* had little to do with the Constitution's ratification. By the time its audience, the people of New York, voted, nine states had already ratified. Historically, it is interesting because it provides a glimpse into the secret chambers of the Constitutional Convention and reveals what delegates thought about the emerging role of commander in chief. The Federalist papers most applicable to the role of the commander in chief are 4, 8, 22–26, 28, 29, 41, 69, and 74.

26. Federalist 25, p. 69.

27. For a fine discussion of this competition see Louis Smith, *American Democracy and Military Power: A Study of Civil Control of the Military Power in the United States* (Chicago: University of Chicago Press, 1951), p. 169.

28. For a discussion of this point, see Ward, *The Department of War*, especially p. 96.

29. Federalist 23, p. 59.

CHAPTER 4

1. John C. Fitzpatrick, ed., *The Writings of George Washington* (Washington: Government Printing Office, 1931–1944), vol. 32, To William Moultrie, May 5, 1792, pp. 34–35.

2. Winthrop Sargent, "Winthrop Sargent's Diary While with General Arthur St. Clair's Expedition Against the Indians," *Ohio Archaeological and Historical Publications*, XXXIII (1924), p. 253.

3. See: *Writings of George Washington*, vol. 30, Sentiments Expressed to the Senate Committee . . . on the Mode of Communication, August 10, 1789, pp. 377–379.

4. William Maclay, *The Journal of William Maclay* (New York: Albert and Charles Boni, 1927), pp. 125–129. See also George Washington's proposals in *Writings of George Washington*, vol. 30, pp. 378–379 and 385–390; and in Walter Lowrie and Matthew St. Clair Clarke, eds., *American State Papers, Class II, Indian Affairs* (Washington: Gales and Seaton, 1832), vol. 1, pp. 54–55. His second visit to Congress is documented in *Annals of Congress*, vol. 1 (Washington, 1834), August 24, 1789, pp. 71–72.

5. Randolph C. Downes, *Council Fires on the Upper Ohio* (Pittsburgh: University of Pittsburgh Press, 1940), p. 312.

6. *Writings of George Washington*, vol. 30, Washington to St. Clair, October 6, 1789, pp. 429–431.

7. St. Clair's circular letter to the county lieutenants calling out the militia captures the spirit of the times. See *American State Papers, Indian Affairs*, vol. 1, pp. 94–95.

8. *American State Papers, Indian Affairs*, vol. 1, The Secretary of War to Brigadier General Harmar, August 24, 1790, p. 99.

9. Howard H. Peckham, 'Josiah Harmar and His Indian Expedition," *Ohio Archaeological and Historical Quarterly*, LV:3 (July–September 1946), 236.

10. *Writings of George Washington*, vol. 31, To the Secretary of War, November 19, 1790, pp. 156–157.

11. James D. Richardson, ed., *A Compilation of the Messages and Papers of the Presidents 1789–1897*, vol. 1 (Washington: 1898–1908). The second annual message, December 8, 1790, is on p. 82; the Senate's reply is on p. 84.

12. *Writings of George Washington*, vol. 31, To David Humphreys, March 16, 1791, pp. 241–243.

13. Wiley Sword, *President Washington's Indian War: The Struggle for the Old Northwest, 1790–1795* (Norman, Okla.: University of Oklahoma Press, 1985), p. 145.

14. See *American State Papers, Indian Affairs*, vol. 1, Instructions to Major General Arthur St. Clair, p. 172.

15. Harry M. Ward, *The Department of War, 1781–1795* (Pittsburgh: University of Pittsburgh Press, 1962), p. 135.

16. William Henry Smith, ed., *The St. Clair Papers: The Life and Public Services of Arthur St. Clair* (Cincinnati: Robert Clarke & Co., 1882), vol. 2, pp. 206–210; and James Ripley Jacobs, *The Beginning of the U.S. Army 1783–1812* (Port Washington, N.Y.: Kennikat Press, 1947), p. 87.

17. Sargent, "Winthrop Sargent's Diary," p. 242.

18. Cited in Sword, *President Washington's Indian War*, p. 180.

19. Sargent, "Winthrop Sargent's Diary," pp. 255–256.

20. Sword, *President Washington's Indian War*, p. 183.

21. Ibid. p. 186.

22. Sargent, "Winthrop Sargent's Diary," pp. 268–269.

23. Jacobs, *The Beginning of the U.S. Army*, p. 109

24. *American State Papers, Indian Affairs*, vol. 1, p. 137; and Freeman, *George Washington*, vol. 6, p. 336.

25. Richardson, *Messages and Papers of the Presidents*, vol. 1, To Congress, December 12, 1791, p. 113.

26. P. L. Ford, ed., *Jefferson's Writings* (New York: Federal Edition, 1904), vol. 2, pp. 213–214.

27. *Writings of George Washington*, vol. 31, To David Humphreys, July 20, 1791, pp. 317–321.

28. *Writings of George Washington*, vol. 31, Opinion of the General Officers, March 9, 1792, pp. 509–515.

29. Franklin B. Sawvel, ed., *The Complete Anas of Thomas Jefferson* (New York: Round Table Press, 1903), p. 61.

30. Paul David Nelson, *Anthony Wayne: Soldier of the Early Republic* (Bloomington, Ind.: Indiana University Press, 1985), p. 2.

31. This was the phraseology Secretary of War Knox used to pass Washington's wishes on to Wayne. See Richard C. Knopf, *Anthony Wayne: A Name in Arms* (Pittsburgh: University of Pittsburgh Press, 1960), Knox to Wayne, June 15, 1792, p. 19.

32. Knopf, *Anthony Wayne*, Knox to Wayne, June 29, 1792, p. 25.

33. *Writings of George Washington*, Vol. 32, To the Secretary of State, August 23, 1792, pp. 128–132.

34. *Writings of George Washington*, vol. 32, To the Secretary of the Treasury, August 26, 1792, pp. 132–134.

35. For a typical example of Washington's attention to the army's training see *Writings of George Washington*, vol. 32, To the Secretary of War, August 1, 1792, pp. 103–105.

36. Knopf, *Anthony Wayne*, Wayne to Knox, August 10, 1792, p. 64.

37. Ibid., Wayne to Knox, September 7, 1792, p. 89.

38. See *Writings of George Washington*, vol. 32, To the Secretary of War, September 7, 1792, pp. 145–147.

39. See *Writings of George Washington*, vol. 32, To the Secretary of War, September 28, 1792, pp. 167–169.

40. See *Writings of George Washington*, vol. 33, To Governor William Moultrie, August 28, 1793, pp. 73–74.

41. *Writings of George Washington*, vol. 32, To the Senate and the House of Representatives, December 7, 1792, p. 253.

42. Knopf, *Anthony Wayne*, Knox to Wayne, December 7, 1792, p. 148.

43. Ibid., Knox to Wayne, January 5, 1793, p. 165.

44. *Writings of George Washington*, vol. 32, To the Secretaries of State, Treasury, War, and the Attorney General, March 21, 1793, pp. 395–397.

45. Richardson, *Messages and Papers of the Presidents*, vol. 1, third annual address, p. 104.

46. Simcoe journal, cited in Richard H. Kohn, *Eagle and Sword: The Federalists and the Creation of the Military Establishment, 1783–1802* (New York: The Free Press, 1975), p. 150.

47. *Writings of George Washington*, vol. 32, To Governor Henry Lee, May 6, 1793, pp. 448–450.

48. Sawvel, *The Complete Anas of Thomas Jefferson*, p. 108.

49. Knopf, *Anthony Wayne*, Wayne to Knox, May 9, 1793, p. 235.

50. Ibid., Wayne to Knox, June 20, 1793, p. 247.

51. Ibid., Knox to Wayne, September 3, 1793, p. 271.

52. Ibid., Wayne to Knox, August 24, 1792, pp. 73–74.

53. Ibid., Wayne to Knox, October 23, 1793, p. 279.

54. Richardson, *Messages and Papers of the Presidents*, vol. 1, fifth annual address, December 3, 1793, p. 140.

55. Knox reported to Wayne: ". . . a greater degree of unanimity will hereafter prevail with respect to supporting the Indian War, than has hitherto existed." Knopf, *Anthony Wayne*, Knox to Wayne, December 7, 1793, p. 290.

56. Ibid., Knox to Wayne, May 16, 1794, p. 327.

57. American losses in this action were twenty-two killed and thirty wounded. See *American State Papers, Indian Affairs*, vol. 1, p. 488. Wayne's battle report begins on p. 487.

58. Lieutenant William Clark, who later found fame during the Lewis and Clark expedition, severely criticizes this formation. See his "A Journal of Major-General Anthony Wayne's Campaign Against the Shawnee Indians in Ohio in 1794–1795," *Mississippi Valley Historical Review* I (1914–1915), p. 428. Recall that Clark was a Wilkinson partisan.

59. A good eyewitness description of the confused initial encounter is in "Daily Journal of Wayne's Campaign," *American Pioneer* I (September 1842), p. 318.

60. For Wilkinson's account see M. Quaife, ed., "General James Wilkinson's Narrative of the Fallen Timbers Campaign," *Mississippi Valley Historical Review* XVI:1 (1929–1930). Recall that Wilkinson detested Wayne.

61. Sword, *President Washington's Indian War*, p. 303.

62. Nelson, *Anthony Wayne*, p. 266.

63. Legion losses were twenty-six killed, eighty-seven wounded, nine of whom later died. The Kentucky Volunteers lost seven killed, thirteen wounded, two of whom later died. See *American State Papers, Indian Affairs*, vol. 1, p. 492. Wayne's battle report begins on p. 491 and glosses over the battle's difficult moments.

64. For these latter pivotal decisions see *Writings of George Washington*, vol. 3, To the Massachusetts Legislature, July 31, 1775, pp. 379–381; and vol. 6, To the President of Congress, September 8, 1776, pp. 27–33.

CHAPTER 5

1. William C. Davis, *Jefferson Davis: The Man and His Hour* (New York: HarperCollins Publishers, 1991), p. 128.
2. James D. Richardson, ed., *A Compilation of the Messages and Papers of the Presidents 1789–1897* (Washington: 1898–1908), vol. 4, p. 380.
3. Richardson, *Messages and Papers of the Presidents*, vol. 4, p. 413.
4. John S. D. Eisenhower, *So Far from God: The U.S. War with Mexico 1846–1848* (New York: Random House, 1989), p. 49.
5. Milo M. Quaife, ed., *The Diary of James K. Polk* (Chicago: 1910), vol. 1, April 25, 1846, p. 354.
6. *Diary of James K. Polk*, vol. 1, May 9, 1846, p. 384.
7. Richardson, *Messages and Papers of the Presidents*, vol. 4, p. 443.
8. *Diary of James K. Polk*, vol. 1, May 11, 1846, p. 392.
9. John H. Schroeder, *Mr. Polk's War: American Opposition and Dissent, 1846–1848* (Madison, Wis.: University of Wisconsin Press, 1973), p. 15.
10. *Diary of James K. Polk*, vol. 1, May 14, 1846, p. 401.
11. *Diary of James K. Polk*, vol. 1, May 19, 1846, p. 408.
12. *Diary of James K. Polk*, vol. 1, May 19, 1846, p. 407.
13. *Diary of James K. Polk*, vol. 1, May 21, 1846, p. 415.
14. *Diary of James K. Polk*, vol. 1, May 30, 1846, p. 438.
15. Ulysses S. Grant, *Personal Memoirs of U. S. Grant* (New York: Charles L. Webster and Co., 1885), vol. 1, p. 92.
16. Rhoda Van B. Tanner, ed., *Journals of the Late Brevet Major Philip Norbourne Barbour* (New York: G. P. Putnam's Sons, 1936), p. 55.
17. Cited in Eisenhower, *So Far from God*, p. 83.
18. Robert H. Ferrell, ed., *Monterrey Is Ours: The Mexican War Letters of Lieutenant Dana, 1845–1847* (Lexington, Ky.: University Press of Kentucky, 1990), p. 68.
19. Tanner, *Journals of the Late Brevet Major*, p. 60.
20. Cited in Maurice Matloff, ed., *American Military History* (Washington: Government Printing Office, 1969), p. 166.
21. Eisenhower, *So Far from God*, p. 84.
22. Matloff, *American Military History*, p. 167.
23. *Diary of James K. Polk*, vol. 1, May 25, 1846, p. 427.
24. *Diary of James K. Polk*, vol. 1, June 22, 1846, p. 483.
25. *Diary of James K. Polk*, vol. 2, September 5, 1846, p. 117.
26. *Diary of James K. Polk*, vol. 2, September 5, 1846, p. 119.
27. *Diary of James K. Polk*, vol. 2, September 22, 1846, p. 151.
28. See Winfield Scott, *Memoirs of Lieut.-General Scott* (New York: Sheldon and Co., 1864), vol. 2, p. 384.
29. *Diary of James K. Polk*, vol. 2, November 7, 1846, pp. 222–223.
30. *Diary of James K. Polk*, vol. 2, November 18, 1846, p. 242.
31. *Diary of James K. Polk*, vol. 2, November 20, 1846, p. 248.

32. *Diary of James K. Polk*, vol. 2, November 21, 1846, p. 249.

33. *Diary of James K. Polk*, vol. 2, November 21, 1846, p. 250.

34. See Scott, *Memoirs*, vol. 2, pp. 397–398.

35. Scott, *Memoirs*, vol. 2, p. 403.

36. Richardson, *Messages and Papers of the Presidents*, vol. 4, p. 508.

37. Scott, *Memoirs*, vol. 2, p. 385.

38. Richardson, *Messages and Papers of the Presidents*, vol. 4, p. 473.

39. *Diary of James K. Polk*, vol. 2, February 5, 1847, p. 368.

40. *Diary of James K. Polk*, vol. 2, March 20, 1847, p. 432.

41. Joseph E. Chance, *Jefferson Davis's Mexican War Regiment* (Jackson, Miss.: University Press of Mississippi, 1991), p. 98.

42. Santa Ana lost 1,500 to 2,000 men while the Americans suffered 264 killed, 450 wounded, and 26 missing.

43. *Diary of James K. Polk*, vol. 2, April 10, 1847, p. 465.

44. *Diary of James K. Polk*, vol. 2, April 20, 1847, p. 482.

45. Scott, *Memoirs*, vol. 2, p. 454.

46. Cited in Russell F. Weigley, *The American Way of War: A History of United States Military Strategy and Policy* (Bloomington, Ind.: Indiana University Press, 1973), p. 75.

47. *Diary of James K. Polk*, vol. 2, April 16, 1847, p. 479.

48. Richardson, *Messages and Papers of the Presidents*, vol. 4, p. 547.

49. Scott, *Memoirs*, vol. 2, p. 578.

50. Scott, *Memoirs*, vol. 2, p. 498.

51. Robert R. Miller, ed., *The Mexican War Journal and Letters of Ralph W. Kirkham* (College Station, Tex.: Texas A&M Press, 1991), pp. 57–58.

52. Richardson, *Messages and Papers of the Presidents*, vol. 4, p. 541.

53. Ibid., p. 542.

54. *Diary of James K. Polk*, vol. 3, February 28, 1848, p. 366.

55. Eisenhower, *So Far from God*, p. 364.

56. *Diary of James K. Polk*, vol. 3, February 28, 1848, p. 366.

57. Thomas Hart Benton, *Thirty Years' View: A History of the Working of the American Government for Thirty Years, from 1820 to 1850* (New York: D. Appleton and Co., 1856), vol. 2, p. 680.

58. Eisenhower, *So Far from God*, p. 357.

59. Richardson, *Messages and Papers of the Presidents*, vol. 4, p. 632.

60. Ibid., p. 588.

61. Schroeder, *Mr. Polk's War*, p. 159.

62. Benton, *Thirty Years' View*, p. 724.

CHAPTER 6

1. James D. Richardson, ed., *A Compilation of the Messages and Papers of the Confederacy 1861–1865* (Nashville: United States Publishing Co., 1906), vol. 1, Message of April 29, 1861, p. 82.
2. William C. Davis, *Jefferson Davis: The Man and His Hour* (New York: HarperCollins Publishers, 1991), p. 53.
3. Varina Davis, *Jefferson Davis: Ex-President of the Confederate States of America. A Memoir by his Wife* (New York: Belford Co. Publishers, 1890), vol. 1, p. 191.
4. Varina Davis, *Jefferson Davis*, vol. 1, p. 199.
5. James T. McIntosh, *The Papers of Jefferson Davis* (Baton Rouge: Louisiana State University Press, 1974), vol. 2, p. 508.
6. William Davis, *Jefferson Davis*, p. 157.
7. Ibid., p. 169.
8. Varina Davis, *Jefferson Davis*, vol. 2, p. 19.
9. Douglas B. Ball, *Financial Failure and Confederate Defeat* (Chicago: University of Illinois Press, 1991), p. 6.
10. Richardson, *Papers of the Confederacy*, vol. 1, Message of April 29, 1861, p. 82.
11. Jefferson Davis, *The Rise and Fall of the Confederate Government* (New York: Da Capo Press, 1990), vol. 2, pp. 109–110.
12. Attributed to James Chesnut by his wife in C. Vann Woodward, *Mary Chesnut's Civil War* (New Haven, Conn.: Yale University Press, 1981), p. 109.
13. William Davis, *Jefferson Davis*, p. 352.
14. For a detailed discussion of this dispute see William Davis, *Jefferson Davis*, pp. 356–360, and Craig L. Symonds, *Joseph E. Johnston: A Civil War Biography* (New York: W. W. Norton and Co., 1992), pp. 126–129.
15. On March 6, 1861, Congress gave Davis the authority to appoint brigadier and major generals subject to congressional confirmation.
16. Symonds, *Joseph E. Johnston*, p. 88. Other factors bearing on this feud included Davis's action while Secretary of War that endorsed his predecessor's decision to deny Johnston's claim regarding a brevet promotion earned in Mexico, and the fact that Johnston had been chosen Quartermaster General in 1860 ahead of two other candidates named R. E. Lee and A. S. Johnston.
17. William Davis, *Jefferson Davis*, p. 357.
18. For another glimpse at Davis's attitude toward Beauregard and his respect for Bragg and A. S. Johnston, see Thomas Bragg, *Diary of Thomas Bragg* (Chapel Hill, N.C.: Southern Historical Society, University of North Carolina Library, 1966), January 8, 1862, p. 104.
19. William Howard Russell, *My Diary North and South* (New York: Harper and Brothers, 1863), p. 43.

20. Russell, *My Diary North and South*, p. 70.

21. See James D. Richardson, ed., *A Compilation of the Messages and Papers of the Presidents 1789–1897* (Washington: 1898–1908), vol. 6, p. 45.

22. Frank Lawrence Owsley, *King Cotton Diplomacy: Foreign Relations of the Confederate States of America* (Chicago: University of Chicago Press, 1931), p. 557.

23. Jefferson Davis, *Rise and Fall of the Confederate Government*, vol. 1, p. 209.

24. Ball, *Financial Failure and Confederate Defeat*, p. 238.

25. Richardson, *Papers of the Confederacy*, vol. 1, Message of January 12, 1863, p. 293.

26. Edward A. Pollard, *The Lost Cause; A New Southern History of the War of the Confederates* (New York: E. B. Treat and Co., 1867), p. 656.

27. *Diary of Thomas Bragg*, December 6, 1861, p. 79.

28. *Diary of Thomas Bragg*, January 17, 1862, p. 115.

29. W. Buck Yearns, ed., *The Confederate Governors* (Athens, Ga.: University of Georgia Press, 1985), p. 74.

CHAPTER 7

1. United States War Department, *War of the Rebellion: A Compilation of the Official Records of the Union and Confederate Armies*, ser. I, vol. 4 (Washington: Government Printing Office, 1880–1901), Polk to Harris, September 4, 1861, p. 180. (Hereafter cited as *Official Records*.)

2. *Official Records* I:4, Davis to Polk, September 5, 1861, p. 181.

3. William C. Davis, *Jefferson Davis: The Man and His Hour* (New York: HarperCollins Publishers, 1991), p. 396.

4. *Official Records* I:7, Johnston to Cooper, January 22, 1862, p. 845.

5. *Battles and Leaders of the Civil War* (New York: Thomas Yoseloff, 1956), vol. 1, p. 550.

6. William Davis, *Jefferson Davis*, p. 398.

7. *Official Records* I:6, Bragg to Benjamin, February 15, 1862, pp. 826–827.

8. Regarding Davis's support for this, see for example *Official Records* I:6, Benjamin to Lovell, February 8, 1862, p. 824; and Benjamin to Bragg, February 18, 1862, p. 828.

9. *Official Records* I:10, part 2, Johnston to Davis, April 3, 1862, p. 387; and Davis to Johnston, April 5, 1862, p. 394.

10. Wiley Sword, *Shiloh: Bloody April* (Dayton, Ohio: Morningside Bookshop, 1988), p. 148.

11. Sword, *Shiloh*, p. 436. A similar remark is found in Jefferson Davis, *The Rise and Fall of the Confederate Government* (New York: Da Capo Press, 1990), vol. 2, p. 55.

12. Bruce Catton, *Terrible Swift Sword* (Garden City, N.Y.: Doubleday and Company, 1963), p. 310.

13. Dunbar Rowland, ed., *Jefferson Davis, Constitutionalist: His Letters, Papers and Speeches* (Jackson, Miss.: Mississippi Department of Archives and History, 1923), vol. 5, Davis to Brooks, March 13, 1862, pp. 216–217.

14. For a typical example involving the governor of North Carolina, who pleaded: "We see just over our lines in Virginia ... two or three North Carolina Regiments, well-armed, and well-drilled, who are not allowed to come to the defense of their homes," see W. Buck Yearns, ed., *The Confederate Governors* (Athens, Ga.: University of Georgia Press, 1985), pp. 146–147.

15. See *Official Records* I:5, Lee to Holmes, March 16, 1862, p. 1103.

16. Cited in Joseph T. Durkin, *Confederate Navy Chief: Stephen R. Mallory* (Columbia, S.C.: University of South Carolina Press, 1954), p. 176.

17. Regarding inefficient use of Cabinet time, see Durkin citing Mallory, pp. 176–177. For a charming and instructive account of Davis's work habits see John B. Jones, *A Rebel War Clerk's Diary* (New York: Sagamore Press, 1958), p. 29.

18. John H. Reagan, *Memoirs: With Special Reference to Secession and the Civil War* (New York: Neale Publishing Co., 1906), p. 137.

19. See Thomas Bragg, *Diary of Thomas Bragg* (Chapel Hill, N.C.: Southern Historical Society, University of North Carolina Library, 1966), December 6, 1861, p. 79, for a first mention of Johnston's fear regarding spies.

20. Edward A. Pollard, *The Lost Cause; A New Southern History of the War of the Confederates* (New York: E. B. Treat and Co., 1867), p. 656.

21. For an excellent discussion of this point, see Thomas Lawrence Connelly and Archer Jones, *The Politics of Command: Factions and Ideas in Confederate Strategy* (Baton Rouge: Louisiana State University Press, 1973), pp. 33–38.

22. Reagan, *Memoirs*, p. 139.

23. A. L. Long, *Memoirs of Robert E. Lee* (Secaucus, N.J.: The Blue and Grey Press, 1983), pp. 167–168.

24. *Diary of Thomas Bragg*, January 31, 1862, p. 130.

25. C. Vann Woodward, *Mary Chesnut's Civil War* (New Haven, Conn.: Yale University Press, 1981), p. 411.

26. He rode the lines frequently before and during the Seven Days and again during Butler's Bermuda Hundred Campaign of 1864.

27. Harry M. Henderson, *Texas in the Confederacy* (San Antonio, Tex.: Naylor Co., 1955), p. 12. A slightly different version appears in Clifford Dowdey, *The Seven Days* (Wilmington, N.C.: Broadfoot Publishing, 1988), p. 236.

28. Mamie Yeary, ed., *Reminiscences of the Boys in Gray, 1861–1865* (McGregor, Tex.: Morningside, 1986), p. 815.

29. Harold B. Simpson, *Gaines' Mill to Appomattox* (Waco, Tex.: Texian Press, 1963), p. 89.

30. Simpson gives the losses as 75 killed or mortally wounded, 180 wounded. Henderson, not separating out the mortally wounded, gives 44 killed and 207 wounded. It was not an all-Texas affair; the 18th Georgia lost 16 killed and 126 wounded.

31. Yeary, *Reminiscences of the Boys in Gray*, pp. 815–816.

32. Henderson, *Texas in the Confederacy*, p. 13.

33. *Official Records* I:17, no. 2, Bragg to Cooper, July 23, 1862, pp. 655–656.

34. Frank Lawrence Owsley, *King Cotton Diplomacy: Foreign Relations of the Confederate States of America* (Chicago: University of Chicago Press, 1931), p. 341.

35. Frank E. Vandiver, *Their Tattered Flags: The Epic of the Confederacy* (New York: Harper's Magazine Press, 1970), p. 150.

36. Edward Younger, ed., *Inside the Confederate Government: The Diary of Robert Garlick Hill Kean* (New York: Oxford University Press, 1957), p. 28.

37. Rowland, *Jefferson Davis*, vol. 5, Davis to Holmes, December 21, 1862, pp. 386–388.

38. William Davis, *Jefferson Davis*, p. 474.

39. He told Johnston, "You will perceive how small is the field of selection if a new man is to be sought whose rank is superior to that of the Lieut. Generals now in Tenn." (Rowland, *Jefferson Davis*, vol. 5, Davis to Johnston, February 19, 1863, pp. 433–435.)

40. An exception was Bragg, whose rare willingness to send trained troops from his command to other more threatened areas attracted the president's favorable attention. See *Diary of Thomas Bragg*, November 30, 1861, pp. 72–73; and Rowland, *Jefferson Davis*, vol. 5, Davis to A. S. Johnston, March 12, 1862, p. 216.

41. For a good example of Davis's deference, see Rowland, *Jefferson Davis*, vol. 5, Davis to Holmes, December 21, 1862, pp. 386–388.

42. See Rowland, *Jefferson Davis*, vol. 5, Davis to Seddon, December 18, 1862, p. 386.

43. For a discussion of this, see Younger, *Inside the Confederate Government*, p. 66.

44. *Battles and Leaders*, vol. 2, Pemberton to Davis, January 5, 1863, p. 474.

45. Kean, quoting Judge Campbell, in Younger, *Inside the Confederate Government*, p. 119.

46. See *Official Records* I:24/3, Johnston to Pemberton, May 17, 1863, p. 888; and Pemberton to Johnston, May 18, 1863, pp. 889–890.

47. *Official Records* I:25/2, Lee to Seddon, May 10, 1863, p. 790.

48. Reagan's account of this is in his *Memoirs*, pp. 150–153.

49. *Official Records* I:51/2, Lee to David, August 8, 1863, pp. 752–753.

50. *Official Records* I:29/2, Davis to Lee, August 11, 1863, pp. 639–640.

51. Craig L. Symonds, *Joseph E. Johnston: A Civil War Biography* (New York: W. W. Norton and Co., 1992), p. 217.

52. See Rowland, *Jefferson Davis*, vol. 5, Davis to Holmes, December 21, 1862, pp. 386–387.

53. See *Official Records* I:23/2, Davis to J. Johnston, January 22, 1863, pp. 613–614; and Rowland, *Jefferson Davis*, vol. 5, Davis to J. Johnston, February 19, 1863, pp. 433–435.

54. William Davis, *Jefferson Davis*, p. 499.

55. Phrases used in his letter refusing to relieve Lee; see *Official Records* I:29/2, Davis to Lee, August 11, 1863, pp. 639–640.

56. Porter Alexander observed: "... the immense possibilities of the situation show the soundness of the strategy"; it would "have been best to have played that game in June instead of the Gettysburg campaign." See Gary W. Gallagher, ed., *Fighting for the Confederacy: The Personal Recollections of General Edward Porter Alexander,* (Chapel Hill, N.C.: University of North Carolina Press, 1989), p. 296.

57. See *Official Records* I:30/2, Jack to Polk, October 28, 1863, p. 70.

58. *Official Records* I:17/2, Cooper to Bragg, July 22, 1862, pp. 654–655.

59. See *Official Records*, I:30/4, Polk to Lee, September 27, 1863, p. 708; and the letter to Davis of October 4, 1863, in *Official Records* I:30/2, pp. 65–66. Longstreet also requested Lee; see *Official Records* I:30/4, Longstreet to Seddon, September 26, 1863, pp. 705–706.

60. G. Moxley Sorrell, *Recollections of a Confederate Staff Officer* (New York: Neale Publishing Co., 1905), p. 191.

61. Durkin, *Confederate Navy Chief,* p. 177.

62. See *Official Records* I:31/3, Lee to Davis, December 7, 1863, p. 792.

63. Woodward, *Mary Chesnut's Civil War*, pp. 482–483.

64. Larry E. Nelson, *Bullets, Ballots, and Rhetoric: Confederate Policy for the United States Presidential Contest of 1864* (University, Ala.: University of Alabama, 1980), p. 11.

65. See Long, *Memoirs of Robert E. Lee*, Lee to Davis, September 8, 1862, p. 538.

66. See Long, *Memoirs of Robert E. Lee*, Lee to Davis, June 10, 1863, pp. 620–621.

67. Nelson, p. 14.

68. *Official Records*, I:51/2, Davis to Vance, January 8, 1864, p. 810.

69. See Long, *Memoirs of Robert E. Lee*, Lee to Davis, February 3, 1864, pp. 641–642.

70. *Official Records*, I:32/3, Longstreet to Lawton, March 5, 1864, p. 588.

71. Nelson, *Bullets, Ballots, and Rhetoric*, p. 107.

72. See Douglas S. Freeman, ed., *Lee's Dispatches to Jefferson Davis* (New York: G. P. Putnam's Sons, 1957), May, 1864, p. 185.

73. Cited in Shelby Foote, *The Civil War: Red River to Appomattox* (New York, Random House, 1974), p. 550.

74. Nelson, *Bullets, Ballots, and Rhetoric*, p. 109.

75. Hill's actions are in *The Rise and Fall of the Confederate Government*, vol. 2, pp. 472–474.

76. Symonds, *Joseph E. Johnston*, p. 321.

77. Woodward, *Mary Chesnut's Civil War*, p. 565.

78. For an interesting insight into this decision, see Woodward, *Mary Chesnut's Civil War*, p. 635.

79. William Davis, *Jefferson Davis*, p. 600.

80. Varina Davis, *Jefferson Davis: Ex-President of the Confederate States of America. A Memoir by His Wife* (New York: Belford Co. Publishers, 1890), vol. 2, p. 575.

81. Burke Davis, *The Long Surrender* (New York: Random House, 1985), p. 67.

82. Rowland, *Jefferson Davis*, vol. 6, pp. 559–562.

83. William Davis, *Jefferson Davis*, p. 669.

84. *The Rise and Fall of the Confederate Government*, vol. 2, p. 645.

85. "Judge Turney on Mr. Davis," *Confederate Veteran* I:1 (January 1893), 15.

86. *Battles and Leaders*, vol. 1, p. 110.

87. *Battles and Leaders*, vol. 1, p. 226.

88. *Official Records* I:46/2, p. 1143. Kean lists it as the primary cause of Confederate failure; see Younger, *Inside the Confederate Government*, p. 213.

89. Younger, *Inside the Confederate Government*, p. 72.

90. Kean, quoting Seddon in Younger, *Inside the Confederate Government*, p. 153.

91. Durkin, *Confederate Navy Chief*, p. 179.

92. Jones, *A Rebel War Clerk's Diary*, January 1, 1865, p. 471.

93. Kean observes that Davis relieved Secretary Randolph because he was jealous. See Younger, *Inside the Confederate Government*, p. 30.

94. Joseph H. Parks, *General Leonidas Polk C.S.A.* (Baton Rouge: Louisiana State University Press, 1962), p. 321.

95. Davis told Lee that the new command "renders it necessary to interfere temporarily with the duties to which you were assigned in connection with the general service, but only so far as to make you available for command in the field ..." (*Official Records* I:11/3, Davis to Lee, June 1, 1862, pp. 568–569.)

96. Robert E. Lee, *Recollections and Letters of General Robert E. Lee* (New York: Doubleday and Page, 1909), p. 103.

97. *Official Records* I:5, Council of War at Centreville, October 1, 1861, p. 885.

98. Clifford Dowdey and Louis Manarin, eds., *The Wartime Papers of Robert E. Lee* (Boston: Little, Brown, 1961), Lee to Davis, May 11, 1863, p. 483.

99. For an example, see Long, *Memoirs of Robert E. Lee*, Lee to Davis, September 14, 1863, pp. 626–627.

100. Dowdey, *Wartime Papers*, Lee to Bragg, April 7, 1864, p. 692.

101. See Long, *Memoirs of Robert E. Lee*, Lee to Davis, December 3, 1863, p. 633.

102. When pondering the wisdom of Lee's Virginia fixation, consider that this total exceeded the Army of Tennessee's entire strength over this period.

103. Long, *Memoirs of Robert E. Lee*, Lee to Davis, June 10, 1863, pp. 620–621.

104. Connelly and Jones, *The Politics of Command*, p. 181.

105. William Davis, *Jefferson Davis*, p. 504.

106. Burke Davis, *The Long Surrender*, p. 107.

107. Harry T. Williams, *Lincoln and His Generals* New York: Alfred A. Knopf, 1952), p. 86.

108. William Davis, *Jefferson Davis*, p. 697.

109. "The Rebel Yell," *Confederate Veteran* I:1 (January 1893), 15.

CHAPTER 8

1. Leslie H. Gelb and Richard K. Betts, *The Irony of Vietnam: The System Worked* (Washington: Brookings Institution, 1979), p. 287.

2. Margaret Leech, *In the Days of McKinley* (New York: Harper and Brothers, 1959), p. 184.

3. Ibid., p. 266.

4. John Dos Passos, *Mr. Wilson's War* (Garden City, N.Y.: Doubleday and Co., 1962), p. 196.

5. Wilson's request for war is in Charles F. Horne, ed., *Source Records of the Great War* (National Alumni, 1923), vol. 5, p. 107.

6. American pride and concurrent tactical naïveté was brought to my attention by Dr. Paddy Griffith, who explores this issue in a forthcoming book about the tactics of the Western Front to be published by Frank Cass Ltd. in 1994.

7. Dos Passos, *Mr. Wilson's War*, p. 235.

8. Ibid., p. 486.

9. Eric Larrabee, *Commander in Chief: Franklin Delano Roosevelt. His Lieutenants and Their War* (New York: Harper and Row, 1987), p. 33.

10. Ibid., p. 42.

11. Kenneth J. Hagan, *This People's Navy: The Making of American Sea Power* (New York: The Free Press, 1991), p. 288.

12. Ibid., p. 289.

13. Larrabee, *Commander in Chief*, p. 639.

14. Stark's description to Ghormley, the top naval attaché serving in Britain, cited in Hagan, *This People's Navy*, p. 293.

15. See James R. Arnold, *The First Domino: Eisenhower, the Military, and America's Intervention in Vietnam* (New York: William Morrow, 1991), pp. 18, 23, 25.

16. James F. Schnabel, *Policy and Direction: The First Year* (Washington: U.S. Army, 1972), pp. 66–67.

17. Ibid., p. 214.

18. For a discussion of this, see D. Clayton James, *Refighting the Last War: Command and Crisis in Korea 1950–1953* (New York: The Free Press, 1993), pp. 221–223.

19. See Arnold, *The First Domino*, pp. 62–65.

20. The Desoto patrols originated in 1962 as an intelligence-gathering effort and to "serve as a minor cold war irritant to CHICOMS."

21. This round is now held by the Navy Memorial Museum in Washington.

22. For a well-researched analysis of this entire incident, see Edward J. Marolda and Oscar P. Fitzgerald, *The United States Navy and the Vietnam Conflict* (Washington: U.S. Department of the Navy, 1986), vol. 2, chapter XIV, pp. 393–436.

23. Jim Stockdale and Sybil Stockdale, *In Love and War* (New York: Harper and Row, 1984), pp. 26–27, 88–89.

24. Arnold, *The First Domino*, p. 44.

25. Ibid., pp. 167, 201.

26. Trip report to Kennedy, "Mission to Southeast Asia, India and Pakistan," 5/23/61, boxes 18–19, files of McGeorge Bundy, National Security File, LBJ Library.

27. Recall that when Kennedy assumed office there were about 900 military advisers in Vietnam. When he died the number had risen to 16,700.

28. Douglas Kinnard, *The Certain Trumpet: Maxwell Taylor and the American Experience in Vietnam* [Washington: Brassey's (U.S.), 1991], p. 102.

29. Cited in Kinnard, *The Certain Trumpet*, p. 123.

30. National Security Action Memorandum (NSAM) 273 is partially reproduced in Lyndon B. Johnson, *The Vantage Point: Perspectives on the Presidency, 1963–1969* (New York: Holt, Rinehart and Winston, 1971), p. 45.

31. NSAM 273.

32. In 1970 LBJ said: "Everything I knew about history told me that if I got out of Vietnam and let Ho Chi Minh run through the streets of Saigon, then I'd be doing exactly what Chamberlain did in World War II" (in Doris Kearns, *Lyndon Johnson and the American Dream* [New York: New American Library, 1976], p. 264). Rusk compared

Chinese rhetoric to *Mein Kampf*; George Ball called it a "do-it-yourself kit" for global revolution.

33. Lin Piao's article, "Long Live the Victory of the People's War," seemed a blueprint for the Communist offensive. See Janos Radvanyi, "Vietnam War Diplomacy: Reflections of a Former Iron Curtain Official," in Lloyd J. Matthews, ed., *Assessing the Vietnam War: A Collection from the Journal of the U.S. Army War College.* (Washington: Pergamon-Brasseys, 1987), p. 61.

34. Memorandum for the Record, 11/25/63, "South Vietnam Situation," box 1, Meeting Notes File, LBJ Library.

35. Text of Joint Resolution, August 7, 1964, reproduced in *The Pentagon Papers: The Defense Department History of United States Decisionmaking on Vietnam*, Senator Gravel ed. (Boston: Beacon Press, 1971), vol. 3, p. 722.

36. Brian VanDeMark, *Into the Quaqmire: Lyndon Johnson and the Escalation of the Vietnam War* (New York: Oxford University Press, 1991), p. 19.

37. Memos for the Record, 12/7/64, boxes 18–19, files of McGeorge Bundy, National Security File, LBJ Library.

38. William C. Westmoreland, *A Soldier Reports* (Garden City, N.Y.: Doubleday and Co., 1976), p. 120.

39. Eric F. Goldman, *The Tragedy of Lyndon Johnson* (New York: Alfred A. Knopf, 1969), p. 404.

40. For LBJ's first impressions of South Vietnamese political turmoil, see Memorandum for the Record, "South Vietnam Situation," 11/25/63, box 1, Meeting Notes File, LBJ Library.

41. This debate mirrors that which occurred during the Eisenhower administration; see Arnold, *The First Domino*, chapters IX and X. For the Johnson administration, see VanDeMark, *Into the Quagmire*, pp. 27, 36–37.

42. The tortuous but critical discussion and analysis can be found in Memorandum for the President, 2/7/65, "Deployment of Major U.S. Forces to Vietnam," vol. 1, box 40, NSC Histories, National Security File, LBJ Library. See in particular tab 3 and tab 22.

43. Memorandum for the President, 1/27/65, "Deployment of Major U.S. Forces to Vietnam," vol. 1, tab 10, box 40, NSC Histories, National Security File, LBJ Library.

44. Johnson, *The Vantage Point*, p. 125.

45. For Sharp's case, see *The Pentagon Papers*, vol. 4, p. 415.

46. The intelligence community presented a different view, saying that mining et al. was unlikely to significantly change Hanoi's war-making ability. See *The Pentagon Papers*, vol. 4, p. 355.

47. Jack Valenti, *A Very Human President* (New York: W. W. Norton and Co., 1975), p. 362.

48. From beginning to end LBJ endorsed the policy described in McNamara to the President, July 29, 1965, in *The Pentagon Papers*, vol. 3, p. 388.

49. One such adviser was McCone's successor at the CIA, Vice Admiral William F. Raborn. See his May 6, 1965, memo to Rusk and McNamara, in U.S. Department of Defense, *United States–Vietnam Relations, 1945–1967: A Study Prepared by the Department of Defense* (Washington: Government Printing Office, 1971), vol. 4, C.3, p. 109.

50. Memorandum for the President, 5/21/65, "Deployment of Major U.S. Forces to Vietnam, July 1965," vol 1, tab 417, box 43, NSC Histories, National Security File, LBJ Library.

51. Luncheons with the President, 3/23/65, box 1, papers of McGeorge Bundy, LBJ Library.

52. For a clear example of this, see U. S. Grant Sharp, *Strategy for Defeat: Vietnam in Retrospect* (San Rafael, Calif.: Presidio Press, 1978), p. 94.

53. VanDeMark, *Into the Quagmire*, p. 78.

54. 3/10/65, 4/1/65, and 4/2/65, box 1, papers of McGeorge Bundy, LBJ Library.

55. For the JCS appeal for tactical flexibility, see "Deployment of Major U.S. Forces to Vietnam," vol. 1, tab 125, box 41, NSC Histories, National Security File, LBJ Library.

56. Cabinet Room, 7/26/65, box 1, Meeting Notes File, LBJ Library.

57. Sharp, *Strategy for Defeat*, pp. 115–116. See also *The Pentagon Papers*, vol. 4, pp. 40–41. Afterward, airpower enthusiasts, notably the admiral in charge of Rolling Thunder, U. S. Grant Sharp, would argue that unrestricted bombing would have changed the course of the war. On the other hand, the Communists demonstrated a superb capacity to conceal their operations from probing American aircraft. Commodore Stockdale recalls that following his shootdown his guards moved him in a truck convoy along a road that he and his mates had been targeting. From the air they had seldom seen anything and had concluded that this road was not a productive target. Once on the ground, Stockdale witnessed how readily the truck convoys avoided the aerial patrols and experienced the mortification of watching his fellow pilots pass overhead while the trucks hid in adjacent jungle. Likewise, several chokepoints along the Ho Chi Minh Trail received the full aerial arsenal that the U.S. military could bring to bear in an effort to block infiltration. These efforts failed.

58. For McNamara's analysis, see *The Pentagon Papers*, vol. 3, p. 388.

59. Jack Broughton, *Thud Ridge* (New York: Bantam, 1969), p. 136.

60. Bundy advised him that even if the bombing policy failed, it "would damp down" conservative criticism that Johnson had not done all he should have if Vietnam fell. See VanDeMark, *Into the Quagmire*, p. 67.

61. Clark Clifford, *Counsel to the President* (New York: Random House, 1991), p. 417.
62. Napoleon to General Hedouville, 1799, cited in J. Christopher Herold, ed., *The Mind of Napoleon: A Selection from His Written and Spoken Words* (New York: Columbia University Press, 1955), p. 208.
63. For LBJ's comment, see 3/10/65 box 1, papers of McGeorge Bundy, LBJ Library.
64. Taylor to Department of State, 2/23/65, "Deployment of Major U.S. Forces to Vietnam," vol. 1, tab 80, box 40, NSC Histories, National Security File, LBJ Library.
65. Current Trends in Vietnam, 4/30/65, "Deployment of Major U.S. Forces to Vietnam," vol. 1, tab 211, box 41, NSC Histories, National Security Files, LBJ Library.
66. 6/10/65, box 1, papers of McGeorge Bundy, LBJ Library.

CHAPTER 9

1. Karl von Clausewitz, *On War* (Princeton: Princeton University Press, 1976), p. 579. The exact time he wrote this particular phrase is difficult to ascertain.
2. Lady Bird Johnson, *A White House Diary* (New York: Holt, Rinehart and Winston, 1970), p. 248. For a characterization of Johnson at this time, see Chapter 27, p. 14, box 1, papers of William Bundy, LBJ Library. For the amount of time Johnson devoted to this problem, see McNamara's testimony cited in Larry Berman, *Planning a Tragedy: The Americanization of the War in Vietnam* (New York: W. W. Norton, 1982), p. xii.
3. See his comments on 12/1/64 in box 1, Meeting Notes File, LBJ Library.
4. "After 15 months we all agree we have to do more." 3/9/65, box 1, papers of McGeorge Bundy, LBJ Library.
5. Taylor to Johnson, 1/6/65, "Deployment of Major U.S. Forces to Vietnam, July 1965," vol. 1, tab 3; and Taylor to JCS, 2/22/65, tab 74, box 40, NSC Histories, National Security File, LBJ Library. Also see History Backup, 1/1/65–1/22/65, box 4, papers of William Westmoreland, LBJ Library.
6. Westmoreland to Sharp and Wheeler, 2/24/65, "Deployment of Major U.S. Forces to Vietnam, July 1965," vol. 1, tab 75, box 40, NSC Histories, National Security File, LBJ Library.
7. When President Ronald Reagan sent Marines to Beruit, the consequences of passive defense became apparent after a car bomb inflicted heavy losses while the Marines slept.
8. Wheeler to Sharp and Westmoreland, 220/65, History Backup,

January 21 to February 28, 1965, box 5, papers of William C. Westmoreland, LBJ Library.

9. Brian VanDeMark, *Into the Quagmire: Lyndon Johnson and the Escalation of the Vietnam War* (New York: Oxford University Press, 1991), pp. 74, 144.

10. Regarding LBJ's lingering uncertainty, see Bundy to LBJ, 5/14/65, "Deployment of Major U.S. Forces to Vietnam, July 1965," vol. 1, tab 163, box 41, NSC Histories, National Security File, LBJ Library.

11. William C. Westmoreland, *A Soldier Reports* (Garden City, N.Y.: Doubleday and Co., 1976), p. 98.

12. VanDeMark, *Into the Quagmire*, p. 180.

13. Doris Kearns, *Lyndon Johnson and the American Dream* (New York: New American Library, 1976), p. 296.

14. News conference of April 27, 1965, cited in Lyndon B. Johnson, *Public Papers of the Presidents of the United States: Lyndon B. Johnson 1965, II* (Washington: Government Printing Office, 1966), p. 456.

15. Rusk to Taylor, 5/3/65, "Deployment of Major U.S. Forces to Vietnam, July 1965," vol. 1, tab 139, box 41, NSC Histories, National Security File, LBJ Library.

16. Westmoreland's impression, cited in Edwin H. Simmons, *Marines* (New York: Bantam Books, 1987), p. 13.

17. "Ground War in Asia," *New York Times*, 9 June 1965, p. 46.

18. VanDeMark, *Into the Quagmire*, p. 95; and Westmoreland, *A Soldier Reports*, p. 125.

19. See comments of McNamara and Wheeler on 7/21/65, box 1, Meeting Notes File, LBJ Library. Also see Taylor to Department of State, 4/12/65, "Deployment of Major U.S. Forces to Vietnam, July 1965," vol. 1, tab 158, box 41, NSC Histories, National Security File, LBJ Library.

20. Douglas Kinnard, *The War Managers* (Hanover, N.H.: University Press of New England, 1977), p. 36.

21. Cited in Harry G. Summers, Jr., *On Strategy II. A Critical Analysis of the Gulf War* (New York: Dell, 1992), p. 54.

22. Arguing against the possibility of effective protest at this time are the results of a secret public opinion survey LBJ commissioned showing better than two-to-one support for sending more troops.

23. "Commander's Estimate of the Military Situation in South Vietnam," 3/26/65, History Backup, March 1 to 26, 1965, box 5, papers of William C. Westmoreland, LBJ Library.

24. Memorandum for the President, 5/20/65, "Deployment of Major U.S. Forces to Vietnam, July 1965," vol. 1, tab 417, Box 43, NSC Histories, National Security File, LBJ Library. Also in *The Pentagon Papers*, vol. 3, pp. 705–706; and cited in Lyndon B. Johnson, *The Vantage Point: Perspectives on the Presidency, 1963–1969* (New York: Holt,

Rinehart and Winston, 1971), p. 141. Eisenhower had suggested the same objective in an earlier conversation with LBJ; see conversation of 2/17/65, box 1, Meeting Notes File, LBJ Library.

25. Memorandum of telephone conversation, 7/2/65, box 2, Post-presidential Papers: Gettysburg, Indochina, Dwight D. Eisenhower Library.

26. It would only lead to "an ever-increasing commitment of U.S. personnel without materially improving the chances of victory ... we will find ourselves mired down in combat in the jungle in a military effort that we cannot win, and from which we will have extreme difficulty in extracting ourselves." See McCone to Secretaries of State and Defense, 4/2/65, "Deployment of Major U.S. Forces to Vietnam, July 1965," vol. 1, tab 135, box 41, NSC Histories, National Security File, LBJ Library; *The Pentagon Papers*, vol. 3, pp. 352–353; and U. S. Grant Sharp, *Strategy for Defeat: Vietnam in Retrospect*, (San Rafael, Calif.: Presidio Press, 1978), pp. 72–73.

27. Memorandum for the United States Intelligence Board, 7/20/65, "Deployment of Major U.S. Forces to Vietnam, July 1965," vol. 1, tab 398, box 43, NSC Histories, National Security File, LBJ Library.

28. McNamara's specific wording states that the VC were winning "largely because the ratio of guerrilla to anti-guerrilla forces is unfavorable to the government." See Memorandum for the President, 6/26/65, "Deployment of Major U.S. Forces to Vietnam, July 1965," vol. 1, tab 353, box 43, NSC Histories, National Security File, LBJ Library.

29. McNamara's brief is in McNamara to President, 7/20/65, "Deployment of Major U.S. Forces to Vietnam, July 1965," vol. 1, tab 396, box 43, NSC Histories, National Security File, LBJ Library. The dialogue is from a July 21 meeting recorded in Cabinet Room Meeting Notes Files, box 1, and is noted in Jack Valenti, *A Very Human President* (New York: W. W. Norton and Co., 1975), pp. 327–328. Additional discussion is in "Summary Notes of 553rd NSC Meeting," 7/27/65, "Deployment of Major U.S. Forces to Vietnam, July 1965," vol. 1, tab 426, box 43, NSC Histories, National Security File, LBJ Library.

30. See comments at the 552d NSC meeting, 6/11/65, vol. 3, tab 34, box 1, NSC Histories, National Security File, LBJ Library.

31. Summary notes of 553rd NSC meeting, 7/27/65, "Deployment of Major U.S. Forces to Vietnam, July 1965," vol. 1, tab 426, box 43, NSC Histories, National Security File, LBJ Library.

32. The language comes from the official summary: "Deployment of Major U.S. Forces to Vietnam, July 1965," vol. 1, box 40, NSC Histories, National Security File, LBJ Library.

33. The president's news conference of July 28, 1965, in Johnson, *Public Papers*, p. 795.

34. "We told them to get the best man they had—three of them about the same: Westmoreland, General Johnson, the Chief of Staff, and General Abrams. And they felt that Westmoreland would be the best man for it and that's who we sent." Transcript, Lyndon B. Johnson Oral History Interview, 8/12/69, by William Jorden, LBJ Library.

35. McNamara heartily endorsed Westmoreland as Deputy Commander, USMACV. See "Memorandum for the President," 1/10/64, box 224, WHCF Name File (Westmoreland), LBJ Library. On 6/8/65 McNamara said, "We ought to keep Westmoreland and change Ambassadors" (box 1, Meeting Notes File, LBJ Library).

36. Westmoreland, *A Soldier Reports*, p. 250.

37. W. W. Rostow, *The Diffusion of Power: An Essay in Recent History* (New York: Macmillan, 1972), pp. 451–452.

38. Westmoreland acknowledges: "President Johnson and Secretary McNamara afforded me marked independence in how I ran the war within the borders of South Vietnam." See Westmoreland, *A Soldier Reports*, p. 261.

39. For an elaboration on his strategy, see "Deployment of Additional US/Allied Combat and Logistic Support Forces to South Vietnam," box 5, History Backup, March 1–26, 1965, papers of William C. Westmoreland, LBJ Library; Concept of Counterinsurgency Operations in South Vietnam, 6/12/65, "Deployment of Major U.S. Forces to Vietnam, July 1965," vol. 1, tab 293, box 42, NSC Histories, National Security File, LBJ Library; also tab 296 in same source.

40. For insight into this strategy, see Nhu Tang Truong et al., *A Vietcong Memoir* (San Diego: Harcourt Brace Jovanovich, 1985), p. 86.

41. Westmoreland, *A Soldier Reports*, p. 83.

42. General William DePuy recalls that the introduction of U.S. forces caused MACV to change quickly "from a staff that originally was very much concerned with counterinsurgency ... to a staff concerned with [large-scale] operations." Cited in Andrew F. Krepinevich, Jr., *The Army and Vietnam* (Baltimore: Johns Hopkins University Press, 1986), p. 139.

43. H. Norman Schwarzkopf and Peter Petre, *It Doesn't Take a Hero* (New York: Bantam, 1992), p. 126.

44. "It is not our concept that the US would take exclusive control or responsibility for any entire province although, in practice, only token South Vietnamese forces might remain" (from "Deployment of Major U.S. Forces to Vietnam, July 1965," vol. 1, tab 296, box 42, NSC Histories, National Security File, LBJ Library.

45. "Deployment of Major U.S. Forces to Vietnam, July 1965," vol. 1, tab 296, box 42, NSC Histories, National Security File, LBJ Library.

46. Sharp to Westmoreland, 6/13/65, box 6, History Backup, May 10 to June 30, 1965, papers of William C. Westmoreland, LBJ Library.

47. Box 7, History File, October 25 to December 20, 1965, papers of William C. Westmoreland, LBJ Library.

48. Harold G. Moore and Joseph L. Galloway, *We Were Soldiers Once . . . and Young—Ia Drang: The Battle that Changed the War in Vietnam* (New York: Random House, 1992), p. 62.

49. Moore and Galloway, *We Were Soldiers Once*, p. 104.

50. Box 7, History File, October 25 to December 20, 1965, papers of William C. Westmoreland, LBJ Library.

51. In partial compensation, and like the 1/7, the battalion had a leavening of experienced, veteran NCOs.

52. Moore and Galloway, *We Were Soldiers Once*, p. 217.

53. Jack P. Smith, "Death in the Ia Drang Valley," *Saturday Evening Post,* 240 (January 28, 1967), pp. 80–85.

54. Ibid.

55. Box 7, History File, October 25 to December 20, 1965, papers of William C. Westmoreland, LBJ Library.

56. Neil Sheehan, "U.S. Troops Renew Search for Enemy in Vietnam Valley," *New York Times,* 20 November 1965, p. 1.

57. John G. Norris, "Big Iadrang Victory Held Turning Point," *Washington Post,* 20 November 1965, p. 1.

58. Moore and Galloway, *We Were Soldiers Once*, p. 216.

59. In a personal correspondence of May 24, 1993, with General Moore in which I inquired about this point, the general explained that initially he, like myself, believed the NVA assertion was historical revisionism. However, he changed his mind while conducting his book research and has convinced me to change mine.

60. Harry Maurer, *Strange Ground: An Oral History of Americans in Vietnam 1945–1975* (New York: Avon, 1989), p. 12.

61. Moore and Galloway, *We Were Soldiers Once*, p. 339.

62. Westmoreland, *A Soldier Reports*, p. 140.

63. von Clausewitz, *On War*, p. 613. For a fuller discussion of this point, see Summers, *On Strategy*, chapter 8, and particularly pp. 56–57.

CHAPTER 10

1. Jim Stockdale and Sybil Stockdale, *In Love and War* (New York: Harper and Row, 1984), p. 181.

2. U. S. Grant Sharp, *Strategy for Defeat: Vietnam in Retrospect* (San Rafael, Calif.: Presidio Press, 1978), p. 109.

3. Jack Valenti, *A Very Human President* (New York: W. W. Norton and Co., 1975), p. 227.

4. Lady Bird Johnson, *A White House Diary* (New York: Holt, Rinehart and Winston, 1970), p. 264.

5. Valenti, *A Very Human President*, p. 227.

6. Lady Bird Johnson, *A White House Diary*, p. 362.

7. Rusk used close to this phrase in urging military persistence. See Valenti, *A Very Human President*, p. 239. For "find a way," see Ibid., p. 228.

8. Ibid., p. 226.

9. See, for example, Lady Bird Johnson, *A White House Diary*, p. 347.

10. William C. Westmoreland, *A Soldier Reports* (Garden City, N.Y.: Doubleday and Co., 1976), p. 120.

11. The DIA director called CINCPAC "a hindrance, and in no way did it help the conduct of the war." William Colby observed that CINCPAC was "halfway between the action and the policy—and effective in neither." See Lewis Sorley, *Thunderbolt: General Creighton Abrams and the Army of His Times* (New York: Simon and Schuster, 1992), p. 327.

12. Westmoreland, *A Soldier Reports*, p. 159.

13. See 2/6/66 and 2/7/66, box 5, The President's Daily Diary, Special Files, LBJ Library.

14. 8/13/66, box 1, Tom Johnson's Notes of Meetings, Special Files, LBJ Library.

15. See, for example, Lady Bird Johnson, *A White House Diary*, pp. 359, 371.

16. For examples, see Johnson to Westmoreland, 11/17/66; Westmoreland to Johnson, 3/25/67; and Johnson to USO Chairman, 3/27/67; all in box 224, WHCF Name File (Westmoreland), LBJ Library.

17. See *The Pentagon Papers*, vol. 4, pp. 304–305.

18. See Memorandum for Secretary of Defense, May 4, 1967, in *The Pentagon Papers*, vol. 4, pp. 461–462.

19. For a 1966 example, see a chart in *The Pentagon Papers*, vol. 4, p. 308.

20. For example, see JCS to McNamara, "Concept for Vietnam," 8/27/65, "Deployment of Major U.S. Forces to Vietnam, July 1965," vol. 1, tab 436, box 43, NSC Histories, National Security File, LBJ Library.

21. See *The Pentagon Papers*, vol. 4, p. 306.

22. Leslie H. Gelb and Richard K. Betts, *The Irony of Vietnam: The System Worked* (Washington: Brookings Institution, 1979), p. 267; and "Annual Message to the Congress on the State of the Union, January 12, 1966," in Lyndon B. Johnson, *Public Papers of the Presidents of the United States: Lyndon B. Johnson 1966* (Washington: Government Printing Office, 1967), p. 4.

23. See *The Pentagon Papers*, vol. 4, p. 369.

24. *New York Times*, 10 March 1968, provided in *The Pentagon Papers*, vol. 4, p. 587.

25. Karl von Clausewitz, *On War* (Princeton: Princeton University Press, 1976), p. 586.

26. George Reedy, *Lyndon B. Johnson: A Memoir* (New York: Andrews and McMeel, 1982), p. 149.

27. Lady Bird Johnson, *A White House Diary*, p. 371.

28. Reedy, *Lyndon B. Johnson*, p. 148.

29. Westmoreland, *A Soldier Reports*, p. 214.

30. For LBJ's response, see comments of 4/21/65, box 1, papers of McGeorge Bundy, LBJ Library.

31. For example, see comments of 12/17/65, box 1, Meeting Notes File, LBJ Library.

32. Lady Bird Johnson, *A White House Diary*, p. 262.

33. Ibid., p. 360.

34. See 7/12/67, box 1, Tom Johnson's Notes of Meetings, Special Files, LBJ Library.

35. See Lyndon B. Johnson, *The Vantage Point: Perspectives on the Presidency, 1963–1969* (New York: Holt, Rinehart and Winston, 1971), p. 259.

36. Conversation cited in *The Pentagon Papers*, vol. 4, p. 442.

37. See Panzer to Johnson, 5/3/67, box 224, WHCF Name File (Westmoreland), LBJ Library. The public telegrams are in the same box.

38. Cited in Gelb and Betts, *The Irony of Vietnam*, p. 337.

39. This possibility had long vexed Johnson. For example, see chapter 26, p. 8, box 1, papers of William P. Bundy, LBJ Library. For William P. Bundy's comments on the Draft Presidential Memorandum dated June 2, 1967, see *The Pentagon Papers*, vol. 4, pp. 502–503. Also of interest is Giap's comment, published in 1967: "The more the war of aggression is Americanized, the more disintegrated the puppet Saigon army and administration becomes."

40. Of general officers surveyed by Kinnard, 73 percent said Vietnamization should have been emphasized years earlier. See Douglas Kinnard, *The War Managers* (Hanover, N.H.: University Press of New England, 1977).

41. The Communist high command's exact expectations remain, as of 1993, obscured by propaganda and the difficulty of accessing North Vietnamese records.

42. "Public Statements," July to December 1967, box 21, papers of William C. Westmoreland, LBJ Library.

43. History File, November 13–28, 1967, box 14, papers of William C. Westmoreland, LBJ Library; also see Westmoreland's November 1967 "Notes for Talk with the President," in box 14; and *A Soldier Reports*, p. 234.

44. History File, December 17–26, 1967, box 14, papers of William C. Westmoreland, LBJ Library.

45. Westmoreland, *A Soldier Reports*, p. 239. Rostow to LBJ, 12/8/67, box 26, Memos to the President, National Security File, LBJ Library, contains an explicit warning to the president of an unprecedented enemy offensive.

46. History File, December 27 to January 31, 1968, box 15, papers of William C. Westmoreland, LBJ Library.

47. For two different assessments of enemy intentions that underscore the schism between military intelligence in Saigon and the CIA, see Rostow to LBJ, 12/16/67, box 26, Memos to the President, National Security File, LBJ Library.

48. A document captured on November 6, 1967, revealed that the enemy planned a coordinated offensive. See Message 0150726Z, Abrams to Westmoreland, History File, November 13–28, 1967, box 14, papers of William C. Westmoreland, LBJ Library. Other indications are reviewed in VNIT-159, 2/25/68, on file at the U.S. Army Center of Military History.

49. History File, December 27 to January 31, 1967–68, box 15, papers of William C. Westmoreland, LBJ Library.

50. Westmoreland says "he frankly did not believe he would do this" [attack at Tet] because in the past he had adhered to the Tet ceasefire. History File, December 27 to January 31, 1967–68, box 15, papers of William C. Westmoreland, LBJ Library.

51. For a candid analysis of the intelligence failure, see Colonel Hoang Ngoc Luong, *The General Offensives of 1968–69* (Washington: U.S. Army Center of Military History, 1981).

52. P. Son, ed., *The Viet Cong Tet Offensive 1968* (Saigon: 1969). The official South Vietnamese history, lacking in perspective given the publication date and prevailing political climate, but full of invaluable detail about ARVN operations.

53. James R. Arnold, *Tet Offensive 1968* (London: Osprey, 1990), p. 50.

54. For the embassy battle, see oral interviews conducted with the 716 MP Battalion on file at U.S. Army Center of Military History, Washington, D.C.; and *Military Police Journal*, April 1968, pp. 22–23.

55. Arnold, *Tet Offensive 1968*, p. 55.

56. Ibid, page 57.

57. "In the course of the next several weeks," he wrote, "I put in extraordinarily long hours." History File, February 1–29, 1968, box 16, papers of William C. Westmoreland, LBJ Library.

58. COMUSMACV Public Statements 1968, box 21, papers of William C. Westmoreland, LBJ Library.

59. John Prados and Ray W. Stubbe, *Valley of Decision: The Siege of Khe Sanh* (Boston: Houghton Mifflin Co., 1991), p. 359.

60. For a detailed dialogue, see Prados and Stubbe, *Valley of Decision*, pp. 355–356.

61. Ibid. p. 289.

62. Ibid. p. 359.

63. Comments of 2/11/68, History File, February 1–29, 1968, box 16, papers of William C. Westmoreland, LBJ Library.

64. Major General Lowell English, who commanded at Khe Sanh, called it a "trap . . . to force you into the expenditure of absolutely unreasonable amounts of men and material to defend a piece of terrain that wasn't worth a damn." Cited in Stanley Karnow, *Vietnam: A History* (New York: Viking, 1983), p. 542.

65. Prados and Stubbe, *Valley of Decision*, p. 367.

66. Ibid., p. 451.

67. In January, I Corps held 40 percent of MACV's entire strength, a figure rising to 50 percent by March. The other three corps areas were designated an economy of force zone.

68. Westmoreland, *A Soldier Reports*, p. 354.

69. *The Pentagon Papers*, vol. 4, p. 547.

70. See *The Pentagon Papers*, vol. 4, p. 580; and Clark Clifford, "A Vietnam Reappraisal," *Foreign Affairs*, vol. 47 (July 1969), pp. 611–612.

71. See chart reproduced in Gelb and Betts, *The Irony of Vietnam*, p. 161.

72. *The Pentagon Papers*, vol. 4, p. 591.

73. McGeorge Bundy's summary comments of 3/20/68, box 2, Meeting Notes File, LBJ Library.

74. Comment on 3/20/68, box 2, Meeting Notes File, LBJ Library.

75. "The President's Address to the Nation," March 31, 1968, Lyndon B. Johnson, *Public Papers of the Presidents of the United States: Lyndon B. Johnson 1968, I* (Washington: Government Printing Office, 1970), pp. 469–476.

76. Privately, he confided his doubts that he could unite the country, and well before his public announcement had told a select handful, including General Westmoreland, that he did not plan to be a candidate in the 1968 election. See History File, November 13–28, 1967, box 14, papers of William C. Westmoreland, LBJ Library.

77. 4/7/68, box 95, Diary Backup, Special Files, LBJ Library.

78. Arnold, *Tet Offensive 1968*, p. 85.

79. Jefferson Davis, *The Rise and Fall of the Confederate Government* (New York: Da Capo Press, 1990), vol. 2, p. 378.

80. Westmoreland's recollection is provided in transcript "An Evening with William C. Westmoreland," 3/10/86, LBJ Library.

81. Arnold, *Tet Offensive 1968*, p. 6.

82. For insight into this approach, see Nhu Tang Truong, et al., *A Vietcong Memoir* (San Diego: Harcourt Brace Jovanovich, 1985), pp. 87, 210.

83. LBJ claimed it was McNamara's idea, proposed before Tet. See Johnson to Westmoreland, 1/19/68, box 224, WHCF Name File (Westmoreland), LBJ Library.

84. The Joint Chiefs of Staff formally announced this change on April 16, 1968.
85. Westmoreland, *A Soldier Reports*, p. 121.
86. Cited in Arnold, *Tet Offensive 1968*, p. 91.
87. Stanley Karnow, "Giap Remembers," *New York Times Magazine*, 24 June 1990, p. 60.
88. Transcript, Lyndon B. Johnson Oral History Interview, 8/12/69, by William Jorden, LBJ Library.

CHAPTER 11

1. Harry G. Summers, Jr., *On Strategy: The Vietnam War in Context* (Carlisle, Pa.: U.S. Army War College, 1981), p. 121.
2. See "Clinton Ignores History's Lessons in Vietnam," *Wall Street Journal*, 9 September 1992, p. A14.
3. Lewis Sorley, *Thunderbolt: General Creighton Abrams and the Army of His Times* (New York: Simon and Schuster, 1992), p. 364.
4. The discussion of the "remarkable trinity" appears in Carl von Clausewitz, *On War* (Princeton: Princeton University Press, 1976), p. 89. Harry G. Summers's comment appears in *On Strategy II: A Critical Analysis of the Gulf War* (New York: Dell, 1992), p. 72.
5. The round-out idea received an acid test in 1990. One reserve brigade went to the National Training Center in the Mojave Desert to see how long it would take to be war-ready. After sixty days it still was not combat-ready.
6. H. Norman Schwarzkopf and Peter Petre, *It Doesn't Take a Hero* (New York: Bantam, 1992), p. 378.
7. Milo M. Quaife, ed., *The Diary of James K. Polk* (Chicago, 1910), vol. 1, May 11, 1846, p. 392.
8. See *Conduct of the Persian Gulf Conflict: An Interim Report to Congress* (Washington: Government Printing Office, 1991), p. 1–1.
9. Schwarzkopf and Petre, *It Doesn't Take a Hero*, p. 318.
10. Ibid., p. 354.
11. Ibid., p. 361.
12. Stephen W. Sears, *To the Gates of Richmond* (New York: Ticknor and Fields, 1992), p. 154.
13. John Prados and Ray W. Stubbe, *Valley of Decision: The Siege of Khe Sanh* (Boston: Houghton Mifflin Co., 1991), p. 294.
14. Besides the usual classified secrets there is this: in his memoirs, Schwarzkopf reveals that he and Colin Powell frequently communicated "outside normal Pentagon channels." Whether these exchanges were preserved and will eventually become reliably available

to researchers is doubtful. See Schwarzkopf and Petre, *It Doesn't Take a Hero,* p. 325.

15. Ibid., p. 381.

16. Ibid., p. 468.

17. von Clausewitz, *On War,* p. 584.

18. Walter Lord, ed., *The Fremantle Diary* (Boston: Little, Brown and Co., 1954), p. 175.

19. Johnson's comment is related in Transcript, "An Evening with William C. Westmoreland," 3/10/86, p. 11, LBJ Library.

20. See Johnson's comment that there is a need for a colorful general "to go to Saigon and argue" with the press in 8/18/67, box 1, Meeting Notes File, LBJ Library.

21. Schwarzkopf and Petre, *It Doesn't Take a Hero,* p. 344.

22. Cited in Summers, *On Strategy II,* p. 224.

23. von Clausewitz, *On War,* p. 87.

24. Richard K. Showman, ed., *The Papers of Nathanael Greene* (Chapel Hill, N.C.: University of North Carolina Press, 1976), vol. 2, Nathanael Greene to Jacob Greene, January 3, 1778, p. 244.

25. John C. Fitzpatrick, ed., *The Writings of George Washington,* (Washington: Government Printing Office, 1931–1944), vol. 32, To the Secretary of War, August 22, 1792, p. 126.

26. James D. Richardson, ed., *A Compilation of the Messages and Papers of the Presidents 1789–1897* (Washington, 1898–1908), vol. 4, pp. 542–543.

27. For an example of how this worked in Vietnam, see George Reedy, *Lyndon B. Johnson: A Memoir* (New York: Andrews and McMeel, 1982), p. 147.

28. Summers, *On Strategy,* p. 7.

29. Summers, *On Strategy II,* p. 27.

30. Barton Gellman, "Rumblings of Discord heard in Pentagon," *Washington Post,* 20 June 1993, p. 1.

BIBLIOGRAPHY

"Your desire of obtaining truth is very laudable. . . . Many circumstances will unavoidably be misconceived and misrepresented. Nothwithstanding most of the Papers which may properly be deemed official are preserved; yet the knowledge of innumerable things, of a more delicate and secret nature, is confined to the perishable remembrance of some few of the present generation."

GEORGE WASHINGTON TO NOAH WEBSTER REGARDING WEBSTER'S HISTORY OF THE YORKTOWN CAMPAIGN, JULY 31, 1788, IN THE WRITINGS OF GEORGE WASHINGTON, VOL. 30, PP. 26–28.

PART ONE. GEORGE WASHINGTON AND HIS REVOLUTIONARY TIMES

Adams, Charles Francis. *The Works of John Adams.* 10 vols. Boston: Little, Brown, 1854.

Adams, Randolph G. "The Harmar Expedition of 1790." *The Ohio State Archaeological and Historical Quarterly,* vol. L (1941), pp. 60–241.

Allen, Gardner W. *A Naval History of the American Revolution.* 2 vols. Boston: Houghton Mifflin Co., 1913.

Annals of Congress: The Debates and Proceedings in the Congress of the United States. 42 vols. Washington: 1834–1856.

Blanchard, Claude. *Guerre d'Amerique.* Paris: 1881.

Boyd, Julian P., ed. *The Papers of Thomas Jefferson.* 24 vols. Princeton, N.J.: Princeton University Press, 1950–1990.

Brant, Irving. *James Madison: Commander in Chief, 1812–1836.* New York: Bobbs-Merrill Co., 1961.

Burnett, Edmund Cody. *Letters of Members of the Continental Congress.* 8 vols. Washington: Carnegie Institute, 1936.

Butterfield, L. H., ed. *The Adams Papers: Series I: Diary and Autobiography of John Adams.* 4 vols. Cambridge, Mass.: Belknap Press, 1961.

———. *Letters of Benjamin Rush.* 2 vols. Princeton, N.J.: Princeton University Press, 1951.

327

Cappon, Lester J., ed. *The Adams-Jefferson Letters: The Complete Correspondence Between Thomas Jefferson and Abigail and John Adams.* 2 vols. New York: Simon and Schuster, 1959.

Chinard, Gilbert, ed. *George Washington as the French Knew Him.* New York: Greenwood Press, 1940.

Clark, William. "A Journal of Major-General Anthony Wayne's Campaign Against the Shawnee Indians in Ohio in 1794–1795." *Mississippi Valley Historical Review,* vol. 1 (1914–1915), pp. 418–433.

Collier, Christopher, and Lincoln, James. *The Constitutional Convention of 1787.* New York: Reader's Digest Press and Random House, 1986.

Corner, George W., ed. *The Autobiography of Benjamin Rush.* Westport, Conn.: Greenwood Press, 1948.

Cunliffe, Marcus. *Soldiers and Civilians: The Martial Spirit in America. 1775–1865.* Boston: Little Brown, 1968.

Cushing, Henry A., ed. *The Writings of Samuel Adams.* 4 vols. New York: G. P. Putnam's Sons, 1904–1908.

"Daily Journal of Wayne's Campaign." *The American Pioneer,* vol. 1 (September 1842), pp. 315–322.

DeConde, Alexander. *The Quasi-War: The Politics and Diplomacy of the Undeclared War with France 1797–1801.* New York: Charles Scribner's Sons, 1966.

Doniol, Henri. *Histoire de la Participation de la France a L'Establissment des Etats-Unis d'Amerique.* 5 vols. Paris: Imprimerie Nationale, 1842. Volume 5 has most of Rochambeau's correspondence.

Dos Passos, John. *The Shackles of Power: Three Jeffersonian Decades.* Garden City, N.Y.: Doubleday and Company, 1966. Informative, entertaining look at America and its government to the 1830s.

Douglas, Robert B., ed. *A French Volunteer of the War of Independence Chevalier de Pontgibaud.* New York: The New York Times and Arno Press, 1969.

Downes, Randolph C. *Council Fires on the Upper Ohio.* Pittsburgh: University of Pittsburgh Press, 1940. A fine account.

Farrand, Max. *The Records of the Federal Convention of 1787.* 4 vols. New Haven: Yale University Press, 1986.

Fitzpatrick, John C., ed. *The Diaries of George Washington.* 4 vols. Boston: Houghton Mifflin Co., 1925.

———. *The Writings of George Washington.* 39 vols. Washington: Government Printing Office, 1931–1944.

Force, Peter, ed. *American Archives. 4th Series.* 6 vols. Washington: 1837–46.

———. *American Archives. 5th Series.* vol. 3, 1776. Washington: 1853.

Ford, P. L., ed. *Jefferson's Writings.* New York: Federal Edition, 1904.

Ford, Worthington C., ed. *Journals of the Continental Congress 1774–1789.* 34 vols. Washington: Government Printing Office, 1904–1937.

Fortescue, Sir John. *A History of the British Army.* 14 vols. London: 1910–1930.

Franklin, Benjamin. *The Autobiography of Benjamin Franklin.* Edited by Leonard W. Labaree et al., New Haven: Yale University Press, 1964.

Freeman, Douglas S. *George Washington: A Biography.* 7 vols. New York: Charles Scribner's Sons, 1948–1957. The author's loving bias aside, still a fine work and a wonderful read.

Frothingham, Thomas G. *Washington: Commander in Chief.* Boston: Houghton Mifflin Co., 1930.

Hagan, Kenneth J. *This People's Navy: The Making of American Sea Power.* New York: The Free Press, 1991.

Hamilton, Alexander; Jay, John; and Madison, James. *The Federalist Papers.* Garden City, N.Y.: Doubleday and Co., 1961.

Hamilton, Stanislaus M., ed. *The Writings of James Monroe.* 7 vols. New York: G. P. Putnam's Sons, 1901.

Higginbotham, Don R. *Daniel Morgan: Revolutionary Rifleman.* Chapel Hill, N.C.: University of North Carolina Press, 1961.

———. *George Washington and the American Military Tradition.* Athens, Ga.: University of Georgia Press, 1985.

———. *The War of American Independence: Military Attitudes, Policies, and Practice, 1763–1789.* New York: Macmillan, 1971.

Jacobs, James Ripley. *The Beginning of the U.S. Army 1783–1812.* Port Washington, N.Y.: Kennikat Press, 1947.

Ketchum, Richard M. *The Winter Soldiers.* Garden City, N.Y.: Doubleday and Co., 1973. Another fine read.

Knopf, Richard C. *Anthony Wayne: A Name in Arms.* Pittsburgh: University of Pittsburgh Press, 1960.

Kohn, Richard H. *Eagle and Sword: The Federalists and the Creation of the Military Establishment, 1783–1802.* New York: The Free Press, 1975.

The Lee Papers. 4 vols. New York: Collections of the New York Historical Society, 1872–1875.

Lewis, Charles Lee. *Admiral de Grasse and American Independence.* Annapolis: United States Naval Institute, 1945. Contains a fine account of the evolution of the strategy of Yorktown. However, p. 129 misses the point of the king's instructions to Rochambeau regarding what to do should Washington's army collapse.

Lowrie, Walter, and Clarke, Matthew St. Clair, eds. *American State Papers. Class II. Indian Affairs.* vol. 1. Washington: Gales and Seaton, 1832.

MacGregor, Morris J., and Wright, Robert K. *Soldier-Statesmen of the Constitution.* Washington: Government Printing Office, 1987.

Maclay, William. *The Journal of William Maclay.* New York: Albert and Charles Boni, 1927.

Mahon, John K. *History of the Militia and the National Guard.* New York: Macmillan, 1983.

Nelson, Paul David. *Anthony Wayne: Soldier of the Early Republic.* Bloomington, Ind.: Indiana University Press, 1985.

————. *General Horatio Gates.* Baton Rouge: Louisiana State University Press, 1976.

Nourse, Harry S. *The Military Annals of Lancaster, Massachusetts.* Lancaster, Mass.: 1889.

Padover, Saul K., ed. *The World of the Founding Fathers.* Cranbury, N.J.: A. S. Barnes and Co., 1960.

Palmer, Michael A. *Stoddert's War: Naval Operations During the Quasi-War with France, 1798–1801.* Columbia, S.C.: University of South Carolina Press, 1987.

Parkman, Francis. *Montcalm and Wolfe.* New York: Atheneum, 1984.

Paullin, Charles Oscar. *Out-letters of the Continental Marine Committee and Board of Admiralty.* 2 vols. New York: De Vinne Press, 1914.

Peckham, Howard H. "Josiah Harmar and His Indian Expedition." *Ohio Archaeological and Historical Quarterly,* vol. LV, no. 3 (July–September, 1946), pp. 227–241.

Pickering, Octavius, ed. *The Life of Thomas Pickering.* 4 vols. Boston: Little, Brown and Co., 1867.

Quaife, M., ed. "General James Wilkinson's Narrative of the Fallen Timbers Campaign." *Mississippi Valley Historical Review,* vol. 16, no. 1 (1929–1930), 81–87.

Rankin, Hugh F. *Narratives of the American Revolution.* Chicago: Lakeside Press, 1976.

Rochambeau, Marshal Count de. *Memoirs of the Marshal Count de Rochambeau Relative to the War of Independence of the United States.* Translated by M. Wright. Paris: 1838.

Rossie, Jonathan G. *The Politics of Command in the American Revolution.* Syracuse, N.Y.: Syracuse University Press, 1975.

Sanders, Jennings B. *Evolution of Executive Departments of the Continental Congress 1774–1789.* Chapel Hill, N.C.: University of North Carolina Press, 1935.

Sargent, Winthrop. "Winthrop Sargent's Diary While with General Arthur St. Clair's Expedition Against the Indians." *Ohio Archaeological and Historical Publications,* vol. XXXIII (1924), pp. 237–273.

Sawvel, Franklin B., ed. *The Complete Anas of Thomas Jefferson.* New York: Round Table Press, 1903.

Showman, Richard K., ed. *The Papers of Nathanael Greene.* Chapel Hill, N.C.: University of North Carolina Press, 1976.

Smith, Joseph E. *History of Pittsfield, Massachusetts.* Boston: 1869.

Smith, Page. *John Adams.* vol. 2: 1784–1826. Garden City, N.Y.: Doubleday and Co., 1963.

Smith, William Henry, ed. *The St. Clair Papers: The Life and Public Services of Arthur St. Clair.* 2 vols. Cincinnati: Robert Clarke and Co., 1882.

Steiner, Bernard. *The Life and Correspondence of James McHenry.* Cleveland: Burrows Brothers, 1907.

Stryker, William S. *The Battle of Monmouth.* Princeton, N.J.: Princeton University Press, 1927.

Sword, Wiley. *President Washington's Indian War: The Struggle for the Old Northwest, 1790–1795.* Norman, Okla.: University of Oklahoma Press, 1985.

Thompson, Ray. *Washington Along the Delaware.* Fort Washington, Pa.: The Bicentennial Press, 1970.

Tornquist, Karl Gustaf. *The Naval Campaigns of Count De Grasse.* Philadelphia: Swedish Colonial Society, 1942.

Ward, Harry M. *The Department of War, 1781–1795.* Pittsburgh: University of Pittsburgh Press, 1962.

Whitridge, Arnold. *Rochambeau.* New York: Collier Books, 1965.

PART TWO. JAMES POLK'S MANIFEST DESTINY

Benton, Thomas Hart. *Thirty Years' View: A History of the Working of the American Government for Thirty Years, from 1820 to 1850.* vol. 2. New York: D. Appleton and Co., 1856.

Chance, Joseph E. *Jefferson Davis's Mexican War Regiment.* Jackson, Miss.: University Press of Mississippi, 1991.

Eisenhower, John S. D. *So Far from God: The U.S. War with Mexico 1846–1848.* New York: Random House, 1989.

Ferrell, Robert H., ed. *Monterrey Is Ours: The Mexican War Letters of Lieutenant Dana, 1845–1847.* Lexington, Ky.: University Press of Kentucky, 1990.

Miller, Robert R., ed. *The Mexican War Journal and Letters of Ralph W. Kirkham.* College Station, Tex.: Texas A&M Press, 1991.

Quaife, Milo M., ed. *The Diary of James K. Polk.* 4 vols. Chicago: 1910.

Richardson, James D., ed. *A Compilation of the Messages and Papers of the Presidents 1789–1897.* 11 vols. Washington: 1898–1908.

Schroeder, John H. *Mr. Polk's War: American Opposition and Dissent, 1846–1848.* Madison, Wis.: University of Wisconsin Press, 1973.

Scott, Winfield. *Memoirs of Lieut.-General Scott.* 2 vols. New York: Sheldon and Co., 1864.

Smith, Elbert B. *Magnificent Missourian: The Life of Thomas Hart Benton.* New York: J. B. Lippincott Co., 1958.

Tanner, Rhoda Van B., ed. *Journals of the Late Brevet Major Philip Norbourne Barbour.* New York: G. P. Putnam's Sons, 1936. Honest contemporary battle reporting.

Weigley, Russell F. *The American Way of War: A History of United States Military Strategy and Policy.* Bloomington, Ind.: Indiana University Press, 1973. A strong overview.

PART THREE. JEFFERSON DAVIS'S LOST CAUSE

Ball, Douglas B. *Financial Failure and Confederate Defeat*. Chicago: University of Illinois Press, 1991. A difficult subject made accessible for the layman.

Battles and Leaders of the Civil War. 4 vols. New York: Thomas Yoseloff, 1956.

Beringer, Richard E. et al. *Why the South Lost the Civil War*. Athens, Ga.: The University of Georgia Press, 1986. Challenging perspectives to be treated with caution.

Bragg, Thomas. *Diary of Thomas Bragg*. Chapel Hill, N.C.: Southern Historical Society, University of North Carolina Library, 1966. Illuminating insights from Braxton's brother.

Catton, Bruce. *Terrible Swift Sword*. Garden City, N.Y.: Doubleday and Co., 1963.

Connelly, Thomas Lawrence, and Jones, Archer. *The Politics of Command: Factions and Ideas in Confederate Strategy*. Baton Rouge: Louisiana State University Press, 1973. Full of good synthetic thinking.

Craven, Avery O., and Vandiver, Frank E. *The American Tragedy: The Civil War in Retrospect*. Hampden-Sydney, Va.: Hampden-Sydney College, 1959.

Daniel, Larry J. *Cannoneers in Gray: The Field Artillery of the Army of Tennessee, 1861–1865*. Tuscaloosa, Ala.: University of Alabama Press, 1984.

Daniel, Larry J. *Soldiering in the Army of the Tennessee*. Chapel Hill, N.C.: University of North Carolina Press, 1991.

Davis, Burke. *The Long Surrender*. New York: Random House, 1985.

Davis, Jefferson. *Private Letters*. New York: Harcourt, 1966.

———. *The Rise and Fall of the Confederate Government*. 2 vols. New York: Da Capo Press, 1990. Tedious and illuminating.

Davis, Varina. *Jefferson Davis: Ex-President of the Confederate States of America. A Memoir by His Wife*. 2 vols. New York: Belford Co. Publishers, 1890.

Davis, William C. *Jefferson Davis: The Man and His Hour*. New York: HarperCollins Publishers, 1991. An excellent recent addition.

Dowdey, Clifford. *The Seven Days*. Wilmington, N.C.: Broadfoot Publishing, 1988.

Dowdey, Clifford, and Manarin, Louis, eds. *The Wartime Papers of Robert E. Lee*. Boston: Little, Brown, 1961.

Durkin, Joseph T. *Confederate Navy Chief: Stephen R. Mallory*. Columbia, S.C.: University of South Carolina Press, 1954.

Foote, Shelby. *The Civil War: Red River to Appomattox*. New York: Random House, 1974. With a novelist's touch, Foote provides a fine counterpoint to Catton's works.

Freeman, Douglas S., ed. *Lee's Dispatches to Jefferson Davis.* New York: G. P. Putnam's Sons, 1957.

Gallagher, Gary W., ed. *Fighting for the Confederacy: The Personal Recollections of General Edward Porter Alexander.* Chapel Hill, N.C.: University of North Carolina Press, 1989.

Grant, Ulysses S. *Personal Memoirs of U. S. Grant.* New York: Charles Webster and Co., 1885. A classic.

Hattaway, Herman, and Jones, Archer *How the North Won.* Urbana, Ill.: University of Illinois Press, 1983.

Heleniak, Roman, and Hewitt, Lawrence L., eds. *The Confederate High Command and Related Topics.* Shippensburg, Pa.: White Mane Publishing, 1988.

Henderson, Harry M. *Texas in the Confederacy.* San Antonio, Tex.: Naylor Co., 1955.

Hendrick, Burton. *Statesmen of the Lost Cause: Jefferson Davis and His Cabinet.* New York: Literary Guild of America, 1939.

Jones, John B. *A Rebel War Clerk's Diary.* New York: Sagamore Press, 1958. Memoirs from a man who worked with Davis.

"Judge Turney on Mr. Davis." *Confederate Veteran* (January 1893), p. 15.

Lee, Robert E. *Recollections and Letters of General Robert E. Lee.* New York: Doubleday and Page, 1909.

Long, A. L. *Memoirs of Robert E. Lee.* Secaucus, N.J.: Blue and Grey Press, 1983.

Lord, Walter, ed. *The Fremantle Diary.* Boston: Little, Brown and Co., 1954. The highly entertaining account of a British tourist in 1863.

McIntosh, James T., ed. *The Papers of Jefferson Davis.* Baton Rouge: Louisiana State University Press, 1974.

McWhiney, Grady. *Braxton Bragg and Confederate Defeat.* 2 vols. New York: Columbia University Press, 1969.

Nelson, Larry E. *Bullets, Ballots, and Rhetoric: Confederate Policy for the United States Presidential Contest of 1864.* University, Ala.: University of Alabama, 1980.

Nolan, Alan T. *Lee Considered.* Chapel Hill, N.C.: University of North Carolina Press, 1991. An iconoclastic view of the marble man.

Owsley, Frank Lawrence. *King Cotton Diplomacy: Foreign Relations of the Confederate States of America.* Chicago: University of Chicago Press, 1931.

Parks, Joseph H. *General Leonidas Polk C.S.A.* Baton Rouge: Louisiana State University Press, 1962.

Pollard, Edward A. *The Lost Cause: A New Southern History of the War of the Confederates.* New York: E. B. Treat and Co., 1867.

Reagan, John H. *Memoirs: With Special Reference to Secession and the Civil War.* New York: Neale Publishing Co., 1906.

"The Rebel Yell." *Confederate Veteran.* 1 (January 1893), pp. 14–15.

Richardson, James D., ed. *A Compilation of the Messages and Papers of the Confederacy 1861–1865*. 2 vols. Nashville: United States Publishing Co., 1906.

Rowland, Dunbar, ed. *Jefferson Davis, Constitutionalist: His Letters, Papers and Speeches*. 10 vols. Jackson, Miss.: Mississippi Department of Archives and History, 1923.

Russell, William Howard. *My Diary North and South*. New York: Harper and Brothers, 1863.

Sears, Stephen W. *To the Gates of Richmond*. New York: Ticknor and Fields, 1992.

Simpson, Harold B. *Gaines' Mill to Appomattox*. Waco, Tex.: Texian Press, 1963.

Sorrell, G. Moxley. *Recollections of a Confederate Staff Officer*. New York: Neale Publishing Co., 1905.

Sword, Wiley. *Shiloh: Bloody April*. Dayton, Ohio: Morningside Bookshop, 1988. The best battle account.

Symonds, Craig L. *Joseph E. Johnston: A Civil War Biography*. New York: W. W. Norton and Co., 1992. A good book about one of the South's most important figures.

United States War Department. *War of the Rebellion: A Compilation of the Official Records of the Union and Confederate Armies*. 128 vols. Washington: Government Printing Office, 1880–1901. The indispensable source.

Vandiver, Frank E. *Rebel Brass: The Confederate Command System*. Baton Rouge: Louisiana State University Press, 1956.

———. *Their Tattered Flags: The Epic of the Confederacy*. New York: Harper's Magazine Press, 1970.

———, ed. *The Civil War Diary of General Josiah Gorgas*. University, Ala.: University of Alabama, 1947.

Von Abele, Rudolph. *Alexander H. Stephens: A Biography*. Westport, Conn.: Negro Universities Press, 1971.

Williams, T. Harry. *Lincoln and His Generals*. New York: Alfred A. Knopf, 1952.

Woodward, C. Vann. *Mary Chesnut's Civil War*. New Haven, Conn.: Yale University Press, 1981.

Yearns, W. Buck, ed. *The Confederate Governors*. Athens, Ga.: University of Georgia Press, 1985.

Yeary, Mamie, ed. *Reminiscences of the Boys in Gray, 1861–1865*. McGregor, Tex.: Morningside, 1986. Revealing stories from the Texans who served.

Younger, Edward, ed. *Inside the Confederate Government: The Diary of Robert Garlick Hill Kean*. New York: Oxford University Press, 1957. Fascinating contemporary commentary, underutilized by Civil War scholars.

PART FOUR. LYNDON JOHNSON'S STRATEGY FOR DEFEAT

DOCUMENTS

Lyndon Baines Johnson Library (National Archives and Records Administration) collections:
Meeting Notes File
National Security File: Country File, Vietnam
National Security File: Files of McGeorge Bundy
National Security File: Memos to the President
National Security File: National Security Council Histories
Papers of McGeorge Bundy
Papers of William Bundy
Papers of William C. Westmoreland
Special Files: Diaries and Appointment Logs of Lyndon B. Johnson
Special Files: Tom Johnson's Notes of Meetings
White House Central File: Confidential File
White House Central File: Name File
Collections of the U.S. Army Center of Military History, Washington, D.C.

BOOKS

Arnold, James R. *Armor*. New York: Bantam, 1987.
———. *The First Domino: Eisenhower, the Military, and America's Intervention in Vietnam*. New York: William Morrow and Co., 1991.
———. *Tet Offensive 1968*. London: Osprey, 1990.
Berman, Larry. *Planning a Tragedy: The Americanization of the War in Vietnam*. New York: W. W. Norton, 1982.
Berry, F. Clifton, Jr. *Sky Soldiers*. New York: Bantam, 1987.
Broughton, Jack. *Thud Ridge*. New York: Bantam, 1969.
Broyles, William, Jr. *Brothers in Arms: A Journey from War to Peace*. New York: Avon, 1987.
Carlson, Paul H. *Pecos Bill: A Military Biography of William R. Shafter*. College Station, Tex.: Texas A&M University Press, 1989.
Clifford, Clark. *Counsel to the President*. New York: Random House, 1991.
Coleman, J. D. *Pleiku: The Dawn of Helicopter Warfare in Vietnam*. New York: St. Martin's Press, 1988.
Divine, Robert A. *Roosevelt and World War II*. Baltimore: Penguin, 1970.
Donovan, Robert J. *Nemesis: Truman and Johnson in the Coils of War in Asia*. New York: St. Martin's Press, 1984.
Dos Passos, John. *Mr. Wilson's War*. Garden City, N.Y.: Doubleday and Co., 1962.

Friedel, Frank B. *The Splendid Little War*. Boston: Little, Brown, 1958.

Gelb, Leslie H., and Betts, Richard K. *The Irony of Vietnam: The System Worked*. Washington: Brookings Institution, 1979. A fine analysis of bureaucratic pressures influencing presidential decision making.

Goldman, Eric F. *The Tragedy of Lyndon Johnson*. New York: Alfred A. Knopf, 1969.

Horne, Charles F., ed. *Source Records of the Great War*. 7 vols. National Alumni, 1923.

James, D. Clayton. *Refighting the Last War: Command and Crisis in Korea 1950–1953*. New York: The Free Press, 1993.

Johnson, Lady Bird. *A White House Diary*. New York: Holt, Rinehart and Winston, 1970.

Johnson, Lyndon B. *Public Papers of the Presidents of the United States: Lyndon B. Johnson 1963–1964, II*. Washington: Government Printing Office, 1965.

———. *Public Papers of the Presidents of the United States: Lyndon B. Johnson 1965, II*. Washington: Government Printing Office, 1966.

———. *Public Papers of the Presidents of the United States: Lyndon B. Johnson 1966*. Washington: Government Printing Office, 1967.

———. *Public Papers of the Presidents of the United States: Lyndon B. Johnson 1968, I*. Washington: Government Printing Office, 1970.

———. *The Vantage Point: Perspectives on the Presidency. 1963–1969*. New York: Holt, Rinehart and Winston, 1971.

Johnson, Virginia W. *The Unregimented General: A Biography of Nelson A. Miles*. Boston: Houghton Mifflin, 1962.

Karnow, Stanley. *Vietnam: A History*. New York: Viking, 1983.

Kearns, Doris. *Lyndon Johnson and the American Dream*. New York: New American Library, 1976. The best biography so far.

Kinnard, Douglas. *The Certain Trumpet: Maxwell Taylor and the American Experience in Vietnam*. Washington: Brassey's (U.S.), 1991.

Kinnard, Douglas. *The War Managers*. Hanover, N.H.: University Press of New England, 1977. A mine of valuable information for the Vietnam scholar.

Krepinevich, Andrew F., Jr. *The Army and Vietnam*. Baltimore: Johns Hopkins University Press, 1986. Controversial, a challenge to Summers.

Larrabee, Eric. *Commander in Chief: Franklin Delano Roosevelt. His Lieutenants and Their War*. New York: Harper and Row, 1987.

Leech, Margaret. *In the Days of McKinley*. New York: Harper and Brothers, 1959.

Lofgren, Charles A. *Government from Reflection and Choice: Constitutional Essays on War, Foreign Relations and Federalism*. New York, Oxford University Press, 1986.

Luong, Colonel Hoang Ngoc. *The General Offensives of 1968–69*. Washington: U.S. Army Center of Military History, 1981.

Marolda, Edward J., and Fitzgerald, Oscar P. *The United States Navy and the Vietnam Conflict*, vol. 2. Washington: U.S. Department of the Navy, 1986.

Matthews, Lloyd J., ed. *Assessing the Vietnam War: A Collection from the Journal of the U.S. Army War College*. Washington: Pergamon-Brassey's, 1987. Insight into the Russian and Chinese attitudes toward the Vietnam War.

Maurer, Harry. *Strange Ground: An Oral History of Americans in Vietnam 1945–1975*. New York: Avon, 1989. A fine example of the genre.

Miles, Nelson A. *Serving the Republic*. New York: Harper, 1911.

Moore, Harold G., and Galloway, Joseph L. *We Were Soldiers Once . . . and Young—Ia Drang: The Battle that Changed the War in Vietnam*. New York: Random House, 1992. Gripping battle account.

Olcott, Charles S. *The Life of William McKinley*. 2 vols. Boston: Houghton Mifflin, 1916.

O'Toole, G. J. A. *The Spanish War: An American Epic—1898*. New York: Norton, 1984.

The Pentagon Papers: The Defense Department History of United States Decisionmaking on Vietnam. The Senator Gravel Edition. Boston: Beacon Press, 1971.

Pohanka, Brian, ed. *Nelson A. Miles: A Documentary Biography of His Military Career, 1861–1903*. Glendale, Calif.: A. H. Clark Co., 1985.

Prados, John, and Stubbe, Ray W. *Valley of Decision: The Siege of Khe Sanh*. Boston: Houghton Mifflin Co., 1991. A well-researched account of Westmoreland's greatest battle and a story of Marine valor.

Reedy, George. *Lyndon B. Johnson: A Memoir*. New York: Andrews and McMeel, 1982.

Rhodes, James F. *The McKinley and Roosevelt Administrations, 1897–1909*. New York: Macmillan, 1922.

Ridgway, Matthew B. *Soldier: The Memoirs of Matthew B. Ridgway*. New York: Harper and Bros., 1956.

Rogers, Bernard William. *Cedar Falls–Junction City: A Turning Point*. Washington: Department of the Army, 1974.

Rostow, W. W. *The Diffusion of Power: An Essay in Recent History*. New York: Macmillan, 1972.

Schnabel, James F. *Policy and Direction: The First Year*. Washington: U.S. Army, 1972. The official army history of command and control in Korea.

Sharp, U. S. Grant. *Strategy for Defeat: Vietnam in Retrospect*. San Rafael, Calif.: Presidio Press, 1978. The thought-provoking account of an "unreconstructed" airpower enthusiast.

Sheehan, Neil. *After the War Was Over: Hanoi and Saigon*. New York: Random House, 1991. Strong biases aside, an excellent glimpse of what happened to Vietnam's people after America left.

Simmons, Edwin H. *Marines*. New York: Bantam Books, 1987.

Son, P., ed. *The Viet Cong Tet Offensive 1968*. Saigon: 1969.

Sorley, Lewis. *Thunderbolt: General Creighton Abrams and the Army of His Times*. New York: Simon and Schuster, 1992. Includes a hostile, very unflattering depiction of Westmoreland, many assertions unverifiable from the footnotes.

Stanton, Shelby L. *The Rise and Fall of an American Army: U.S. Ground Forces in Vietnam, 1965–1973*. Novato, Calif.: Presidio Press, 1985. A good overview of the army's war.

Stockdale, Jim, and Stockdale, Sybil. *In Love and War*. New York: Harper and Row, 1984. A must read to understand how decisions made in the rarified Washington air affected the lives of American servicemen and POWs in Vietnam.

Summers, Harry G., Jr. *On Strategy: The Vietnam War in Context*. Carlisle, Pa.: U.S. Army War College, 1981. Extracting Vietnam's strategic lessons, a fine contribution to the rebirth of American strategic thinking.

———. *On Strategy II: A Critical Analysis of the Gulf War*. New York: Dell, 1992.

———. *Vietnam War Almanac*. New York: Facts On File Publications, 1985.

Truong, Nhu Tang et al. *A Vietcong Memoir*. San Diego: Harcourt Brace Jovanovich, 1985.

U.S. Adjutant General's Office. *Correspondence Relating to the War With Spain*. 2 vols. Washington: Government Printing Office, 1902.

U.S. Army. *Annual Report of the Major General Commanding the Army*. Washington: 1898.

U.S. Department of Defense. *United States–Vietnam Relations, 1945–1967: A Study Prepared by the Department of Defense*. 12 vols. Washington: Government Printing Office, 1971.

U.S. Senate. 56th Congress, 1st Session, Senate Document 221. *Report of the Commission . . . to Investigate the Conduct of the War Department*. 8 vols. Washington: Government Printing Office, 1900.

Valenti, Jack. *A Very Human President*. New York: W. W. Norton and Co., 1975.

VanDeMark, Brian. *Into the Quagmire: Lyndon Johnson and the Escalation of the Vietnam War*. New York: Oxford University Press, 1991. Finely researched account of LBJ's decision to escalate the war in 1964–1965.

Walt, Lewis W. *Strange War, Strange Strategy: A General's Report on Vietnam*. New York: Funk and Wagnalls, 1970.

Westmoreland, William C. *A Soldier Reports*. Garden City, N.Y.: Doubleday and Co., 1976.

Willets, Gilson. *Inside Story of the White House*. New York: 1908.

ARTICLES

Ball, George W. "Top Secret: The Prophecy the President Rejected." *Atlantic Monthly,* vol. 230 (July 1972), pp. 33–49.

Brodie, Bernard. "Why Were We So (Strategically) Wrong." *Military Review,* vol. 52 (June 1972), pp. 40–46. Insight into the influence of systems analysts in McNamara's Pentagon.

Clifford, Clark M. "A Viet Nam Reappraisal." *Foreign Affairs,* vol. 47 (July 1969), pp. 601–622. Reflections of a hawk turned dove.

Grinter, Laurence E. "How They Lost: Doctrines, Strategies and Outcomes of the Vietnam War." *Asian Survey,* vol. 15 (December 1975), pp. 1114–1132. An interesting counterpoint to Summers's ideas.

Humphrey, David C. "Tuesday Lunch at the Johnson White House: A Preliminary Assessment." *Diplomatic History,* vol. 8 (Winter 1984), pp. 81–101. Useful research directions for finding the real Lyndon Johnson.

Karnow, Stanley. "Giap Remembers." *New York Times Magazine,* June 24 1990, p. 22. An old general recalls his greatest victories.

Kissinger, Henry. "The Viet Nam Negotiations." *Foreign Affairs,* vol. 47 (January 1969), pp. 211–234.

Moyers, Bill. "Bill Moyers Talks about LBJ, Power, Poverty, War, and the Young." *Atlantic Monthly,* vol. 222 (July 1968), pp. 29–37. Insights into the LBJ style, written when memories were still fresh.

Norris, John G. "Big Iadrang Victory Held Turning Point." *Washington Post,* 20 November 1965, p. 1.

Sheehan, Neil. "Battalion of G.I.s Battered in Trap." *New York Times,* 19 November 1965, p. 1.

———. "U.S. Troops Renew Search for Enemy in Vietnam Valley." *New York Times,* 20 November 1965, p. 1.

"Skirmishes Flare Up After Bitter Five-Day Iadrang Valley Battle." *Washington Post,* 19 November 1965, p. 1.

Smith, Jack P. "Death in the Ia Drang Valley." *Saturday Evening Post,* vol. 240 (28 January 1967), pp. 80–85.

Summers, Harry G., Jr. "The Bitter Triumph of Ia Drang." *American Heritage,* vol. 35 (February–March 1984), pp. 50–58.

PART FIVE. PRESIDENTS UNDER FIRE

"Clinton Ignores History's Lessons in Vietnam." *Wall Street Journal,* 9 September 1992, p. A14.

Conduct of the Persian Gulf Conflict: An Interim Report to Congress. Washington: Government Printing Office, 1991.

Gellman, Barton. "Rumblings of Discord Heard in Pentagon." *Washington Post,* 20 June 1993, p. 1.

Huntington, Samuel P. *The Soldier and the State: The Theory and Politics of Civil-Military Relations.* Cambridge, Mass.: 1957.

Herold, J. Christopher, ed. *The Mind of Napoleon: A Selection from His Written and Spoken Words.* New York: Columbia University Press, 1955.

MacArthur, John R. *Second Front: Censorship and Propaganda in the Gulf War.* New York: Hill and Wang, 1992.

Matloff, Maurice, ed. *American Military History.* Washington: Government Printing Office, 1969.

Neustadt, Richard E. *Presidential Power: The Politics of Leadership.* New York: Wiley, 1960.

Pusey, Merlo J. *The Way We Go to War.* Boston: Houghton Mifflin Co., 1971.

Schwarzkopf, H. Norman, and Petre, Peter. *It Doesn't Take a Hero.* New York: Bantam, 1992. Fine critical insights from Vietnam to the Gulf, far less critical about the Gulf War itself.

Smith, Louis. *American Democracy and Military Power: A Study of Civil Control of the Military Power in the United States.* Chicago: University of Chicago Press, 1951.

Summers, Harry G., Jr. *On Strategy II: A Critical Analysis of the Gulf War.* New York: Dell, 1992. How the military revenged Vietnam.

Tugwell, Rexford G. *The Enlargement of the Presidency.* Garden City, N.Y.: Doubleday, 1960.

von Clausewitz, Carl. *On War.* Princeton, N.J.: Princeton University Press, 1976. Still the classic strategic primer.

Woodward, Bob. *The Commanders.* New York: Simon and Schuster, 1991. An interesting story lacking reliable documentation.

INDEX